Theory and Interpretation of Narrative
James Phelan and Peter J. Rabinowitz, Series Editors

UNDERSTANDING NATIONALISM
On Narrative, Cognitive Science, and Identity

PATRICK COLM HOGAN

THE OHIO STATE UNIVERSITY PRESS
COLUMBUS

Copyright © 2009 by The Ohio State University.
All rights reserved.

Library of Congress Cataloging-in-Publication Data
Hogan, Patrick Colm.
  Understanding nationalism : on narrative, cognitive science, and identity / Patrick Colm Hogan.
    p. cm. — (Theory and interpretation of narrative)
  Includes bibliographical references and index.
  ISBN-13: 978-0-8142-1107-6 (cloth : alk. paper)
  ISBN-10: 0-8142-1107-0 (cloth : alk. paper)
  1. Nationalism—Cross-cultural studies. 2. Nationalism in literature. 3. Cognition and culture—Cross-cultural studies. I. Title.
  JC311.H595 2009
  320.54—dc22

                              2008055805

This book is available in the following editions:
Cloth (ISBN 0-978-08142-1107-6)
CD-ROM (ISBN 0-978-08142-9204-4)

Cover design by Laurence J. Nozik
Type set in Gandhari Unicode
Text design by Juliet Williams

In memory of my mother-in-law, Kamalavati Pandit (1918–2008)

दमी दीठम नद वहवनी
दमी डयूठुम सुम नत तार ।
दमी दीठम थर फवलवनी
दमी डयूठुम गुल नत खार ॥

Lalleśvari
(Kashmir, 14th Century)

Mo Tzu said: What the man of humanity devotes himself to surely lies in the promotion of benefits for the world and the removal of harm from the world. . . . But what are the benefits and the harm of the world? . . . Because of want of mutual love, all the calamities, usurpations, hatred, and animosity in the world have arisen. . . . It should be replaced by the way of universal love and mutual benefit. What is the way of universal love and mutual benefit? It is to regard other people's countries as one's own.

CONTENTS

Acknowledgments   xi

INTRODUCTION
Nationalism and the Cognitive Sciences   1

CHAPTER 1
Understanding Identity:
What It Is and What It Does   23

CHAPTER 2
Hierarchizing Identities:
Techniques of Nationalization   66

CHAPTER 3
Metaphors and Selves:
Forefathers, Roots, and the Voice of the People   124

CHAPTER 4
Emplotting the Nation:
The Narrative Structures of Patriotism   167

CHAPTER 5
Heroic Nationalism and the Necessity of War
from King David to George W. Bush   213

CHAPTER 6
Sacrificial Nationalism and Its Victims:
Sin and Death in Germany and India   264

CHAPTER 7
Romantic Love and the End of Nationalism:
Walt Whitman and Emma Goldman   305

Works Cited   339
Index   359

ACKNOWLEDGMENTS

An earlier version of part of chapter 5 was delivered at the Lechter Institute for Literary Research at Bar-Ilan University, Ramat-Gan, Israel. I am grateful to Ellen Spolsky and to audience members for their comments and suggestions. An earlier version of part of chapter 6 was delivered at Harvard University and at Tulane University. I am grateful to Alan Richardson, Elaine Scarry, and the participants in the Harvard seminar on cognitive theory and the arts, as well as faculty and graduate students at Tulane, for lively and illuminating discussions of these issues. An earlier version of part of chapter 4 was delivered at the Modern Language Association Convention in Philadelphia. I am grateful to Brian Richardson and to the participants for their comments and questions. An earlier version of part of chapter 7 was presented at the International Conference on Narrative in Austin, Texas. I am grateful to Brian McHale and the participants for their stimulating observations.

As always, I am indebted to my wife, Lalita Pandit, for reading earlier versions of parts of the manuscript and making extremely valuable suggestions for improvement.

I am grateful to Alan Richardson and an anonymous reviewer for reading an earlier draft of the manuscript and making careful, helpful comments. James Phelan and Peter Rabinowitz devoted a great deal of time to attentively reading different versions of the manuscript with sharp critical eyes. Their comments and suggestions have significantly improved many sections of the book.

I am grateful to Sandy Crooms of The Ohio State University Press for her care in handling the manuscript.

An earlier version of part of chapter 4 was published in *Narrative Beginnings,* ed. Brian Richardson (Lincoln: University of Nebraska Press, 2008).

INTRODUCTION

NATIONALISM AND THE COGNITIVE SCIENCES

FROM THE RISE OF Nazism through the anticolonial movements of mid-twentieth century to the disintegration of Yugoslavia and the current war in Iraq, nationalism has been one of the most important social forces in recent history. Wimmer refers to nationalism as "the most powerful ideology in the history of modernity" (32). Dittmer and Kim cite Steven Rosen's 1969 *Survey of World Conflicts*, which explains that, at the time, "nationalist and ethnic conflict accounted for some 70 percent of 160 significant disputes with a probability of culminating in large-scale violence." A decade and a half later, the situation was much the same, perhaps worse. In connection with this, they cite Ernest Gellner's 1983 *Nations and Nationalisms*, stating that "there may be as many as eight hundred irredentist movements in the contemporary world" ("In Search" 8).

By the end of the 1980s, however, it had become something of a commonplace among many writers that nationalism was dead. The main argument for the disappearance of nationalism was the growth of globalization. But the relation between the two is not that simple. For example, in a 2003 essay, István Mészáros argued that global integration remains inseparable from a nation/state system. It may be true that the nation is less crucial as an economic unit than it was in the recent past. As Habermas put it, "Individual states are less and less able to control the national economies" (292). However, the insularity and uniformity of national economies was probably never as great as we commonly imagine. As Mann notes, "Transnational relations are not merely 'postmodern'; they have always undercut the sovereignty of all states. . . . Neither the capitalist economy nor modern culture has ever been greatly constrained by national boundaries" (298; see also Amin 24–27).

More important, nationalist feelings and nationalist conflicts have hardly disappeared, nor has their intensity diminished. In 1991, Benedict Anderson wrote that "the 'end of the era of nationalism,' so long prophesied, is not remotely in sight. Indeed, nation-ness is the most universally legitimate value in the political life of our time" (3). Wimmer notes that "in three-quarters of all wars worldwide between 1985 and 1992 ethno-nationalist factors predominated" (85). Around the same time, Michael Mann argued that "The nation-state is . . . not in any *general* decline, *anywhere*" (298; emphasis in original). In their 1995 collection, published at perhaps the height of the claims that nationalism is dead, François, Siegrist, and Vogel noted that there had been much talk about "the end of the nation" ("Die Nation" 22; my translation). However, they point to a striking countertrend—"nationalism again growing virulent throughout Europe" (13). Eight years later, Chaim Gans pointed out that "It is a well-known fact that cultural nationalism has enjoyed a revival in many parts of the world in the last fifteen years" (1). More recently still, Aviel Roshwald noted that "the break-up of the Soviet Union, the Yugoslav wars, China's growing preoccupation with the Taiwan question, and the surge of collective emotion in the United States following the September 11 attacks have highlighted nationalism's enduring power" (1). As I write, in 2008, the "end of the nation" seems no nearer than it did when Anderson was writing in 1991, or when Gellner was writing in 1983. People around the world continue to kill one another in the name of patriotism. To a great extent, the crucial allegiances that drive people to both heroic and despicable actions remain national. Human emotions, motivations, commitments, and consequent actions—these are what make nationalism a topic of continuing, indeed vital concern, not the insularity or autonomy of national economic systems. To take a prominent recent example, the U.S. government insisted that it must invade Iraq in order to protect its national interests. Many Americans supported the war precisely because they felt devotion to the nation.

Many Iraqis attack U.S. forces out of loyalty, not to Saddam Hussein, but to Iraq (see, for example, Jamail). Nationalism is hardly unimportant in these cases because the economies of the two nations are interrelated or because Iraq's national autonomy is limited by its relation to other nations.[1]

As the distinction between economic autonomy and personal allegiance suggests, "nationalism" has many different meanings.[2] One critical task in discussing the theoretical and practical problems of nationalism is to explain just what constitutes nationalism. That is, in part, the task of the first chapter. However, it is important to set out a preliminary definition here, especially as my use of the word *nationalism* in some ways goes against common usage. Most authors today confine the idea of the nation to modern states (see Anthony Smith, "Nationalism" 191–92). Many confine it to specifically democratic states or at least states in which there is some assertion of popular self-determination. For example, Mitchison distinguishes nationalism from ethnicity most significantly by the "stress" on "popular political sovereignty" ("Some" 164). There is nothing wrong with this usage in itself. However, it leaves us without any straightforward way of referring to the attitudes expressed by, say, the eleventh-century Persian *Shâhnâme*, which celebrates Iran and lionizes those who are willing to fight and die in Iran's conflicts with its enemies. Moreover, the presumption of much writing on nationalism is that modern nationalism is discontinuous with the various personal commitments to states and state-based communities that went before.[3] My contention is precisely the

---

1. Indeed, that economic interrelation and that political limitation are likely to enhance nationalist feeling—as anyone familiar with the history of colonialism could have predicted. For example, Dreyfus recently pointed out that there has been an upsurge in Iraqi nationalism, due in part to the attempt to partition Iraq, further degrading national political autonomy, and in part to "American pressure to force the partial privatization of Iraq's oil" (6), thus further degrading national economic autonomy. More generally, drawing on Hannah Arendt's work, Graham MacPhee writes that "the decline of the nation-state as the operative unit of political sovereignty" gives rise to a "tendency to manage the resultant social disorientation and crises by appealing to nationalism" (200–201). Along the same lines, David Sirota recently observed that "full-throated nationalism is now lodged in the ideological center of American Politics," in part as a response to "global economic policies written by, and for, a transnational elite" (32).

2. Indeed, the ambiguity of the term nationalism is recognized as a significant problem in discussions of the topic. See, for example, chapter 1 of David Brown and citations.

3. There are certainly exceptions to this. For example, David Kaplan writes that, "although they did not generate the mass horizontal allegiance of nationalism, many empires did foster a sense of a larger identity that transcended smaller scale clan, ethnic, or religious ties. For instance, the Roman Empire became more of a political community over time, leading to where residents felt themselves part of a common civilization and offered their willing allegiance" (39–40; see also Breuilly, "Approaches to Nationalism" 153 and, most significantly, Roshwald 8–44). I would only add that even "smaller scale clan, ethnic, or religious"

opposite.[4] In my view, the similarities between modern, democratic nationalism and earlier commitments to states and state-based communities are more extensive and more consequential than the differences.

I use "nationalism," then, to refer to *any form of in-group identification for a group defined in part by reference to a geographical area along with some form of sovereign government over that area*. This definition is roughly in keeping with general principles of international law. As summarized by Levi, "There is far-reaching agreement on some conditions that must exist before a group is entitled to being a state. There must be a territory, though it need not be contiguous. There must be a population, though its size seems to be irrelevant. And there must be a government in control of territory and population" (66). The main difference is that I am referring to a sense of identification rather than a political structure. I should explain that, by "geographical area," I do not necessarily mean an area marked by strict boundaries. There can be considerable leeway in the degree to which boundaries are considered precise and fixed. Writers on nationalism often stress that strict boundaries are a modern phenomenon (see, for example, Anderson 170–78 on maps). This is significant, and points to one difference between the modern period and earlier periods.[5] However, the vagueness of boundaries does not mean that earlier societies lacked a sense of national territory. By "sovereign government," I mean a structure of social authority that supersedes other forms of social authority when conflicts arise (e.g., there is a structure of social authority defined by a family, but in cases of conflict with the legal system, the authority of the legal system supersedes that of the family). Sovereignty in this sense need not involve any form of popular participation in governance. Finally, I take it to be obvious that the sovereignty in question also need not be actual or current. It may be an imagined or desired form of sovereignty. Thus, nationalism may inspire an anticolonial movement to establish a state.

As I am using the term, then, nationalism has been around as long as there have been complex, hierarchically structured, nonnomadic societies.

---

identifications share crucial features with nationalism. Cognitively, the differences are almost insignificant.

4. I do not mean that the specific nations formed today are continuous with earlier ethnic groups (cf. Anthony Smith *Ethnic*). That is sometimes the case, sometimes not. But, either way, it is irrelevant to my concerns. My point is that the general structures are continuous in relying on the same cognitive processes and involving the same fundamental principles of social psychological dynamics.

5. On the other hand, boundaries are not absolute, even in the modern period. There is much more fluidity and complexity in our geographical identifications than one might imagine, as the essays collected by Herb and Kaplan make clear.

Moreover, it has always followed the cognitive and affective principles of in-group/out-group division.[6] It is very likely that the development of print, mass literacy, and other factors have greatly expanded the extent and intensity of nationalist feeling. Moreover, that expansion was far from insignificant. It made nationalism a popular force in modern society, a force with consequences that engage large bodies of people for extended periods. Writers interested in broad geopolitical patterns may reasonably restrict their use of the term nationalism to modernity, when the effects of nationalist ideas and feelings became particularly widespread and systematic. But, if print and other factors contributed to the scope and durability of nationalist feeling, they did not create such feeling, giving it its first appearance on earth. They necessarily bore on preexisting cognitive and affective processes. My interest is in those processes—the motives that drive nationalism and the patterns of understanding and inference that organize it. Thus, I necessarily view nationalism as operating over a much longer time scale. Even if nationalist feelings and ideas in the past were less expansive and stable, and less systematically consequential for political economy, they are continuous with modern nationalism. Indeed, without these prior motivations and understandings, it would be very difficult to see how modern nationalist motives and understandings could have developed, no matter how much literacy spread or what other technological and social changes occurred.

The mention of "cognitive and affective processes" leads us to the topic of theory and to the fundamental theoretical presuppositions of this work, presuppositions drawn from cognitive neuroscience. Up to now, the academic study of nationalism has been largely historical. Certainly, historical research is crucial. However, it is insufficient in two ways. First, it indicates why nationalism changes, why it becomes widespread in certain periods, why some nationalist movements succeed and others fail. But it does not indicate why nationalism is possible in the first place, how it has any existence at all that may then be affected by historical change.[7] The second problem is related. History leaves out the micro-level that must always underlie social trends.[8] Specifically, research on the human mind and the

6. On these principles see my *Culture* 95–104 and citations.

7. For example, Snyder brilliantly analyzes factors that contributed to differences between Belarussian and Lithuanian nationalisms. But these factors would not, so to speak, have any effect on stones. They have effects on people, and they do so because of human cognitive and emotional processes—processes that simply do not fall within the scope of historical works, such as Snyder's.

8. As Bloom puts it, "*whatever* the configuration of socio-economic and political realities, and no matter how powerful and determining they may appear, there always remains the

human brain suggests that a great deal of our social behavior is shaped by aspects of our cognitive architecture. In order to have significant consequences, nationalism must work itself out through attention, inference, feeling, understanding, and other aspects of cognition and emotion that are repeated with adequate consistency across individuals. It is, after all, the ideas and actions of individuals that, collectively, make up a functional (or, for that matter, dysfunctional) society. Conversely, no social patterns can develop if they would be inconsistent with the structures and processes that govern human thought and action.

More exactly, in considering human cognitive architecture (i.e., the general organization of the human mind as it emerges from the operation of the human brain), we need to distinguish structures, processes, and contents. Structures are the basic systems that organize the mind. For example, there are perceptual systems (visual, auditory, etc.), memory systems (for meanings, personal experiences, skills), and so forth. Processes are the operations performed by these systems. Thus, the storing and retrieval of personal memories in "episodic memory," the development of meanings (e.g., the averaging of individual experiences that generates prototypes), and the circulation of information in "working memory" are all cognitive processes. Finally, contents are the objects of processes. Thus, individual episodic memories (which are stored or retrieved in episodic memory) are contents, as are particular skills, particular semantic prototypes, and so on. Among contents, we need to distinguish those that are representational and those that are procedural. Representational memories are possible objects of certain processes, prominently including attentional focus. Procedural memories are possible objects of other processes—most important, those that involve enactment. More simply, representations are things we might think about whereas procedures are things we might do or, rather, the skills that allow us to do things.

Structures and processes are universal. At least some contents are universal as well. Technically, then, studies of nationalism have focused almost entirely on contents. Moreover, even that study has been rather narrow, for it has concentrated almost entirely on variable contents rather than cross-culturally constant contents. This is unsurprising for cognitive reasons. Our minds are designed to focus our attention on difference, on

---

psychological dimension" (4; emphasis in original). Bloom goes on to say that there has been a "lack of clarity" regarding this dimension (4). In responding to this situation, Bloom himself draws on psychoanalytic and other theories that, however insightful, were formulated before the recent advances in cognitive neuroscience and related fields. The same point applies to David Brown, who states bluntly that "the psychological dimension [of nationalism] demands more attention" (23).

variation. As Frijda points out, "Strangeness per se motivates cognitive activity: It is one of the situational meaning components shaping the feature of interestingness" (214). Specifically, our "orienting reaction," which includes attentional focus, occurs "in response to novel or unexpected stimuli" (131; see also, Kahneman and Miller 148, on when we ask "why questions"). But one cannot understand variable contents without understanding the larger architectural principles that encompass them. Studying the different histories of nationalisms without understanding their shared cognitive underpinnings is in some ways like studying vocabulary items in different languages (largely the result of historical accidents) without studying the universal principles of linguistic structure.[9]

In the following pages, I will, of course, consider cultural and historical particulars. Moreover, when discussing specific cases, my primary interest is in the modern period and particularly in the present. Again, in my view, nationalism is longstanding, even if it assumes different forms in different periods. However, I will not be focusing on ancient nationalisms. Rather, when I turn to particular cases—ancient or modern—I will be exploring nationalisms that have had significant impact on the world today. Indeed, my focus is even narrower than this suggests. The bulk of my analyses take up current American nationalism, because it is simply the most globally consequential nationalism right now. Nationalism in, say, the Yüan dynasty is of interest primarily to a particular group of Sinologists.[10] In contrast, contemporary American nationalism—particularly in a time of unbounded war[11]—is of concern to virtually everyone on the planet. I take up analyses of other nations only when there are no suitable American instances of relevant magnitude. Here, too, I have selected cases that have had significant impact on the world as it is now.

On the other hand, my overriding concern throughout the following pages is not with historical, cultural, or other particulars, even in the case

---

9. In saying this, I do not mean to imply that historically particular studies of nationalism are not worthwhile. Quite the contrary. For example, I have found the particular analyses of writers such as Breuilly (*Nationalism*), Nairn, Snyder, and others to be greatly illuminating. To continue with the analogy, it is crucial to know the different meanings of vocabulary items. The point is simply that one does not have a very good linguistic theory—or even a very good comprehension of the broader semantic structure of a particular language—if one does not also understand the universal principles of speech production and comprehension, including the universal principles of semantics.

10. I have discussed some aspects of nationalism during the Yüan dynasty in "Narrative Universals, National Sacrifice." The topic is no less intellectually important than current U.S. nationalism. But it is less politically consequential at the moment.

11. Led by policy makers who have been characterized as "radical nationalists" (see Chomsky *Hegemony* 37 and citations).

of the United States. Rather, my primary interest is in the common principles, the structures, processes, and shared contents that make nationalism possible in the first place. Indeed, even in the case of differences, my main concern is with what principles govern these differences, what larger patterns are instantiated in the variations. For example, I consider why Germany and India developed sacrificial versions of nationalism so extensively. I pay some attention to why these versions were different from one another. However, I am concerned, first of all, with what conditions were shared by these societies. My contention is that a focus on common principles provides us not only with a deeper understanding of nationalism at the micro-level—one that goes to the cognitive substrate of the politics—but a more adequate understanding at every level. In other words, it helps us to explain a range of macro-level, thus apparently noncognitive, phenomena. These range from the instability of nationalism (in the face of subnationalisms) to the general failure of movements for international solidarity. Indeed, here as elsewhere, I believe that attention to shared patterns is the only means by which we can come to understand historical particularity and cultural difference. Historical particularity and cultural difference are not matters of absolute alienness and singularity. They are distinct specifications of common principles. Without those common principles, we could make no sense of any historically and culturally different society. Such a society would be simply opaque to us.

The first chapter, then, presents a general account of identity formation. It begins by drawing a fundamental distinction between categorial and practical identity. Roughly, practical identity comprises what we do or can do. It is the total of our capacities, propensities, interests, routines—most important, those that bear on our interactions with others. Categorial identity is our inclusion of ourselves in particular sets of people, our location of ourselves in terms of in-group/out-group divisions.[12] The chapter goes on to explore the nature of categorial identity, its motivational force, and its relation to practical identity.[13] It considers the ways in which categorial

---

12. The general distinction between practical and categorial identity is both obvious (at least once stated) and highly consequential. Nonetheless, it seems to have been almost entirely ignored by writers on identity. For an overview of theories of identity, which tend to combine these in unclear and shifting ways, see Monroe, Hankin, and Van Vechten.

13. One reader of my manuscript asked about the relation of categorial and practical identity to individual identity. We use *individual identity* in two senses. One refers to one's activities and capacities. This is the same as practical identity—though, in discussing practical identity, I stress the interpersonal integration of people's activities and capacities rather than their private idiosyncrasies (which may be emphasized in treatments of individual identity). The more common use of individual identity refers to one's self-conscious sense of being the same individual—thus one's sense of continuity in memories, feelings, interests, and so forth.

identification is bound up with the articulation of group norms, the formation of out-group prototypes, and the development of in-group hierarchies. It then sets out to define nationalism as a particular form of categorial identification. The chapter concludes by broaching the question of how we hierarchize different categorial identifications in cases of conflict. Suppose Smith's religious identity conflicts with his or her national identity. How does it happen that Smith fights on the side of his or her nation against his or her coreligionists (or vice versa)? I argue that the hierarchization of identity categories (i.e., their ordering in terms of motivational force) is governed by specifiable parameters. I isolate five that are particularly important: salience, functionality (with respect to the distribution of goods, services, and opportunities in society), opposability (i.e., the degree to which an in-group category is contrasted with one or more out-group categories), durability, and affectivity (or emotional force).[14]

The second chapter goes through these parameters in sequence, considering how ordinary routines of daily life as well as unusual events serve to enhance the salience, functionality, opposability, durability, and affectivity of one or another identity category. Specifically, the chapter examines what I call "techniques of nationalization," which is to say, the means of hierarchizing identity categories in such a way as to make the national category preeminent. In connection with this, it considers social phenomena ranging from flag ceremonies to national legal systems. The argument of the chapter is that societies such as the United States are pervaded by practices that enhance the motivational force of national identifications. In keeping with this, the chapter focuses particularly on the motivationally crucial parameter of affectivity.

This is related to categorial identity in referring to one's ideas about oneself. However, it is different also, for the ideas, in this case, concern one's distinctiveness, not what one has in common with others. One's sense of individual identity is an important topic (and one closely related to narrative, cognition, and emotion). But it is also the topic for a different book.

14. Relatively little work has been done on emotion and categorial identity, especially from a cognitive perspective. Consider, for example, the collection on *Identity and Emotion*, edited by Bosma and Kunnen. Most of the chapters take up identity in a very different sense. They bear first of all on an emergent, experiential, and active sense of self, which is related to practical identity. They do not focus on the idea of oneself as defined by a particular group category. Indeed, even treatments of emotions in politics have tended to focus on a small number of particular issues (for an overview, see G. E. Marcus; for a range of specific topics see Goodwin, Jasper, and Polletta, *Passionate Politics*). François, Siegrist, and Vogel have put together a fascinating volume, *Nation und Emotion*. The essays have a great deal to say about some ways of fostering nationalism (e.g., particular national festivals) in their specific historical contexts. However, despite the title, there is little systematic treatment of particular emotions and their precise function in nationalist politics. (They also presuppose the "social, cultural and historical character of emotions" [François, Siegrist, and Vogel, "Die Nation" 20; my translation], which is, I believe, incompatible with the neurocognitive evidence.)

The second chapter leaves out two crucial factors in the way we think about and respond to nations. First, nations are obviously vast and multifarious entities, far too large for us to encounter directly. As Benedict Anderson famously put it, the nation is an "imagined community," not an experiential one. Our inability to know the nation in a personal way inhibits our thought about nationalist undertakings or possibilities and, even more important, our emotional relation to the nation. In general, when faced with an abstract entity that no one can experience, we turn to models. We compare what is vast and amorphous to something that is more concrete and familiar. In short, we use metaphor. Chapter 3 considers the nationalist operation of "conceptual metaphor," metaphor that organizes our thought and, in some cases, orients our feeling as well.

More exactly, in this chapter, I argue that there are a few standard metaphors for nationhood or for a citizen's relation to the nation. Such metaphors may derive from the distinguishing characteristics of nationalism as opposed to other types of identity category. Perhaps the most prominent of these distinguishing characteristics is the connection of nationalism to the land. Religion or class is not bound up with a specific territory in the way that nationhood is. In keeping with this, one of the most common types of nationalist metaphor parallels the citizen's relation to the national territory with a plant's relation to the earth—for example, through the image of roots. Metaphors of this sort cultivate a sense of belonging to the nation and its culture, as well as the national territory itself. A second prominent source for metaphors of national identity is the converse of this—distinguishing characteristics of competing identity categories. The purpose of these metaphors is, presumably, to preempt the force of those competing categories. Thus, one common metaphor for the nation is the family. This works to take over some of the intellectual and emotive power of ethnic categorization, which is distinguished from class, religion, or even nation by the putatively common ancestry of members of the ethnic group. Prominent cases of this in nationalism include the metaphor of the founding fathers. The third domain from which we commonly draw nationalist metaphors is the paradigm of human unity—the individual. This serves in an obvious way to occlude divisions within the nation and to foster a feeling of oneness. It gives rise to such common metaphors as "the voice of the people" and "the will of the nation." The chapter includes examples from a range of sources, including Abraham Lincoln's "Address at the Dedication of the Gettysburg National Cemetery." It ends with an analysis of metaphor in one of the most prominent national songs in the United States, "My Country 'tis of Thee."

Metaphor is crucial, both conceptually and emotionally. However, it is, so to speak, temporally localized. It gives us a way of thinking about and responding to an object or situation. But nationalism involves extensively elaborated sequences of events and actions undertaken in the pursuit of goals. This leads us to the second crucial factor left out from chapter 2—narrative.[15] When we think about national goals and actions in pursuit of those goals, we think in terms of stories.[16] Like metaphor, narrative

15. Some readers of this manuscript have been concerned that I have opposed metaphors and narratives too sharply. Of course, metaphors are not entirely separate from narratives. Indeed, the two are often integrated. This occurs most obviously in allegory. But it is common elsewhere as well. My point here is simply that examining metaphors as such does not tell us much about the narrative structures through which complex causal sequences are organized in nationalist thought and action. For example, THE NATION IS A MOTHER may be taken up in an Irish nationalist story where, say, the hero's mother is kidnapped by British soldiers and the hero must rescue her. In this case, the history of British colonialism in Ireland is simultaneously metaphorized and emplotted. The basic narrative structure includes a set of characters—a protagonist, a family of the protagonist, and an antagonist. More important, it includes a series of events or conditions—normalcy, followed by kidnapping, followed by anxiety and suffering, followed by rescue (and perhaps punishment of the antagonist), followed by normalcy. That basic narrative structure may be combined with the metaphor in that the metaphor may be used as one means of specifying and developing the narrative structure. Thus, it may lead to an author making the mother the one who is kidnapped; it may lead to the specification of the captors as British, and so on. Alternatively, one might say that the narrative structure allows one to expand the metaphor to a series of historical events. It allows us to think of colonial conquest as kidnapping the mother; it facilitates our imagination of achieving independence in terms of freeing the mother. However, either way, the metaphor itself does not produce this sequence of events. The point is clear when we simply recognize that the kidnapping narrative structure may be used literally or may be metaphorized in countless other ways (e.g., a wartime draft may be allegorized as kidnapping; a successful deceptive electoral campaign may be allegorized as kidnapping, and so on). Conversely, the metaphorical structure THE NATION IS A MOTHER may be narrativized in various ways (e.g., she may be brutalized by a landlord who takes all her money so that she can barely feed her children; she may be a promiscuous woman who sleeps with a wealthy man for her own benefit while ignoring her hungry children, and so on—note also that THE NATION IS A MOTHER may be specified to mean that the land, the citizens, or the government is a mother). In short, I am not claiming that metaphors and narratives are antithetical. They are simply different and thus need to be discussed separately. A similar point could be made about almost any mental contents or processes. For example, remembering the past and imagining the future are not wholly unrelated activities. Indeed, they are closely interrelated. But we would not, for that reason, want to act as if they were the same.

16. Over the past decade or so, researchers have devoted increasing attention to the relation between narrative and nationalism. However, this attention has for the most part focused on isolating nationalist concerns in specific narratives (e.g., particular novels). This is certainly valuable, but it does not really tell us much at a theoretical level. Sometimes researchers have asserted more general connections between narrative and nationalism. However, in these cases, the use of the term *narrative* often seems overly broad. For example, the "narratives" discussed by some writers seem to be largely a matter of causal inference. As a result, the narrative nature of nationalism seems to entail the somewhat banal observation that nationalism involves causal inference. There are certainly valuable treatments of narrative and

too guides the way we understand and respond to the nation. Moreover, as with metaphor, there are patterns to our use of narrative structures. In the fourth chapter, I consider first of all the implications of general narrative organization. For example, stories have beginnings and endings. The point may seem banal; however, it has consequences for the way we think about causality. Consider the most intense and destructive form of national conflict, war. We explain a war by telling the story of the war. The story has a particular starting point. In real life, wars are the result of multiple, temporally staggered precedents that are themselves the result of multiple, temporally staggered precedents, and so on *ad infinitum*. The bombing of the World Trade Center was a heinous crime. But it was not an absolute beginning. It was preceded by U.S. actions, and actions by other nations and by other subnational and transnational groups. Similarly, there are no real endings. Causes produce effects that are themselves causes of further effects. Consequences multiply endlessly. Thus, the conflict in Afghanistan continues, despite its supposed conclusion. It does not, and indeed cannot, have a storybook ending. Nonetheless, we tend to think about wars as if they have such endings. This bounding of wars within story structure has concrete effects, not only on people's understanding of historical events, but on their actions of supporting and pursuing war as well. In short, even at this general level, the emplotment of nationalism is highly consequential.

Of course, the effects of narrative structure do not stop with these very general or "schematic" features, properties that are common to stories simply in that they are stories. Narratives fall into more particular categories or genres as well. I conclude chapter 4 by outlining the three most common narrative prototypes worldwide.[17] These are heroic, sacrificial, and romantic tragicomedy. The heroic structure involves a sequence of events bearing on the usurpation of in-group authority and a sequence of events concerning threats posed by an out-group. The sacrificial structure concerns some sin by the in-group, the resulting devastation of the in-group society, and the necessity of a sacrifice to end that devastation. Finally, the romantic

---

nationalism (see, for example, Khalidi, Reichmann, and Mary Green). Moreover, there are illuminating explorations of narrative and other aspects of politics. For example, the essays in Dennis Mumby's collection, *Narrative and Social Control*, help to explain such topics as the operation of conformity in the workplace and the social communication of racist belief. But this research does not appear to have significant theoretical consequences for the relation between narrative (its distinguishing forms, structural principles, etc.) and nationalism. There are only very rare exceptions, such as Kevin Foster's treatment of romantic quest structures in the Malvinas/Falkland Islands War.

17. On the universality of these prototypes, see my *The Mind and Its Stories*.

structure is a fairly ordinary love story in which society (often in the form of oppressive parents) prevents two lovers from uniting. I argue that these universal structures are the most common structures by which nationalism is emplotted. I should emphasize here that they are not the only structures by which nationalism may be emplotted. Our narrative capacities are not determined by these three prototypes. However, these structures are the ones that recur across cultures and across historical periods. They appear to guide the majority of canonical literary narratives worldwide.

The reason for the predominance of these prototypes is simple. We may tell stories about anything—and, indeed, we do. I come home from the grocery store and tell my wife how the price of feta cheese has gone up and how this led me to wonder whether or not I would buy it. The story is interesting enough to my wife (or at least she feels compelled to pretend that it is interesting enough). However, it is probably not interesting enough for, say, most readers of this book. Individually, among intimates, many narrative topics and developments will engage us, perhaps even motivate us to action. However, as one moves out from one's circle of family and friends, the list of engaging and motivating topics and developments will diminish. More precisely, narratives are formed around happiness goals. For example, heroic tragicomedy draws on the happiness goal of social prestige and power (for the in-group over out-groups and for an individual within an in-group). My story about the grocery story draws on the happiness goal of getting cheese that I like. There are two crucial variables here: (1) the extent to which the goal is shared by different people and (2) the importance of the goal for individuals who share it. The goal of acquiring social prestige and power is widely shared and it is important for most people. The goal of getting feta cheese is not widely shared and it is not all that weighty even for those who have it. Stories are likely to have greater emotional force and motivational impact for larger groups of people for longer periods of time if they concern goals that are important and widely shared. For this reason (and due to the nature of our emotion systems), a limited number of narrative prototypes are likely to have disproportionate force across cultures and across time periods. Drawing on narrative and psychological research, I have argued that there are three such prototypes. Since these are the prototypes that have the broadest and most enduring force in general, they should also be the prototypes that have the broadest and most enduring force in the emplotment of nationalism in particular.

Of course, a number of writers have referred to a narrower set of narratives that appear to be consequential for social ideas and practices. In some cases, they refer to particular stories. Particular stories that have social impact need not conform to one of the prototypes. In this way, a particular book may come to have great social influence outside the narrative structures I am considering. On the other hand, more often than not, such paradigmatic works do conform to standard narrative structures. For example, the (obviously pervasive) Christian story of the fall and redemption of humanity is a highly prototypical sacrificial narrative; the Hindu epic *Rāmāyaṇa*—a socially and politically crucial text in India—combines highly prototypical heroic and romantic narratives.

Indeed, the point holds even for narratives that appear very narrowly bound to cultural and historical particulars. For example, James Phelan refers to "cultural narratives," such as the Barbie doll being a dangerous role model for young girls (9). What could be more nonuniversal than a narrative structure centering on a particular toy manufactured at a particular time and place? But, on reflection, we may decide that it is not so simply culturally bound. (Phelan is not claiming that it is simply culturally bound. However, I think most readers would be likely to take this as a good instance of a nonuniversal narrative.) First of all, the structure may be more aptly referred to as a narrative of female emaciation, for which the Barbie doll serves simply as one prominent instance. Needless to say, this narrative, too, is not universal. But it is more clearly related to an ethical element of the sacrificial prototype, an element according to which the ethics of self-sacrifice are bound up with self-denial of food (see my *The Mind* 200 for discussion). In conjunction with this universal prototype, a social ideology that assigns women a role of greater self-sacrifice may contribute to the development of cultural narratives bearing on female emaciation. In this way, even such apparently particularistic structures as the Barbie narrative may be seen as deriving at least part of their social force from their relation to universal prototypes.

Of course, one might wonder if "Dangerous Role Model Barbie" is aptly considered a narrative at all. Barbie comes to serve as a paradigm or ideal of female beauty. That ideal presumably has consequences for one's behavior (as ideals do generally). Does the sequence of establishing and pursuing an ideal truly constitute a narrative? I agree with Phelan that it does. Put very crudely, the "Dangerous Role Model Barbie" narrative runs something like this. Young women form an ideal of female beauty by exposure to Barbie dolls, emaciated fashion models, and so on. They compare their own bodies to this ideal. Finding themselves too thick—even when they are at a healthy weight—they begin to diet. In some cases, this dieting becomes obsessive, even to the point where some young women risk (or succumb to) starvation.

To understand why this constitutes a narrative, we need to define "story." Like other words of ordinary language, "story" may be defined at different levels of specificity. The most basic levels give bare minimal conditions for being a story. But we do not consider all stories to be equally good instances of "storyness," even if they satisfy the minimal conditions. In other words, not all stories are equally prototypical. One fairly basic level of story definition would be as follows. A story is a sequence of non-normal, causally related events and actions that emerge from normalcy and return to normalcy. In other words, we have certain expectations about the way the world will ordinarily operate. We have a possible story whenever things do not happen the way they are supposed to. Driving to work, I expect to encounter some red and some green lights. If I encounter all green or all red lights, that is abnormal and I have the seed of a story. I begin with the normal world when I am at home. I return to the normal sequence of things when I arrive at work. However, in the interim, I experience a series of events that are non-normal. A slightly more prototypical level would delimit stories in the following way. We have a story when an agent desires the achievement of some goal and passes through a series of nonordinary events and actions before achieving that goal or establishing that the goal is not achievable. (Either achieving the goal or finding it to be unachievable should have the function of returning the agent's situation to normalcy.) Note that the goal is presumably something that will contribute to the protagonist's happiness. In consequence, the middle of the story—in which the protagonist lacks that goal—should be emotionally aversive for the protagonist. This is the level at which "Dangerous Role Model Barbie" is a narrative. It involves a goal of achieving a certain physical ideal, an aversive emotional condition (disgust with one's appearance), and pursuit of the goal (through dieting). A peculiar thing about this narrative is that it rarely has a comic conclusion, a conclusion in which the young woman achieves the goal and lives happily ever after. Rather, dieting itself becomes "normal," if more tragic consequences do not follow.

Beyond the types of story considered thus far, we have a still more prototypical story when the goal, the events, and the actions are emotionally engaging, not only for the protagonist, but for readers or listeners as well. We therefore have the most highly prototypical stories when the goals are standard happiness prototypes. This begins to account for the existence of the three cross-cultural narrative prototypes, for these are linked with happiness prototypes—enduring romantic union for the romantic prototype; individual and in-group power and esteem for the heroic prototype; plenty of life's necessities in the sacrificial prototype.

Of the three cross-cultural prototypes, it should come as no surprise that heroic tragicomedy is the default form for nationalism. In other words, our tendency is first of all to imagine our nation—its organization, its relation to enemies, its past, its future—through a heroic structure. In particular conditions, people shift to a sacrificial or romantic mode. Specifically, when the society has been devastated and there is no longer any hope of social domination over out-groups, nationalists may take up the sacrificial structure. When the nation is divided by subnational oppositions, then the romantic mode may become important, as writers envision the union of the subnational groups through stories of romantic love.[18] On the other hand, the romantic plot is strongly individualistic and antihierarchical. Thus, it often works against nationalism, opposing identity divisions between in- and out-groups and opposing in-group hierarchies. As a result, the romantic structure may operate, not only as a narrative of national reconciliation, but as a narrative of internationalism. Put differently, it may serve as a means of opposing national divisions just as it may serve as a means of opposing subnational divisions. Indeed, the logic of the romantic plot seems to push inevitably toward undermining categorial identifications of any sort, including national identifications (and toward challenging group hierarchies of any sort).

In referring to subnational reconciliation, I mentioned "stories of romantic love." One very common way of opposing subnational divisions is through the literary representation of romantic love that crosses such subnational boundaries (e.g., love uniting a Hindu and a Muslim in India or an African American and a European American in the United States). The nationalist use of literature is not confined to romantic emplotment. Heroic and sacrificial forms of nationalism are also frequently expressed in such explicit, fictional stories—narrative poems, plays, movies, and so forth. It may be less obvious that narrative structures of all three sorts serve to emplot histories as well,[19] guiding our selection of historical details, orienting our causal inferences, and so forth. Perhaps most important, these structures even provide implicit organizing principles for nationalist policies and practices. This is particularly striking because, unlike fictions or histories, policies and practices do not have an obvious, overt narrative

---

18. As far as I am aware, this is the only one of the three patterns that has been discussed by other writers. Specifically, Doris Sommer has treated this topic in relation to Latin American literature.

19. The emplotment of history was explored by Hayden White in his path-breaking *Metahistory*. I am deeply indebted to White's work, though my own understanding of the key narrative structures, and the way they operate in nationalist thought and feeling, is obviously different from White's.

organization. Put differently, when we look at a policy statement, we do not commonly see a plot (at least not in the narratological sense). In the final chapters, I consider the three narrative prototypes in turn, examining cases of both explicit narratives (in stories and/or histories) and implicit narratives (in policy statements and related works).

Chapter 5 takes up heroic emplotment. It begins with some general points about the nationalist operation of narrative genres. Specifically, all three genres operate at two levels. We might refer to these as the "prototypical" and "exemplary" levels. The prototypes just outlined provide general, cross-culturally constant structures for imagining the nation. More exactly, the heroic prototype provides a general structure for imagining the internal social hierarchy of the nation and the relation of the nation to its external enemies. The sacrificial prototype provides the broad principles for imagining social devastation and regeneration. The romantic prototype provides guidelines for imagining national division and reconciliation. But emplotments do not proceed solely from prototypes. They draw on particular, exemplary narratives as well. These exemplars, which differ from nation to nation, are especially important in the case of heroic emplotment. Specifically, nations often adopt one or two ancient heroic plots as paradigms for nationalist thought and action.

After briefly treating these general issues, chapter 5 turns to a paradigm of this sort, the story of King David. This story illustrates the heroic structure and its nationalist use remarkably well. It has obvious importance for contemporary Israeli nationalism, including the Israeli relation to Palestine and the Palestinian people. But it is also consequential for a range of European and American nationalisms, including that of the United States. In the case of the United States, it seems clear that biblical stories have had greater national importance than any subsequent epic or related narratives. (For example, no work of American literature—heroic or otherwise—has had anything like the influence of the Bible on American political life.) Moreover, the importance of biblical stories has only increased in recent years. Indeed, they are central to the increasingly influential Christian nationalist movements. As Goldberg points out, "Veterans of the Christian nationalist movement occupy positions throughout the federal bureaucracy, making crucial decisions about our national life" (16). Regarding Israel itself, Moyers notes that millions of conservative Christian Americans actively support Israel because of their deep belief in biblical narratives. More generally, today the nationalisms of the United States and Israel are intertwined, particularly in foreign policy. One could even argue that there is no single issue of greater importance for American, or global, peace than the resolution of the Israel-Palestine conflict.

In the second part of the chapter, I turn to a recent American film, *Independence Day*. This is, of course, an explicit, fictional narrative, and a highly popular one—indeed, it is one of the twenty top grossing films of all time in the United States.[20] I have chosen this film for two main reasons. First, it is different from the biblical story of David in obvious ways. It is modern, popular, and enacted rather than ancient, high canonical, and written. But it shows us the same prototypical structure operating toward nationalist ends. On the other hand, while the prototypical structure is shared, there are clear differences in the details of the story. Some of these are incidental. (Stories have to have some differences.) But some are not incidental. Some are systematic and politically consequential. This leads to my second reason for choosing this film. It allows us to explore the particularity of U.S. nationalism. While nationalism follows common principles everywhere, those principles are always particularized in distinct ways. Thus, the nationalism of the United States is not identical with that of Israel or any other country. It has a different historical development, and a different cultural and political context. *Independence Day* presents the heroic plot in a highly prototypical form—hence its similarity to the story of David. But it also specifies that form in a way that reveals distinctive aspects of U.S. nationalism. (A third, less important reason for choosing the film is that it draws on—or at least alludes to—the story of David. Though the connections are very limited, they do suggest the paradigmatic status of the David story in American nationalism.)

The treatment of *Independence Day*, with its specifically American nationalism, prepares us for the third section of the chapter, which examines the tacit heroic emplotment of the nation in George W. Bush's national speech three days after the September 11 bombings.

Before continuing on to the sacrificial plot, I briefly treat the "epilogue of suffering." A surprising part of explicit heroic stories (discussed at length in chapter 4 of my *The Mind*) is the addition of an epilogue that questions the heroic actions and values of the rest of the work. This epilogue typically presents the hero as suffering from remorse for the innocents killed during the heroic conflict. It is clear that such epilogues occur outside explicit stories as well (e.g., in nationalist policies). To illustrate the point, I consider an historically consequential, public instance of this epilogue. The Winter Soldier Investigation took place in January and February of 1971. It convened over one hundred witnesses to war crimes in Vietnam. The witnesses were primarily soldiers who had often taken part

---

20. See http://www.the-movie-times.com (accessed June 2, 2006).

in these crimes, under orders from superior officers. In 1972, a selection of these testimonies was edited by the Vietnam Veterans Against the War and published by Beacon Press. Of course, this book does not form a single, coherent narrative. However, when one is aware of the structure of the epilogue of suffering, it is easy to recognize that the work does indeed manifest an opposition not only to the Vietnam War, but to its heroic emplotment. Moreover, it manifests traces of its own narrative organization as well—and these traces follow the structure of the epilogue.

Chapter 6 considers sacrificial narratives. The military preeminence of the United States has meant that the United States has never been in a position where sacrificial emplotment became nationally significant. I have therefore taken up two diametrically opposed and historically consequential cases from other parts of the world—one from Germany, and one from India.

Some versions of sacrificial nationalism involve the deaths of both out-group and in-group members. However, many versions of sacrificial nationalism focus on one or the other. In some cases, sacrificial nationalism isolates an "internal enemy" that is taken to be the cause of national devastation. That internal enemy must, then, be purged. In other cases, sacrificial nationalism sees the in-group itself as collectively responsible for the devastation. That in-group must, then, sacrifice from itself. In the first section of this chapter, I consider the former, "purgative" sacrificial nationalism. Specifically, I take up what is probably the most extended and horrifying example of such emplotment in the history of the world—Hitler's Germany. To discuss this case, I work through the first book of *Mein Kampf*, examining the implicit sacrificial emplotment that rationalizes the authoritarianism and genocide that marked Nazi policy.

In the second section of the chapter, I turn to Gandhi, one of the most widely revered political figures ever, a nationalist politician whose ideas and practices have had significant impact around the world—including the United States, by way of such activists as Martin Luther King. Gandhi may seem to have nothing at all in common with Hitler. However, the two share a fundamentally sacrificial approach to nationalism. The crucial difference is that Gandhi's nationalism is a nationalism of penitential *self*-sacrifice. It is not a nationalism of purging an internal enemy. In order to explore Gandhi's sacrificial emplotment of nationalism, I consider a series of lectures he delivered on the *Bhagavad Gītā*, a Hindu religious text that was of central importance in the development of Indian nationalism.

In the cases of both Hitler and Gandhi, a recognition of sacrificial emplotment allows us to see patterns in and implications of their principles and policies that we would otherwise have missed. It also suggests some reasons for their great popular appeal. As David Brown pointed out, it is important to explain "not only why state elites articulated" a particular "ideology of nationalism, but also why these invented nationalist ideologies resonated in the imaginings of civil society" (34). In this case, both explanations are bound up with the conditions in which sacrificial emplotments tend to arise and take hold. In addition, as I have already noted, the default mode of nationalist narrative is heroic. The heroic plot remains important even in sacrificial nationalism. Indeed, it effectively underlies sacrificial narratives. Put differently, nationalism is never purely sacrificial. It is sacrificial only insofar as an heroic emplotment appears impossible. Various aspects of both Hitler's and Gandhi's thought (e.g., Gandhi's sometimes equivocal statements about violence or weapons)—and some aspects of their followers' commitments and actions—become much more comprehensible when we recognize this.

The final chapter considers the romantic plot. As Doris Sommer has suggested, one of the most common uses of the romantic plot is to oppose subnational division—racial, religious, regional, and so forth. Again, just as conditions of national devastation tend to trigger a sacrificial emplotment, conditions of national division tend to trigger a romantic emplotment. In connection with this, I consider the work that is perhaps the closest thing Americans have to a national epic—Walt Whitman's *Leaves of Grass,* specifically the key poem, "Song of Myself." Whitman is widely viewed as the "poet of America" (see Miller 5) and "Song of Myself" is "the most acclaimed and influential poem written by an American," as Greenspan has remarked (1). Whitman was keenly aware of the growing estrangement of different segments of the American population, specifically those who opposed slavery (concentrated in the North) and those who supported it (concentrated in the South). Even more important, he was deeply disturbed by the racial divisions in the nation. Many cases of literary works involve an explicit romantic emplotment of nationalism, some discussed by Sommer. "Song of Myself" involves a much more subdued version of the narrative structure, a tacit emplotment that is visible only at certain points in the poem. But this is precisely why it is valuable to examine that emplotment. It helps us to discern and understand aspects of the poem and the poem's nationalism that would otherwise go unnoticed or that we would sense only vaguely and inarticulately. It also helps us to recognize and more fully understand the inexplicit operation of such emplotment.

As I have already indicated, a distinctive feature of the romantic plot is that it has an antidivisive or incorporative tendency that tends to repeat itself with increasingly large groups all the way up to humanity as a whole. Simply put, if romantic emplotment offers us an argument against regional subnationalism, then it must equally offer us an argument against nationalism. If it works against the oppositions among different racial groups in the United States, then it must work against the oppositions among different national groups globally. For this reason, the tacit romantic emplotment of politics tends, not toward nationalism, but toward internationalism. In fact, we see this tendency in Whitman. At certain points, "Song of Myself" is a song of America. But it repeatedly expands beyond America to the world. Some authors have followed through on the implications of this extension, self-consciously advocating a vigorous internationalism and elaborating on the antihierarchical elements of romantic emplotment as well. I conclude with a case of this sort—Emma Goldman, a Russian immigrant to the United States and a widely influential activist. Her important essays on Anarchism reveal a consistent romantic emplotment of social ideas and practices. This emplotment not only helps to explain various aspects of Goldman's own thought and action. It also suggests alternatives to the destructive nationalisms of the heroic and sacrificial modes, nationalisms that have caused such terrible, human suffering across the ages, and particularly in the past century.[21]

21. Earlier, I responded briefly to the idea that globalization has spelled the end of nationalism. The brevity of this response was troubling to some, who felt a deeper engagement with the most prominent theorists of this orientation—particularly Hardt and Negri—is important to establish the continuing political relevance of nationalism. I initially added a lengthy discussion of work by Hardt and Negri, with whom I have many political agreements and share a sense of political solidarity, despite our sometimes significant intellectual divergences. Hardt and Negri, however, are treating a different topic and are therefore largely irrelevant to this book. Specifically, they are discussing governmental autonomy, not the motivational force of categorial identification, which is the topic of the present work. Moreover, as I have already noted, governmental autonomy is not straightforwardly correlated with group solidarity or emotional engagement. Again, the motivational force of national identification may actually be enhanced by a decline in national autonomy, a point well illustrated by the growth of nationalist feeling under colonial domination. For this reason, a lengthy discussion of Hardt and Negri, or any other theorist arguing that the authority of national governments has declined, is simply beside the point. Treating Hardt and Negri at length would take us on a detour from the main argument and add extra pages to an already bulky manuscript.

I have therefore removed this discussion here, and transformed it into a separate article. The key points of that article are as follows. (1) Hardt and Negri are discussing *nationalism* in the somewhat peculiar sense of the autonomy of one national government relative to other national governments—"the sovereignty of the nation-state," as they put it (*Multitude* xii). This is surely an important topic, but it should not be confused with *nationalism* in the sense of a motivating force. (2) Hardt and Negri view the decline in national sovereignty as related to the development of a "new form" (xii) of world structure, the network. I agree that there is a network aspect to intergovernmental relations. But I disagree with Hardt and Negri in two respects. First, I believe that this has always been the case. Second, their use of network theory is somewhat loose and metaphorical, leading them to conclusions about a decline in national autonomy that simply do not follow. (3) Their conclusions about the novelty of the multitude as a network also rely on the loose and metaphorical use of network theory and their conclusion that states must become networks to fight networks appears simply to be a non sequitur. (4) Their treatment of recent coalition-building efforts by the United States understates the development of coalitions in the past and overstates the need of the United States for coalition partners. It also understates the coercive force of such coalition-building in a "unipolar" world (a point that could be treated productively through a more technical use of network theory). (5) Part of the reason for coalition-building, in the view of Hardt and Negri, is the need for justification and the primacy of humanitarian concerns (see 26, 60). The facts surrounding "humanitarian interventions" seem to speak against the seriousness of the humanitarian concerns (see Chomsky, *New*, and Herman and Peterson on the paradigmatic case of Yugoslavia). (6) When Hardt and Negri turn from governments to the multitude, their analysis seems to rely on inadequate causal analyses. For example, their key explanatory category of "immaterial labor" includes scientific research, psychotherapy, and serving fast food. This does not seem to be a causally coherent category—nor does it seem to be particularly immaterial (thus profoundly different from what went before). (7) The conclusions they draw from their notion of immaterial labor—for example, that the "construction of social relationships" by "the poor" becomes "directly productive" (131)—seem to be non sequiturs. This is important because these conclusions make social transformation (e.g., the development of "economic self-management"; 336) appear much easier than it is. (8) Hardt and Negri present an inspiring vision of antiauthoritarian, mass movements for social, economic, and political transformation. This vision is itself derived from various popular movements that have arisen in recent years. Unfortunately, it is not clear that their optimism is justified. (9) Finally, I ask—if a number of Hardt and Negri's conclusions do not follow from their premises, what do they follow from? I believe their conclusions follow most directly from their preferred form of tacit emplotment, in much the way predicted by the analyses set out in the following pages. Specifically, like Whitman and Goldman, Hardt and Negri's understanding of and response to nationalism are oriented and organized by a tacit romantic narrative. Indeed, this is one reason why their work also holds out an, in many ways, inspiring vision for a more humane future.

1

UNDERSTANDING IDENTITY

What It Is and What It Does

PATRIOTISM IS, FIRST OF ALL, the assertion of a certain sort of identification. Specifically, it is a form of commitment to a particular national identity. The common view of identity, at least of national identity, is that it is best understood as a way of life. Thus, a patriot is someone committed to a particular society's culture, institutions, political philosophy. But there are numerous problems with this view. First, no society has a single way of life. Different segments of society have different rights, privileges, obligations, and restrictions. Moreover, patriotism is often affirmed most acutely in times of international conflict, thus in opposition to a national enemy. But the national enemy, too, does not represent a single, invariant way of life. Indeed, in some cases, a patriot for one side may have greater sympathy with certain ideas and practices on the enemy side. However, he or she is, it seems, unlikely to recognize such sympathy if the practices are explicitly associated with the enemy side. Consider, for example, the recent conflict between the United States and France over the Iraq war. Obviously, the United States and France were not themselves at war. However, in the United States, it was widely considered patriotic to oppose all things French—hence, for example, the spectacle of Americans pouring out bottles of French wine. The crux of this conflict was the French view of the situation in Iraq. However, when Americans were presented with a statement of the French position on Iraq, they largely agreed with it. Or, rather, they largely agreed *as long as the position was not identified as French.*[1] As this example suggests, the crucial factor for a patriot is not the position or practice of his or her country, nor the position or practice of the enemy. Rather, the crucial factor is the labels, the names attached to those positions and practices.

The same point applies to ethnic, religious, and other group loyalties. I suspect that most Catholics do not have a strong commitment to the defining theological positions of their church. But, depending on the degree of their commitment to a Catholic identity, they would be inclined to favor positions labeled "Catholic" and to demur from positions labeled "Protestant." This is true whether the labeling is direct ("Catholics believe that . . .") or implied. For example, I suspect that many Catholics would accept the doctrine of papal infallibility or that of the Immaculate Conception, and that many Protestants would reject them, because they know to associate these doctrines with Catholicism. On the other hand, at least some of the Protestants may agree to the statement "Mary was born without sin," if they are not told that this is the doctrine of the Immaculate Conception. Conversely, many Catholics seem unaware of just what the doctrine of the Immaculate Conception is.

This distinction between mere labels and ways of life (encompassing cultural practices, political institutions, and so forth) is crucial for understanding national or any other sort of group identification. Contrary to our intuitions, the labels are the more consequential of the two. In the following pages, I set out this division in more technical terms, examining its implications for group formation. Specifically, the first section considers

---

1. For example, CBS News polls on February 10–12, February 24–25, March 4–5, and March 7–9, 2003, all show a majority of Americans saying that the United States should not "take military action fairly soon," but should "wait and give the United Nations and weapons inspectors more time." A FOX News/Opinion Dynamics Poll on February 11–12, 2003 explained that "France and Germany have made a proposal that would put United Nations troops in Iraq to back up the inspectors, increase the number of inspectors, and give inspections a longer time to work." Only 37% of those polled felt this was a "good plan." Moreover, when faced with the statement that "Several U.S. allies, such as France, Germany, and Russia, oppose taking military action against Iraq at this time," only 18% agreed; 77% disagreed with these allies, including 35% who were "Angry that [France, Germany, and Russia] are not supporting the United States." (For the poll data, see www.pollingreport.com; on the French position, see, for example, the "Joint declaration by France, Russia and Germany on Iraq" [February 10, 2003], available at www.iraqcrisis.co.uk.)

the operation of labels or categorial identities and their difference from practical identities (roughly, our individual, interpersonally coordinated forms of life—our routines, capacities, expectations, and so forth). It argues that group oppositions or conflicts are not primarily a matter of practical incompatibilities (the so-called clash of cultures). Instead, they are fundamentally a matter of mere labeling or vacuous categorization. In connection with this, I outline the cognitive and neurocognitive structures underlying these two forms of identity. The next section examines the interaction between categorial identity and practical identity. Specifically, it addresses the effects of categorial identification on the diversity or homogeneity of practical identities in a given group. Subsequent parts treat group inclusion criteria (i.e., ways of defining who has what categorial identity), the formation of in-group and out-group prototypes (or stereotypes), the development of group ideals, and the operation of structures of authority within identity groups. The last two sections consider what happens when we face contradictions among our identity categories (e.g., what happens when we encounter a conflict between our national and religious identities). The first of these sections sets out the most common nationalist strategies for dealing with potentially divided loyalties. The final section outlines five critical parameters governing which identity category comes to dominate our thought and action in cases of conflict. Throughout these analyses, I draw on a range of sources from cognitive science, neurobiology, social psychology, political economy, and elsewhere, which, I argue, provide converging evidence for the present account of identity.

CATEGORIAL IDENTITIES AND PRACTICAL IDENTITIES

In the preceding paragraphs, I treated a basic division in identity through the use of ordinary language terms and commonsense ideas. I spoke about "ways of life" and "labels." Here, I need to introduce some more technical terms. What I initially referred to as a way of life roughly approximates what I have elsewhere called "practical identity." Practical identity is the set of habits, skills, concepts, ideas, and so forth, which allow me to act physically and mentally, most importantly insofar as such action bears on interaction with others.[2] More technically, practical identity is the complex

---

2. The idea of practical identity is related to the notion of the *habitus* as developed by Bourdieu and others. This idea has been taken up by theorists of nationalism. For example, Treibel discusses the ways in which the habitus cultivated by schooling in the Federal

of representations and procedural competences that enable my thought and action. In the following pages, I am concerned only with that part of practical identity that bears, not on isolated or wholly private activities, but on fluid interaction with others. Obviously, this is a complex concept and requires some unpacking.

As I noted in the introduction, our "cognitive architecture" or the organization of our minds involves several components. To a great extent, these components are universal. For example, we all have episodic and semantic memories (see Schacter 17, 134–35), that is, memories of particular events and memories of concepts. However, some components are not universal. For example, there are differences in the contents of our episodic and semantic memories, thus the precise events and concepts we remember. Memory contents may be divided into memories that we recall in thought and memories that we enact—on the one hand, memories of what happened at a certain time, what something means, and so on, and, on the other hand, memories of how to do something. The former are *representational* memories. The latter are *procedural* memories (or "skills"; see Johnson-Laird 156). The memory of my last birthday dinner or the meaning of "anapest" is representational. The memory of how to ride a bicycle is procedural. When I "activate" a representational memory, I think about that memory. When I activate a procedural memory, I engage in a certain activity (e.g., ride a bicycle).

Representational memories may be further subdivided into schemas, prototypes, and exempla. *Schemas* are broad structures that give general conditions for an object, event, or action.[3] *Prototypes* are standard cases. *Exempla* are particular instances. (Obviously, all our episodic memories are exempla in this sense, for they are particular, experiential instances—of, for example, birthday dinners.) A great deal of research indicates that we tend to think most consistently through prototypes or standard cases (see Holland et al. 182ff. and citations). For example, when we identify something as a bird, we do not (in ordinary life) begin with an abstract schema for birdness. Nor do we begin with particular instances (e.g., Polly, my pet canary). Rather, we begin with a standard case. In identifying birds, think-

---

Republic of Germany was different from that developed by schooling in the German Democratic Republic (322). The two concepts differ in their precise extension and theoretical specification.

3. When a schema concerns a relatively routine set of actions (with defaults, alternatives, and so forth), it is often referred to as a *script*. Thus, we might refer to the script for going to a restaurant (to take the standard example). The classical discussion of scripts is to be found in Schank and Abelson. For a brief overview of the current understanding of scripts, see Schank.

ing about birds, talking about birds, we begin with an idea of birds that is roughly "things like robins." In other words, we have some idea of a prototypical bird (which, it turns out, is very similar to a robin). That prototype serves us as a default. Unless we are given reason to think differently about birds (e.g., if we are doing ornithology), we stick with this prototype.[4]

In contrast with representations, procedures are generally understood as purely schematic. In other words, cognitive scientists do not generally refer to procedural prototypes or exempla. Rather, they refer only to procedural schemas. Of course, these schemas must be broad and flexible enough to accommodate a range of prototypical and nonprototypical objects and unusual instances (e.g., the procedural schema for riding a bicycle should allow us to ride different sorts of bicycles).[5]

Practical identity is someone's entire set of representational and procedural structures, most importantly insofar as these enable his or her interaction with others. Thus, two people share practical identity to the degree that their representational and procedural memories enable them to achieve common purposes. Suppose Smith needs to find the nearest hospital and asks Doe. Doe then gives Smith directions. This is a routine interaction. But it is very complicated. Doe must understand Smith's request and must be able to give Smith the information in a way Smith will understand. This involves a shared language. It also involves shared practical presuppositions—such as how to drive and what sorts of things one is likely to notice or miss while driving (as when Doe says, "get into the right lane immediately or you'll miss the turn").

Practical identity is only partially shared by any group of people. Moreover, one (partially) shares different practical identities with different groups. I share an ability to discuss cognitive science with some people,

---

4. In fact, things are not as simple as this suggests. Complex issues surround the precise nature of prototypes. For example, some writers reject the idea that there are prototypes, instead seeing only "prototype effects" (see, for example, Lakoff, *Women*). There are also differences between writers who discuss prototypes or prototype effects in terms of representations or symbols and writers who discuss prototypes or prototype effects in terms of neural networks (for an influential case of the latter sort, see Rogers and McClelland on "typicality" and "typicality effects" [198–204]; for an intermediate case, see Barsalou). I have discussed some of these issues elsewhere (see *The Mind* 58–60n.2). Here and below, I tend to adopt a representationalist idiom, even when drawing on neurobiological research. However, so far as I can tell, nothing in my argument rests on adopting a particular view of the cognitive existence of prototypes. Moreover, my personal view is that intentional, representational or symbolic, connectionist or subsymbolic, and neurobiological accounts can all be valid, capturing different patterns at different levels of analysis (see Hogan, "On the Very Idea").

5. For further discussion of procedural and representational schemas, see my *Cognitive Science* 44–45.

a (limited) ability to play water polo with others. My competence in English is broadly shared by other English speakers. But here, too, there are differences. Indeed, language is a prime case of practical identity—and it perfectly illustrates the way that such identity is incompletely shared. We tend to think that language is simply held in common by a given speech community. But even brief reflection on our differences in, say, vocabulary, shows that this is not true. Moreover, there are theoretical reasons for recognizing this. For example, Noam Chomsky has stressed that "a person's language should be defined" as "the grammar represented in his/her mind" (*Rules* 120; see also *Knowledge* 25). The point is made even by sociolinguists, such as Hudson, who writes that "*no two speakers have the same language*" (12; emphasis in original).

Of course, many features of one's practical identity are more likely to be shared by people within one's own society than by people outside that society. Thus, the way I speak, drive, eat, gesture, and make presumptions about social space are all likely to fit better with the ways other people do these things in my own society than with the way people in other societies do them. However, this is never entirely uniform. For example, my presumptions and ways of arguing about the war in Iraq are, it seems, much closer to those most common in Africa or Asia than to those most common in the United States.

We are ordinarily not self-conscious about practical identity. We tend to become aware of practical identity at points where it breaks down. In other words, we do not usually become aware of shared practical identity, but only of different practical identities. At a family reunion in Missouri, a cousin expects me to be able to discuss the results of the most recent Superbowl, but I am only vaguely aware that it has even occurred. In India, my sister-in-law sends me into the kitchen with some clicking apparatus, evidently expecting me to light the stove, but I have no idea what to do with it. In cases such as these, we become aware that there is some sort of practical discrepancy. When it has a national pattern (e.g., when many people from one society exhibit the same inability to light a stove), we say that it is a cultural difference. When there is a pattern within a nation, we might refer to it as a regional or class difference. In any event, practical identity comes to our attention only through individual cases, and those individual cases are most often negative. (In some cases, we may expect differences in practical identity. Then we will become aware of practical identity in individual cases where it is shared—for instance, if we encounter someone who happens to speak English in a remote Chinese village. We will consider cases of this sort further below.)

Categorial identity, in contrast, is any group membership that I take to be definitive of who I am. It is the way I locate myself socially—as American, Irish, Catholic, or whatever. It is what I answer when I am asked questions about my identity. The crucial thing here is that an identity-specifying group membership is defined, in the first place, only by a name. As I have already suggested, it is, roughly, a form of labeling. More exactly, categorial identification is the acceptance of a category label as a representation of what one is, as a name for some crucially important quality of one's nature. The label names this quality by placing one in a group with other people who share that quality. It may be religious, ethnic, national, a matter of sex or sexual orientation, or something else. In any case, it is critical for one's self-concept, and it defines an in-group—along with an out-group of people who do not share the quality in question.

There are obviously relations between practical identity and categorial identity. If Jones identifies categorially as a gay man, that almost certainly means that he has some aspects of practical identity in common with other categorially identified gay men. Specifically, it indicates that he finds men sexually attractive, that he is disposed to pursue men or, in particular cases, to respond favorably to sexual pursuit by men. However, it is crucial that the categorial and practical identity are by no means the same. I was once at a psychoanalytic conference where an analyst was speaking about two patients. One, he explained, regularly went out and had sex with men. The other had had a single homosexual encounter many years earlier. The first man adamantly refused to identify himself as gay. The second man, in contrast, did identify himself as gay—with great feelings of guilt. One might argue that these men were misconstruing their own propensities due to the homophobia of the larger society. That seems perfectly reasonable, and probably correct. However, it does not affect the fact that the relation between practical identity and categorial identity is not direct; it does not affect the fact that these two cases clearly illustrate the discrepancy between practical and categorial identity. Moreover, even when two men say that they are gay and routinely act on their sexual preference, it does not follow that anything else in their practical identities is shared. Their precise sexual preferences, the ways in which they act on those preferences, the precise nature of their interests and enjoyments—none of this has to be the same (cf. Butler 17). Indeed, queer theory has repeatedly emphasized such diversity (see, for example, Cohen).

Of course, the fact that categorial identification diverges from practical identity does not warrant the conclusion that they are unrelated. Taking up the case of sexual preference, one might argue that categorial identification, at least in this case, is not solely a matter of labeling. It has some content. That is true. But it is important to recognize that the content is very limited. Moreover, in other cases, that content may be entirely absent. Research has shown that in-group/out-group divisions can be created with no practical group differences whatsoever. Test subjects have been assigned to two groups based on an explicitly arbitrary principle (e.g., the penultimate digit of their social security numbers). They did not know one another before the groups were determined and they were not allowed to interact with one another after the groups were determined. As a result, the groups were indistinguishable in terms of practical identity. Nonetheless, in their judgments and actions, the subjects identified with their in-group, showing the standard prejudices in favor of in-group members and against out-group members (see Hirschfeld 1 and Duckitt 68–69).[6] In other experiments, researchers tested whether or not subjects discriminated on the basis of similarity (roughly, practical identity) in the way they did on the basis of group membership (categorial identity). As Horowitz summarizes, there was "no statistically significant tendency to discriminate on the basis of similarity. Plainly, what counts is group membership and not demonstrated similarity" (145).[7]

Neurobiological research converges with social psychological research on these points. First of all, it suggests that we categorize individuals very quickly in terms of at least certain in-group/out-group divisions, prominently those that involve high visual salience. Mitchell et al. explain that the medial prefrontal cortex is strongly activated when one simulates another person's mind—thus when one views that person as an intending subject, parallel to oneself. They undertook a study of medial prefrontal activation in subjects looking at photographs of faces. The research demonstrated that "activity in the medial [prefrontal cortex] was higher for faces that participants judged to be" like themselves "than for faces judged to be" unlike themselves (77). Clearly, judgments of likeness in this

6. One might ask, "What made an individual feel she or he was part of Group A other than being assigned to that group?" This is an excellent question, for it gets to the heart of these studies. The answer is *nothing.* Merely being told that you, Jones, Smith, and so on, constitute Group A, while Doe, Jenkins, and so on, constitute Group B, produces in-group/out-group prejudice (e.g., more favorable evaluations of other people assigned to Group A, relative to those assigned to Group B). That is precisely the point of the experiments.

7. Horowitz is perhaps the most important writer in this general area of political analysis to have drawn on social psychological research to discuss politically consequential group divisions—in his case, ethnic groups in conflict. In this way, Horowitz's book is an important precursor to the present study. However, his concerns are rather different and his use of this research is more limited—and necessarily not combined with cognitive neuroscientific research that has taken place in the intervening two decades.

context cannot refer to propensities and preferences, hence practical identity. Given only photographs, the participants were able to judge only physical likeness or unlikeness, thus such categorial properties as race.

Work by Ito and her colleagues extends these points. These researchers set out to consider a real political problem—the killing of unarmed black men by police. By measuring electrocortical activity, they were able to demonstrate that "attention is directed to race and gender cues at early processing stages regardless of the dimension to which participants are explicitly attending" (193). Moreover, responses to blacks suggested "initial covert orienting to targets heuristically associated with the greater potential for threat" as early as 100 to 200 milliseconds after exposure to the image (193). The point is related to the finding there is "greater amygdala activation to racial out-group than in-group faces" (196, citing work by Wheeler and Fiske). The amygdala activation suggests either heightened fear or anger, or both. (On fear and the amygdala, see LeDoux and Phelps; on anger, see Panksepp, "Emotions" 144, 146–47). Note, again, that this cannot be a function of practical identity of the people in the photographs. Given the test conditions, it is necessarily a matter of their categorial identity.

These cognitive and emotional points have practical consequences. Kunda cites research indicating that "the mere exposure to an African American face can suffice for other Americans to activate the construct of hostility, which, in turn, can lead them to behave in a more hostile manner" (321). She goes on to summarize studies in which such in-group/out-group divisions had harmful effects on behavior toward African Americans in job interviews (323).

Other work brings speech into the analysis. As Nusbaum and Small explain, citing research by D. L. Rubin, "for Caucasians, seeing an Asian face identified as a talker reduces the intelligibility and comprehensibility of a speech signal, compared with seeing a Caucasian face . . . paired with the same speech" (142–43). Here, the researcher explicitly controlled for practical identity by using the same speech. We can only conclude that the discrepancy in response is purely categorial.

While all this is bad enough, other research points to even more disturbing consequences. For example, in a simulation discussed by Ito and her colleagues, "Behavioral results showed a consistent bias against blacks relative to whites. Participants were faster and more accurate in 'shooting' armed blacks compared with armed whites. By contrast, they were faster and more accurate in 'not shooting' unarmed whites than unarmed blacks" (198, citing work by Correll et al.). Differences extend even to responses that follow the discovery that one has made an error—for example, in "shooting" an unarmed black (200).

Though much of this research has focused on race or ethnicity, the divisions at issue are not confined to race and ethnicity. Ito et al. refer more generally to "automatically encoded social category cues" (204), which is to say, in-group/out-group divisions. Moreover, responses to out-groups are not confined to fear-related amygdala activation, but may include, for example, disgust-related insula activation.[8] Krendl et al. used functional magnetic resonance imaging to investigate brain activity in response to several visually isolable, but nonracial out-groups (e.g., transsexuals). They found that these stigmatized groups tend to elicit amygdala and insula activation, suggesting fear, disgust, or other forms of aversion. This response was more robust in implicit conditions (i.e., conditions that did not involve any explicit evaluation of the person from the stigmatized out-group). However, those implicit conditions may be more significant. As Krendl et al. explain, "Implicit attitudes have consistently been shown to be more accurate predictors of affective state than explicit attitudes because we are highly motivated to inhibit societally undesirable explicit attitudes" (13; we will return to the issue of inhibition below).

In sum, as Fiske, Harris, and Cuddy put it, "Categorization of people as interchangeable members of an outgroup promotes an amygdala response characteristic of vigilance and alarm and an insula response characteristic of disgust or arousal" (1482–83).

We can, of course, observe the same patterns, if necessarily less clearly, in real political life, outside controlled studies. Consider, for example, the identity category "Hindu," which is deeply important in Indian national politics today. B. R. Ambedkar, chair of the committee that drafted India's constitution (see Wolpert, *New* 356), wrote that "Hindu society is a myth. The name 'Hindu' . . . was given by the Mohamedans to the natives for the purpose of distinguishing themselves" (quoted in Sharma 37). Partha Chatterjee argues that "'Hindu-ness' . . . cannot be . . . defined by any religious criteria at all. There are no specific beliefs or practices that characterize this 'Hindu'" (110). Much of Indian politics today is animated by the sharp opposition between Hindu and Muslim. But as Nandy et al. point out, "Even religious divisions within the two aggregates ['Hindu' and 'Muslim'] often bear 'peculiar' relationships with divisions within the other community. Thus, the Pranami sect in Gujarat (the one in which Gandhi was born) is

---

8. The practical importance of disgust in the treatment of out-groups has been explored valuably by Nussbaum. See, for example, her discussion of disgust in anti-Semitism and homophobia (*Upheavals* 347–49).

in many ways closer to Islam than it is to many other sects within Hinduism; likewise, most versions of Sindhi Hinduism look terribly Islamic to many South Indian Hindus and many Muslim communities in Rajasthan, Gujarat, and Bengal look disturbingly Hindu to Muslims in other parts of India" (51–52). Pascal Boyer makes a similar point. Speaking of Java, he writes that "the division between Muslim, Javanist and Hindu is to some extent internal to most individuals. That is, the various viewpoints and normative ideals that can be identified with these different traditions are tools that people combine [in practical identity] much more freely than a description in terms of affiliation [i.e., categorial identification] would suggest" (268).

But suppose there are riots in India. Will the Pranami Hindus join with Muslims while the Rajasthani Muslims join with Hindus? Will people join together with others in a community of shared practical identity? No, not at all. They will join together on the basis of prominent identity categories—in this case, "Hindu" and "Muslim." Tacitly recognizing the individual, idiolectal character of practical identity, Gandhi once wrote that "In reality, there are as many religions as there are individuals" (quoted in Daniel 57). But categorial identification supersedes this individuality, segmenting our identifications into "Muslim," "Hindu," "Christian," and so forth, independent of our practical similarities and differences.

In order to clarify my argument here, it may be useful to contrast my claims with those of two writers who have recently addressed related topics—Bruce Wexler, a neurocognitive researcher and psychiatrist, and Amartya Sen, a Nobel laureate in economics. Wexler has treated neuroscience and culture in a very valuable way. He is undoubtedly correct that intergroup conflicts can result from "internal neuropsychological structures created to conform with an individual's sensory and interpersonal environment at the time of development" (228). However, he does not distinguish between practical and categorial identity. As a result, he assumes that the relevant neuropsychological structures are a matter of culture, thus practical identity. In keeping with this, he writes that "Most of the violent conflicts raging around the world today are between peoples of different cultures and belief systems: Protestants versus Catholics in Northern Ireland; Muslims versus Hindus in India and Pakistan," and so forth (246). Though this analysis has intuitive plausibility, the research cited above indicates that it takes the wrong type of identity to be causally important. As we will discuss below, there are circumstances when conflicts in practical identity are consequential. However, they are consequential only in making categorial identities salient. When Ram and Narayan find their attitudes and habits incompatible, they are likely to understand this as a purely personal conflict. However, when Ram and Ali have the same experience, there is a good chance that they will become more aware of their different religious categories, even if these are entirely irrelevant to the practical incompatibilities. Thus, even when cultural differences exist and have social consequences, they have those consequences as a result of categorial identifications. In short, even here, the crucial factor is categorial identity.

My view is closer to that of Amartya Sen, who also treats Hindu-Muslim communalism. However, there are some significant differences. Sen rightly emphasizes the multiplicity of any given person's identities. But he is right in two very different ways. Each of us has multiple competencies and inclinations, thus multiple practical identities. In addition, each of us may be categorized or labeled in many ways. Though there are points where Sen begins to touch on this difference, he does not fully articulate it. As a result, his treatment of the nature of identity is never entirely clear. Thus, Sen writes of his "disturbing memories of Hindu-Muslim riots in India in the 1940s," which "include seeing . . . the massive identity shifts that followed divisive politics. A great many persons' identities as Indians, as subcontinentals, as Asians, or as members of the human race, seemed to give way—quite suddenly—to sectarian identification with Hindu, Muslim, or Sikh communities" (9–10). Such changes, of course, need to be explained. Part of what I hope to do in this book is explain how such changes occur. But it should already be clear that they are allowed by the fact that the "identities" in question are only labels. None is a matter of actual cultural practice. In other words, the problem is not simply one of people failing to recognize that they have numerous real (thus practical) identities. It is a matter of people organizing the social world into categorial identities at all.

Sen's memory of the Hindu-Muslim riots leads us to a more general point. The discrepancy between practical and categorial identity suggests why one type of identity may change without affecting the other. Practices alter while categories continue unchanged; categories shift while practices remain. At least for certain sorts of category, categorial identity changes more readily than practical identity. Indeed, change in categorial identification is often undertaken directly by political activists. Feminist educators seek to develop a categorial identification among women as women. Marxist "consciousness raising" sets out, among other things, to create a categorial identification of all workers as workers. Nationalist activists work to spread national identification throughout a society. The other side of this is that, once established, such categorial identifications may be unstable. In many cases, the effort to secure a certain sort of categorial identification (e.g., class or national identification) must be constantly renewed.

In a very general way, some of these points have been recognized by writers on nationalism and related topics. As just noted, Sen touches on these ideas in places. For example, he remarks that identity "categorization" may be "arbitrary," and he quotes Pierre Bourdieu on the way that "social action can end up 'producing a difference when none existed'" (27; quoting Bourdieu 160). But even here, there is ambiguity. The phrase "producing a difference" can mean one of two things. In the present analysis, it is important to distinguish between making a difference in practical identity and making a difference in categorial identity.

Sometimes parallel observations arise in connection with the analysis of a particular national or subnational group. For example, Wachtel maintains that people belong to a nation, "not because of any objective identifying criteria such as common language, history, or cultural heritage . . . but because they think they do" (2). Actually, things are more complex than this, but this rightly suggests that national identity categories can have little or even no content. Speaking of the former Yugoslavia, Wachtel writes that "no one at the turn of the nineteenth century would have identified him- or herself as a Yugoslav, whereas studies in the 1960s showed that the majority of the country's citizens held some form of Yugoslav national identity. Beginning in the late 1960s, however, the idea lost popularity precipitously, and at present it is preserved almost exclusively in the consciousness of émigrés scattered thinly all over the world" (1).

Along the same lines, Kasfir points out that many criteria have been used to define national groups—"Language, territory, social structure, cultural patterns, external administrative classification, and an active sense of identification" (56). Note that language, social structure, and cultural patterns are all components of practical identity. In contrast, the "sense of identification" refers to categorial identity. Kasfir goes on to state that "an active sense of identification with a particular group"—thus categorial identification—is "the most conclusive indicator of political behavior." This is why, for example, "Batoro and Banyoro regard themselves as separate 'tribes' . . . in spite of speaking the same language and sharing the same customs." In contrast, "some groups, such as the Baamba, speak two languages . . . and speakers of one may not be able to understand speakers of the other" (57). How, then, do such categorial definitions come about? Kasfir points to colonial administrative categories. "The use of 'tribal' classifications in gathering census information and establishing county and district boundaries," he argues, "has reified ethnic consciousness along official lines" (61). Speaking of the Congo, Olorunsola comes to similar conclusions. Subnational conflicts there derive from "ethnic identities and antagonisms." However, these "have a relatively short history." Specifically, "Ethnic labels were learned by the Belgians and applied to various peoples. Such labels were used to unify or divide a people and to distinguish favored ethnic groups from the less 'desirable' allies" (191). Put simply, the divisions are the result of labeling, not discrepancies in practical identity.[9]

As these references to religious riots and ethnic antagonisms suggest, and as the neurocognitive studies attest, categorial identifications—thus in-group/out-group divisions—involve a strong emotional component and are highly motivating. Indeed, they frequently overrule self-interest. The point is supported by a great deal of social psychological research. As Monroe, Hankin, and van Vechten put it, "The thousands of experiments underlying social identity theory have consistently shown that individuals identify with the in-group, support group norms, and derogate out-group members along stereotypical lines, even when there is no individual gain at stake" (435). Indeed, in-group bias holds even in cases where there is individual loss. As Duckitt summarizes, "group members . . . seek maximum relative advantage for the ingroup over the outgroup, even when this interferes with the achievement of maximum absolute outcomes for the subjects." Moreover, in some studies, subjects "are categorized into minimal groups," that is, arbitrary groups distinguished only by name (e.g. "A" and "B"). In these studies, when members of one group "are given the opportunity to discriminate [against members of other groups], they . . . show increased self-esteem" (Duckitt 85). In keeping with this, T. A. Wills has argued that "downward comparison," that is, comparison with inferiors in a hierarchy, is highly consequential for one's self-evaluation; thus we "can increase [our] subjective well-being through comparison with a less fortunate other" (245).

These points hold directly for national identification. For example, Greenfeld explains that the modern sense of "[n]ationality elevated every member of the community which it made sovereign. It guaranteed status. *National identity is, fundamentally, a matter of dignity.* It gives people reasons to be proud" (487; emphasis in original). The research on in-group definition agrees with Greenfeld, except on her claim about sovereignty. Intuitively, one might expect that group membership would bestow a sense of dignity only insofar as one is somehow responsible for the achievements

---

9. Of course, none of this is to say that labeling is, in general practice, a simple or wholly arbitrary matter. For example, on some complexities of the labeling process in colonial Africa, see Hastings 148–66.

of the group—here, only insofar as one participates in the governance of the nation as a citizen. People undoubtedly do have democratic aspirations, desires to have a say in matters of importance to them (though the aspirations are somewhat more complicated than one might initially imagine; see Baer and Jaros). However, their pride in a group does not seem to rest on such participation. Consider sports teams. Ortony, Clore, and Collins explain that "in a series of studies Cialdini et al. (1976) found that after a victory of their college football team, students were more likely to wear school colors, and were more likely to use the first person pronoun, 'we,' than the third person pronoun, 'they,' in referring to the football team" (136). In short, they were more likely to feel proud. It makes no difference whatsoever that they had nothing to do with the team's victory. Greenfeld goes on to link self-esteem with categorial identification more simply, stating that, "It would be a strong statement, but no overstatement, to say that the world in which we live was brought into being by vanity" (488) and "Nationality makes people feel good" (490). Earlier, Greenfeld had cited Tocqueville to the same effect. Tocqueville wrote in *Democracy in America* that "For the last fifty years no pains have been spared to convince the inhabitants of the United States that they are the only religious, enlightened, and free people . . . hence they conceive a high opinion of their superiority and are not very remote from believing themselves to be a distinct species of mankind" (quoted in Greenfeld 444). Tocqueville sees this as a specifically American inclination. The details no doubt differ from group to group and country to country. But the general feeling is part of all in-group definition.

The flip side of in-group pride is the denigration of out-groups. Thinking that we are good goes along with thinking they are bad. Believing that we are trustworthy is consequential only insofar as we think of them as untrustworthy. Viewing ourselves as benevolent is continuous with viewing them as malevolent. Thus Monroe, Hankin, and van Vechten explain that, according to "social identity theory . . . genocide and racism may in fact be extreme manifestations of normal group identification and behavior" (436). We have already seen that ample neuroscientific research is consistent with this conclusion.

DEFINING IDENTITY GROUPS AND ORGANIZING CULTURAL PRACTICES

Yet, despite my emphasis up to this point, in-group definition does not result from the mere existence of labels—national, ethnic, or whatever.

It is not even a simple matter of someone identifying himself or herself with a particular label, believing that the label defines something essential about him or her. For anyone to function as part of a particular in-group, it must be possible to isolate members of that group. One need not be able to isolate all of them, or to isolate them with absolute certainty all the time. However, one must have a general ability to differentiate in-group members from out-group members. Thus, every functional identity category must comprise not only a label, but an inclusion criterion.[10]

This inclusion criterion may be otherwise vacuous. It may involve no information beyond the bare principle that says who falls into the category and who does not. Moreover, that inclusion criterion may be entirely arbitrary, as in the "minimal group" studies mentioned earlier. On the other hand, vacuous and/or arbitrary categorial identifications tend to be extremely unstable. They continually risk disruption. This is where practical identity enters again. We expect certain behavioral, linguistic, conceptual, attitudinal, and other continuities within identification groups. Put differently, we tend to expect a certain degree of connection between categorial and practical identity. When expected continuities of practical identity fail, that failure produces a sense of alienation. A very similar point is made by Treibel in her discussion of reunified Germany. She writes that "The 'We'"—marking people's shared categorial identification as Germans—"sounds strange" (319; my translation). She goes on to explain that "After reunification, the new experience of strangeness confirmed that the East German habitus [thus, practical identity] and the West German habitus had developed ever further away from one another" (320). When repeated across a number of cases, that sense of alienation can create fissures in categorial identification. An obvious example of this is language in nationality. When individuals in two subnational groups cannot communicate through a shared language, some sense of mutual alienation may result. The alienation is likely to worsen when the clash in practical identities extends to conflicts over governmental language, the language of schools, and so forth.[11]

---

10. The inclusion criterion is related to the notion of social closure, set forth by Max Weber and recently taken up by Andreas Wimmer. Social closure defines the boundary between the in-group and the out-group. Moreover, it is a general concept, covering "ethnic groups, nations, social classes, estates, village communities and so on" (Wimmer 8). However, as Wimmer's discussion makes clear, it involves a more extensive and elaborated set of in-group connections than I envision here.

11. The point is far from merely academic. As Spolsky points out, "countries monolingual in both practice and management are quite rare" (159). Ways of resolving the problems that arise from this situation are far from obvious, as Spolsky's work makes clear.

The result of "practical alienation," as we may call it, is twofold. First, it tends to challenge the categorial identification on which we based our initial expectations of shared practical identity. For example, encountering linguistic incompatibilities may lead us to question our assumption of shared national identity. This may lead us to question the centrality of the shared category for our own national identity, as when conflicts over language led many Francophone Canadians to question their own Canadianness. Alternatively, encountering practical incompatibilities may lead us to question the appropriateness of using the initial category to include members of the other group. For example, conflicts over language may lead Anglophone Americans to question the Americanness of Spanish speakers. The second result of practical alienation is the converse of this. Such alienation enhances our awareness of categories that align more adequately with our practical identity, at least in the particular area of alienation. Thus, a conflict over language may lead us to become more aware of our identification with a language category. For example, when Gujarati speakers and Marathi speakers conflict in Mumbai, that is likely to make members of each group more conscious of, and thus more committed to, their linguistic category.

Before examining this alienation further, we need to back up for a moment and consider the ways in which categorial identification develops initially. Any group category defines some in-group/out-group division. However, people are not equally aware of all such categories, nor are they equally committed to all of them. I live in Connecticut. Thus, I necessarily have some sort of Connecticut-based protoidentification. But it really has no great motivating force for me right now. On the other hand, the protoidentification is there and that could serve as the basis for a strong sense of Connecticut identity. In keeping with this, protonationalist feelings may be widespread in a population. However, full-fledged nationalist feelings and commitments do not simply arise on their own in an entire population. So, what happens? Commonly, full-blown nationalist commitments arise in a few people who undertake the conversion of others to their attitude. Thus, nationalist movements—for example, anticolonial nationalist movements—commonly begin with a limited number of activists who work to create a sense of national identification in the populace as a whole.[12] This

---

12. A number of writers have stressed the importance of activists for the development of nationalism. For example, "the class of literati and urban professionals that formed the nuclei of nationalist movements" (Wimmer 75) are critical for Wimmer's account. Similarly, David Brown stresses the importance of elites, particularly "displaced traditional elites" and "aspiring educated elites" (27), in certain sorts of nationalism. He convincingly demonstrates their

is not to say that activists are necessary. Nationalist identifications may arise spontaneously through complex, unplanned developments. However, nationalisms that are socially consequential for extended periods of time do involve activists. As Breuilly explains, "the emergence of national sentiments has to be related to far more complex changes than the diffusion of a doctrine from its intellectual creators to broader populations" ("Approaches to Nationalism," 147). However, "national sentiments . . . .are so diffuse and varied that they normally are only selected for study by historians when they are mobilized by a political movement" (148)—for those are the cases in which such sentiments have sustained social effects.

One of the first concerns of an identity movement is practical alienation. Though they do not conceive of the issue in precisely these terms, all identity movements of any size—nationalist, religious, feminist, socialist, whatever—face the problem of splitting. At a certain point, an identity movement will spread beyond a very local, homogenous in-group—a group from the same region, speaking the same language, holding the same beliefs, and so forth. As the movement spreads, members with different languages, religious beliefs, ethnic backgrounds, and other potentially conflicting aspects of practical identity will enter the group. This broadening of membership almost invariably threatens to disrupt the sense of group identification through practical alienation (as well as through competing categorial identifications, which we will discuss below). Activists typically respond to this by a combination of homogenization and "tolerance" or accommodation to diversity. Thus, they first seek to create some sort of common group culture or, in our terms, shared practical identity. In the case of nationalism, this common culture usually involves a range of practices relating to language, religion, literature, music, art, food, dress, and so on. An illustrative instance, discussed by Santasombat, is the "national policy of homogenization" in Thailand (320), a policy "promoting religious and cultural unity among ethnically distinct subgroups" (321), with programs "designed to convert tribal peoples in north and northeastern Thailand to Buddhism" (320). Gans mentions several cases. "The United States and Australia," he notes, "tried to force their respective aboriginal populations that had survived genocide to assimilate into the majority. Turkey has also recently attempted to do this to its Kurd population, as have post-colonial African states with respect to their populations" (13).[13] Instances of the

---

key role in many cases.

13. Readers familiar with Gans's work will notice that I have not distinguished between "cultural nationalism, which focuses on the interests people have in their own culture," and "statist nationalism," which "focuses on the interests states have in the cultural homogeneity

"relentless press toward homogeneity" (in Verdery's phrase [231]) could be extended almost indefinitely.

More exactly, many socially patterned constraints on and opportunities for individual choice arise spontaneously as part of the social evolution of practical identity. Put simply, societies develop in ways that enable us to do some things, but not others. For example, societies have a wide range of conventions that bear on social interaction, personal appearance, speech, and so forth. In these cases, the constraints and opportunities are usually both vague and implicit. Moreover, many of the constraints are flexible. Language provides a good example. In ordinary speech, we follow standard idioms, common word choice, ordinary syntactic principles. However, most people could not say what any of the usual constraints are. Moreover, there is considerable leeway regarding such constraints in actual practice—not only with respect to idioms and the like, but even with respect to more apparently strict principles. Thus, in conversation, we make grammatical mistakes all the time—not only mistakes from the perspective of prescriptive grammar, but mistakes from the perspective of our own, internal grammatical principles, thus our own linguistic practical identity. (The point is clear from any transcript of actual conversation; see, for example, the cases in Biber, Conrad, and Reppen 69–73 and 144.) Yet, for the most part, no one pays any attention.

In contrast, when homogenization derives from categorial identity, it is systematic and self-conscious. Moreover, it is often quite rigid and self-righteous, as well. This is perhaps most obvious in the case of religious homogenization, as when it is opposed to heresy. We also find it in

---

of their citizenries" (Gans 1). There are certainly contexts in which this distinction is significant. However, my contention here is that nationalism is always a matter of categorial identification. Certainly, people may join in solidarity for practical reasons. These reasons may include matters of practical identity. For example, speakers of a minority language may join together to agitate for schooling in that language, simply as a practical matter (e.g., if schooling in the majority language means that their children learn less or learn more slowly). However, the sorts of attachment and activism that characterize nationalism, including cultural nationalism, result only when the group stops being a temporary coalition to achieve particular pragmatic aims and becomes an identity group. Moreover, once this occurs, homogenization arises as an issue in cultural nationalism—just as it does in "statist nationalism." Practical identities are not homogenous. For example, languages vary dialectally. Even if a group begins with some pragmatic commitment to practical identity, the shift to categorial identification brings with it concerns about homogenization, about not disrupting the sense of categorial identification through conflicts in practical identity. For example, speakers of a minority language may become concerned about forging a standard form of the language that overcomes regional variations. In this way, the issue of homogenization, as discussed here, is constant across both of Gans's types, and for the same reason. As a result, the typological distinction, though undoubtedly consequential elsewhere, is not relevant here.

economic class—for example, when speech practices are homogenized as a sign of class standing in prescriptive grammar. In the case of nationalism, especially anticolonial nationalism, the most extreme forms of zealous strictness regarding homogenized practical identity occur in what I have elsewhere called "reactionary traditionalism" (see *Colonialism* 319). Reactionary traditionalism is (putatively) a rejection of the influence of other national cultures and a reaffirmation of one's own national tradition. But, in fact, one's own national tradition has always been an interacting complex of diverse and changing practical identities (as stressed, in different terms, by writers such as Nandy [*Illegitimacy* 47] and Parekh [19]). Unfortunately, this does the nationalist activist no good. In reactionary traditionalism, this vast array of practices is reduced to a limited set of norms, which activists affirm as the authentic culture of the nation. Indeed, in some cases, this set of norms does not even derive from those earlier practices, but is modeled on colonial stereotypes.

For example, Indian tradition includes a wide variety of beliefs, ranging from materialism and agnosticism to different forms of mysticism. In part because of colonial stereotypes, nationalist activists have tended to affirm a commitment to spirituality as Indian and materialism or agnosticism as European. Moreover, even within mysticism, reactionary traditionalists have been very selective—largely setting aside pacifistic tendencies (e.g., that of Patañjali's *Yoga-Sūtra*) in favor of militaristic mysticism (prominently that of the *Bhagavad Gītā;* we will return to this point in chapter 6).

Of course, nationalist homogenization is not confined to reactionary traditionalism. It may take a number of forms, some of which are much less rigid than others. It may, for example, affirm syncretism. National identity in the United States does not involve an assertion of English or, still less, Native American tradition. Rather, it affirms some sort of synthesis derived from the "melting pot" of immigrant and, to a lesser extent, native cultures along with ideas, routines, and customs formed by American geography and particular historical experiences. Even more strikingly, some forms of nationalist homogenization may affirm tolerance or individual freedom. This, too, is part of the standard view of American identity. For example, imposing one's religion on others is commonly seen as un-American.

The reverse of practical alienation is what I have elsewhere referred to as "situational identification" (see *Empire* 129–32). Again, practical alienation occurs when I expect a smooth interconnection of practical identities but instead encounter incompatibility. Situational identification occurs when I discover practical interconnections beyond what I expected. For example, some of the Pranami Hindus mentioned by Nandy et al. may find that their views and actions do not fit well with those of other Hindus. As a result, they may experience practical alienation from those Hindus. Conversely, they may find that their views and actions do fit well with those of some Muslims. As a result, they may experience situational identification with those Muslims. Either occurrence is disruptive with respect to categorial identity. Practical alienation leads us to question our identification with members of the in-group defined by the relevant category. Situational identification leads us to question our difference from members of the out-group defined by that category. The result of this is that the development of categorial identity cannot homogenize in-group practical identity in just any way. To enhance in-group categorial identification, homogenization must reduce the overlap in practical identity across in- and out-groups. In other words, it is important that our interactions with other members of the in-group be distinctly more continuous than our interactions with members of the out-group.

Here, too, the obvious outcome is reactionary traditionalism. Reactionary traditionalists commonly seek to maximize the differences between in-group and out-group culture. In keeping with this, one major variant of reactionary traditionalism in anticolonial movements involves narrowing indigenous tradition by purging it of any properties or practices that overlap with those of the colonial culture. For example, if the colonizer is seen as sexually liberal, then sexually liberal strains of the indigenous tradition must be suppressed. Alternatively, reactionary anticolonialists may begin with stereotypes about indigenous culture that themselves assert a dichotomy between the indigenous culture and the colonial culture. For example, faced with a colonial stereotype that Africans are communal and interactive, nonrational, in touch with nature, and so forth, some African nationalists may assert that Africans are indeed communal and interactive (not individualistic, like Europeans), nonrational (unlike the logic-bound Europeans), and so forth.

Of course, in-group/out-group dichotomization too need not be a matter of reactionary traditionalism. Indeed, it may be just the opposite. Nationalists may try to base their sense of national difference on radical change and the loosening of constraints, on modernity and liberality. At least in some contexts, Americans see the United States as constantly overcoming the limits of the past and extending freedom—altering technologies, patterns of work, economic policies, social patterns, all in novel and liberating ways. In recent years, the affirmation of this view of American practical identity has been most prominent in contrast with reactionary traditionalist movements in Islam. As such, it has partially underwritten American military actions in the Muslim world.

SELF-CONCEPTS AND GROUP IDEALS

Some of the preceding examples, however, suggest a problem. Up to now, I have been speaking of homogenization of the in-group and differentiation from the out-group as if an in-group's norms actually govern the homogenization of that group's practical identity. But this is clearly untrue. According to a study published in November 2004, the invasion of Iraq had at that point already resulted in over one hundred thousand excess deaths (see Roberts et al.). Despite governmental claims, it is difficult to reconcile this with America's self-defining ideals of benevolent liberality. The PATRIOT Act clearly involves an attempt to homogenize American practical identity. In doing this, it supposedly serves to preserve our freedoms. However, it does this primarily by taking away freedoms. The same point may be made, perhaps even more strongly, about the affirmation of indigenous nonrationality and other stereotypical assertions. After all, nationalist assertions of African irrationality do not serve to homogenize African practical identity by making Africans irrational. In order to take account of such discrepancies, we need to add a further component to our analysis of categorial identity.

As we have seen, the cultivation of categorial identification initially requires nothing more than a label along with some inclusion criterion to define just who belongs in the identity category (e.g., the nation). To stabilize this identification, its advocates—which may be a small elite or a large, popular body—tend to advocate and enforce the homogenization of in-group practices and their differentiation from out-group practices. Put differently, identity groups that move toward such differential homogenization (either spontaneously or by design) are more likely to thrive, while identity groups that sustain high levels of internal practical difference and external practical similarity are more likely to dissipate. But this is not everything that constitutes categorial identification. If they are sustained for any extended period of time, identity categories are likely to develop meaning structures that are consistent with general cognitive principles of semantics. Again, our minds organize and store meanings first and most significantly in prototypes. In keeping with this, our cognitive inclination is always to form prototypes when faced with a category. This is true whether the category is "bird" or "American."

A prototype is, again, a standard or, roughly, average case. The prototypical human has two arms, two legs, is average height, and so on. However, a prototype is not an absolute average; it is, rather, a weighted average. The averaging process occurs unconsciously in our minds and it gives greater weight to distinctive features, those that highlight the differences between the present category and contrasting categories (cf. Tversky; Ortony; and Barsalou 212). In other words, in making prototypes, our minds follow principles parallel to those followed by reactionary traditionalists. For example, our prototypical man will be more masculine than the statistically average man. Thus, he will have a larger jaw and narrower hips. Similarly, the prototypical woman will be more feminine than the statistically average woman.

In keeping with this general feature of prototype formation, our prototypes for identity categories will be weighted and contrastive in precisely the same manner. Indeed, "man" and "woman" are already identity categories—fundamental identity categories, learned from infancy and enforced, often quite rigidly, through parenting, education, and so on. Note that the weighting operates for both the in-group and the out-group prototype. No matter whether one is a man or a woman, one's prototypical man will be more manly than average and one's prototypical woman will be more womanly than average. Whether one is white or black, one's prototypical white person will be more "white" and one's prototypical black person will be more "black" than is statistically accurate.

The preceding reference to statistical accuracy with respect to whites and blacks may have made some readers pause. Aren't our prototypes of whites and blacks little more than stereotypes? Is there any point in speaking about statistical accuracy in such cases? This is, I believe, the right reaction. Of course, at one level, the differentiation in prototypical whites and blacks is entirely innocuous. Our prototypical white man is likely to be a bit blonder than average. Our prototypical black man is likely to have darker skin than the statistical average. But when our prototypes go beyond this simple weighting of skin and hair color, they become problematic. Indeed, a parallel point holds for men and women. Why then speak about averaging at all in these cases? Doesn't "averaging" imply that our deviations are not mere ideology, that they refer, instead, to facts? But surely a racist stereotype of blacks has no basis in facts. Thus, it cannot be the result of averaging.

There are factors that enter into prototype formation beyond averaging, prominently including the biases in evaluation that accompany in-group/out-group categorization. Duckitt explains that "Ingroup members are rated more favorably than outgroup members on evaluative trait ratings" (69). Indeed, in-group members judge the personalities and behavior of in-group members more favorably, even when the groups are formed arbitrarily and the members of a group are not allowed to interact (68–69). These evaluative discrepancies bias our interpretation of specific cases and thus alter the "data" that we average. As Nisbett and Ross note, a white person may see a white man lounging on a park bench in the afternoon and understand him as someone who has been laid off from work. In contrast, he or she may see a black person and understand him as a loafer. Thus, a white person may take identical instances of behavior in white and black individuals, but interpret them differently (Nisbett and Ross 240). Kunda cites a disturbing case of this sort. White test subjects were asked to watch a tape of two men arguing. When one of the men pushes the other, the experimenters stop the tape and ask test subjects to characterize the action. There were two versions of the tape. In one, a black man shoves a white man. In the other, a white man shoves a black man. As Kunda explains, "This made a big difference to how the shove was interpreted: When delivered by a White man, it was viewed most often as 'playing around,' or as 'dramatizes,' but when delivered by a Black man, the identical shove was typically viewed as a violent or aggressive behavior" (347). The interpretation is what contributes to the average. On the other hand, in cases such as these, the skewed interpretation results not only from in-group/out-group biases, but also from preexisting prototypes/stereotypes. Thus, the group biases cannot fully explain those prototypes/stereotypes.

The other crucial factor here, beyond basic in-group/out-group biases, is that weighted averaging is not confined to our direct experience of real people. Our minds spontaneously average over fictions, conjectures, gossip, and anything else that presents relevant information, whether that information is true or false. A European-American's prototypical African American is formed in part from real experiences. But it is probably formed far more from television, film, literature, news, and private conversations (e.g., on the effects of informal, personal anecdotes; see van Dijk 157). To a great extent, our experience of out-groups is indirect, and filtered through other in-group members. Indeed, that separation of in-group from out-group members itself is important. Empirical research shows that one of the best ways to reduce affective bias against out-group members is through cooperative work toward shared goals (see Duckitt 98, 252, 256). In terms of the preceding analyses, this is unsurprising. Such cooperative work is just the sort of thing that is likely to lead to situational identification. Formal or informal segregation of groups prevents that.

So, once we begin to think in terms of certain identity categories, we are likely to form prototypes for those categories. The prototypes will highlight differences between in-group and out-group members. Moreover, those differences may be largely fictional, due to basic in-group/out-group biases and to the development of social ideologies that are then manifest in literature, film, history, and elsewhere. To make matters worse, these prototypes operate even if we do not believe in their validity. As Clore and Ortony point out, prototypes require "corrective processes" to be avoided (Clore and Ortony 35, citing Devine). In other words, even if we do not self-consciously accept the accuracy of a given prototype, it will affect our ideas, attitudes, interpretations, and actions unless we make an effort to correct for the effects of that prototype. At a neurobiological level, this is what the work of Krendl et al. indicates. When asked to evaluate members of stigmatized groups, test subjects evidently made an effort to overcome their prejudices. This was manifest in "robust activation of prefrontal regions." These regions appear to inhibit "activation of the amygdala," thus an aversive emotional attitude, when "perceivers are highly motivated to control their evaluative response" (12). Other research supports this analysis. For example, Ambady et al. used brain imaging and electric field recordings to study responses of low-prejudiced individuals and high-prejudiced individuals. They concluded that "low-prejudiced individuals . . . monitor automatic reactions to negative stereotypes elicited by out-group stimuli" (216–17).

However, even this does not always work. Monitoring and suppression are unreliable. Kunda summarizes research suggesting that, when we suppress one stereotype, we often do so in favor of another stereotype. Put differently, we may simply be choosing one in-group/out-group division over another. For example, a white man may respond to a Chinese woman through a Chinese stereotype, suppressing his stereotype of women, or vice versa (340). More significant, when a "stereotype is activated outside of our awareness, we may be able to do little to curtail" its effects (342). Perhaps most important, monitoring and suppression may backfire. Kunda discusses studies showing that the suppression of a stereotype in one context "led to an increase in its activation and use in other settings encountered shortly thereafter" (344). This, too, has significant behavioral consequences (345).

Again, we not only form prototypes of Others. We form prototypes of ourselves as well. The other side of in-group bias—beyond underestimating the personalities, behavior, accomplishments, and general value of out-group members—is overestimating the personalities, behavior, accomplishments, and general value of in-group members. Moreover, this tendency is exacerbated by a fundamental principle of group dynamics. It is always a compliment to one's addressee to praise his or her identity groups. Indeed, though it is usually considered gauche to praise oneself, praise of one's group is considered generous, at least when one is addressing members of that group. Moreover, when one is speaking to members of out-groups, praise of one's own in-group may be considered bravely defiant, while denigration of one's own in-group is widely considered disloyal. Indeed, in any identity group, one of the greatest crimes one can commit is denigrating that group before the enemy. Humiliating the enemy is noble. Humiliating the in-group is a despicable form of betrayal—even if that humiliation is nothing more than an objective account of the actions of the in-group (e.g., its war crimes against another nation). As we discuss in chapter 2, this dichotomizing tendency reaches its pinnacle (or nadir) in the association of the in-group with divine choice and the linking of the enemy with Satanic or related evil (a cross-cultural tendency).

As these points suggest, there is an ethical component in the discourse surrounding the in-group and the out-group as well. Our lexical entry (i.e., our semantic memory) for a given term is likely to include, not only a prototype, but some set of norms forming an ideal, or paradigm, as well. This, too, is simply an ordinary part of semantic development. At least one property is found in the ideal for members of any in-group—loyalty. The ideal American, the ideal Catholic, the ideal feminist, the ideal socialist—insofar as these are understood as identity categories—is, above all else, loyal. Other aspects of the ideal may vary. Thus, the ideal American may cherish freedom. The ideal Muslim may cherish Islamic tradition. But the valuing of loyalty is constant.

Perhaps somewhat surprisingly, there are prototypes and ideals not only for members of the group, but for the group as a whole. In other words, there is an ideal to which I might aspire as an American. But there is also an ideal for America itself. In-groups have a universal group ideal, parallel to the universal individual ideal of loyalty. That ideal is authority or preference over out-groups.[14] All identity groups share this. Indeed, it is implied by the presumption of in-group superiority. Insofar as my nation is best, it should have a position of authority over other nations. The same point holds for my religion or language. Indeed, the personal ideal of loyalty is inseparable from the collective ideal of dominance. Again, even in

---

14. Of course, this may take different forms. In one case, it may be a matter of direct rule over other nations. In another case, it may be a matter of widely recognized superiority or leadership in some area of politics or culture.

minimal (or contentless) groups, individuals are willing to forgo personal gain so that their in-group will be hierarchized above the out-group (see Duckitt 68–69). Beyond this, ideals for the group may vary.

As should be obvious, in the real world, problems are almost certain to arise in the pursuit of these ideals. It is often impossible to reconcile the pursuit of dominance with the other ideals commonly professed for a nation and for its citizens. Take a society that considers itself Christian—such as the United States, especially in the presidency of George W. Bush. How can a society pursue global authority through military domination and at the same time claim to be following the teachings of Jesus, who famously proclaimed, "To the man who slaps you on one cheek, present the other cheek too" (Luke 6:29 *Jerusalem Bible*)? How do the invasions of Afghanistan or Iraq conform to the teachings of Jesus? The problem is not confined to Christian societies. Every in-group compromises its more peripheral moral principles in pursuit of its basic norm—dominance over out-groups. But how does an in-group understand or imagine what occurs during this compromise? For example, how do the evangelical supporters of President Bush understand themselves as part of a Christian nation and supporters of military invasions?

To answer these questions, we need to isolate a further component of the in-group category. It is, in effect, the opposite of the ideal. It is the set of characteristic sins or faults, both those of members of the group and those of the group as a whole. For instance, Greenwald et al. explain that men identify even with the negative aspects of being "strong" (325). This negative self-image may serve a number of functions. For one thing, it may contribute to in-group/out-group dichotomization. Men's identification with destructiveness is bound up with an identity-based opposition to women's putative gentleness. Most important for our present concerns, this component commonly serves to rationalize actions that would otherwise threaten one's self-evaluation as a member of a group and one's evaluation of the group. The negative self-prototype allows members of the in-group to understand their own individual and collective failures as the result of particular, acceptable, perhaps even unavoidable flaws. Thus, the United States may have the fault of blundering in, lacking cultural sensitivity, failing to fully plan its benevolent invasions. It may have the same fault in Vietnam, Lebanon, and Iraq, never really learning its lesson. This is unfortunate. It may even be tragic. But it is not a violation of such ideal principles as supporting freedom and democracy. It may even be the inescapable consequence of our innocence, optimism, and enthusiastic good will. In any case, admitting these faults into the prototype of "America" allows us to avoid recognizing that the United States has repeatedly invaded other countries for purposes that have little to do with freedom and democracy and that often result in the denial of both.

Before concluding this section, it is important to mention a final norm that arises in connection with social prototypes. This is the norm that adjures members of the in-group to conform, in general, not only to paradigms or ideals, but to the group prototype as well, including, for example, preferences in food or entertainment—and even including the group's putatively characteristic faults.[15] Conformity, here, means fitting one's behavior to group expectations, not necessarily to group behavior per se.[16] This norm is commonly invoked under the rubric of authenticity. Someone who deviates from the prototype too greatly is not a "real" or "authentic" group member. For example, someone who supports socialism or is a practicing Muslim may not be viewed as a "real" American, even when his or her politics or religion does not impinge on practical social interactions or national loyalty.

IDENTITY AND SOCIAL HIERARCHY

In the preceding sections, I have spoken somewhat vaguely about nationalists, activists for an in-group, advocates of a particular categorial identification, and so forth. The point of these references is that there are always some people who are more diligent than others in the propagation of identity categories. This propagation may be self-consciously planned or it may occur spontaneously. In some cases, it is the result of "lateral" connections, interactions among people at roughly the same level of authority or social power. In other cases, it involves economic, political, institutional, or other hierarchies. Indeed, both sorts of connections—vertical and lateral—appear to be necessary for the successful propagation of an identity category. Moreover, both are bound up with the homogenization of practical identities. In the preceding section, I treated homogenization in largely egalitarian terms. But it invariably involves a hierarchical component as well. While some aspects of practical identity may be simply egalitarian,

---

15. There are, of course, exceptions to this. For example, nationalist activists might object to prototypical behavior of the in-group if it is inadequately nationalistic. However, the imperative to conform to prototypical behaviors holds generally. Indeed, when nationalists try to change prototypical behavior, their aim is to establish a new, normatively valid prototype for conformity.

16. For example, in order to be considered an authentic black man, a rap musician might conform to a prototype that has little to do with the actual behavior of ordinary black men.

many involve structures of authority as a necessary element. For example, in religious rituals, the priest or minister has a role different from members of the congregation. That is because the priest or minister has greater authority within the ritual, greater power over the execution of the ritual, and so on.

The final point suggests that the homogenization of practical identity is not a matter of giving everyone the same practical identity. Of course, there is enormous overlap. However, there are crucial points at which practical identities differ. For example, entirely uniform practical identities could operate only in relatively uniform situations that allow for predictable outcomes. If all roads have two lanes and allow for traffic in both directions, then our uniform practical identity (in the United States, "drive on the right") will serve us all pretty well. However, in any situation that is not precisely normal, any situation in which outcomes may differ in consequential ways, some hierarchy is required—or at least useful—for coordinating behavior. If a road narrows to one lane (e.g., due to an accident), then it is usually helpful to set up some sort of hierarchy of authority. Through this hierarchy—for example, through a police officer halting some cars while allowing others to proceed—the flow of traffic may be regulated successfully. Note that this is not something that contradicts practical identity. It is a crucial element of practical identity. Part of our practical identity is knowing what to do in such a situation. In other words, it involves knowing our place in the relevant hierarchy and the places of other people in that hierarchy. Indeed, hierarchy pervades practical identity. A great deal of childrearing involves inculcating the ways one should respond to different groups of people—parents, teachers, priests and ministers, police officers, and so on. A central component in each case is a familiarity with what one can and cannot do to or with members of these groups, what freedom one has with them and what freedom they have in return. In each case, practical identity is bound up with the apportioning and gradation of authority.

At the same time, that apportioning and gradation of authority are themselves inseparable from labeling, from defining some people as parents and others as children, some as teachers and others as students.[17] As a result, practical identity in these cases is inseparable from categorial identity. Most often, one has certain privileges or obligations with respect to someone else, not because of one's practical identity per se, but because of the categories at play in the relationship. I obey the orders of a police

---

17. In connection with this, it is worth noting that the establishment of inegalitarian social equilibrium has been modeled in terms of asymmetrical roles in game theory (see, for example, McAdams and citations).

officer precisely because I categorize him or her as a police officer and I categorize myself as a civilian. I would not (in most cases) obey that same person, making the same gestures and saying the same things, if I categorized him or her—or myself—differently. Indeed, social categories are generally hierarchized and that hierarchization is crucial to the way they figure in practical identity. More technically, the procedures that define our practical identity are not triggered by immediate experiences, but by a particular "encoding" of those experiences. Encoding is the selection and organization of information available in the environment. Hierarchized social categories contribute crucially to the way we encode information. Put simply, when we approach a part of the road where one lane is closed, we do not need to encode details about the foliage on the side of the road, the color of the various vehicles around us, the height of the person directing traffic. However, we do need to encode those details that trigger the category "police officer" (e.g., the color and design of his or her clothing).

Of course, we do not simply obey others because we are told that they have authority. We obey them because their category is associated with the possibility of coercion. That possibility may be many steps removed. But it is nonetheless real. I obey the police officer since he or she might arrest me. I obey a teacher because he or she might give me a bad grade—which could result in my not getting a suitable job, thus harming my ability to achieve other goals in life. In this way, authority is *functional*. Hierarchized categories, insofar as they organize and orient our practical identities, are underwritten by the possibility of practical harm—or, in some cases, practical benefit.

Hierarchization of this sort also enters into the definition of identity prototypes and norms. First, in most cases, our prototype for a group member will be more obedient to group hierarchy than the statistically average member of the group (e.g., our prototypical Catholic is probably more committed to papal authority than the average Catholic). More important, in most cases, our norms for group behavior highly value obedience within the group.

There are certain limitations on this valorization of authority and obedience—or, rather, qualifications of it. For example, some rejection of authority is a crucial part of American national norms, visible in television programs, movies, and the widespread indifference to torture. On the one hand, the United States is, like other groups, highly devoted to group hierarchy. For example, there is a great deal of reverence for the president, primarily because he is the president. Many Americans take offense at criticisms of our commander-in-chief. On the other hand, rugged independence and rejection of authority are a crucial part of American norms as well. In the final analysis, though, this presumptively distinctive American characteristic is less exceptional than it may at first seem. Indeed, it has three characteristics that recur in other nations as well, if in different degrees.

First, the American rejection of authority is often a rejection of foreign authority. Historically, the paradigm case of such independence is the rejection of the English monarchy. However, the practice of repudiating foreign authority continues into the present. Consider the recent condemnation of the U.S. invasion of Iraq, a condemnation that spanned virtually the entire globe. Americans not only rejected world opinion, many seemed quite proud of our nonconformity. A similar point holds for the use of torture in American prisons in Iraq. Americans can be positively pleased that their government is refusing to follow international rules. As the case of France and Iraq suggests, this is not because Americans individually agree with American policies. They may or may not agree. It is, rather, because such defiance is an affirmation of national autonomy.

But Americans do not reject only the authority of out-groups. They also reject the authority of some members of the in-group. This is because those authorities are (putatively) inhibiting the advancement of the goals of the group. This leads to the second component of the American rejection of hierarchy. Groups commonly justify internal hierarchy by reference to the well-being of the group. Thus, it is always possible to reject that hierarchy in cases where group well-being is at stake. This is actually one of the most common, recurring motifs in American national narratives. It is a crucial part of the American national ideal. Indeed, it is perhaps the primary way in which we can think of ourselves as individualistic while simultaneously being almost fanatical about national identity and patriotic loyalty.

Finally, it is important to recognize that American antiauthoritarianism is virtually never very extended in its scope. In other words, it is virtually never revolutionary. The normative rejection of authority in American nationalism tends to be local and subhierarchical or impersonal. In other words, it tends to be the rejection of some lower-level official who is ignorant or corrupt or the rejection of some impersonal agency that has no understanding of the actual of struggles of real people (i.e., is ignorant) or corrupt. The former may be referred to as the "bad boss" scenario; the latter is the "bad bureaucracy" scenario. (Readers should be able to recall numerous examples from film and television. In chapter 5, we consider a prominent American film that illustrates these tendencies.)

The rejection of the bad boss or the bad bureaucracy is, of course, a matter of rejecting authority that does not serve the interests of the group. One result of this is that the local rejection of authority tends to focus on positions that are justified specifically by merit. If someone's position of authority is justified by merit, our rejection of that authority is normative when the person does not in fact have the merit. The supervising officer has his or her position because he or she supposedly understands policing better than the rookie. If that is untrue, his position is undeserved. The crucial point here is that not all positions of authority in a group are justified by merit. Those that are justified in other ways are, then, the ones that demand our most strict allegiance. The obvious case is the presidency. Put differently, some positions of authority are the manifestation, not of merit, but of national autonomy. Those require our more or less unquestioned obedience.

These forms of opposition to authority probably have unusual salience in American nationalist discourse. Moreover, in their current American versions, they are the product of particular historical and cultural developments. However, they are far from uniquely American. Indeed, they are almost certainly found, in some form, in all varieties of nationalism. Indeed, societies not only need ways of establishing and sustaining hierarchies of authority. They need ways of altering such hierarchies in the face of contradictory group interests as well.

NATIONALIST RESPONSES TO CONFLICTS AMONG IDENTITY CATEGORIES

I have been speaking, to this point, about in-group identification generally. I have considered the establishment of such identification through vacuous categories with inclusion criteria, its relation to practical identity and the homogenization of culture, the development of group norms and prototypes, and the establishment of external group oppositions and internal group hierarchies. I have drawn examples from a range of groups, discussing religious, ethnic, linguistic, national, and other categories without distinction. But these different types of group are distinct. And that distinctness has consequences.

Commonly, each of us has only one religion, one nationality, one racial category. Multiplicity may arise within a type of identity category (e.g., in cases of dual citizenship). However, that multiplicity is accidental. In contrast, multiplicity necessarily arises across types of identity category. My national identity category simply is not the same as my religious, racial, or even ethnic identity category. As Sen points out, "There are a great variety of categories to which we simultaneously belong." In some cases "they compete for attention and priority over each other" (19). Indeed, their conflict may give rise to serious practical difficulties for national integration and homogenization. Specifically, our multiple identity categories may generate multiple and contradictory loyalties in cases of social conflict. For example, when the United States attacks a Muslim country, a Muslim American may feel greater categorial identification with his or her fellow Muslims or with his or her fellow Americans. Moreover, different categorial identities tend to be associated with different practical identities in certain areas. Thus, Christian Americans and Muslim Americans may find that they cannot always interact in completely fluid ways. Practical discontinuities may make their different religious identities more obvious or more consequential than their shared national identity. In short, discrepancies across non-national categorial identities may disrupt national homogenization and undermine national identification.

Nationalists facing this dilemma have tended to take one of two approaches. One way of preventing these discontinuities is through alignment, the paralleling of national, ethnic, religious, and other categories. Nationalists who adopt this approach aim for a nation with a common ethnicity, religion, language, and so forth. Since nationalists usually cannot align all categories, they will most often emphasize a few. Depending on the precise categories they stress, there are two ways in which they may go about this. They may try to convert everyone to a single religion, to make one language standard for the entire nation, and so on. In other words, they may try to change the categories of some members of the current population. Obviously, this will work only with "elective" identity categories, categories such as religion that one can in principle choose to change. It will not work with nonelective categories, such as ethnicity or race. Thus, nationalists who stress alignment with nonelective categories tend to advocate separatism (if the desired alignment occurs in geographically localized areas of the current nation); restrictions on immigration (if national alignment is largely intact, but at risk from immigration); and/or "ethnic cleansing," the physical removal of people belonging to the "wrong" (nonelective) groups, such as racial and ethnic minorities, either through deportation or murder.

The elective alignment strategy has been fairly common. Indeed, Philip generalizes the idea, asserting that, "It is accepted wisdom that nationalism needs to be buttressed by certain key factors which distinguish one nation from another. Among these factors are counted a common territory, a common language, a common culture, a common history, and a common religion" (5). The nonelective alignment strategy, too, has been common. Nazism is an obvious case. It, and related forms of fascism, may seem to be the only instances of this sort. However, in somewhat milder versions, nonelective alignment nationalism has arisen much more frequently than one might imagine. Arendt points out that "there was hardly a country left on the Continent that did not pass between the two wars some new legislation which, even if it did not use this right extensively, was phrased to allow for getting rid of a great number of its inhabitants at any opportune moment" (278–79). She goes on to explain that "in the years following Hitler's successful persecution of German Jews," a broad range of "countries began to think in terms of expatriating their minorities" (289). Nor is this solely European. Befu explains that advocates of *Nihonjinron* [Japanese identity] assert the "isomorphism of geography, race, language, and culture." They insist that "carriers of Japanese culture" are necessarily "speakers of the Japanese language" and that they "share 'blood'" and have done so for thousands of years. Moreover, "no significant amount of new blood has been infused into this 'pure' Japanese race" (276). Wimmer notes that forms of ethnic cleansing have been "constants of the European history of nation-building and state formation, from the expulsion of Gypsies under Henry VIII or of Muslims and Jews under Fernando and Isabella to . . . the 'people's exchange,' as it was euphemistically called, after the Treaty of Lausanne between Turkey and Greece" (3). Horowitz refers to numerous cases of this sort—the expulsion of "Indian Tamils" from Sri Lanka, Chinese from Vietnam, Bengalis from Burma, and Asians from Uganda, the attempts to deprive Chinese and Indians of Malaysian citizenship, Ivory Coast riots against Dahomeyans and Togolese (with "some victims . . . offered the 'choice' between departing the country and death" [198]), and so forth (198–99).

A second broad approach to nationalism accepts the diversity of identity categories in the nation, but tries to manage that diversity. It does this, in part, by undertaking to minimize their disruption of practical identity. One standard way of minimizing practical disruption is through the homogenization of public interaction and the localization (or even privatization) of nonhomogenous practices. In such a system, nonhomogenous practices associated with, say, diverse religions would not commonly confront one another in public spaces. For example, Catholic, Protestant, Jewish, Muslim, and Hindu politicians may refer to "God" in public speeches, but confine more sectarian ideas or references to their homes and places of worship. This is not to say that there would never be occasions when non-national identities would arise publicly. The point is simply to minimize and disperse occasions for practical alienation. A nation can sustain a certain amount of internal identity conflict. It is crucial, however, that the conflict not be frequent enough and public enough to inspire large subgroups to reject national identity in favor of some other identity—religious, ethnic, regional, or whatever.

A further, in some ways even more important, method of managing identity diversity is by hierarchizing identity categories. As a number of writers have noted (see, for example, Berezin 83), our self-concept is structured. I think of myself as more centrally a professor than a resident of Connecticut; I think of myself as more centrally a resident of Connecticut than someone who owns a beige desk. In terms of identity categories, I am more likely to be motivated by a sense of identification with professors than by a sense of identification with residents of Connecticut. A hierarchy of this sort is always in place. Managing identity diversity in relation to national identity involves the establishment of national identification above all potentially competing categorial identifications.

I saw a striking example of this recently with my own family. Most members of my family are very devout Catholics. Moreover, several of them have a devotion to the Pope that goes well beyond anything required by Catholic teaching—in one case, treating pictures of the Pope as if they were holy relics. Yet no one in my family was affected in the least by Pope John Paul II's opposition to the wars in Afghanistan and Iraq. (On the Pope's antiwar views, see Scheer, "The Pope," and Carroll.) Their devotion to the Pope was seemingly boundless when there was no conflict between their Catholic identity and their American identity. But, as soon as the two did conflict, their devotion to the Pope virtually evaporated. It seems clear that they have set "American" above "Catholic" in the motivational hierarchy of their identity categories.

Although hierarchization predominates in the second sort of nationalism (i.e., the sort that manages diversity), it is not at all absent from the first sort, the sort that tries to do away with diversity. Even the most extreme variety of alignment nationalism cannot eliminate all subnational categories. If Catholics are gone, different Protestant groups may conflict with one another. If only Baptists remain, different orientations among Baptists will be possible sources of identity conflict. Moreover, there are always regional and other differences. Each of these categories must be subordinated to the national category. In short, category hierarchization is crucial to all forms of nationalism.

This leads us to the issue of just how category hierarchies develop. Referring to a particular case, Monroe, Hankin, and van Vechten put the issue clearly, asking, "What is it that made 'Serbianness' politically salient at a particular time and place, such that this Serb identity came to be understood as a basis for genocidal behavior? Each Serb also had other identities that had the potential to be critical bases for differentiation: class, race, rural/urban, and even Yugoslavian" (439; unfortunately, the question is rather biased, as the work of Herman and Peterson shows, but it illustrates the point nonetheless). The problem is generalizable.

FIVE PARAMETERS IN THE HIERARCHIZATION OF IDENTITY CATEGORIES

Identity hierarchies are by no means unique. Indeed, they are, at one level, merely instances of ordinary categorization processes that occur constantly in our day-to-day activities. Every thing, event, or condition may be named and described in many ways. We choose some names and descriptions over others. Moreover, we understand and respond to things, events, and conditions in terms of some categories rather than others. Hierarchizing categorial identities is, first of all, a matter of doing the same thing with persons, including ourselves.

How, then, do we categorize ordinary objects? (Here and below, I will use "object" in a very broad sense where it includes any target of categorization—thus things, events, and so forth.) The simplest reason that I use one word rather than another, isolate one aspect or element of an object rather than another, is that it occurs to me. Technically, some conceptual categories and some objective properties are more salient than others. Suppose I look into a room. The room has some furniture, a few gum wrappers on the floor, a movie poster, and a corpse. If someone asks me what is in the room, I am likely to ignore the furniture, gum wrappers, and movie poster, mentioning only the dead body. This is because the corpse has a high degree of *salience*. Salience has two aspects. First, it involves the intrinsic properties of the object. Intrinsic salience is a matter of the degree to which the item itself is attention-drawing. For example, things that are smelly or loud tend to be highly salient. Second, salience involves relational characteristics. These are a matter of subjective propensities that link one to the object in attention-eliciting ways.[18] For example, one's name is always salient.

---

18. Technically, all salience is relational in that properties can trigger attention only

Suppose I am having a conversation at a party. Someone behind me, in another conversation, is saying all sorts of things that I do not hear. His words have no salience—in themselves or for me. If he suddenly shouts, I will hear that because the loudness makes it intrinsically salient. Similarly, if he says "Hogan," I will hear that because it has relational salience for me (see LeDoux, *Synaptic* 191). In this case, relational salience results from long-term sensitivities. Relational salience may also be a matter of priming, which is to say, the partial activation of cognitive contents, a partial activation that temporarily renders me more sensitive to the presence of particular objects or the occurrence of particular events. For example, if I am in a conversation about hair loss, then, for a while after that conversation, I will find men's hairlines particularly salient. When I am in the dentist's office, everyone's teeth become salient.

Salience operates in the same way with identity categories. At the level of individual group members, some categories are more intrinsically salient than others. For example, in most cases, race has significantly greater visual salience than nationality. We may become aware of someone's race by looking at him or her. Indeed, the neurobiological research considered earlier shows the great importance of perceptual salience for triggering in-group/out-group divisions. Such perceptual triggering is much less likely to happen with nationality. As nationality generally lacks intrinsic salience, nationalists must work particularly hard at making national identity relationally salient. Indeed, the promotion of salience is one of the tasks undertaken by activists and one of the reasons activists are so important for the development of nationalism.

Of course, there may be many salient properties of any given object. But we do not value all such properties equally. What other criteria, then, affect our categorizations of ordinary objects? More precisely, what properties are we likely to exclude, even when they are salient? In choosing one name or description out of many possibilities, we are, first of all, disposed to ignore ephemera. If a property is likely to change quickly, we are unlikely to use that property for purposes of categorization. The point is well established in, for example, studies of childhood development. As Pascal Boyer points out, children "start with some definite biases about what aspects of the environment they should attend to, and what they should infer from these cues" (107). Specifically, they categorize objects

---

because of their relation to the human senses and cognition. The difference is that intrinsic salience requires only the ordinary functioning of our common sensory and cognitive systems (e.g., hearing). Relational salience, in contrast, relies on variable contents of cognition (e.g., specific memories).

by drawing on tacit expectations about the constancy of "essential" properties (108). Obviously, this is a default tendency that may be overridden in particular cases. However, it is a very robust and resilient tendency. This leads us to our second parameter, *durability*. Other things being equal, we prefer categories that refer to more durable properties. In connection with categorial identity, we need to distinguish two levels of durability. On the one hand, there is the degree to which an individual's category status may change. On the other hand, there is the degree to which the social group isolated by the category is itself enduring. If the group itself has developed only recently, then its own stability may be uncertain. In the case of identity categories, then, high durability means that I am unlikely to leave the group and the group itself is unlikely to dissolve.[19] With respect to both levels, nonelective identity categories, such as race, tend to have an advantage over elective categories, such as religion, nation, or class.[20]

But durability too is insufficient. Consider a very simple case. I am presented with a $100 bill in a plastic bag. Paper is not very durable. Plastic bags (I gather) are. However, I am very unlikely to categorize this gift as "plastic." I am likely to say, "Wow! One hundred dollars!" The reason for this is straightforward: We also choose characterizations based on importance, usefulness, value. Note that this is not confined to positive value. A large credit card bill in a plastic bag would have the same consequences. In the case of identity categories, it is not quite accurate to speak of value. Rather, we would say that categories have greater or lesser *functionality*. Functionality is the degree to which a particular category affects one's freedom of action or choice and one's receipt of goods and services in a given society.[21] The more functional a category, the more likely it is to be high in the hierarchy of one's self-concept. The operation of legal systems, which govern the use of violence and the flow of goods and services, more or less

---

19. The sense of group durability is bound up with the importance of significant historical events, often involving relations between the in-group and some out-group. These events give us a sense of the group's past, and thus a sense of its enduring nature. Such "historical memories" have been stressed by a number of writers on nationalism (see, for example, Wimmer 105), though in a noncognitive context.

20. Horowitz suggests a similar point when he refers to "the more immutable and therefore reliable" cues to group identity (47; he also touches on saliency when he refers to cues that are "more visible"). Needless to say, in contrast with Horowitz, my claim here has nothing to do with "reliability." Durability gives properties a greater effect on our categorization processes. It does not give the corresponding categories any greater validity.

21. Note that I am referring to the social function of categories here. I am not referring to the "psychological function" of identity. Thus, I am not presenting what is sometimes called a "functionalist" account of nationalism, according to which nationalism satisfies a psychological need (see Breuilly, "Approaches to Nationalism" 154–57).

guarantees that nationality is a highly functional category.[22] This is less commonly the case for, say, religious categories. For this reason, activists for religious identity have to exert a special effort to make religious identity appear functional. The obvious way of doing this is through appeals to suffering or reward in an afterlife. This has at times been supplemented by the more material functionality of heresy inquisitions or communal conflict (as in India or Northern Ireland today). Despite the abolition of race-based slavery, race continues to be a highly functional category in the United States and elsewhere. However, there is no intrinsic reason for this. Unlike nationality, there is nothing in the nature of racial categories that makes them particularly likely candidates for an enhanced social function. An important and complex case of functionality may be found in sex. Sex is always functional in society because of its place in reproduction. Indeed, sex categories are always functional in such a way as to bear directly on nations, religions, ethnicities, and so forth, for the reproduction of these groups is in part contingent on the biological reproduction of their members. In this way, sex is an identity category that all identity groups must address and incorporate, because of its functional consequences.[23]

Of course, a very common property may be highly functional, durable, and salient. But it is unlikely to trigger categorization. When we are treating identity, one of our main concerns is distinctiveness. Except in very

22. In different theoretical contexts, other writers have implicitly recognized the importance of social function. For example, Wimmer's account of ethnic conflict takes up function in this sense. In speaking of the ethnicization of national bureaucracy, he explains that "it is not the unequal representation of different ethnic groups in the state apparatus as such that leads to a politicisation of ethnic differences. Only when those in power favour their own ethnic groups to the cost of others is a fertile ground for the politicisation of ethnicity prepared" (92). However, in most cases, writers treating function have set out to isolate what the different parties in, say, ethnic conflict have to gain through that conflict. My analysis says nothing about gain from conflict. It says only that functionality increases the likelihood that one identity category will be hierarchized above others. For example, war—such as the current war in Iraq—contributes to the functionality of national identity categories. It thereby increases the likelihood that Jones, a U.S. citizen, will categorize himself preeminently as an American. This does not mean that Jones himself, or Americans generally, have anything to gain from this war. Horowitz notes that the main theories of ethnic conflict stress such factors as "economic interest" (140). He also explains that these theories have limited success in explaining actual ethnic conflict. One reason for this is that the theories are taking up functionality in an overly limited way. Issues of, say, resource control are certainly important in governmental deliberations on war. However, at the level of individual citizens' commitment to war or other forms of identity-based conflict, identity categorization is the crucial factor. That categorization is often functional, due to the broad organization of society or common social practices. But it need not involve any systematic possibilities for material gain or loss in the particular case at hand.

23. For a discussion of gender and nationalism, in a very different theoretical context, see Walby.

unusual contexts, we are unlikely to characterize a person as having eyes. Eyes are certainly functional; they are durable; they are salient. The difficulty is that most people have eyes. Moreover, most nonhuman animals have eyes. Thus, having eyes is not a good differentiating feature, not a feature that is appropriate for defining identity. Moreover, not any difference will serve well for categorization. The sharper and more discrete the distinction, the better. If a particular feature varies in slight increments from one person to another, then it is a less likely choice for categorization than if a feature varies in large steps. The limiting case of this is bipolar division. Thus, a sharp, bipolar division is more likely to be high in our hierarchy of categories than is a more smoothly graduated set of differences. I refer to this as *opposability*. One type of identity category scores very high in opposability—sex. Though hermaphrodites do present an intermediate case, the great majority of people are male or female. Sexual orientation comes close. Even including a large number of bisexuals, the division is relatively sharp and involves only three categories. Depending on just how it is interpreted, a category such as class may rank very low on opposability. If it is interpreted in terms of income, as is common in the United States, then there is clearly a relatively smooth gradient of class categories or possible categories. Indeed, virtually every household has a different income. Categories such as nation are intermediate. There are sharp divisions, due to legal requirements for citizenship and the relative rarity of dual citizenship. However, there are many nations, so the division is not close to bipolar.

Here, an interesting complication enters. Even in ordinary categorization, we try to quantify gradients. Thus, we speak of "tall," "average," and "short" people, though people come in a variety of heights. We find the same thing in identity categories. The world does not divide into a black race and a white race. However, in the United States, we tend to treat these categories as if they were sharply different. Moreover, in cases where there is quantization, the tendency is strong to reduce the alternatives to two or three. As Horowitz remarks, "despite the plurality of groups in an environment (rarely are there only two), polarity frequently emerges" (182). In the case of American racial categorization, we see this in the white/nonwhite division. In religion, we see this in the Protestant/Catholic opposition in Northern Ireland, the Christian/Jewish division in much of Europe at different times, and the Hindu/Muslim divide in India. We also see this in the nationalist tendency to isolate one or two national enemies against which the national in-group may be defined. Indeed, this is part of the propaganda function of cultivating a collective imagination of a great enemy—the

Soviet Union during the Cold War or international terrorism (or fundamentalist Islam) in the war on terror, to take two American examples.

In sum, when there is some potential conflict among our identity categories, we are more likely to think of ourselves in terms of the category that is most salient, enduring, functional, and opposable. If nationalists are to succeed in lifting the national category above racial, religious, ethnic, or other categories, they must engage in the sorts of actions that enhance salience, perceived durability, perceived functionality, and opposability. (I say "perceived durability" and "perceived functionality" because in each case it is not the objective, worldly fact, but our experience and understanding of the world that are crucial. "Salience" and "opposability" already refer to our experience and understanding. Thus, the qualification is not necessary in those cases.)

On the other hand, none of this matters if we are not moved to act on this categorization. At the beginning of this section, I wrote that identity hierarchies are, *at one level,* instances of ordinary categorization processes. But that level is inadequate to create nationalism, or any other operative group identification. The hierarchy of categorial identities is not simply a matter of thinking about ourselves and others in a particular way. It is a matter of acting on that categorization. It is not, then, simply a matter of ideas. It is also a matter of motives. These motives derive their force from our emotional engagements[24] or the category's *affectivity,* our final parameter.

In order for nationalism to have concrete, practical effects, citizens must feel something about that national category. Our emotional response is in part a simple result of labeling, as we have already seen. It is a matter of categorial identification triggering responses in the amygdala or insula in the case of out-groups, and perhaps regions such as the basal ganglia (which are connected with trust; see King-Casas et al.), in the case of in-groups. In addition, labels become associated with particular emotional experiences (e.g., in war). These emotional experiences serve to specify and intensify the motivational force of the categories. Moreover, beyond the categories themselves, we have emotional responses to the routines of homogenized practical identities, to in-group and out-group prototypes, to the land, and to other components of national identification. These responses, too, are

---

24. Horowitz makes a similar point in the (different, but related) context of ethnic conflicts, when he writes that such conflicts require "an explanation that takes account of the emotional concomitants of group traits and interactions" (181–82).

in part a result of mere categorization and in part the product of particular emotional experiences. In both cases, the relevant experiences may derive from our engagement with the world itself or from our engagements with representations of the world in literature, media, ordinary discourse, and so forth.[25]

---

25. The preceding analysis should indicate the ways in which my cognitive account of national identification differs from the accounts of other writers. Consider, for example, Wimmer's four "models of explanation and interpretation" for ethnicity and nationalism (see 51–52). The first is a matter of "rational choice." Rational self-interest—including group self-interest—certainly enters into the calculation of individuals (including government officials) engaging in action bearing on the nation. However, our individual and collective behaviors are motivated in much more complex ways. Again, research shows that, given a choice, people opt for hierarchizing the in-group above the out-group rather than maximizing their own or their in-group's gain (see Duckitt 68–69). In keeping with this, as I have stressed, functionality enters nationalism, not in terms of possible individual or even group benefit in particular cases, but in terms of likely self-categorization across cases. Thus, rational self-interest is largely irrelevant to my account. It enters only when distinctive concerns of categorial identification are absent—thus, when we are not really talking about nationalism at all. Two of Wimmer's other three models make "ethnic and nationalist politics" part of "modern society" (51). As I noted in the introduction, one can certainly define nationalism in such a way that it applies only to categorial identifications found in the modern period. Moreover, the historical differences in categorial identifications are very important. However, modern nationalism does not arise out of nothing. It arises from the same neurocognitive structures and processes, as well as the same general principles of group dynamics, as all earlier human group identifications. Historicist accounts almost necessarily leave out all this. The final model isolated by Wimmer treats ethnicity as "a constant factor of human life" such that "Politics has always been a matter of ethnic pride and rivalry" (51). In my account, categorial identification has been a continuous and central factor of human life and politics has always involved categorial identification. However, no one type of identity category (e.g., ethnicity) has necessarily been dominant. Different categories and types of categories have formed shifting, variable configurations even among the same people over short periods of time. Finally, as we will see more clearly in the following chapters, the emotions that bear on categorial identification are not reducible to pride and rivalry.

Similar points apply to David Brown's "three conceptual languages which see nationalism as, respectively, an instinct (primordialism), an interest (situationalism) and an ideology (constructivism)" (5). Brown's "primordialism" is roughly the same as Wimmer's ethnicity-based model. Again, I agree that categorial identification is a cross-cultural and transhistorical propensity of humans. But that says nothing about the precise nature of the identification. Moreover, it is very far from suggesting that ethnic identifications are somehow representative of genuinely natural groupings—quite the contrary, in fact. His situationalist category is more or less identical with Wimmer's rational choice model. Brown's third category, which sees nationalism as ideological, is perhaps closest to my own view, depending on how one defines ideology. *Ideology* may be understood as having two characteristics. First, it is a complex of false ideas or overly limited alternatives for understanding the world along with a set of aspirations that are not in the best interest of the people who have adopted those aspirations. Second, ideology is socially functional in establishing or preserving nonmeritocratic social hierarchies. I would certainly say that nationalism commonly has both characteristics. However, this is quite general and does not in any way explain nationalism—its components, causes, varieties, etc. Moreover, this does not seem to fit Brown's account of nationalism as

Again, we all fall into countless categories. In this way, each of us has countless identities. But these do not have equal importance in our self-concepts and they do not have equal motivational force. I have isolated five parameters governing the hierarchization of identity categories—salience, durability, functionality, opposability, and affectivity. We must now consider how nationalist practices serve to manipulate these parameters toward nationalist ends, and how processes of nationalization are so successful in elevating the national identity category that people—many people—are willing to sacrifice their own lives (and, of course, the lives of others) for what they see as service to the nation.

"simplistic formulas" presented by nationalist leaders to "otherwise confused or insecure individuals" (20). This is not entirely out of keeping with my account of the conditions for the rise of sacrificial nationalism. Moreover, it fits many cases of heroic nationalism (e.g., much American nationalist fervor after the September 11 crimes). However, I would not accept such a formulation generally. (I should note that, though I do not agree with the framework presented by Brown, that framework does help him to present insightful analyses of a number of cases of nationalism.)

2

HIERARCHIZING IDENTITIES

Techniques of Nationalization

IN THE PRECEDING chapter, I set out a series of parameters that govern the hierarchization of identity categories. In this chapter, I examine each of those parameters in greater detail, considering some of the standard practices that serve to establish the national category as preeminent. I refer to these practices as "techniques of nationalization." Some of these techniques are self-consciously deployed by nationalist activists for the express purpose of fostering patriotism. Others arise more spontaneously through the interaction of individuals and institutions in societies where national identity categories are becoming important. In each case, the crucial thing is not the individual intent with which a given action is performed. Rather, the crucial thing is the effect of the action. Suppose Doe is killed in Iraq. Jones may urge that the town put up a monument to Doe's memory. Perhaps he wants to honor a dead friend. Perhaps urging such a thing seems an effective way of getting votes in the next election. For our purposes, these motives do not matter. Whatever the motives may be, the establishment of a monument to a soldier in a national war serves as a technique of nationalization, operating through salience and affectivity, and perhaps through other parameters as well.

I will consider each of the parameters in turn, examining relevant techniques under each heading.[1] I have not tried to cover every technique of nationalization. I have, rather, sought to present a broad range of the most widespread and effective techniques. There are two particularly crucial techniques that I do not consider in the present chapter—metaphor and narrative. They are pervasive and highly consequential. Moreover, they have not been explored in detail by other authors. For these reasons, I give them—particularly narrative—a fuller, separate treatment in the remaining chapters of the book.

In order to give the discussion a clearer shape, I have divided the treatment of most parameters into techniques bearing on ordinary life and techniques bearing on extraordinary events. The division is rough. Some events are recurrent, thus not precisely extraordinary, but also not exactly part of everyday life. Nonetheless, the broad division is useful in calling to mind the fact that techniques of nationalization are ubiquitous. They are, of course, bound up with large and highly dramatic events, such as war. But they are no less bound up with our quotidian routines. The only exception to this division is in the final section on affectivity. It is, I believe, more useful to organize emotions by reference to their objects, which, in this case, fall into four main groups—other in-group members, the in-group hierarchy, the national out-group, and the land.

SALIENCE

Salience may at first seem to be the least important of the five parameters. But that is only because its necessity is so obvious. If we are oblivious to our national category, it simply will not play much of a role in our thought and action. More technically, if there are not multiple and strong connections between our national category and other, ordinary items in our semantic and episodic memories (roughly, our memories of ideas and of events), then the national category is unlikely to be activated and we are unlikely to think about the world, our lives, our feelings in relation to that category. Far from being unimportant, the cultivation of salience is fundamental to the cultivation of nationalism.

---

1. Needless to say, most techniques operate on more than one parameter. Thus, there will necessarily be some overlap in the discussion of those different parameters.

Daily Life

As I have just suggested, it is crucial that the national category become highly salient in ordinary life. In part, this is because subnational categories, such as race, are likely to be salient on their own. It is also because it is important that we spontaneously interpret events in nationalistic terms. For example, people could easily have interpreted the September 11 bombings in several ways. They could have interpreted them as an attack on commerce, on wealth, on the Judeo-Christian world, or—as is most accurate—on the policies of the U.S. government and those who accept such policies. (Obviously, it was a terrible crime, murdering thousands of people who have no particular responsibility for the deaths in Iraq or Palestine. To say that the bombers had a particular motive is not to say that the motive justified the crime.) But people rarely interpreted the bombings in any of these ways. Americans interpreted them as an attack on their nation. A rare critic argued that the motives were not some vague, generalized hatred of Americans or the American way of life, but anger over specific U.S. government policies. However, the position of these writers was both distorted and immediately appropriated toward nationalistic ends. Noam Chomsky and others who tried to determine just what led to the bombings were referred to as the "blame America first" group. But, of course, their point was not to blame America. It was to argue that the U.S. government had followed destructive policies in Iraq, Palestine, and elsewhere, policies that gave rise to anger and despair throughout the Muslim world. That anger and despair led to the bombings. Thus, the policies help to explain the bombings. They do not serve to justify them. After all, part of the point such writers made is that murder is wrong, whether it is Americans murdering Iraqis or Arabs murdering Americans. Yet the argument seemed impossible for most people to follow. In part, this was because the national category was so salient that the event itself, and any response to the event (e.g., an attempt at analyzing its origins), were immediately interpreted in terms of national categorial identity.

Perhaps the most obvious way of making the national category salient is by displaying the national flag. The presence of the flag above public buildings, outside private homes, at rallies and sporting events, on pins, on clothing, on cars is a constant reminder of the nation. Even in ordinary times, it is difficult to walk through any American city without having one's national category repeatedly primed (i.e., partially activated and thus made readily available for use in interpretation, causal attribution, etc.). The display of flags proliferated after the September 11 bombings. This contributed to the way people thought about the bombings and thus to the consolidation of a nationalist interpretation of the events.²

Of course, the salience of the national category, both before and after September 11, was due not only to the display of flags. It was the result of many factors in daily life. A number of these, like displaying the flag, involve a simple physical presence that serves to remind us of the nation. As several writers have stressed, monuments have an important role in this regard. Thus, Anderson writes that "No more arresting emblems of the modern culture of nationalism exist than cenotaphs and tombs of Unknown Soldiers" (9). In his extremely important discussion of nationalist "invention of tradition," Hobsbawm isolates "three major innovations," one of which was "the mass production of public monuments" ("Mass-Producing Traditions" 271). The same general point holds not only for monuments per se, but for national buildings (e.g., government facilities), parks, and other national public objects.

All national public objects become part of ordinary life and thus serve as constant reminders of the national identity category. In addition, many of them also call to mind particular ideas about the nation—narratives, metaphors, associated feelings, and so forth. Wachtel gives a striking example of a single work that had a significant place in the formation of Yugoslav national identity, the Kosovo Temple of Ivan Meštrović. Wachtel quotes one of Meštrović's contemporaries, who wrote that "Meštrović's temple has deep national significance" (56). Specifically, the temple is in "close touch with the national soul . . . our soul, the Yugoslav soul" (59). The work is noteworthy in many ways. Its two names—"Kosovo Temple" and "St. Vitus Day Temple"—commemorate an historical event, the Battle of Kosovo, thereby enhancing a sense of national durability as well as salience. The structure "combined Catholic and Orthodox elements" (55),

---

2. One reader of this discussion complained that the flag is not in fact very salient. It is true that the ordinary display of the flag may not draw self-conscious attentional focus. However, it seems fairly clear that we do perceive the flag and thus experience effects from that perception even in the normal course of events. For example, I suspect that at least many people would notice if, say, the confederate flag were substituted for the U.S. flag at their local post office. Many people do notice when a flag is flown at half mast. If we notice these changes, there must be some degree to which we are experiencing the presence of the flag in ordinary circumstances. Thus, it seems fairly clear that we do indeed perceive the flag. Given this, and given the general principles of human cognition, we can be confident that its presence has the usual consequences for memory, semantic activation, etc. Specifically, it serves to prime (or partially and implicitly activate) national associations. Moreover, in times of crisis or nationalist fervor—whether after events such as those of September 11 or after a national team's victory in some international sporting competition—the multiplication of flags makes their presence highly salient.

thus forestalling a subnational identification with the work by either of these religious groups. Meštrović's "figures [were] inspired by the heroes of South Slavic Oral poetry" (55), hence bound up with national narratives. Meštrović himself said that he "tried to give a single synthesis of the popular folk ideals and their development," memorializing "the greatest moments and most significant events in our history" and doing so in such a way that "The temple cannot be dedicated to any one confession or separate sect" (quoted in Wachtel 59).

National public objects perform their salience-enhancing function most obviously for people living near them. This is particularly true in capitals, which often serve as insistent reminders of the national category through their general design and multiplication of nationalist sites. For example, Cannadine refers to the "large-scale rebuilding of capital cities, as the great powers bolstered their self-esteem in the most visible, ostentatious manner" (126). In relation to this, he refers to the U.S. capital, mentioning "the Washington Memorial, the White House extension, the Union Station, the Lincoln Monument and the scheme for grand government buildings surrounding the Capitol" (127). He also refers to London, where "monumental, commemorative statues proliferated" (128; here as elsewhere commemorative works enhance not only salience, but our sense of the endurance of the nation through time). Beyond this, he explains that the relevant aspects of capitals are not confined to monuments and buildings, but include their broad avenues, squares, and related aspects of city design (126).

On the other hand, the salience-enhancing effects of monuments, buildings, and so forth are not confined to local inhabitants. They enter into the ordinary lives of people from across the nation in many ways. One of the most important is tourism. In general, the "sights" visited by tourists tend to be national or religious. The latter is unsurprising, since the premodern parallel to tourism was the pilgrimage, which also had an identity function. To a great extent, however, nationalism has displaced religion even in the case of religious sights. Thus, today religious monuments tend to take on a national coloring. For example, I suspect that most visitors to the Chartres cathedral view it not only as Catholic, but also—and perhaps more importantly—as French.

The contribution of tourism to national saliency is not confined to monuments, public buildings, and other artifacts. It commonly extends to national geography as well. The landscape of a place may be understood explicitly or implicitly as specifically *national* land. When this occurs, a tour of the countryside can serve to make the national category more salient. It can also foster an affective relation to the national land, thereby enhancing the affectivity of national categorical identification. For example, discussing the case of Wales, Morgan explains that there was "a wide movement which tried to make the Welsh understand that their landscape must be cherished." In consequence, "each stick and stone" was assigned "historical . . .interest" (86). In these cases, the national landscape was not merely a general reminder of the national category. It was a reminder of historical particulars bearing on the nation. Thus, it contributed not only to salience, but to the sense of durability as well. Morgan goes on to explain that this nationalizing of the landscape was bound up with tourism in the eighteenth century (see 87).

Returning to artifacts, we find that the same points hold, not only for statues, buildings, and parks, but also for much smaller items. These include national heirlooms and symbols, such as the throne of a past monarch, the original copy of the constitution, a letter written by a past president. Even ordinary roads and squares can enhance saliency, most obviously through their names (e.g., Abraham Lincoln Highway, Constitution Plaza). New buildings can stand on memorial spaces, marked by plaques of the "George Washington slept here" variety. Particular types of tree (e.g., the maple in Canada), flower, arrangement of foliage (e.g., an English garden) can have the same sort of effect. None of this has to have been developed by self-conscious nationalist design. It strikes someone as a good idea to memorialize where Washington slept (perhaps he or she owns the shop next door and hopes for some extra business) or to rename a road in honor of a president. Who would disagree? The plaque is set on the spot or the road is given its name and that plaque or name functions to recall our national category, and to support our sense of the durability of the nation, whatever the initial intent.

For the most part, public objects of this sort are stationary. Even the smaller items tend to be housed in museums or otherwise located in a fixed place. For the relevant cues to activate national categories, people have to experience the objects. Again, this is often a matter of people seeing the objects directly, thus visiting national historic sites. In other cases, however, saliency is enhanced by reproductions—on postcards, newscasts, television programs or films, or through the mass-marketing of miniatures (e.g., tiny replicas of the White House).

François, Siegrist, and Vogel point out that techniques for "symbolic integration" of the nation operate through "identification and affective binding with 'national' symbols," including "material symbols such as memorials, buildings, and landscapes, as well as works of art and ordinary objects." Among ordinary objects, they stress "coins and postage stamps" ("Die Nation" 19; my translation). They are right to do so. Money and stamps are the two "most universal" forms of "public imagery," as Hobsbawm puts it. They serve to bring the national category into our everyday lives in wholly unexceptional ways, as part of our most basic routines. They do not require us to travel to the capital, but only that we buy something in the market or receive a letter. Moreover, the nationalist effects do not result solely from their function in national economic and postal systems (i.e., from the mere fact that they are the national currency and national postage). Their designs involve a series of representations that themselves have nationalist associations, such as depictions of presidents and national heroes or inscriptions of nationalist slogans. Cannadine points out the bearing of special commemorative stamps on nationalism (155). From our perspective, such stamps clearly enhance salience. They may also foster a sense of durability, if the event commemorated involves historical reference, as in a bicentennial. In keeping with this, Hobsbawm explains that anniversaries "often provided for the first issue of historical or similar images on postage stamps" ("Mass-Producing" 281). Beyond this, postage stamps may contribute to the metaphorical unification of the nation, as when they feature a representation of the nation as a person (a standard form of nationalist metaphor, as we will discuss in the next chapter). For example, Hobsbawm cites the case of "'Germania,' who played no notable role in sculpture," but "figured extensively on postage stamps" ("Mass-Producing" 276). Stamps may even enhance (however slightly) the heroic emplotment of national aspirations, if they happen to commemorate war heroes or battles.

National media are, of course, important to the enhancement of salience as well, and not only in reproducing images of national landmarks. Perhaps most significant, newspapers (and other news media) commonly orient reporting toward a particular national audience. They focus on news relevant to Americans, Germans, or Indians, depending on whether they are American, German, or Indian newspapers. This may seem unremarkable. But there is nothing in the nature of newspapers that requires this. We do have newspapers geared toward workers, toward professions, toward particular ethnic groups. So a non-national orientation toward news reporting is certainly possible. But these newspapers are seen as specialized, as catering to an unusual audience. The common view is that the nationally oriented newspaper (or news broadcast) is the norm. What this means is that newspapers and other news media almost invariably present the news from the perspective of the nation, thus from the perspective of national interests. American news media report stories that involve Americans, that bear on the American economy, and so forth. As such, they serve to make the national category highly salient. At the same time, the national organization of news reporting gives national categorization a sense of normalcy or naturalness. News appears to be national by its nature. Alternatives (e.g., ethnic or class-based news) are defined against national news as the norm or default.³ In this context, it is unsurprising that newspapers are often bound up with the earliest development of widespread national identification. Thus, Glanmor Williams writes of "The experience of a Galician peasant," that "neither he nor many of his fellows had fully realised that they were Poles until they started reading books and newspapers" (122).⁴

The same point also holds for various routine collective activities. In some cases, the content is not greatly significant. In other cases, it is. Obvious instances of the latter would include the recitation of the Pledge of Allegiance—"a daily ritual in the country's schools" (Hobsbawm, "Mass-Producing" 280)—and the singing of the national anthem at sporting events. The singing of the national anthem is particularly interesting. During domestic contests, the entire crowd sings the anthem. It thus serves to remind them of their common identity even as some other form of identity difference (e.g., by city) is suggested by the contest itself. This sense of national identification may be enhanced still further if the sport in question is a "national" sport, such as American football or baseball (see Hobsbawm, "Mass-Producing" 300, on the development of national sports). Specifically, national sports render the national category more salient by the simple fact that they are seen as national. Moreover, by their differentiation from the national sports of other nations (e.g., Gaelic football's difference from English football), they may enhance opposability as well. In contrast with domestic contests, the national anthems of both sides are played

---

3. The same point holds for history. History appears naturally to be national. Other forms of history are then defined against the national norm.

4. One might object here that news may be local also. That is perfectly true. The point isn't that all news operates at the national level of organization. The point is that there are many sorts of news that might be of interest to people. Local news is an obvious case of this. Moving outside of local news, what larger units might we expect to find? We might expect to find, say, union-related news, or professional news, or ethnic news. But typically what we find above the level of local news is national news. Moreover, even local news is selective, and a large part of that selection is national. For example, if a local newspaper reports on local representatives, it will far more commonly report on local representatives to the national government—not to unions, professional societies, ethnic pride groups, language revival societies. Even local news often focuses on local government, which is, of course, part of the national system. In other words, even a great deal of apparently purely local reporting has an implicit national orientation.

during international competitions. Fans of one national team sing one national anthem; fans of the other national team sing another national anthem. In this way, the anthem serves to define the contest in national terms and to recruit the contest to nationalist ends, first of all by rendering the national category more salient and opposable.

Events

The repetitive rituals of a daily pledge or a weekly song are still part of ordinary life. That is what makes them routine. There are also extraordinary events, such as the September 11 bombings, that provide an occasion for enhancing the salience of national categories. Less frequent periodic rituals and "common collective practices" (as Hobsbawm puts it; see *Nations* 71) serve as a sort of transition between the habitual and the truly extraordinary. In being nonquotidian, they serve as moments of particular nationalist intensity. In this way, they are similar to the emotion spikes that are necessary to sustain a mood (see Greg Smith 37–44). Indeed, they often include such moments of strong national feeling. At the same time, they are highly routinized. They are not the huge shocks of September 11 or the unique celebrations that mark the end of a war. Their impact is more controlled.

Clear examples of this sort may be found, first of all, in the nationalist organization of the calendar. As Anderson has discussed, nations make national festivals in the way religions do.[5] They commemorate battles, births and deaths, and other events with particular national significance. An obvious case from the United States would be Presidents' Day. Being released from work to celebrate Washington and Lincoln serves to emphasize the national category, and to imbue it with positive emotion. Since the process has become so ingrained, we may not recognize that it could be otherwise. Imagine instead a society in which we were given days off to celebrate, say, Louis Pasteur and Edward Jenner for developing a vaccination against smallpox. One might say that the addition of Martin Luther King Day is somewhat comparable. But, in fact, Martin Luther King Day is a nationalist holiday as well. It serves to incorporate King—and thus African Americans more generally—into national unity. Insofar as he has been honored by a national holiday, King is perhaps less readily available for

---

5. There is not merely a parallel, but an historical connection between religious and nationalist practices (see François, Siegrist, and Vogel, "Die Nation" 24–27, and the essays by Vogel, Maas, Ben-Amos, Ackermann, and Abélès, as well as Berezin 88–90).

subnational appropriation. Labor Day in the United States operates similarly. It takes up a day putatively celebrating a transnational group, workers, then nationalizes the day, in part by shifting it away from the international day of labor solidarity, May 1.

The nationalistic operation of Memorial Day is no less explicit than that of Presidents' Day. It is obvious that the parades on that day serve to make the national category salient. With their strings of veterans of different ages and from different wars, Memorial Day parades also stress the durability of the nation. In terms of affectivity, the mere presence of a crowd may foster a "yielding" or "submission response" (see Tan and Frijda 53, 54, 62–63). In a nationalist context, such a response would involve a sense of "losing oneself," not merely in "something greater" (62), but specifically in the greater national community. Finally, Memorial Day incorporates all this into a tacit heroic emplotment of the national purpose, for it is necessarily a day celebrating the nation at war.

The connection between national holidays and war is, of course, not unique to Memorial Day. National celebrations routinely involve the military. Military parades, displays of weaponry, and so forth contribute in obvious ways to the salience of the national category, to the sort of heroic emplotment just mentioned, and to a sense of national unity across regions, races, religions, and other subnational categories (due to the constitution of the armed forces). For example, examining Germany and France in 1871–1914, Jakob Vogel writes about "the ascent of the army to a central symbol of the nation." He explains that, "Regularly held, public military parades developed at this time into the most important rituals, through which the state leadership not only propagated a national cult around the army, but, going further, celebrated the nation as a unified, battle-ready community as well" (199; my translation).

The most obviously nationalistic American holiday is Independence Day, a day of communal festivities, a huge birthday party for the nation, ending with fireworks from Maine to Hawaii and the singing of nationalist songs. Here, too, the national category is highly salient—as people dress in red, white, and blue; children have their faces painted with the flag; and hundreds of thousands of people join in singing the national anthem. There is also emotional arousal—feelings of attachment to the group, and heroic thrill at the fireworks that harmlessly mimic the many battles we as a nation have fought against our enemies.

Before going on, it is worth pausing for a moment over communal song and other coordinated collective activities. Song is often involved in the establishment of a sense of in-group identification, as is dance. Goodwin and Pfaff point out the value of song in fostering a sense of unity (291; see also Barker 187). François, Siegrist, and Vogel note that, "In gymnastic festivals, parades, and mass dancing, the nation . . . embodied itself in forms and in synchronous movement" ("Die Nation" 28; my translation). Conversely, one main purpose of song and other coordinated activities is to inhibit any sense of subnational difference. We find a nice example of this use of coordinated activity in the Commemoration of the Leipzig People's Battle of 1813, discussed by Hoffmann. As Hoffmann explains, Ernst Moritz Arndt proposed the remembrance of this battle on October 18 and 19, with October 18 "a pure folk festival . . . to symbolize the unity of all Germans and to make it something that can be experienced through the senses." In order to accomplish this, "in the evening, on nearby mountains or hills throughout Germany celebratory fires should be lit." This coordinated exhibition of "signs of love and joy," Arndt claimed, would "announce . . . that now all German people have only one feeling and one thought." Thus, "social differences will be overcome . . . to stress the unity of the nation" (113; my translation). In cases such as this, the national category is rendered salient through the unexpected coordination of practical identities among citizens. (This also contributes to opposability, for reasons that will become clear below.)

Of course, not all recurrent collective activities are so narrowly political. For example, some serve nationalist ends through arts or culture. Thus, speaking of Welsh nationalists, Glanmor Williams explains that "Two of their most typical activities were to celebrate the national day—Saint David's Day (1 March)—and to organise *eisteddfodau*. The *eisteddfod* (an assembly for competitions in literature and music) was an exceptionally lively institution in nineteenth-century Wales," including "the national *Eisteddfod* held once a year" (122).

Perhaps the most obvious ritual day in democracies is not annual. Rather, it takes place at longer (sometimes regular, sometimes irregular) intervals—election day. Elections serve to make the national identity category more salient, to homogenize the national in-group (no citizen has more than one vote), to polarize in-group and out-group (here, noncitizens, who have no vote), to memorialize the continuity of the system, to stress the functionality of citizenship, and to create a sense of emotional involvement in the nation. Finally, elections have the specific effect of reenforcing the social hierarchy by linking it with popularity.[6]

---

6. Nondemocratic rituals, too, can operate to support hierarchy. (For some examples from India and Africa, see Cohn 172 and Ranger 221.)

FUNCTIONALITY

These references to democracy and voting rights lead us nicely to the topic of function. The functionality of the national category—its bearing on access to opportunities, services, and goods—is fairly self-evident. For that reason, I will treat it only briefly. However, before treating this topic, I should note that there is an ambiguity in the way we understand the concept of national identity category. We tend to equate national identity category with citizenship. In most cases, this is perfectly reasonable. However, suppose Smith is an Australian citizen, but has been raised in the United States and currently lives there. If someone asks about his nationality, he may say something like, "Well, I'm officially an Australian citizen. But I've lived most of my life in the U.S." Statements of this sort show that our national identity categories are not confined to our citizenship. This is particularly consequential for the functionality of that national category. Both in daily life and in unusual events, my relation to a nation may be highly functional even if I am not a citizen.

Daily Life

Once a national state is established, the functionality of the national hierarchy usually supersedes that of all other group categories in a broad range of areas. The obvious place where the nation shows its functionality is in law. Virtually everything we do is in some way qualified by the laws of the state. The functional impact of other identity group structures—ethnic, religious, racial, regional, linguistic—is very limited in comparison. Where I live is governed by housing codes; how I live there is governed by laws pertaining to ownership, construction, taxation; when I drive to work, laws of the road structure my trip (along with laws bearing on the ownership of my car and national policies relating to oil); at work, I am governed by labor laws, laws relating to interaction with my coworkers, laws regarding contracts; when I return home, even my most private moments are qualified by law—rules governing possible sexual partners, laws governing where I can perform certain bodily functions. There are laws governing dress, food, comportment, interaction with others. These laws may be oppressive or they may serve to protect us (e.g., against unsanitary practices in restaurants). But, in any case, they are pervasive. And they are largely national laws. Even when the laws are local, they must be the sort of laws permitted and, indeed, underwritten by the national legal structure.

For the most part, the legal system is an area in which my national identity category is most importantly a matter of where I live, rather than what my citizenship status might be. But, of course, there are areas of law where this is not the case. Indeed, the entire apparatus of citizenship makes the functionality of the national category still clearer. The use of passports—which became compulsory in the United States only in 1918 (Higgins and Leps 122)—and the resulting restriction on freedom of international movement provide a striking case of the extension of national functionality (for a discussion of the history and nationalist functionality of passports, see Higgins and Leps). Indeed, citizenship law is broadly illuminating with respect to the functionality of national identity categories, which is hardly surprising. There have generally been two criteria for citizenship, *jus sanguinis* (or law of blood) and *jus soli* (or law of territory). The former defines citizenship by parentage. It served initially to align the national identity category with an ethnic identity category. *Jus soli,* in contrast, takes up one distinctive feature of nationhood—its relation to a geographical place—and defines citizenship in terms of birth in a particular area. For example, until recently, Benhabib explains, "most German citizenship was granted only if one parent—usually the father—was a German, a vivid continuation of the *jus sanguinis,* which had been formalized in 1913 to withhold citizenship from Polish guest workers and East European Jews." In 1999, a law was passed that "grants German citizenship to almost anyone born on German soil to parents who have resided and worked in the country for at least eight years, potentially including the children of millions of *Gastarbeiter*" (6). Such cases demonstrate—and increase people's awareness of—the functionality of the national category.[7]

Another option for citizenship is naturalization. This is an interesting case also, for naturalization involves complex qualifications and formal procedures. For example, in the United States, to be naturalized as a citizen, one must satisfy a series of requirements, including a particular "period of continuous residence and physical presence in the United States"; "an ability to read, write, and speak English"; "a knowledge and understanding of U.S. history and government"; "good moral character"; "attachment to the principles of the U.S. Constitution"; and "favorable disposition toward the

---

7. The awareness of functionality is crucial. Again, functionality does not enhance national identification if that functionality is simply present. People have to believe that nationality is functional—even if they are mistaken. On the other hand, making nationality functional in reality is usually a very good way of producing a belief in its functionality.

United States" (website for the U.S. Citizenship and Immigration Services, http://www.uscis.gov). The final two require, among other things, an Oath of Allegiance, which includes renunciation of "any foreign allegiance" and an agreement to "bear arms for the Armed Forces of the U.S." None of this is required for those who are citizens by birth, whether by *jus sanguinis* or *jus soli* criteria. Thus, in some ways, the functionality of the nation is enhanced and made particularly salient by naturalization. This is true most obviously for the new citizens who go through the process of naturalization. But it is true to a lesser degree for those who are citizens by birth, for they are commonly aware, at least in a general way, of the processes involved in naturalization and of the requirements and exclusions that these processes involve.

Thus, it seems impossible not to recognize the functionality of the nation in one's daily life, and, in most cases, its overwhelmingly greater functionality than that of other identity groups.

Events

A range of events may express the functionality of the nation—particularly, the nation as hierarchically structured in a state. We may see the functionality of the nation-state in certain sorts of international agreements, temporary internal changes (e.g., states of emergency), and the like. However, the most significant events of this sort are, commonly, wars. Indeed, one might argue that the functionality of any group identity is largely a matter of the degree to which the group is able to exert and control violence through its hierarchy. The nation-state commonly claims a monopoly or near monopoly on physical violence within its boundaries. This is established, first of all, through the legal system. Nations in effect claim a monopoly on international violence as well. This is bound up with the virtually universal claim that "our" decision to go to war is a defensive response to the illegitimate aggression (or threatened aggression) of the enemy. War is obviously inseparable from a whole series of other national structures and practices that also manifest functionality—the armed forces, the draft, and so forth.

We will consider nationalism and war in more detail in subsequent chapters. Here, the crucial point is simply that war brings home the functionality of the national category. The ways in which it does this are, I take it, too obvious to require enumeration.

OPPOSABILITY

Opposability involves two things: (1) polarization or near polarization of in-group and out-group and (2) categorial unification of the in-group and, to a lesser extent, categorial unification of the out-group.

By "polarization or near polarization," I mean simply that opposability increases to the degree that it reduces the number of in-group/out-group oppositions. The highest opposability comes with full polarization, that is, opposition of the in-group to a single out-group. However, polarization is often too simple for actual national relations. Thus, national in-groups frequently define themselves against two out-groups. An obvious case is the opposition between the United States, the Soviet Union, and China during parts of the Cold War. This is "near polarization." It involves a lower degree of opposability. However, it allows for greater ideological and practical flexibility. Specifically, a fully polarized opposition tends to establish the enemy as eternal and immutable. It does not allow much leeway for diplomacy or for spontaneously changing relations resulting from shared interests. In a triadic division, it is commonly the case that one of the two enemies is viewed as more antagonistic than the other. This difference can be used strategically, as was obviously the case with the United States, USSR, and China. In some cases, the division into two out-groups recurs, in a slightly different form, within a single national enemy. For example, in colonial situations, the colonizer often divides the colonized populace into two groups, the smaller of which serves as a sort of buffer between the colonizer and the majority of the colonized population. Thus, in the Caribbean and in South Africa, whites distinguished between full Africans and people with mixed racial ancestry. The latter had a status intermediate between that of the whites and that of the majority black population.

Again, such triadic divisions do not give the same degree of opposability as a dyadic division. However, they allow practical benefits over pure dualism. Generally, these benefits diminish with the introduction of further out-groups. Moreover, the loss of polarization becomes more consequential. As a result, it seems fairly uncommon for a nation to consistently represent itself as opposed to three main enemies, and virtually unheard of for it to define itself against four or more groups.

By "categorial unification," I mean the occlusion of sub- and transnational categories of the in-group or, equivalently, the minimization of situations in which sub- and transnational categories would become obtrusive. Thus, a national category has greater opposability to the extent that racial, ethnic, religious, or similar non-national categories are unlikely to be recognized or invoked. This is primarily important for the in-group. Subdivisions in the out-group are significant for in-group self-categorization only insofar as they are connected to transnational identifications with members of the in-group, or insofar as they are recruited to divide the enemy, as already noted. In other words, as far as the in-group's self-identification goes, religious, racial, ethnic, and related differences in the out-group are insignificant in themselves.[8] They affect in-group national identification only when they mirror such differences in the in-group, and thus might give salience to those in-group differences, or when they may be viewed as defining two out-groups that may be set against one another.

All national identifications are fragile. Some nations appear to have aligned national, racial, religious, and other identity categories. However, as I have already noted, this is never entirely true. If India rid itself of Muslims, Christians, and Sikhs, then Vaiṣṇavites and Śaivites or different castes could form subnational identity groups. If the United States were all white and Christian, then Catholics and Protestants, northern and southern Europeans, and other identity rifts could open up. In other words, all nations have subnational divisions. Thus, every nation faces the task of creating a sense of homogeneity.

Crude as it may seem, the best way to foster a sense of in-group homogeneity is simply to divert attention from subnational categories. There are two obvious ways of doing this, one negative, the other positive. The negative way is to avoid occasions when subnational divisions would become salient, functional, and so forth. This is the purpose of homogenizing practical identities. As discussed in the preceding chapter, any conflict in practical identities is likely to draw attention to relevant categorical differences (or even, in some cases, irrelevant differences[9]). The positive way is to lead attention to some other identity division. This is why polarization and the creation of internal categorial identification come together in opposability. Part of opposing ourselves to the national enemy is a matter of thinking of "us" as falling under a single identity category. Part of thinking about "us" as a single identity is thinking not about our various differences from one another, but instead about our collective difference from the national

8. Moreover, our spontaneous, un-self-conscious assumption is that out-groups are highly homogenous, indeed virtually uniform. As Duckitt points out, we assume out-groups are "less complex, less variable, less individuated" (81). We will return to the point below in connection with emotion.

9. For example, a European American and an African American may experience a conflict in practical identities that is related to purely individual idiosyncrasies. However, they may understand that conflict in racial terms.

enemy. (It should be clear why, in this context, the unity of the enemy figures is unimportant in itself.)

In sum, an identity category will have the highest degree of opposability, and thus contribute most powerfully to the privileging of that category in identity hierarchies, in circumstances where it is contrasted directly and definitively with one or, perhaps, two out-groups, where the practices of its members are coordinated, and where the attentional focus of those members is on the out-group. The homogenization of practices is most obviously a function of daily life, though it may be enhanced by particular events (e.g., there are ways in which practical life becomes more homogenous during wartime). The diversion of attentional focus to the out-group is most obvious during periods of crisis, such as war, though it may occur outside that context as well.

Before going on, I should stress once again that when I refer to "homogenizing" practical identities, I do not mean making them all the same. Rather, I mean coordinating them so that they work smoothly together. We all have certain capabilities and certain expectations about how society will operate. The general patterns of the expectations, and our understanding of the ways in which these fit with individual capabilities, should be roughly the same. However, this does not mean that everyone has the same capabilities or that everyone is subjected to the same expectations. For example, part of a homogenous American culture is seeing certain sorts of intrusive medical examination as normal and even necessary. This does not mean that everyone is capable of performing such exams or is expected—or allowed—to do so.

Daily Life

The most obvious and probably most crucial area of practical identity coordination in daily life is language. There is nothing that is more disruptive of shared identification than an inability to communicate. Indeed, even lesser forms of linguistic discontinuity—due to regional differences in vocabulary or idiom—can make subnational categories obtrusive. This is why nationalists almost invariably assert the importance of national language. This is true not only of English advocates in the United States. It is true of the Yugoslav nationalists who worked to homogenize Serbo-Croatian, Turkish nationalists who criminalized the use of Kurdish (see Chomsky, *New* 52), Chinese nationalists who "forced . . . standard Mandarin as the official language of everyday communication" in Taiwan (Chun

86). Needless to say, these efforts are not always successful. Indeed, suppression of a language, as in the case of Kurdish, serves to make use of the language more functional even for polyglot speakers (i.e., in this case, even for Kurdish speakers who are fluent in Turkish). If being a Kurdish speaker can land you in jail (for speaking Kurdish), the category is clearly very functional (i.e., very consequential for one's access to opportunities, services, and goods). Moreover, these sorts of repression are likely to increase the affectivity, opposability, and salience of the language category. The only thing they may not enhance is the sense of durability—though even here the threat to the language, the danger to its continuation, may bring to mind its ancestry. In any case, such acts of suppression often have the opposite effect from that desired. This does not mean that linguistic homogeneity is not valuable for nationalism. It simply means that coercive suppression of non-national languages—with their associated identity categories—is most often not a good way of advancing that homogeneity.

In contrast, education, particularly literacy education, may be effective in fostering linguistic homogeneity. Judit Kádár-Fülop explains that, "Literacy education has three interrelated functions." Two are relevant here. The first is "to diminish *language distance* between the members of society by developing communicative competence in at least one standard written language: the language of national literacy." This is, precisely, national linguistic coordination. Kádár-Fülop's second function is "to *develop language loyalty* toward the language of literacy" (31–32). In our terms, this is a form of language-based categorial identification. Such identification serves nationalist purposes if and only if language and nation are aligned. She goes on to explain that, "State school systems were established in many countries in the hope that instruction and education in the standard written language would diminish language barriers between communicants. The history of nations and languages shows that these were not unrealistic expectations" (32). Haugland provides an apt example from Norwegian nationalism, explaining that "the greatest effort for the cause of *Landsmal* [Norwegian national language] came from the Folk High Schools through their influence on thousands of young pupils. When the boys and girls returned home from these schools, many had become keen *Landsmal* adherents" (28).

Needless to say, the effects of education in homogenizing practical identity go well beyond language coordination. Thus, Hobsbawm maintains that, "The standardization of administration and law within it, and, in particular, state education, transformed people into citizens of a particular country" ("Mass-Producing" 264). There are countless examples. For instance,

Cullen points out that, "The precise character which Irish nationalist aspirations acquired is closely tied up with the impact of school teaching. Teachers were in fact of immense importance in the growth of nationalism" (101). As Chua and Kuo explain, Singapore instituted a "national system" in education. Specifically, "Common curriculum and syllabi were introduced." As a result, "The possibility of forging a common political, economic, and social orientation among the population through education was in place for the first time," in contrast with earlier "vernacular schools," which were "divided along political, cultural, and linguistic orientations" and thus had "divisive effects on the population" (50).

The coordination of practical identities is, of course, not confined to education. It touches almost everything in daily life. For example, food commonly operates to enhance opposability. National cuisines establish commonalities of taste and consumption within a nation and differences of taste and consumption between nations. Sometimes the differences lead people from one culture to find the cuisine of another culture inedible— too hot, too bland, even simply disgusting. Indeed, sharing food is one of the most fundamental ways of bonding personally. When one does not share a cuisine, it may be difficult to share food. When one does not share food, it may be difficult to form personal bonds across identity divisions. In some cases, the separation of cuisines and the nonsharing of food are formalized in food taboos. For example, the strict dietary restrictions on Orthodox Jews helped to prevent the commingling of Jews and gentiles by restricting the possibilities for sharing meals. This in turn helped to strengthen the identity category of "Jew," by making it more salient, functional, and opposable. The same point could be made for Hindus in relation to Muslims, or caste Hindus with regard to untouchables. (Steven Pinker has discussed this aspect of food taboos insightfully; see 385.)

Food taboos are relatively rare for nations. Moreover, today many nations are becoming increasingly cosmopolitan in food. However, the opposability of national cuisines still operates and has effects. French haute cuisine has not disappeared with the introduction of Vietnamese restaurants and Kentucky Fried Chicken. Indian food continues to be the mainstay of Indians even if they occasionally stop in McDonald's. Indeed, even McDonald's in India has been partially Indianized, through the introduction of such items as Chicken McCurry and McAloo Tikki (see www.mcdonaldsindia.com). Such variations on McDonald's standard menu serve the same nationalizing function as a more purely national cuisine.[10]

10. One reader of this manuscript objected that in Maine McDonald's serves lobster rolls. I suppose the point is that not everything McDonald's does contributes to national identifica-

Moreover, for simple practical reasons, there is virtually always some close relation between the diversity of cuisines in a nation and the ethnic diversity in the nation. Of course, here as elsewhere, a nation may pursue a policy of alignment. However, it is unlikely that a nation will institute policies that allow diverse ethnic groups to enter a nation while excluding the cuisines of those groups. Thus, it is commonly the case that initially foreign cuisines are simply incorporated into the national cuisine. For example, in the United States, spaghetti and egg rolls are as much part of the national cuisine as roast beef. Such incorporation diminishes opposability along one axis, reducing differences between the national in-group and national out-groups (in these cases, differences between the United States and China or Italy). However, it increases opposability by homogenizing the practical identities of the in-group (e.g., making all Americans into consumers of spaghetti and egg rolls). Moreover, the "indigenization" of the various cuisines partially restores national differences, as when Chinese or Italian food is Americanized.

The preceding point is obviously parallel to the Indianization of McDonald's, though McDonald's spread to India due to economic globalization and is not associated with a nationalized ethnic group. However, an in some ways more revealing variation on the incorporation of different national cuisines did occur in India. As Appadurai discusses, the definition of a national Indian cuisine has involved the simultaneous definition of regional cuisines. The latter is an important part of the process whereby the great diversity of cultural practices in the area is organized into manageable units and made the common property of the nation. Here, too, opposability is both inhibited and enhanced, though in a way that is slightly different from the transnational case. The definition of regional cuisines (e.g., through selection out of diverse local and even familial practices) does make regional subnational categories more salient. However, the integration of these regional cuisines into a national cuisine compensates for this by coordinating the practical identities of Indians (as eaters of many types of "regional" food).[11]

There are also aspects of housing that operate to cultivate in-group identification, including opposability. However, these are commonly sub-

---

tion. That is true, and I certainly don't wish to sound as if I am claiming nationalism is the only function of food. The point is simply that food often does have the effect of enhancing opposability. Of course, here as elsewhere, such effects depend in part on the larger social context. Suppose, for example, that Maine developed a separatist movement. In that case, McDonald's lobster rolls may have nationalist consequences in Maine in a way that they do not now.

11. A similar point applies to Maine and lobster.

national. Consider, for example, the organization of neighborhoods. The racial ghettos of the United States are an obvious instance of the way housing patterns may enhance subnational identification. But the phenomenon is hardly unique to the United States. Nandy et al. point to a similar pattern that has developed recently in Jaipur (147). Here, the division is religious, thus a matter of the major subnational opposition in India. Hindus and Muslims have increasingly divided into distinct neighborhoods. The division is inseparable from the communal riots that have pitted these groups against one another. Thus, it results from a form of subnational opposability, but it also intensifies that opposability.

In some cases, nationalists have tried to inhibit or reverse such developments. An interesting case of this may be found in Singapore. Chua and Kuo explain that the Singapore government set up a policy of demolishing squatter settlements, which were ethnically based, and setting up public housing that prevented the clustering of ethnic groups (53). Indeed, the government set up quotas at the level of the block. "One is constrained to sell only to a household from the race that is not already over-represented in the block" (54). The policy is also interesting for it highlights a paradox that is inherent in some self-conscious nationalizing techniques. The policy makes ethnicity highly salient and functional at the time of sales in order to reduce its saliency and opposability at other times.

Of course, some nations actually pursue neighborhood division. We find this in Nazi Germany, Apartheid South Africa, and the segregationist southern United States. It may seem that in these cases the nationalists are incoherently fostering subnationalism. However, these are in fact cases where the nationalists in question are pursuing a policy of alignment. Rather than occluding ethnic, racial, or other differences, their goal is to make the nation identical with a particular race or ethnicity. In order to do this, the nationalists need to cultivate opposability not only externally, with respect to other nations, but internally with respect to putatively nonnational ethnic or racial groups. Put simply, "Aryan" Germans are unlikely to support the extermination of Jewish Germans if they simply consider the members of both groups to be Germans (i.e., if they consider them to be members of one identity group, rather than two). It is crucial that the "Aryans" distinguish themselves sharply from the Jews. Neighborhood division contributes to such internal opposability.

Another aspect of daily life that has functioned to foster opposability is dress. Trevor-Roper explains that Scots asserted "national identity" through the kilt (15). This enhanced not only opposability, but the sense of durability as well, for Scottish nationalists claimed the costume was of ancient provenance, though in fact "the kilt is a purely modern costume" (22), "a recent English invention" (23). Moreover, the contribution of Scottish nationalist dress to the opposability of the national category was furthered by the British outlawing of Scottish national dress—"imprisonment without bail for six months and, for a second offense, transportation for seven years" (24). Obviously, this made the clothing, and thus the national category for which it stood, highly functional as well. Similar points apply to Welsh national dress. In the nineteenth century, Augusta Waddington thought that there should be a Welsh national "costume which would be distinctive and picturesque" (Morgan 80). She and some colleagues "evolved a homogenized national costume from the various Welsh peasant dresses." Opposability was fostered by its homogeneity and distinctiveness. This was combined with salience, through "an enormous red cloak . . . and a very tall black beaver hat" (80). The effect on identity categorization was further enhanced by the implication of durability—for example, through "a sprig of mistletoe" used to show "connection with the Druids" (81).

The point extends throughout Europe (see, for example, Laver 82 and 86 on differences between English and French dress in the eighteenth century). Moreover, it is not at all confined to Europe. For instance, Ghurye explains that there was a gradual influence of Western clothing on Indian dress. This development tended to inhibit opposability. However, while the East/West synthesis "was on its way to stabilize itself," an "upsurge of national feeling" led to the rejection of "some of its features as non-national" (210). In connection with this, Mahatma Gandhi "proclaimed the need for the use of a cap of white cotton cloth called 'khadi' as a national symbol." This "was avidly taken up not only by strict adherents" of the nationalist Congress party, but also "by some other sections of the population" (211). Ghurye goes on to discuss the issue of defining a "national dress" that is "sufficiently distinctive" and that combines "aesthetics with functionalism, tradition with modernity, and grace with martial appeal" (213).[12]

---

12. Most often, distinctive clothing serves to coordinate practical identities (as with official uniforms) and/or to render the national category salient. In some cases, it may operate to draw attentional focus to the out-group. However, this is likely to occur only when a dominant in-group, committed to a policy of alignment, is living in one society with a subordinated out-group. In these cases, the clothing of the out-group may be distinctively homogenized, rather than that of the in-group. In this way, the practice is the inverse of that employed in the fashioning of a national costume for the in-group. The obvious instance here is the Nazi requirement that Jews wear a star of David. But this was not a unique occurrence. *The New Standard Jewish Encyclopedia* notes that "Moslem rulers, from the 7th cent., ordered that Jews and Christians should wear special clothing to distinguish them from 'believers.' . . . The

The final point is worth emphasizing. Martial appeal is an important aspect of national clothing. Indeed, the standardized and distinctive uniform of a national military is one of the most important forms of dress contributing to opposability. This is obviously true in times of war, but it applies generally—for example, in military parades on national holidays. I take it that both the homogenization and polarization in this case are too obvious to require comment.

Events

The reference to military uniforms leads us to the topic of events. The crucial events affecting opposability are events of intergroup conflict. Once again, the most intense version of such events comes in war, though we find more temperate versions ranging from diplomatic controversies to sporting contests. I will not discuss war, as its relation to opposability is self-evident. However, there are a few points worth mentioning on other events.

Sporting contests between national teams are a good case of vacuous categorial identification in general and a striking instance of opposability in particular. First, the entire point of, say, a soccer or basketball team is that it behaves in a coordinated way, the various members working together against a common enemy. Insofar as the team is successful, individual members have integrated their practical identities (their complexes of procedural schemas, etc.) with one another. Moreover, this homogenization has incorporated a strict hierarchy of authority. Perhaps even more important, the fans have integrated their practical identities. Whatever their individual idiosyncrasies or sub- and transnational affiliations, they largely behave in the same way. They cheer or hiss at the same moments and in more or less the same manner. They sing the same songs, chant the same chants. It may seem that sporting contests do not involve attentional focus on the out-group. True, we pay attention to our own team. However, I suspect that our attention is more likely to be drawn to out-group fans rather than to fans on our own side. Certainly, this is what occurs when violent

---

conception was officially introduced into Christian Europe by the Fourth Lateran Council (1215) which ordered that Jews (and other infidels) should be distinguished from Christians by their clothing" (Wigoder 105). In these cases, the distinction was obviously religious, not national, but the principle is the same. In early South Asian society, parallel instances may be found in certain prescriptions regarding caste. For example, the "ornaments" of untouchables "should be made of black iron" and, in general, untouchables should be "recognizable by distinctive marks," as one ancient law text had it (*Laws* 242). In each case, the distinguished group is distinguished as in some sense outside the society.

clashes take place after a game. The responses of the rival team's spectators—their cheers and boos—may be experienced as a sort of provocation. Our own cheers and boos may go almost unnoticed, at least insofar as they are properly coordinated (e.g., when everyone in our part of the bleachers stands at the right moment to produce a "wave").

Diplomatic differences also provide an interesting case. In its decision to invade Iraq, the United States came into conflict with a number of countries. However, the popular imagination of this disagreement in effect polarized conflict within the United States, pitting the U.S. virtually alone against France.

DURABILITY

It is well known that one of the primary tasks of nationalists is to project the nation back into the past, to create a sense that the nation has an enduring existence. In many cases, this goes so far as to present the nation as having always existed, even if it has not always been recognized or allowed to exist in its proper form. Perhaps it was divided or conquered, dispersed or subsumed, but it has always been there. Obviously, this does not hold for all nations. For example, the United States does not follow this particular pattern of projection into the indefinite past. Indeed, some aspects of U.S. nationalism result in part from the fact that the nation did not always exist. In any case, there is always some projection into the past—even if it is only a projection of ideals coming to realize themselves in the course of history. In this way nationalism is bound up with "the invention of tradition," as Hobsbawm and Ranger put it. In his novel, *Midnight's Children*, Salman Rushdie makes the point very well. Speaking of the nationalist imagination on the eve of India's independence, Rushdie explains that "a nation which had never previously existed was about to win its freedom, catapulting us into a world which, although it had five thousand years of history, although it had invented the game of chess and traded with Middle Kingdom Egypt, was nevertheless quite imaginary" (129). The other side of this idea is that the nation, once properly instituted, will always exist in the future.

Daily Life

Though it may seem that our daily lives are entirely divorced from history, this is not in fact true. Rather, our daily lives repeatedly lead us to encounter history. This is most obvious in our experience of monuments.

Monuments are designed to last into the future and they usually come to us from the past. Their own enduring character is bound up with the enduring character of the nation. More important, they often memorialize historical events or persons—founding fathers, great battles, and so on. A similar point may be made about museums. First, the mere existence of national museums is important, even for people who never visit any of them. Second, museums are visited by millions of people every year. Still more are affected by them through television, books, or word of mouth. For example, the Smithsonian Museums (which include the National Portrait Gallery, the Smithsonian American Art Museum, and the National Museum of American History) saw 20.4 million visitors in 2004. There were 78.8 million visitors to their website (see www.si.edu, including their 2004 annual report, entitled "Uniquely American"). There are also national historical sites that operate in much the same way as museums. An American example is Gettysburg. An Indian instance is the Taj Mahal. Maas discusses a late nineteenth-century example from Germany. As part of a drive toward legitimating its annexation, "the battlefields of Lothringen [Lorraine] were systematically made out as national pilgrimage sites" (218).

Perhaps even more obviously, written histories—including popular works, such as biographies of presidents—enhance the sense of national durability. In addition, there are historical novels, historical films, televised histories. Collectively, these are probably the major source of our sense of national durability today. Obviously, films and television are modern developments. Greenfeld outlines some earlier instances of the same sort. Among the Elizabethans in England, "A whole new class of people emerged whose main preoccupation was to do research and write—chronicles, treatises, poems, novels, and plays—in English about England" (67). At this time, "The Society of Antiquaries was formed. Holinshed, Warner, Camden, and others wrote general histories of England and histories of specific periods. Playwrights—whose number included Shakespeare and Marlowe—dramatized episodes of national history" (67).

As this suggests, literature is crucial to this process. So is literary history. The writing of national literary history and the related development of national literary canons are important for creating a sense of national durability. The establishment of national literary paradigms—such as Shakespeare in England, Homer in Greece, Vālmīki in India—has been particularly consequential. Even if one never reads Homer, his mere existence serves to foster a sense of the ancientness of the Greek nation. The same point holds for Vālmīki and India. Shakespeare is, of course, more recent. But, by adopting the right models or metaphors, nations can accommodate variations in the narrative of duration. For example, by drawing on the model of an individual life, nationalists can suggest that relative youth implies a longer and more vigorous future. If Greece and India are older, that only means that they are "past their prime," unlike England. In keeping with this, Ashis Nandy has discussed the ways in which the putative adulthood of English national society was contrasted with the supposed senescence of Indian national society, invariably in such a way as to support British colonial domination (see *Intimate* 16–18 and *Traditions* 39).

In addition to literature proper, orature was often particularly important for establishing national ancestry. Thus, myths and ancient poetic forms were often recruited to nationalist ends. A well-known example of this is Ireland in the late nineteenth and early twentieth centuries. Writers of the Irish Renaissance drew extensively on Irish myth, some preserved in ancient texts, some preserved in oral tradition. Another apt example is Finland. In his article on the "Birth of Finland's National Culture," Klinge discusses the project of making a "compilation of Finnish Mythology" (70).

Perhaps the most important means of conveying nationally functional historical information (or pseudo-information) is formal education. We have already seen that education is critical for increasing practical homogenization. It operates equally to communicate national or other in-group narratives (thus fostering affectivity and opposability), to enhance the salience of the identity category—and to expand the sense of durability. This function may be discerned at virtually every educational level, and in different types of institution. For example, Anderson links the spread of modern nationalism with the development of history as a university discipline including "academic chairs" and an "elaborate array of professional journals" (194).

Events

Events too have important effects on our sense of the durability of a nation. The events that operate in this way are often recurring celebrations or memorials that recall some historical occurrence—a battle, the birth of a national leader, or the like. Thus, people in the United States have celebrated Columbus Day as the discovery of America. (These celebrations have been toned down recently as they were inflaming some subnational divisions, due to the simple falsity of the claim that Columbus discovered

America, and due to the fact that his arrival led to genocide.) The nationalist function of the celebration has been in part a matter of establishing durability. The same point holds for Thanksgiving, which in part commemorates the joining of settlers and Native Americans at a shared feast in 1621. The holiday serves to memorialize an historical event in a way that enhances the sense of national durability—extending it back well before national independence—while also occluding subnational categorial conflicts. The annual celebrations of Independence Day and Presidents' Day have the same general function.

Needless to say, the United States is by no means unique in ritualizing historical events in this way. For example, Kerr and Chifunyise point to "historical re-enactments" in southern Africa that undoubtedly served the purpose of enhancing the sense of durability. They mention in particular the *Umutomboko* ceremony of the eighteenth-century Lunda empire and the Swazi *Incwala* ceremony, also from the eighteenth century, which reenacted early Swazi life (272). (Both ceremonies also served to reaffirm political hierarchies.)

Major anniversaries may be particularly powerful in promoting a sense of durability. Cannadine cites celebrations for "the six hundredth anniversary of the Hapsburg monarchy" in Austria, "the millennium of the kingdom of Hungary," and "the tercentenary celebration of the Romanov dynasty" in Russia (127–28). He goes on to "republican régimes," citing "the centennial of the revolution" in France and the "lavishly commemorated" U.S. anniversaries that marked the "centennial of the revolution and the four hundredth anniversary of Columbus's discovery of America" (128).

Inaugurations and coronations are relevant and effective here as well, for they simultaneously commemorate an entire history (of inaugurations or coronations) and continue that history. Malinowski discusses the coronation of George VI, maintaining that it promoted "an increased feeling of security, of stability, and the permanence of the British Empire" (quoted in Cannadine 149). All three properties—security, stability, and permanence—involve durability. Similarly, Harold Nicolson describes the Silver Jubilee of George V as "a guarantee of stability, security, continuity" (quoted in Cannadine 156).

More generally, one great value of emphasizing national tradition is that the mere existence of tradition shows the durability of the nation. This is one primary reason that it is so important, and so common, for nations to invent traditions, as Hobsbawm and his collaborators have discussed.

AFFECTIVITY

Affectivity is the infusion of emotion into our ideas about identity. It is the fundamental motivational parameter. Without emotion, the other parameters would have no practical effects. At the same time, emotion is, at least in certain respects, much more cognitively complex than the other parameters. At one level, it is a matter of direct experiential triggers and emotional memories, which is to say memories that make us feel the relevant emotion again (see LeDoux, *Emotional* 182, and Schacter 171–72). For example, sudden explosions (direct experiential triggers) are frightening and recollections of a friend's death (emotional memories) are sad. But emotions occur in larger trajectories as well. They are inseparable from hopes, plans, expectations. As Oatley puts it, "emotions depend on evaluations of what has happened in relation to the person's goals and beliefs" (*Best* 19) and "Emotions emerge at . . . significant junctures in plans" (25). Put differently, emotions are involved with narrative—specifically, our ongoing narratives of our own lives. In Martha Nussbaum's words, "Emotions . . . have a narrative structure. The understanding of any single emotion is incomplete unless its narrative history is grasped" (*Upheavals* 236).

In a very narrow sense, emotions are punctual. They are stabs of fear, bursts of joy, flashes of embarrassment. But those momentary emotions are not what is most crucial for large patterns in social life, such as the development of national identity. In the case of such patterns, more sustained and systematically organized emotions are crucial. Sustained emotions are no doubt marked by periodic spikes of momentary intensity, as for example, Greg Smith has argued. However, they are not a matter of random spikes. These emotionally intense moments are systematically organized, integrated with goals and efforts. That organization is largely a matter of narrative. This is why emotion in nationalism is crucially bound up with the narrative structures we will consider in later chapters.

On the other hand, to say this is not to say that we cannot examine nationalism and emotion at all outside the context of narrative analysis. In this section, I wish to consider the most important emotions in the development and operation of nationalism. I will indicate some of the techniques that bear on these emotions, other than narrative and metaphor. Perhaps the best way of organizing these emotions is by their primary object. Any functioning identity group (e.g., an ethnic identity group) must foster certain emotional attitudes in its members toward two distinct objects—first, toward other members of the in-group; second, toward members of the out-group. A specifically national identity group must add emotional attitudes toward the in-group hierarchy or the authorities in that hierarchy and toward the national land. I will consider each in turn. I conclude with a brief section on the incorporation of religion into nationalism because such incorporation is a particularly powerful and widespread technique for enhancing affectivity. In fact, this incorporation may bear on our response to all the objects of national emotion.

Needless to say, the list of emotions that might have a role in nationalism is quite long. Indeed, anything from acrimony to zeal might be cultivated for nationalist purposes. I will concentrate on a more confined set of emotions. Specifically, I have argued in *The Mind and Its Stories* that there is a limited set of protoemotion systems that are innate (see 253–64). Protoemotion systems develop into full-blown emotion systems through maturation and individual experience, including, of course, cultural experience. These innate systems are happiness and sadness (emotions bearing on outcomes of actions and events in the context of goals); hunger, lust, and disgust (emotions bearing on things); anger, affection, and fear (emotions bearing on agents); boredom/curiosity, wonder, and sensitivity (emotions bearing on ambient conditions). In the following analysis, I will focus primarily on the fundamental emotions of these emotion systems (leaving aside only boredom/curiosity and sensitivity, which play more limited roles in nationalism[13]). This does not mean that other emotions—complex emotions, derived from the interaction of these innate systems with experience—are irrelevant for nationalist identification. In fact, they are often relevant. However, I will consider these only when they have a particularly important and constant role in nationalism, as they do in the cases of pride, shame, and awe.

In-Group Members

The most obvious dilemma for the development of a functional in-group is the reconciliation of in-group members with one another. Individually, we have different and often contradictory interests. Moreover, a large in-group, such as a nation, must reconcile contradictions among subgroups,

---

13. This is not to say that they play no role whatsoever. For example, there is a degree to which some people become enthusiastic about war simply because it is novel, thus stimulating, thus a change from the tedium of normalcy. However, these emotions are not usually of central importance for the cultivation of national over other allegiances, or even for the cultivation of any particular national allegiance.

such as ethnic communities, that themselves involve sometimes intense emotional attachments.

As Benedict Anderson has famously stressed, a nation is an imaginary community. It is not a "face-to-face" community in the manner of a village (or a family). As I will discuss in chapter 4, we have a default tendency to distrust anyone who is strange or unfamiliar. Numerous empirical studies demonstrate that we have a more positive response to the familiar than the unfamiliar. For example, as Zajonc explains, "when a particular stimulus is shown over and over again . . . it gets to be better liked" (35). The point applies to people as well (with some disturbing exceptions; see Oatley's *Emotions* 73, on the persistence of racial bias even after repeated exposure). The first emotional barrier that national identification must overcome is this default distrust. Put differently, if we are to have a functional national identification, we must have that minimal form of attachment that we call "trust." The dilemma comes from the fact that the national community cannot be familiar. It is necessarily composed almost entirely of strangers.

The distrust of strangers cannot be entirely overcome. However, it can be mitigated. The diminution of national strangeness may be developed in two areas. First, it may be developed in relation to actual interactions among citizens. This occurs primarily through the sorts of homogenization discussed earlier. If I share language, dress, food, and various habits with my fellow citizens, unknown individuals will appear less unfamiliar to me. If our practical identities mesh without disruption, my tendencies toward suspicion will be minimized.

The second area of mitigation is general rather than particular. When I imagine any group, I will have some sort of attitude toward that group. This is true if I imagine engineers, faculty at Harvard, or Canadians. In each case, my attitude will be affected by two sorts of cognitive structure—prototypes and exempla. Again, the prototypes are roughly average or standard cases of a given category. With respect to national categories, prototypes are most often stereotypes. Exempla are instances of a given category. If I imagine Canadians, my emotions will be affected by my prototype of a Canadian (white, moderately liberal, competent) and by any salient exempla of Canadians (e.g., Margaret Atwood). Personally, I tend to have relatively warm feelings for Canadians since I support national health care and like Margaret Atwood's novels and poetry.

One way in which feelings of national trust—and, indeed, feelings of national affection—may be developed is through the cultivation of prototypes and exempla that inspire these feelings. Exempla seem particularly crucial in this regard. For instance, when I think of Canada, my evaluation of the country is bound up with such issues as national health care. However, my feelings are much more closely connected with my response to Atwood's writings. Exempla bring us almost invariably to narrative. Traditionally, one function of nationalist history has been to associate our thought about the nation with emotionally powerful exempla—for instance, leaders and soldiers who protect us, thus figures that we can trust and admire. Much early education, when developed in a nationalist framework, involves the cultivation of such national prototypes and exempla, emotion-triggering ideas and memories that will arise in our minds spontaneously when we think about the nation. Insofar as we understand, imagine, respond to the nation as a whole through these more particular cognitive contents, our emotional relation to the nation as a whole will be bound up with our emotional relation to those particular contents. If "America" brings to mind Abraham Lincoln, then my emotional response to Lincoln—that particular American with his particular life (as developed through narratives)—will affect my emotional response to America as a whole, and thereby to other individual Americans. Indeed, in many ways, it does not matter how I interact with real, individual Americans. My response to national issues will be more a matter of my emotional attitude toward individuals that I think of as exemplary of America. Lincoln is no more of an American than the people I interact with at a restaurant. But, cognitively, my idea of Lincoln and my emotional response to Lincoln are bound up with my judgments about and actions regarding America. This is not true of the waitress at Pizza Hut or the teller at Wells Fargo.

Exempla in fact allow us to go beyond trust to more motivationally imperative forms of empathy. It may seem that empathy is a difficult and rare thing. In fact, we have a strong, neurocognitive propensity toward empathy. For example, "mirror neurons" in our brains "fire when a certain type of action is performed, but also when another agent is observed performing the same type of action" (Hurley and Chater 3). Because of this coordination, "sensations and emotions displayed by others can also be empathized with, and therefore implicitly understood, through a mirror matching mechanism" (Gallese 114). Among other things, mirror systems apparently help foster an inclination to mimic the movements of people we witness (see Brothers 78, and Prinz 274). It is well-established that certain imitations of this sort tend to induce emotions that parallel those of the person imitated. Thus, as Plantinga points out, "Viewing the human face," as well as human posture, action, and so forth, may "*elicit* an emotional response in the viewer" through "the processes of 'emotional contagion' as induced by 'affective mimicry' and 'facial feedback'" (242; emphasis in original). Affective mimicry is our "tendency automatically to mimic and synchronize expressions, vocalizations, postures, and movements with those of another person" (Hatfield, Cacioppo, and Rapson 48). Facial feedback is our tendency to feel the emotion that we imitate through facial expressions (see Plantinga 243). When we are conversing with someone and he or she laughs, that inclines us to laugh as well. If he or she screams in fear, we may or may not scream, but we partially imitate his or her expression, experience a moment of fright, and become more inclined to feel afraid.

Obviously, many factors may override this empathy, just as many factors may enhance empathy. Perhaps the most fundamental factor in both enhancing and overriding empathy is our preliminary categorization of agents into benevolent and malevolent, along with the related (but not identical) categorization into opportunities and threats. The establishment of broad, *prima facie* trust for the in-group fosters the categorization of in-group members as benevolent. It thus "uninhibits" our propensity toward empathy. Conversely, an enhanced distrust of the out-group will foster the categorization of out-group members as malevolent. (As Horowitz points out, "general attitudes of distrust are correlated with inter-ethnic antipathy" [194]; the point presumably applies to other identity groups, such as nations, as well.) A categorization as malevolent will, in turn, intensify the inhibition of our empathic tendencies. Indeed, in the case of certain emotions, the categorization of someone as hostile may change our response to an opposite or complement of the emotion he or she is expressing. For example, if the putatively hostile out-group member expresses anger, this is likely to provoke fear or antagonistic anger, not empathic anger.

Neurocognitive research reported by Ambady et al. may point toward this sort of attitude adjustment. A study by Chiao and colleagues showed that Caucasian subjects had greater amygdala activity when faced with "Caucasian and Asian American faces showing fear" than African American faces showing fear (Ambady et al. 213). Thus, Caucasian subjects experienced a parallel emotion (here, fear) when faced with other Caucasians or Asian Americans. This was not the case when they saw African American faces. A separate study found that Caucasian test subjects "detected angry expressions most accurately in African American and Caucasian faces relative to Asian American faces." This sensitivity may result from experiencing a complementary emotion with the African Americans. Unsurprisingly, in this context, "neutral expressions were recognized equally well across the three racial groups" (213).

On the other hand, there are some emotions for which categorization has only very limited consequences—primarily emotions that inhibit or disable aggression, such as grief. Suppose I have categorized someone as hostile due to his membership in a particular out-group (e.g., another nation). That categorization will change my relation to his or her anger or fear. It is likely to have a much more limited impact on my response to his or her pain. This is particularly true if the pain is disabling, so that he or she cannot act on hostile impulses—that is, so that I no longer categorize him or her as a threat.

Yet, even here, there are complications. Empathic grief is likely to overcome malevolent categorization only if I directly experience or concretely imagine the other person's expression of pain—cries, body movements, facial contortions. (Decety and Chaminade point out that "empathy and sympathy most commonly arise when people directly perceive individuals in trouble" [132]. However, imagination can produce a version of the emotions ordinarily triggered by direct experience, since it activates the same brain areas as direct experience; see Kosslyn 295, 301, 325, and David Rubin 41–46, 57–59.) The concreteness is crucial. Innate emotion triggers are tied closely to concrete features of the environment. Moreover, our own emotional memories are usually activated only by particulars. Put differently, statistics do not, most often, frighten or sadden us. A concrete experience of someone's terror or grief, however, does. As a result, our empathy will be inspired by someone's emotional expressions when we experience those expressions directly or imagine them concretely. It will not be inspired if we do not experience them directly and imagine them only vaguely and inconsistently. Moreover, such vague and inconsistent imagination is particularly likely when one is experiencing fear (see, for example, Preston and de Waal 8, on fear and the inhibition of taking other people's perspective). This includes fear due to out-group categorization. Preston and de Waal give a striking example. As they explain, "In experiments with adults, human subjects who witness" shocks to other people "offer to take the shocks . . . if their similarity is manipulated with demographic descriptions." In other words, they offer to take the shocks themselves if they believe that they share categorial identity with the person receiving the shocks. "If they do not feel similar"—that is, if they do not feel categorial identification—"they only offer to take the shocks if they have to watch the [other person] receive the remaining shocks" (16). In short, test subjects are willing to take someone else's pain in two types of case. First, when they share a categorial identification with the person and second, when they directly perceive the person's suffering.

This brings us to a simple, common, and obvious technique for enhancing empathy with the in-group and inhibiting empathy with the out-group—the presentation of concrete images or detailed accounts of the emotions of in-group members, and the occlusion of details of the emotions of out-group members. For example, after the bombings on September 11, 2001, the *New York Times* ran a series of articles on the victims. This fostered a deep sense of empathy with those who died and with their bereaved families, as the stories delved into the particularity of the people involved, triggering our own emotional memories and encouraging us to imagine each loss concretely. In contrast, as Howard Zinn pointed out, the "[v]ictims of our bombing in Afghanistan have not been humanized in the same way" (33). More generally, he asks, "what if all those people who declare their support for Bush's 'war on terrorism' could see the real human beings dying under our bombs . . . ? What if they learned . . . the names of the dead, images of the villages that were bombed, the words of a father who lost his children, the ages of the children?" (34). We do not imagine any of this concretely. We do not imagine the dead; we do not imagine their families' grief. Again, this is not simply because our empathy is inhibited by categorizing these people as enemies. It is also because their particularity has been occluded. Speaking of the Malvinas/Falkland Islands war, Kevin Foster puts the point this way: "The first-hand accounts of those who actually confronted and combated one another are full of equivalent moments of mutual recognition, when the fabricated antagonisms of politics and nationalism fall away in the face of the irresistible empathy of the troops and the inescapable likeness of the enemy" (145). He cites a particular case where a soldier "found that his personal responses to the enemy were more complex than the ritualised antagonisms of the training ground. His natural empathy for a frightened and wounded man threatened his ability to discharge his professional responsibilities" (145; see also 147).

Of course, such empathy-inspiring particularity is not confined to sorrow. We also share the joy of other Americans—through television pictures and interviews, through stories that present happy events concretely and in such a way as to provoke detailed imagination. We lack that experience for other nations. When an American soldier escapes from enemy captivity, we see the rejoicing troops, family, and the soldier himself or herself. In contrast, if an Iraqi or Afghani soldier escapes from American detention, we are likely to have only vague details about the escapee, along with images of the somber, angry officers who discuss the escape.

Here, someone might object that I am asking too much. After all, news reports cover what is of interest to the home audience. "Our" soldiers—

thus American soldiers, in the case of the United States—are of interest to the home audience; enemy soldiers are not. In fact, the reasons for such dissymmetrical reporting are more complex than this suggests. However, if one accepts the basic claim about reporting, it only indicates again that the media are nationalist by their very organization and that national identity categories usurp broader human identifications.

The sharing of joy leads us to one of the complex emotions that are particularly important for in-group identification—pride. I take pride to be a sort of joy derived from imagined superiority to others, first of all in emotionally consequential areas, such as greater power, which itself bears on both anger and fear. Pride can be confirmed and thus enhanced by successful activity (e.g., in a competition). Conversely, it can be undermined by failure. Depending on the intensity of the failure, the gradient of change from expected success to failure, and other factors, such undermining may produce shame. Pride is most obviously an individual emotion. However, it is crucial in group definition as well. Indeed, it seems reasonable to say that one does not have a socially functioning in-group or identity group if the members of the group do not have a strong sense of group pride. (One may have a functioning coalition or alliance without pride, but a coalition is different from an identity group.) Insofar as it operates nationally, pride is inseparable from heroic narratives. Similarly, insofar as it operates nationally, shame is inseparable from sacrificial narratives. But, as with emotion generally, that does not mean there is nothing to say about identity-based pride and shame outside of those narratives.

The development of in-group pride appears natural and straightforward for a species that engages in cooperation or is, as Keith Oatley puts it, "cognitively specialized for interacting with other cognitive beings in joint plans" (*Best* 13). Whenever we engage successfully in a joint project, we share pride at least to some extent. But things are more complex than this suggests. Perhaps most important, our sense of self has a great deal of plasticity when it comes to pride and shame. We may feel ashamed of having failed to resist our own cravings. In this case, we define our self very narrowly so that the self includes only our deliberations, and not our appetites. (After all, appetite is what "I" failed to resist when I ate that jar of fudge.) On the other hand, we may feel proud of our children's success in their professions. Then, we are implicitly expanding our sense of self to our offspring. The case of the children may seem to suggest that such expansion must involve some causal connection, starting with me as the cause. My children have my genes. Moreover, I raised them. Therefore, I am to some extent responsible for their success. But this is not, in fact, necessary. I may also feel proud of my parents or my siblings—or my father-in-law, or my college's football team. Causal relations are not crucial. There are, rather, two important factors in the extension of pride. The first is simply shared joy. In order to be proud of my father-in-law, it is important that I be able to share my father-in-law's joy when he achieves something. The second factor is a function of the social distribution of prestige. I am likely to be proud insofar as my father-in-law does something that will cause other people to respect me. Put differently, I am likely to be proud insofar as having an accomplished father-in-law has some comparative social value or can be seen as suggesting my own superiority. This goes along with our converse tendency to limit our sense of self in cases of reduced prestige. It is nicely illustrated by the study of pronoun usage and college sports cited above. That study showed that college students were more likely to refer to the football team as "we" when the team won, but "they" when the team lost (Cialdini et al.).

The techniques used by nationalists to foster shared pride are largely straightforward in this context. We commonly share the joys of other Americans, particularly when these joys involve superiority over members of national out-groups. Obvious examples of this include international sporting events, such as the Olympics, where media coverage is nationally oriented in obvious ways (e.g., through constantly updated tallies of medals won by one's nation, the ranking of one's nation in the medal count, and so forth). More important, we are all socially recognized for such accomplishments. This recognition is often self-produced. Americans feel buoyed up after defeating other nations in the Olympics. They then announce enthusiastically to one another that "We're number one!" Whether other nations share this enthusiasm is largely irrelevant. The same point holds for wars, both current and historical. Celebrations of past victories serve not only to make the national identity category salient. They serve equally to foster shared pride by socially affirming the superiority of all citizens with respect to the historically defeated enemy. Moreover, victory enhances the in-group's power in obvious ways, thus its ability to provoke fear. (Again, pride is most importantly a matter of superiority in emotionally consequential areas, such as power.)

The national cultivation of shared pride is not confined to such obviously competitive and emotional events as wars or sports. In fact, nations show remarkable ingenuity in creating occasions for national pride. For example, in the United States, an election provides the occasion for months of self-congratulatory assertions about American democracy. Political parties and nonpartisan groups cite the electoral process as evidence that the

United States is the greatest nation on the earth. In the 2004 election, this proved particularly valuable as we had gone to war against two nations that did not have democratic institutions. The assertions about "our" greatness as a democracy fostered collective national pride, and helped extend that pride to those national conflicts, so that we could be proud of spreading democracy to other parts of the world.

Perhaps the most basic way of establishing such pride is through simple assertion, removed from any context, as in bumper stickers that say "Proud to be an American." This is part of the symbolism of the flag as well. The flag does not merely call to mind the nation. It suggests pride. (For those who display the flag, flag burning may then suggest shame, which begins to indicate why it gives rise to such angry and, at times, violent opposition.) Every such assertion of national pride serves to enhance the social valorization of national identity. In other words, every time someone affirms national pride, that affirmation serves to tell others that their national identity has social value, that it is something to be proud of. It thereby fosters the spread of national pride. Of course, this is largely vacuous. Some people are proud to be Americans because other people are proud to be Americans, because still other people (or perhaps even the same people) are proud to be Americans, and so on. But, then again, vacuity is a standard part of national identification.

The Land

Before going on to treat the in-group hierarchy and the out-group, we should briefly consider the cultivation of emotions toward the nation as a physical place. Herb points out that, "Territory is vital to national feeling" (17). In keeping with this, "All national anthems make reference to the special qualities of their natural environment to underline their unique character" (18).[14] It may at first seem odd to speak of enhancing affectivity regarding territory rather than regarding people. However, the two are in fact inseparable. Our fundamental feeling of trust and attachment, the feeling that defines our automatic division of the world into benevolent and malevolent agents, applies equally to places. We automatically divide the

---

14. Peter Rabinowitz pointed out to me that this may be an overstatement. "The Star-Spangled Banner" does not seem to make any reference to the "special qualities of their natural environment," if this refers to distinctive physical features (e.g., the Grand Canyon). On the other hand, it does refer to special political and spiritual qualities of the natural environment by stressing "the land of the free" and the "Heav'n-rescued land."

world into home and away, safe and unsafe places. For example, flight is not only a flight from malevolent attackers toward benevolent protectors, it is equally escape from an unsafe place to security. As Nesse points out, "The direction of flight" is both toward "trusted kin" (or, more generally, in-group members) and toward "home" (77S). Indeed, this sense of place is not peripheral, but central to our emotional lives. As Panksepp points out, "separation-distress systems may be evolutionarily related to ancient mechanisms of place attachment" (*Affective Neuroscience* 265) or, as he puts it elsewhere, "it is possible that the ancient mechanisms of place attachment provided a neural impetus for the emergence of social attachments" (407n.93). Oatley notes that one primary function of the corpus striatum, one of the evolutionarily older parts of the brain, is "the establishment of a home site" (*Emotions* 64). Nationalism draws on this sense of home. The difficulty is getting us to extend our sense of home to the entire national territory. As Edward Said put it, "space acquires emotional . . . sense by a kind of poetic process, whereby the . . . anonymous reaches of distance are converted into meaning for us here" (*Orientalism* 55). But how does this occur?

As we just discussed, familiarity is crucial to the emotional relations among citizens. Compatriots should not see one another as strangers. They should relate to other citizens with a sense of comfort and trust, thus a mild form of attachment. There is a direct parallel with the land. Again, the citizenry is too numerous to experience in the way one experiences a family or a small village. Similarly, the physical space of the nation is too large for one to experience it as home. One aspect of promoting nationalist identification is making the nation familiar as a physical space. This will not produce the intense attachment of one's familial home. However, here as elsewhere, familiarity fosters fondness and trust. Strange places are as suspicious as strange people. The "framing" of national landscapes through painting, photography, film, songs, poems, novels, school geography lessons, and so forth serves to make the nation familiar in a way that fosters a sense of security and builds affection. Herb explains that, in poetry and history, "The soil is soaked with the blood of national heroes, the mountains are sacred, the rivers carry the national soul" (19). Of course, the investment of the land with feeling is accomplished by direct experience as well. Tourism guided by natural beauties or wonders, such as the Grand Canyon, familiarizes us with the national land, creating emotional associations and attachments.

Following most writers on the topic, I have been referring to the national "land." However, monuments and skyscrapers can be familiar markers of place as well. Indeed, many people felt this way about the twin towers in New York. In addition to the terrible loss of life, the September 11 bombings constituted a destruction of something familiar, and in that sense a violation of home. I myself remember seeing a television program a few weeks after the bombings. The program had evidently been filmed over the preceding summer. It began with a panorama of Manhattan. My eyes fixed on the towers and I thought how fragile home is—something many Iraqis must have felt when surveying the ruins in Basra or Baghdad.

Of course, our relation to the national place is not solely a matter of familiarity and attachment. It is also a matter of pride. If our skyscrapers are bigger or our canyons deeper, if our temples are more exquisitely crafted or our rivers more sacred—if there is any way we can see our physical space as superior to that of an out-group, then we take pride in it. Here, as elsewhere, nations are tremendously resourceful in finding ways of imagining their land or monuments, their rivers or houses, their mountains or palaces to be better than those of everyone else.

Finally, the land, and even artifacts, inspire a particular emotional attitude that we rarely have toward fellow citizens—what I have referred to as "wonder." Wonder is a pleasure in the experience of ambient conditions that do not elicit a desire for the alteration of those conditions or for our relation to those conditions.[15] For the most part, emotions lead to actions. For example, fear makes us withdraw from an object, while anger makes us approach it. Wonder interrupts our ongoing activities, not so that we will act in another way (e.g., fleeing out of fear), but rather so that we may continue experiencing passively what is before us or around us.[16] Aesthetic appreciation is a version of wonder. We may experience it before a painting or in a musical performance (either of which may, in a particular case, be national). Most important for our purposes, we may experience it before landscapes, mountains, rivers, forests, or national monuments and buildings. Thus, nationalism cultivates an aestheticization of the nation as a physical place, first of all as a landscape. It fosters a sense of wonder, focused on selected sights.

Indeed, in isolating objects or scenes for wonder, a nation helps to define natural beauty for its citizens, focusing it on mountains of a certain

---

15. Of course, the word "wonder" may be used for other emotions. I am using it for this particular emotion, without any claim that this is the single correct usage of the word. Indeed, I do not believe that there is a single correct usage of this or any other word.

16. Of course, as with any emotion, we become habituated to conditions that might elicit wonder, when our experience of those conditions is repeated. Thus, the experience of wonder, like the experience of other emotions, is bound up with expectation, novelty, and other variables. But those are not distinctive features of wonder.

magnitude, rivers of a particular force, heaths and moors, fields of amber grain. One thinks, for example, of James Joyce's wondrous attachment to the Liffey. This attachment is manifest clearly in *Finnegans Wake*, a paradigmatic nationalist work, whatever Joyce's self-conscious political beliefs, affiliations, or intentions. But to an outsider—someone whose paradigmatic river is, say, the Mississippi—the Liffey is unimpressive. When the nationalist fostering of wonder is effective, our attachment to the national place is like our attachment to Mom's home cooking. It is not a matter of intrinsic qualities alone; it is also a matter of just how our taste has developed.

The Out-Group

Affection links us with other people in obvious ways, and wonder ties us to places. Pride, too, when developed socially, binds citizens together. Happiness and sorrow do so as well. As Pindar put it, "We have all kinds of needs for those we love— / most of all in hardships, but joy, too, / strains to track down eyes that it can trust" (*Nemean* VIII.42–44; quoted in Nussbaum, *Fragility* vi). In relation to this, it is unsurprising that nationalism tends to inhibit these binding emotions (e.g., empathic experiences of joy or sorrow) when they might be directed at members of out-groups.

But that is not all. Lust and hunger serve to bring people together as well. National identification is probably not fostered by the direct triggering of these emotions. (One is unlikely to be thinking patriotic thoughts when hungry or sexually aroused.) However, nationalism is fostered by shaping the longer-term specification of our innate protoemotions in these cases.

For instance, ideals of beauty develop somewhat differently in different cultures. To a certain extent, this happens spontaneously. Our sense of beauty is, in part, a matter of weighted averaging. For example, as numerous studies have shown, the most beautiful face is, roughly, the most average face (see Langlois and Roggman). But there are other factors as well, such as socially developed expectations about clothing, build, tone of voice. In all these cases, nationalist identification may be fostered by national specifications of beauty, which tend to limit the degree to which one sees members of out-groups as attractive. In some cases, this affects our response to real individuals. For example, until recently, white Europeans considered black skin and African hair to be unappealing. In other cases, the limitation of intergroup attraction operates by way of prototypes. The German language and a German accent are, supposedly, ugly. The French, in one common stereotype, try to conceal repulsive body odor with perfume. Jews, too, in anti-Semitic belief, are smelly.[17] In these cases, aesthetic preferences are likely to inhibit our general openness to sexual or romantic relations with members of the out-group. To put the point rather crudely, if our stereotype tells us that members of a particular out-group are smelly, we are less likely to put ourselves in such close proximity that we will find out. Thus, we are less likely to cross over identity categories in romantic or sexual relations.

The same point holds for national cuisine and hunger—or, more exactly, national cuisine and desiring to eat a food, finding a food "appetizing" (as opposed to the related, but distinct bodily need to fill one's stomach). For example, Catherine Gallagher and Stephen Greenblatt have discussed the historical rejection of the potato by the English poor, even when hungry—"the poor would accept nothing but white bread even at the height of scarcity" (124). They have tied this rejection to the association of the potato with the Irish diet (see chapter 4 of Gallagher and Greenblatt). If we do not find the out-group's food appealing, we are less likely to share food with them, thus to enter into their ordinary lives in personal relations.

Of course, our emotional attitude toward national out-groups does not result solely from the inhibition of emotions that might otherwise have brought us together. Some emotions operate more directly to separate or oppose us—specifically, fear, anger, and disgust. Just as the binding emotions are crucial for our relation to the national in-group, these distancing emotions are crucial for our relation to the national out-group.

As I have already indicated, low-level wariness is part of the attitude of distrust with which we commonly respond to out-groups. It is limited enough in intensity that it is unlikely to serve as the sole motive for any significant action, such as violence. However, it provides a constant basis for the development of full-blown fear, with its more severe responses. For example, out-group distrust is one reason why a black man reaching for a cell phone might be shot by police, whereas a white man reaching for a cell phone would not. The distrust does not by itself motivate shooting. However, it contextualizes ambiguous behavior such that the act of reaching into one's pocket may be more readily imagined as reaching for a weapon. In this way, distrust prepares us to respond to an out-group with fear.

On the other hand, as the reference to imagination suggests, intense fear is not the product of the events alone, even in the context of prior

---

17. Intra-European stereotypes of this sort were much more important when national opposability in Europe was primarily a matter of other European nations. They have declined in importance as the national enemies have shifted to other parts of the world.

constant distrust. For example, European American police officers may distrust Asians as an out-group. However, they would be unlikely to shoot an Asian man reaching for a cell phone because they would not distrust him in precisely the same way that they distrust black men. Fear, then, results, not only from general distrust, but from our understanding of events. That understanding is clearly prejudiced by factors beyond the mere attitude of out-group distrust, factors such as prototypes (or stereotypes). The point holds even more obviously for events that we do not experience directly, but through media representations, which often serve quite clearly to manipulate our emotional responses. Indeed, such media representations are the usual way in which we experience events of consequence for national feeling.

Consider, for example, the bombings on September 11, 2001. It may seem that the widespread reaction of fear was simply a reasonable response to the events themselves. In part, that is true. Three thousand people were killed. It was undeniably a major tragedy. Moreover, it was not an accident. It was a deliberate, planned attack. However, it is possible to imagine several different ways of treating the bombings. It would have been perfectly possible for the government and the news media to present it as a massive criminal act that required such extensive planning that it would be unlikely to be repeated in the near future. The group responsible for the attacks had made attacks in the past, and these had typically taken several years to develop. Moreover, the government could have acted more quickly than it did in strengthening airport security. Thus, it could have minimized panic while enhancing actual safety. Instead, we were faced with a continual barrage of new warnings and an astonishing aggrandizement of Osama bin Laden and al Qaeda. In the weeks and months after the bombings, we not only saw the images of the towers collapsing again and again, we heard that our water supply would be infected with smallpox, that our nuclear plants would be used against us in the same way as the airplanes, that another attack by air would soon hit another major city. Bill Fletcher referred to "a situation of perpetual anxiety" in the United States (93). Eliot Weinberger wrote that "America doesn't feel like America any more. The climate of militarism and fear, similar to any totalitarian state, permeates everything. . . . Every few weeks there is an announcement that another terrorist attack is imminent, and citizens are urged to take ludicrous measures, like sealing their windows, against biological and chemical attacks, and to report the suspicious activities of their neighbors."[18] The

18. Bernardine Dohrn notes that the condition of fear did not arise simply from the bombings. It is bound up with institutional practices—for instance, practices in schools—that have developed over a longer period of time (as one would expect, given the general nature of

country was kept in a constant state of anxiety through the activation of traumatic memories and through the imagination of scenarios filled with powerful triggers of fear. Such feelings are not slight or inconsequential simply because we experienced the events indirectly. Berkowitz points out that "events portrayed or reported on television, radio, or in the press" bring "ideas . . . actively to the viewers' minds, and these persons . . . have feelings, memories, and even action tendencies that are associated with the depicted occurrences" ("Towards" 22).

The nationalist function of panic in the case of the September 11 bombings—and subsequent wars—is clear. Such emotional extremity is unnecessary for ordinary national coherence. It is, however, important for national mobilization. Fear, in this context, has at least three relevant consequences. First, it intensifies the sense of in-group coherence. As Frijda puts it, "Social affiliation is sought with increased intensity under threat" (351). Second, it dehumanizes the out-group and eliminates whatever concern we might have for their well-being. If we truly believe that some other agents are threatening us, we are likely to wish to stop the threat by whatever means are available (not only whatever means are necessary)—most obviously, by destroying those threatening agents. This is why we repeatedly heard cries to "nuke the Arabs" after September 11 (see, for example, Ismail on people at a cable news network calling "let's kill them all," "let's get those fuckers" and "let's just nuke everyone"; 25). These calls were delivered with great bravado, often by people who characterized any less violent approach as "cowardly." However, these calls showed a profound fear.

The third result of fear is that it leads us to seek protection. When afraid, we are not only inclined to distrust the out-group more intensely and thoroughly. We are also inclined to trust our own group leaders more intensely and thoroughly. Indeed, we are likely to see them as a refuge. We demand of them precisely the violence that we feel is necessary to eradicate the danger. This is why intensified fear is highly functional for facilitating war or other national violence and strengthening the internal hierarchy of a nation (e.g., in enhancing executive powers). It is something

---

social change). "Schools in America," she writes, "have become barricaded places of fear. People who don't have their own youngsters in school today may not realize what's happened to the environment where our young people spend seven hours of their day. You can't get into a school and you can't get out. Surveillance is pervasive. There are lock downs, body searches, and dogs. There are armed guards. And all of this is in schools that have never seen a violent incident. The fear of violence and the notion that it is likely to come from anywhere, including from our young people, has been the precursor and the trial run for what's now happened in all of our public spaces and airports" (132).

of a political commonplace that a fearful populace is a politically passive populace, willing to accept any dictates from their leaders. The claim is not precisely accurate. Emotions certainly limit our action tendencies. Indeed, that is one of their definitive features. However, fear does not typically make us passive. (That is more likely to be the result of certain sorts of depression.) Rather, fear makes us active supporters of (putatively) defensive violence and intensified (putatively) protective hierarchization. Put differently, if you are a leader who wants to move a society toward peace and democracy, cultivating fear will not serve your purpose.

Of course, cultivating fear serves the purposes of war only in very limited ways. Specifically, it enhances support for war. However, it typically enhances support for *other people* fighting the war. If I am deathly afraid of the enemy, I am unlikely to join the army in order to fight that enemy. This is where anger becomes important. Needless to say, many emotions affect the recruitment of soldiers. Fear of hunger, or more generally a sense of anxiety over one's finances, is an obvious instance, what Marxists often call "economic conscription." Pride in one's nation, or indeed in oneself (e.g., as valiant and manly), may play a motivating role as well. But in the case of a particular crisis, the cultivation of anger toward the enemy is often crucial. Indeed, just as broad support for war and internal hierarchization are facilitated by the intensification of fear into panic, the actual prosecution of war may be facilitated by the prolongation of anger into something like ruminative vengefulness (e.g., through the repeated activation of the relevant emotional memories such that the anger is so widely primed, and so readily triggered, that it is almost a habitual state).[19]

Anger may be triggered in a number of ways. The most obvious, perhaps, is physical injury or other aggression. However, the most fundamental seems to be a sort of inhibition—"thwarting and frustrations," in Panksepp's phrase (*Affective Neuroscience* 52). Even physical injury commonly provokes sustained or recurrent anger, as opposed to immediate anger, through inhibition (as when an injury prevents one from engaging in a certain activity for months afterward). Inhibition is a cognitively interesting trigger because it crucially involves imagination. If someone grabs my arm, this counts as inhibition only if I am in the course of intentionally moving away. I recognize it as inhibition due to the contrast of my current state (still standing in the room) with a state that I tacitly imagine as

---

19. Panksepp has roughly the same emotion in mind when he refers to hatred as "little more than the emotion of anger, conditioned to specific cues, that has been cognitively extended in time." It is differentiated from ordinary anger in being "more calculated, behaviorally constrained, and affectively 'colder'" (191).

the outcome of my previous action (exiting through the door). Most anger is immediate. It involves a sort of mirroring aggression (e.g., hitting the person who just hit you) or freeing oneself from inhibition (e.g., pushing away the person who has detained you). We may refer to this as expressive or spontaneous anger. Ruminative or retrospective anger (Panksepp's "hatred"; *Affective Neuroscience* 191) occurs when the injury or inhibition remains with us beyond the exciting cause.

Ruminative anger is perhaps best thought of as a series of emotional spikes of spontaneous anger, spikes that occur when we reexperience the pain or inhibition of the initial event directly (e.g., due to a resulting physical condition, such as a broken limb) or through the triggering of emotional memories. In this way, ruminative anger is bound up with spontaneous anger. However, there is an external inhibition on our "actional response" in ruminative or retrospective anger, for the exciting cause is no longer present. We tacitly imagine a response (e.g., mirroring aggression, such as punching our antagonist). However, we are unable to engage in this response.

This leads us to a peculiar feature of anger. Emotions tend to dissipate spontaneously. Think of joy. You are very happy about something. Then, after a while, you are not so happy. No unhappy event has intervened. The joy has simply dissipated on its own. There are, of course, cases when a particularly traumatic experience continues to trouble us long after the event. These are important, and we find them particularly in cases of great fear and the specific sort of sorrow that bears on attachment (i.e., grief). However, anger is unusual, for it may actually be intensified in retrospect. The reasons have to do with actional and expressive outcomes. When I recall the death of a loved one, I can engage in the usual actions that are part of grief. I can weep or seek comfort from family and friends in almost the same way I could at the time of the death itself. I cannot do anything to rectify the situation (e.g., to bring the dead person back to life). Indeed, that is centrally what makes grief a difficult emotion. However, it is crucial that frustration—in this case, my inability to do anything about the situation—is not itself a trigger of grief. In other words, the reexperiencing of grief does not generate further triggers for grief. That is a crucial difference from anger.

Specifically, the retrospective reexperiencing of anger invariably leads to the imagination of some response to the provoking event (e.g., punching the initial offender). However, the fact that we cannot act on that imagination is itself a cause of frustration and thus a trigger for anger. In this way, whenever we dwell on anger-provoking incidents, we almost necessarily multiply triggers for anger through the discrepancy between our imagined response and our real action. It is this multiplication of frustrations that sustains and even intensifies anger. The point is supported by the work of Bandura. As Clore and Ortony explain, referring to Bandura's conclusions, "whether angry behavior eliminates anger depends not on whether one uses up or drains off a pool of aggressive energy"—as in the folk psychological view—"but on whether it decreases the activation of cognitive material conducive to anger" (Clore and Ortony 50). In short, the crucial factor in sustaining and intensifying anger is the repeated recollection of the anger-provoking incident. This gives rise to action tendencies, which are, in turn, frustrated—generating still further anger.

Moreover, once the process of recollection and intensified frustration has begun, it tends to be self-perpetuating. Every time they are recalled, the relevant memories become more prominent in our emotional life, and thus more likely to be recalled again in the future. This results from two factors. First, the anger memories come to have a wider range of associations. This means that they are more likely to be activated in the future as they are part of a larger and more diverse set of circuits. To take a simple example, suppose I go to a movie and find myself distracted by these anger memories. When I return to the theater later, that may activate memories of my earlier visit—thus the anger memories (along with the additional frustration). The second factor derives from the simple principle that, if a circuit is repeatedly activated, it acquires a higher level of resting activation. Technically, it becomes more highly *primed*. To take a simple, nonemotional example, if I am at a conference on neurology, some lexical items will be activated regularly. That repeated activation will serve to prime those items. Thus, if someone says "emotion," I may immediately think of "amygdala." In contrast, if I have been attending a music conference and someone says "emotion," I might immediately think of "Romanticism." This process affects memories, including emotional memories, no less than lexical items. In the case of anger, as priming effects accumulate and the anger circuit pervades our thought more fully, it comes to affect the way we interpret current conditions and imagine future possibilities, even outside the original context of the incident. For example, it may lead us to interpret ambiguous statements or actions as aggressive, thus as a cause for further anger. As it becomes more of a "normal" or continuous attitude, anger may come to affect our longer-term goals as well. This is, of course, what occurs in the imagination of revenge.

National identification benefits from such ruminative anger in particular circumstances and for particular national out-groups. Specifically, ruminative anger serves to support war and related forms of violence. It is particularly important for the citizens who are engaging directly in the violent actions—for example, soldiers. Again, fear serves national militancy when it is spread throughout the noncombatant population. But it can hardly serve nationalist purposes in the military itself. Some testimonies of Vietnam War veterans, given in the Winter Soldier Investigation, suggest how this ruminative anger—with its sustaining spikes of spontaneous anger—may be cultivated in military training. As one corporal put it, "Marine training starts from the first day you get into boot camp.... When you're told something to do, whether to go to the bathroom or have a cigarette, or whether you go to bed or you get some free time to write a letter, you preface it or you end it with VC, or gook or slope, kill-kill-kill.... [T]hey make you want to kill.... When you're wound up and when your button is pushed, you've gotta react" (Vietnam Veterans 5–6). In the words of one sergeant, "By the time I had left Ft. Polk, Louisiana, I wanted to kill my mother, you know. Or anyone, that, that wasn't, you know, completely in agreement with me. I wanted to kill everything.... I went over to Vietnam with the same attitude because I, I had been trained and I knew I was an effective fighting machine.... I was going to kill everything in my path" (157–58).

It is worth noting that, in general, spontaneous anger does not serve nationalist identification as well as a ruminative devotion to revenge. The former demands immediate action, which is likely to be reckless (as in the calls for "nuking the Arabs" after September 11). Revenge, in contrast, allows for longer-term planning. Moreover, it is more likely to allow for hierarchies of authority. Spontaneous anger is impulsive and rash. The contemplation of revenge, in contrast, is more readily shaped by national authorities, as long as the prescriptions of the authorities lead to violent action that is likely to produce the required pain on the part of the enemy. On the other hand, ruminative vengefulness loses its motivating force if it is not sustained by bursts of anger. This creates a paradoxical situation in which military training must make soldiers experience spikes of immediate or spontaneous anger (as is quite clear in the case of the sergeant just quoted), but act only under the effects of ruminative anger.

Shame often provides a particularly intense provocation for ruminative anger. Again, shame (as I am using the term) is produced by a sharp decline from a particular imagined status to comparative inferiority. It is part of the nature of a shameful event that we cannot change it through the expression of spontaneous anger. The event is over when we feel shame. Indeed, the completion of the event is what gives rise to shame. Put differently, shame implies that one has already responded to some provocation and has been defeated (e.g., in an argument). As a result, shame almost invariably produces retrospective anger. Moreover, this retrospective anger is facilitated by the fact that shame is bound up with our comparative imagination of our character, abilities, and social standing. This imagination is a recurring feature of our ordinary lives as we estimate our ability to perform certain acts or envision different people's expectations of or reactions to us. As a result, ordinary experiences (e.g., situations where we might engage in an argument) repeatedly trigger relevant memories, including emotional memories, which revive the feeling of shame. This, in turn, is likely to produce and enhance anger in the usual way, through the repetition of frustration.

It is not surprising, then, that "violence is linked to the experience of shame and humiliation" (Wilkinson 25), as Wilkinson explains in his treatment of the conflicts between evolved human propensities and social stratification. Moreover, anger that develops out of shame is often bound up with individual self-destruction as well as destruction of the enemy. As Tangney explains, there is some clinical research suggesting that "shame can motivate . . . a kind of hostile, humiliated fury." This suggests why, for example, suicide bombing is often related to a sense of humiliation, as Jessica Stern's study suggests (see her chapter on "Humiliation"; 32–62). Stern is not alone in this view. For example, she cites the work of Mark Juergensmeyer, who "sees suicide bombing as a means to 'dehumiliate' the deeply humiliated and traumatized" (54). (Suicide bombing is also commonly bound up with a particular sort of narrative structure—the sacrificial prototype—which we will discuss in chapter 5. As I have already noted, that prototype is itself bound up with shame—as is clear from the paradigmatic sacrificial narrative of the Judeo-Christian tradition, the story of the Fall.) It is worth noting that humiliation is also inseparable from a sense, not only of frustration, but of impotence. As Frijda points out, "Being, or just feeling, reduced to impotence probably is the most important cause of violent anger" (296).

Up to this point, we have been considering out-groups that are, largely, outside the nation. We may respond to other nations with fear or anger. Of course, we may respond to internal out-groups, internal enemies, in this way as well.[20] Such internal enemies may be supporters of other nations or they may be antinational activists (e.g., advocates of international solidarity among workers). They may also be citizens whose religious, ethnic,

20. A number of analysts, drawing on different theoretical frameworks, have noted the importance of differentiating internal from external enemies (see, for example, Wimmer 218).

linguistic, racial, or other identifications come into conflict with national identification, or simply with the vision of certain nationalists who wish for a religiously, ethnically, linguistically, and racially uniform nation. This returns us to the difference between nationalisms of hierarchization or subordination and nationalisms of alignment.

Anger figures significantly in nationalisms of subordination. Specifically, it is important in the mobilization of national opinion against citizens who do not hierarchize properly, which is to say, citizens who do not place national identity above other identity categories or, worse still, citizens who oppose identity categories generally. Anger may operate in alignment nationalism as well, particularly in those forms of alignment nationalism that focus on elective categories. In these cases, anger is likely to be directed against citizens who do not change group membership appropriately, persisting, for example, in their minority religious affiliation. However, another emotion becomes crucial for alignment nationalisms that stress nonelective categories, such as race. When people are to be expelled or killed—particularly people who have apparently been part of our in-group, perhaps even part of our face-to-face community—we do not want to think of them as agents at all. Anger implies the agency of other persons. While expulsion and extermination may draw on anger, they draw much more readily and much more effectively on the emotion that requires expulsion or extermination—disgust. Martha Nussbaum argues that disgust (along with shame) is crucial to sexism, racism, homophobia, and other forms of discrimination (see *Upheavals* 205–6, 220–22, 346–50, 448–54). I believe she overgeneralizes the point. Nonetheless, she is absolutely correct to point to disgust as centrally important in facilitating certain forms of social brutality. Disgust is particularly functional in ethnic cleansing, as the term itself ("cleansing") suggests. Here, the in-group responds to the out-group as something decayed and disease-bearing, to be expelled like sewage, to be exterminated like vermin.

As the preceding point suggests, the obvious technique for producing disgust is to link the out-group with well-established disgust triggers such as excrement, insects, and rodents. This may be done through metaphor, or through literal links, usually in narrative form. For example, I have argued that films such as *Nosferatu* served, subtly and indirectly, to associate Jews with rats and plague (see "Narrative Universals, Nationalism"). Similarly, Sander Gilman has pointed out that anti-Semitic propaganda linked Jews with syphilis, as well as other forms of physical and mental disease (96). There are more practical techniques as well. Nussbaum explains that "Nazis made Jews do things that would ... associate them with the disgusting.

They were made to scrub latrines.... They were deprived of access to toilet facilities so that they had to squat in the open" (348). This functioned to link Jews more thoroughly with disgust reactions on the part of guards and thus facilitated the execution of Jews.

Of course, the use of disgust is not confined to internal enemies in alignment nationalism. In fact, in-groups commonly claim that out-groups are smelly and unclean. However, this aspect of the relation to out-groups is given intensive development only in cases where the systematic killing of the out-group is a nationalist goal, and where members of that out-group are readily experienced empathically (e.g., through face-to-face interaction). That occurs most commonly in the case of an internal enemy.

Finally, as I have already suggested, prototypes and exempla operate here in much the same way that they do in the case of trust. Our prototypes of out-group members, readily formed through news, film, fiction, and so forth, very easily come to incorporate fear, anger, and disgust triggers. The point is even more obvious for exempla, where real or fictional instances may be socially emphasized in such a way as to produce widespread effects on in-group responses to the out-group. One need only think of the emotional function of Saddam Hussein or Osama bin Laden in the United States. Generalization of such instances to the out-group as a whole is facilitated by the fact that we view out-groups as "less complex, less variable, and less individuated" (Duckitt 81). Thus, we tend to view individual out-group members as representative of the out-group generally. Even when we self-consciously deny this generalization, our intellectual judgments and emotional responses commonly manifest it.

In-Group Hierarchy

Like any other aspect of national identity (or anything else), an in-group hierarchy is operative only insofar as it inspires relevant emotions. The relevant emotions are straightforward. The most obvious is a form of fear.[21] In a nation, the in-group hierarchy is inseparable from coercive force. Indeed, the state—the centerpiece of this hierarchy—commonly asserts a monopoly over certain sorts of violence, particularly the ability to take away human life. For citizens to respect this authority, they must feel a type

---

21. A number of analysts, working in different descriptive and explanatory contexts, have noted that fear is important not only for fostering antagonism toward out-groups, but also for maintaining and extending internal hierarchies (see, for example, Robin 18–20). For a fuller discussion of fear and recent U.S. policy aims since September 11, 2001, see Kateb 60–92.

of fear. However, this is not, typically, the same sort of fear that citizens feel for the out-group. Specifically, fear of the out-group is a fear of generalized hostility. It is based on a lack of trust. Insofar as fear of a national state serves national identification, it must be based on trust.[22] In other words, it must involve a sense that the hierarchy exercises violence in both predictable and reasonable ways.[23] If I violate the national order (e.g., in breaching property guarantees or in harming fellow citizens), then I can expect punishment, because I am guilty and deserve it. However, if I do not violate the national order, I can trust that I will not suffer deprivation or harm from the state. In contrast, the point of out-group violence is that its victims (i.e., its victims in the in-group) are innocent. The techniques for cultivating this positive or trusting fear with respect to the national hierarchy are obvious. They include, for example, the entire judicial system. They also include a wide range of narratives (e.g., on television programs), many of which treat that system.[24]

What I just referred to as our "trusting fear" of the national hierarchy is, in fact, a feeling of trust that is inflected by fear in particular conditions. Trust is the crucial, fundamental emotional attitude required for commitment to a national hierarchy. Specifically, we are motivated to accept national hierarchies as the legitimate hierarchies of our in-groups insofar as we feel that they protect us (i.e., that they protect the national in-group). This is why the power of the national hierarchy tends to increase as we feel a greater threat from national out-groups. Insofar as our need for protection is greater, our attachment to protectors will be greater as well. Exempla are

---

22. Obviously, different forms of fear may be highly functional in a given society, strongly supporting internal hierarchization. My concern here is only with the forms of fear that contribute to national identification. For a broader treatment of the operation of fear in society, specifically the United States, see the second part of Robin's book. Robin also considers such issues as the effects produced by theorizations of fear and the ways in which fear may be used as a pretext—important issues that are beyond the scope of this discussion.

23. It is important to distinguish "reasonable" from "rational" here. There are certainly cases when violence is predictable, and even rational (given the aims of the perpetrators), but not what we would consider "reasonable" in the sense of a generally acceptable way of running a nation (for a discussion of this point, see Robin 208–10). I take it that only predictable and reasonable forms of state violence cultivate trust, thus fostering national loyalty, rather than some sort of panicked conformity.

24. Crime investigations and courtroom dramas range from protoforms in *Oedipus the King* and *The Eumenides* through *CSI* and *Law and Order* and include such non-Euro-American works as *The Injustice Done to Tou Ngo* (an important Chinese drama from the Yüan dynasty). Dramas of this sort may show that there are some problems with the justice system. But, on the whole, they suggest that the system and the people in it are fair, thus trustworthy, and that investigators are smart and thorough, thus posing a serious threat to potential criminals.

particularly consequential here. Our trust and attachment focus naturally on individuals. Moreover, these feelings are particularly inspired by singular incidents of protection. Stories of national heroes serve this function in obvious ways. By the same token, stories of betrayal inspire distrust. In the 2004 election, supporters of John Kerry sought to portray his war record in such a way as to inspire just the sort of trust and attachment that benefit hierarchical order. In contrast, his antagonists portrayed his war record and postwar activities as one of betrayal. It is unsurprising that the antagonists were more successful.[25] Again, our spontaneous tendency for all other people appears to be one of distrust. More important, the stakes are fairly high when it comes to trust. It makes sense in evolutionary terms that we would not be inclined to trust someone with our safety after that person has shown any signs of betrayal. We speak of "breaking" trust precisely because the emotion of trust is fragile. The overall result is that most Americans' emotional response to Kerry was likely to be more influenced by the accusations than by the praise. The case for trust must, in general, be overwhelmingly stronger than the case for distrust if it is going to foster a feeling of trust in us.

As the last points indicate, if the state fails in our protection—or even shows signs that it might fail—there is a good chance that we will reject the state hierarchy. Indeed, the occurrence of revolutions during or just after war (as in Russia and Germany) suggests just this sort of rejection. On the other hand, the precise opposite can occur as well. If there is a sharp gradient from fear of the enemy to domination over the enemy, and if the domination over the enemy is thorough, attachment to national hierarchy may be enhanced to the point of becoming almost religious. Specifically, the spectacular defeat of an enemy produces awe—roughly, joyous relief combined with intense admiration of the power of the state, trusting fear, and even a sense of aesthetic wonder. I take awe to be the ideal feeling for fostering devotion to in-group hierarchy, and for sustaining or extending the authority of that hierarchy.

Awe is commonly fostered by narrative—in news, history, fiction. However, it may also be fostered by other means. Parades of military equipment

---

25. See, for example, Langer on changes in voters' views of Kerry during the relevant period. Questions about Kerry's war record did not elicit a predominantly negative response. However, there was a significant decline in many people's judgments of character attributes bearing on trust (e.g., honesty) during this time. This suggests that the attacks (among other factors) were having effects, even if people were not fully, self-consciously convinced of their accuracy. This is just what one would expect. To lose trust, one need not have an actual conviction in the other person's bad character; one only has to have doubts about his or her good character.

and soldiers, the testing of nuclear weapons, and displays of might outside of war provide examples. But, of course, the primary instances of direct cultivation of awe come in war. The most obvious example is Nazi Germany, particularly during the period of early military success. But there are countless other cases as well. For instance, in the "Shock and Awe" campaign of bombing Baghdad, the U.S. government sought not only to demoralize the Iraqis, convincing them that resistance is futile. The government also sought, through images and descriptions of the bombing, to make Americans feel awe. That sense of awe was important not only for the war in Iraq. It was one part of the U.S. government's response to the Vietnam Syndrome. It served to help overcome the partial American aversion to making war. Awe inspires a sense of national omnipotence that tends to weaken our inhibitions resulting from a rational fear of violent conflict. When we feel awe for the state, we not only feel that it can protect us within our borders. We feel that it can protect us anywhere at any time. Awe, then, is a particularly powerful emotion for fostering and sustaining aggressive, militant nationalism.

God and the Nation

The preceding reference to awe almost necessarily leads us to the issue of just how nationalism relates to religion. To a great extent, nationalism tries to take over religion, in effect substituting for religion. Indeed, one of the most powerful techniques for enhancing nationalist affectivity involves the incorporation of religious ideas, beliefs, and attitudes into nationalism.

Perhaps the most surprising incorporation of this sort concerns the land, which is commonly sanctified and linked directly with God. For example, the Gikuyu of Kenya hold the "belief that the land has been given them, through Gikuyu and Mumbi [the founding ancestors], by God" (Sicherman 41). The Indian nationalist leader Subhash Bose wrote that India was "the holy land" with "sacred rivers" and "sacred cities" (quoted in Daniel 55). The idea recurs in Indian subnationalism also, as in the claims of Tripuran separatists that Tripura is a "Holy Land" (see Debbarma 183). Mark Williams refers to "the Edenic myth of God's Own Country" in New Zealand (261). Hobsbawm mentions beliefs in "Holy Russia," "Holy Tyrol," and "Holy Ireland" (*Nations* 49–51).

The connection derives in part from a metaphorical alignment of religion and nation. Just as religions commonly have holy sites, the nation itself becomes a holy site in its entirety. Indeed, as a number of writers have pointed out, national tours have one precursor in religious pilgrimages. However, there is another source for this connection as well. It is in the intensification, indeed absolutization, of the evaluative—and oppositional—quality of in-group/out-group division. In the case of nationalism, this intensification divinizes the land. But it does not stop with the land. It extends to the national hierarchy and, beyond even that, the in-group generally. Thus, the national hierarchy is sanctioned by God. Indeed, it culminates in God. Moreover, the national in-group is itself divinely chosen, in opposition to national out-groups (which, in consequence, may be demonized). In this way, nationalism does not have to be aligned with religion, even metaphorically. It becomes a sort of religion.

The relation of divinization to internal authority is perhaps the most obvious case, at least in feudal nations. The idea of the Divine Right of Kings is familiar to anyone who took some English history in high school (for an overview of the idea, see chapter 10 of Nicolson). Cannadine explains that the Archbishop of Canterbury felt that "Britain was close to the Kingdom of Heaven on Coronation Day" (154). Cohn discusses the idea of "heaven-blessed British rulers" in colonial India (194). Ranger treats colonial Africa and the representation of the British king as "almost divine" (230). Similar complexes of ideas recur across the globe. Greenfeld notes the belief in "the Divine election of the French king" (94). Peter I of Russia understood his kingdom as "lands subjected by God Almighty to our Government" (Greenfeld 194). The Shah of Iran ruled by grace of God, as shown by the "divine farr" or radiance bestowed by God (see, for example, Ferdowsi 7, 9, 15, and 17). The emperors of China held their authority through the Mandate of Heaven. The Turkish *Book of Dede Korkut* tells us that "Emperors are the shadow of God. None who rebels against his emperor prospers" (153). Nicolson cites examples extending back five-thousand years. "As early as 3000 BC," he writes, "the Sumerian city kings asserted their claim to have been begotten by gods and born of goddesses" (28). He goes on to cite Babylonian (31), Incan (31), Egyptian (31), Roman (32–34), Japanese (34–40), and Chinese (41–46) examples. Other clear cases include the Holy Roman Empire and the Caliphate (a Khalīfah being a successor to the Prophet Muhammad, whose own political authority was clearly inseparable from his claim of receiving divine revelation and being set on a divine mission of witnessing for that revelation).

The point extends, usually in more subtle ways, to nationalist leaders in the modern period. For example, Wachtel cites a statement by the nineteenth-century nationalist epicist, Petar Njegoš, speaking to the Croatian leader Ban Jela: "Everyone who loves our nation . . . stretches out their hands to you as to a heaven-sent Messiah" (103). Of course, Njegoš probably intended his statement metaphorically. In this respect, he was incorporating religion rhetorically, not substantively. But that does not mean all modern cases are similarly metaphorical. For example, George W. Bush repeatedly cites the Lord when discussing U.S. policies, indicating, for example, that "God is not neutral" in the War on Terrorism ("Address"; we will consider further indications of divine preference, drawn from "President's Remarks," in chapter 5). This indirectly suggests the political hierarchy instituting that war has divine authority. Certain Christian nationalist groups believe that "Christians have a God-given right to rule" (Goldberg 13).

Again, the cultivation of popular adherence to national hierarchy is commonly bound up with the cultivation of awe. That cultivation of awe is obviously facilitated by linking our response to the hierarchy with religious devotion. The relation between divinizing national hierarchy and cultivating trust and fear is self-evident. God is, in many ways, little more than the imagination of an ideal in this area, a paradigmatic object of awe. God protects us against our greatest enemies. In doing so, God is perfectly benevolent and omnipotent. At the same time, God punishes our transgressions—in a perfectly reasonable and predictable manner. Associating the state with God fosters the same feeling of awe toward the state.

The divinization of the nation as a whole is no less widespread than the divinization of national hierarchy. Instances are ubiquitous. For example, some Welsh nationalists believed in "a special relationship between Welsh and the Deity" (Glanmor Williams 126), even suggesting that Welsh was the "The Language of Heaven," an idea "still heard to this day" (Morgan 74). Arendt explains that pan-Slavic activists claimed they represented "the true divine people of modern times" (233). Wachtel writes that Serbian nationalists viewed the Serbs "as a people of God" (35), "a special people, chosen by God" (203). Arendt also notes that "Austrian Pan-Germans laid . . . claims to divine chosenness." Hitler said, "God the Almighty has made our nation. We are defending His work by defending its very existence" (Arendt 233). Kevin Foster explains that the military chaplain for the Argentinian troops in the Malvinas/Falkland Islands war "celebrated the recovery of the islands as a triumph of Catholic nationalism, proof that the nation's cause was just and that those who served it were assured of special protection" (124). A bizarre extension of this idea is reported by Greenfeld. "In 1559," she writes, "the future Bishop of London John Aylmer took up Latimer's astonishing claim that God had nationality," declaring that "God is English" (60).

Kohn has maintained that modern nationalism took "the idea of a chosen people" from the Old Testament (Brennan 59). It is no doubt true that modern European (and, of course, Israeli) nationalists were influenced by the biblical precedent. The foregoing cases suggest this already. Other instances are even more straightforward. For example, Trumpener discusses the self-conscious development of a Welsh/Jewish parallel along these lines (2–4). Greenfeld presents numerous examples. She cites the claim in John Foxe's *Book of Martyrs* that "the English people was chosen, separated from others and distinguished by God." She states that this was not some marginal and idiosyncratic work. Rather, "The status of Foxe's book, the influence it was allowed to exert on the minds of sixteenth- and seventeenth-century Englishmen, was far above that of any other work of the age, and comparable only to that of the Bible" (61). Unsurprisingly, the enemies of the English, the French, had the same view of themselves. "In the literature of the crusades," she tells us, "the Franks . . . are represented as . . . 'chosen by God'" (93). Even "The Papacy recognized that 'God chose the kingdom of France among all other peoples'" (94).[26]

On the other hand, the notion of Jews as the chosen people is itself merely one specification of a cross-cultural belief that one's in-group is favored by God. For example, a few years ago, the Japanese Prime Minister said that "Japan is a divine nation with the emperor at its core, and we want the people to recognize this" (French A3). Showing the same idea, but, so to speak, from the other side, one of the Dinka poems collected by Deng ties the group's military defeat to the loss of divine favor (205).

As the Dinka example suggests, the divinization of the in-group is developed most consistently and most powerfully in heroic plots. Heroic plots treat war, and the most consequential and salient way that God shows His preference for our nation is in battle. In keeping with this, the place of divine election in war is straightforward in much nationalist writing. A well-known literary example may be found in King Henry V's characterization of the English victory over the French in Shakespeare's play. Henry gratefully addresses the Supreme Being with the acknowledgment, "God, thy arm was here" (IV.viii.100). He then addresses those around, asserting that "God fought for us" (IV.viii.114). Indeed, he goes so far as to proclaim that, if anyone refuses to accept that God is responsible for the victory, that person will be put to death (IV.viii.108–10).[27] The idea was by no

---

26. For a recent, extensive discussion of national "chosenness," see Roshwald 167–252.

27. It is worth noting that such an attitude is widely considered humble, because the speaker does not assert the group's strategic or martial superiority. However, it is anything but humble, for it affirms a far more important and consequential superiority, a spiritual

means confined to fiction. Greenfeld points out that the English, French, and Germans all thought that God aided them in war. For example, Aylmer claimed of England that "God and his angels fought on her side against her foreign foes" (Greenfeld 60). German nationalists contended that "the triumph of Germany was willed by God" (363). John Milton stressed that the victories of Cromwell proved divine election had fallen with the English (see the "Apology for Smectymnuus," *Works* 3: 340). The general pattern recurs outside Europe (and Dinka poetry) as well. In *The Book of Dede Korkut,* one of the heroes is explicitly aided by an angel of God (160). The great Ainu heroes regularly have divine ancestry. In the Indian *Rāmāyaṇa*, the central text of modern Hindu nationalism, the paradigmatic hero Rāma was himself an incarnation of God.

Unsurprisingly, this divinization of the in-group is commonly paralleled by a demonization of the out-group. Arendt quotes a pan-Slavicist who maintained that, "The German monsters are not only our foes, but God's foes" (233). Greenfeld explains that, at a certain time, French nationalism was inseparable from a "violent and irrational Anglophobia," according to which, the English were "the eternal enemies of our nation" and England was the "artisan of the ills of the world." As a result, "The mission of France was to rid the world of this monster" (183). German nationalists sometimes viewed France similarly. For example, one German nationalist asserted, "I hate all Frenchmen without distinction in the name of God and of my people, I teach this hatred to my son, I teach it to the sons of my people . . . I shall work all my life that the contempt and hatred for this people strike the deepest roots in German hearts and that the German men understand who they are and whom they confront" (376). Milton asserted that the Irish are a "godless" group "cursed and set apart for destruction" (*Works* 5: 190). Moving outside Europe, we find that the enemy of Rāma in the *Rāmāyaṇa*—an enemy that commonly serves as a model for Indian national enemies even today (see, for example, Narayan xii)—is literally a demon. The enemies of Iran in the *Shāh-nāma* are often associated with devils. For example, the first threat to the Shahs is the Black Demon (Ferdowsi 6). More significantly, the first Arab ruler of Iran is a collaborator of Iblis (Satan) and is referred to as Ahriman, "the Maker of Evil" in Zoroastrianism (Ferdowsi 20). The Ainu national hero, Aeoina-kamui, battles for many years against Big Demon.[28] In the Ainu "Epic of Kotan Utunnai,"

---

superiority manifest in divine election.

28. Aeoina-kamui is relevant to our concerns in several ways. His authority is underwritten by the fact that his father is a god. Moreover, his mother is the Ainu land itself (see Philippi 204).

their traditional enemies are directly characterized as "demons" (Philippi 369; see 369n.7) and one of this group's great warriors is referred to as an "evil monster" or an "evil human demon" (Philippi 378, 378n.21; see also 378n.20). The heroes of *The Book of Dede Korkut* must struggle against infidels. The enemy must not only be defeated. Their churches must be destroyed, their priests killed (see 87, 139, 181), and they themselves must be slaughtered in impressive numbers (see 57 and 105). These acts suggest that the enemies are not merely the partially correct Christians, who are tolerated in orthodox Islam. Rather, they are "enemies of religion" (43), as one story puts it.

I take it that the practical consequences of all this are too obvious to require spelling out.

In this chapter, I hope to have shown that techniques of nationalization—techniques that serve to make national categories supersede other identity categories—pervade our ordinary lives and our experience of extraordinary events. In doing so, they constantly affect the key parameters of categorial identification. They systematically enhance the salience, (perceived) functionality, opposability, and (perceived) durability of the nation. Simultaneously, they develop and intensify national pride, attachment to the nation as a physical place, awe before the national hierarchy, fear or anger toward national enemies, and other forms of national affectivity. Moreover, all these effects are commonly enhanced by associations with religion or even the implicit development of a sort of religion of nationalism. Given this, it should be much less surprising that people are so inclined to accept and act on national identity categories, even when those categories come into conflict with non-national (e.g., racial or religious) identities.

3

METAPHORS AND SELVES

Forefathers, Roots, and the Voice of the People

BENEDICT ANDERSON HAS pointed out that we cannot possibly experience the nation directly. It constitutes a community for us, but that community is necessarily imaginary. Given the level at which Anderson is discussing nationalism, it is not necessary for him to spell out precisely what constitutes such imagination. However, this is just the sort of issue that a cognitive scientific account must address.

How, then, do we imagine the nation? How do we conceptualize the unity of diverse individuals, widely dispersed in space and time, understanding them all as part of a single, exclusive entity? How do we think about this national oneness, draw inferences from it, respond to it? My contention here is just what one would expect from cognitive neuroscience. We conceptualize the nation in the same way that we conceptualize other abstract entities—through cognitive modeling or metaphor, specifically what is sometimes called "conceptual metaphor."

Over the last twenty years or so, cognitive theorists, beginning with George Lakoff, have examined the ways in which our thought is organized by a limited number of metaphorical structures. According to Lakoff and his collaborators, these metaphors organize our conceptual categories, guide inferences, incline us to act in certain ways rather than others (see Lakoff and Johnson 3). I am not convinced that metaphors consistently have these effects. Or, more accurately, I am not convinced that the idioms we use in ordinary speech are necessarily operational metaphors that have these consequences in a significant degree. (In fact, all concepts have networks of association that affect our thought and action. This is not to say that all concepts affect our thought and action as metaphors.[1]) However, it is clear that our thought and action are affected whenever we adopt a cognitive model to think through or act on an idea or problem. Genuine metaphors are a species of such models. At the very least, the pattern of structures manifest in metaphors is likely to tell us something about our general conceptual organization of the "target," which is to say the abstract topic we are addressing through those metaphors—here, the topic of the nation. In this chapter, I seek to outline the metaphorical patterns that are most prominent in discourses on national identity and to suggest how these patterns, and the specific metaphors that instantiate them, have consequences for the crucial identity parameters—durability, opposability, salience, functionality, and affectivity.

---

1. For a discussion of some problems with Lakoff's account of metaphor and an alternative analysis, see my "A Minimal, Lexicalist/Constituent Transfer Account of Metaphor." Lakoff has influentially extended his account of metaphor to politics. Obviously, Lakoff's work has been extremely important for the present chapter and readers should consult his *Don't Think of an Elephant* for an alternative analysis of some of the metaphors I consider. However, there are some fundamental differences between Lakoff's approach and mine. It would take a separate essay to develop these. However, here are some main points. First, Lakoff views metaphors as guiding thought about policy alternatives. In my account, one often chooses metaphors because one already holds certain policy views. In this way, Lakoff overstates the cognitive consequences of metaphors. Moreover, metaphors foster certain identifications, which themselves have consequences for policies. Thus, the consequences of metaphors are often more indirect than Lakoff indicates. In short, I do not see the operation of metaphors as simply a matter of framing, as Lakoff does. Nor is it clear to me that framing is an adequately well-specified explanatory concept. Second, in keeping with this, Lakoff's broader theoretical treatment of political thought is, in my view, somewhat reductive. Lakoff stresses the cognitive consequences of metaphors to the virtual exclusion of other equally or more important factors, such as group dynamics, perceptual salience, memory organization, etc. Finally, Lakoff's central typological division seems overly simple. He takes up THE NATION IS A FAMILY metaphor to distinguish "strict father" and "nurturant parent" political orientations. He then groups many advocates of identity politics together with civil libertarians, environmentalists, certain sorts of Marxists, and others under the "nurturant" category (14). This is valuable for coalition building. But it is probably not the best way of theoretically organizing political programs. It is in any case different from—indeed, in many ways opposed to—the account of identity politics presented here.

NATIONS AND THEIR METAPHORS

One of our basic cognitive strategies is to think through new and difficult problems in relation to simpler, previously resolved problems. We set out to establish parallels between the more difficult problem and the easier one, trying to use the latter as a means of understanding and resolving the former. Metaphor—or, more broadly, cognitive modeling—is a version of this general strategy. We use this strategy explicitly when we try to analyze, say, the atom on the model of the solar system. We use it implicitly when we draw unselfconsciously on, for example, hydraulics or pressure dynamics to discuss emotion (as when we say that someone had built up a lot of anger and was bound to explode eventually). The point holds in a straightforward way when our task is establishing unity for such abstract and physically dispersed objects as nations. In this case, the problem is to understand, and relate emotionally to, something that we cannot possibly experience or concretely imagine as a single item. We resolve this dilemma by analogizing the abstract and dispersed entity to something that we can experience more directly as a unit and/or by analogizing our relation with that object to a more readily comprehensible relation.

Clearly, we draw on metaphors in a wide range of situations and in response to a wide range of problems. But the metaphors we take up in these various situations and for these various problems are not as variable as one might expect. The work of Lakoff, Johnson, Turner, and others has shown that metaphorical structures manifest patterns of great consistency. This may seem surprising at first. However, it results from two factors. First, humans tend to be interested in the same sorts of things and, given their nearly identical cognitive capacities, they tend to experience the same difficulties in conceptualizing those things. For example, humans tend to be concerned with emotion. Since emotion is difficult to understand (given human cognitive architecture), its conceptualization is likely to be seen as a problem and related to more readily solved problems. But this only explains why the "targets" of metaphors (i.e., their objects of concern) tend to recur. It does not explain why the "source" domains—the sets of concepts we draw on as models for the targets—tend to recur as well. Why, for example, is analogizing emotion to temperature so common? (See, for example, Kövesces. *Metaphor* 178–81, for cases of ANGER IS HEAT[2] metaphors in a range of unrelated languages—Chinese, Japanese, Hungarian, Polish, Zulu, and English.) Indeed, why do we all do this so extensively and

---

2. It is conventional to print general metaphorical structures in upper case.

easily, even across novel cases (i.e., why is innovation in the use of such metaphors not confined to, say, poets)? For instance, we easily understand John's statement about his boss's recurring bouts of irascibility even after he has been repeatedly placated—"He seems to have come equipped with an automatic re-ignition device." This is not because there is some unique relation between temperature and emotion in general or anger and heat in particular. There are many domains that are more concrete and more comprehensible than emotion. Moreover, it is not clear that the domain of temperature really tells us a lot about emotion. After all, the physics of temperature plays no role in contemporary cognitive accounts of emotion. If there were a significant connection between the two domains, we would expect this to carry over to scientific research.

This leads us to the second factor contributing to the commonality of metaphorical structures. The selection of models or source domains is governed by a shared set of cognitive principles. Of course, in any given case, our minds may select domains in an idiosyncratic manner. However, when this occurs, the resulting choices are unlikely to be passed on and thus preserved, as Pascal Boyer has emphasized (speaking of cultural patterns in general, not conceptual metaphors in particular). Put differently, there are two stages in the social generalization of metaphors. The first is the generation of a metaphor by some individual (or by several individuals independently or collectively). The second is the spreading of the metaphor to other people in the society. The first stage is already governed by human cognitive patterns. However, if idiosyncratic elements work their way in at this level, they are likely to be eliminated at the stage of dissemination, which is also governed by human cognitive patterns, in this case, patterns shared by all those to whom the metaphorical structure is disseminated. Specifically, not all possible models are equally accessible to the mind. Salient properties of the target "prime" or partially activate a number of possible source domains. We are likely to choose a source model from those primed domains. There will be idiosyncrasies in each person's network of lexical connections (i.e., the circuits through which priming passes). However, over enough cases (i.e., over enough different people), those idiosyncrasies should cancel each other out.

But widespread acceptance of individual metaphors is not all there is to the patterning of metaphors. As the example of temperature and emotion suggests, we do not make our metaphors for individual targets in isolation. As Lakoff and his collaborators have shown, we map larger domains onto one another. Thus, in English, we do not merely say that Sally was burning with anger at Bill; we also say that Jane gave John the cold shoulder, that, despite this chilly treatment, John felt warmth for Jane, and so forth. Why do metaphors tend to cluster into recurring source domains? This is because priming operates across both the source and target domains. As a result, related targets come to prime lexical items from related source domains.

Consider a specific case—lust and heat. Sexual arousal leads to reddening and increased localized surface temperature as a result of changes in blood flow distribution (see Frijda 130–31). It also leads to activity that often results in sensations of heat, perspiration, and so forth. In thinking about sexual desire, our lexical networks undoubtedly prime a number of associated items. These are likely to include lexical items that involve redness, heat, and the production of perspiration—such as the item "heat" itself, as well as "fire," "burn," and so forth. As a result, when discussing how desirous someone is, there is a reasonable chance that we will come up with something along the lines of "burning with lust." This is true even if we have never before encountered temperature metaphors for emotion. This sort of metaphor should have good "survivability" in that it fits well with the lexical associations of other English speakers. From here, it is easy to see how a broader mapping of lust onto temperature could ensue. If great desire is fire, then, by simple inferential logic, less desire is parallel to less fire. Ordinary associations lead easily from this to a dousing of the flame, thus a reduction of the heat, a cooling off, and so forth. Moreover, once we have begun to associate temperature with sexual feelings, temperature is primed as a likely source domain for modeling other emotions, such as anger. (I am not proposing that this is the actual genesis of the temperature model for emotion. I am simply trying to illustrate how cognitive operations produce such modeling relations. On the other hand, conceptual metaphor theorists often view our bodily experiences as the origin of metaphor universals. For example, Kövecses argues that "increase in skin temperature" during anger is a key factor in the development of ANGER IS HEAT metaphors ["Metaphor"; see also Lakoff, *Women* 406–8].)

But just what good does this model do? I began by indicating that metaphors have a problem-solving function. They help us to think through ill-understood phenomena by invoking well- or at least better-understood models. The case of emotion and heat suggests that perhaps this is not always the case. One might argue that the model of fire helps us to understand anger as something that dissipates if it does not have fuel. However, it seems as likely—indeed, more likely—that this understanding of anger precedes the metaphor and indeed is part of the reason for using it. On the other hand, there may be other relevant problems with anger. We may understand that anger spontaneously dissipates, unless it is reprovoked in some way (through the actions of an antagonist, through reflection on the angering incident, or whatever). However, it is not always very easy to express an idea of this sort accurately and concisely. It may be easier or more effective to analogize the dissipation of anger to the consuming of fuel in a fire. This is a sort of problem solving. However, it is not conceptual. Rather, it is communicative problem solving. It is not a matter of knowledge per se, but of articulating that knowledge.

The mention of communication suggests another possible function for such metaphors. In some instances, we may use metaphors in order to communicate, not just an idea about a feeling, but some sense of the feeling itself. Again, our emotion systems appear to be set up in such a way that emotions are triggered by actual perceptual experiences or concrete, perceptual imagination (see chapter 7 of my *Cognitive Science*), not by generalities. Moreover, in comparison with abstract ideas, concrete images are more likely to trigger emotional memories. For these reasons, concrete images are more likely to enhance one's emotional response to a statement. "He was burning with anger" primes associations with fire, destruction by fire, and so forth. These associations foster certain sorts of concrete imagination. Moreover, they may include emotional memories. As a result, "He was burning with anger" is more likely to inspire an emotional response than "He was very angry." Similarly, we are more likely to have an emotional response to an image of the soil as "nurturing" than to an image of soil having "appropriate amounts of potassium." In these cases, one might say that metaphors solve a problem, not of conceptualization or articulation, but of rhetorical effect.

Finally, not all metaphors are a matter of problem solving even in this broad sense. In some cases, we make metaphors simply because our minds are set up in such a way as to isolate and elaborate parallels with ease. We notice that humans start out small and grow bigger, eventually drooping over and dying. We notice that plants start out small and grow bigger, eventually drooping over and dying. As a result, we develop one of the most common metaphorical structures, PEOPLE ARE PLANTS (see Lakoff and Turner 6, 12–15). It is difficult to imagine that our ancestors really understood plant growth better than human growth, or that they found it easier to talk about plants than about people. It is also difficult to imagine that the analogy served emotional purposes, since we generally care more about people than about plants.

Thus, we have four types of metaphor. We might refer to them as *inferential* (metaphors that guide our thought about a target), *articulatory* (metaphors that facilitate our communication of ideas about a target), *emotional* (metaphors that facilitate our communicative transferal of feelings regarding a target), and *unmotivated* (metaphors that express a spontaneous recognition of parallels, initially without further functions). All four types have a role in the discourse of nationalism. Our primary concern will be with inferential and emotional metaphors. Common articulatory and unmotivated metaphors certainly enter from areas outside nationalism. However, insofar as they are important in nationalist discourse, they tend to be taken up in inferential or emotional ways. For example, as we will discuss, PEOPLE ARE PLANTS has an important place in nationalist discourse. In its origins, this is almost certainly an unmotivated metaphor. However, its use in nationalism is both inferential and emotional.

Before going on to consider the patterns that recur in nationalist metaphors—first of all, the limited source domains that dominate these metaphors—I should say something more about the inferential consequences of metaphors. There is a common view that metaphors somehow determine our thought about certain topics. Thus, we think of arguments as combative because we use metaphors such as "winning," as if an argument were a war. I do not hold to a view of this sort. First, we have many meanings for terms in our internal lexicons. Even if we learn the word "win" first in the context of battle (which seems unlikely), it is clear that we develop other meanings for the term beyond "defeat in warfare"—including something along the lines of "show superiority along some axis of comparison." Thus, if I say, "Kerry won the debate," I need not be using "won" metaphorically or drawing on a model of warfare. Second, even when we use a term metaphorically, we have a great ability to select meanings from that (metaphorical) term. If I say that Oscar is a big old bear of a man, my auditors know that I am referring to some aspects of his physical presence. They are in no way inclined to suspect that Oscar poses a threat to campers.

However, this is not to say that metaphors make no inferential difference. They do. They do not determine what we think. But, once we hit on a metaphor, it primes certain ideas and not others. Thus, it orients our thought in certain ways. As a result, we are more likely to ask some questions rather than others, more likely to look for answers in certain areas rather than others, more likely to choose certain sorts of actions rather than others. If I say that Oscar is a big old bear of a man, you know not to imagine that he catches fish with his teeth. But "eating raw meat" is primed for you anyway. As a result, you may be surprised to hear that Oscar is a vegetarian—more surprised than if I said nothing about him, or if I said that he is a big old Santa Claus. If Oscar was coming over for dinner, you may even have cooked more meat than usual. All this can occur without you reflecting for a moment on what you believe about Oscar's eating habits. On the other hand, even if you do reflect, that may not make any difference. Reflection on a metaphor does not necessarily undo its inferential consequences. Indeed, it may enhance or extend those consequences, if one self-consciously takes the metaphor to be broadly valid. For example, if one self-consciously accepts the idea that the nation is a sort of person, one may draw more extensive conclusions from the metaphor than if one uses it unreflectively.

Finally, metaphors are particularly consequential for inferential reasoning if we are not thinking through an issue on our own, but rather listening to or reading someone else's arguments. When a nationalist rhetorician uses certain metaphors, we may find his or her conclusions more compelling insofar as those metaphors do not prime relevant alternatives. Put simply, when we have not thought extensively about an issue on our own, the use of certain metaphors can help to inhibit our critical reflection on that issue, particularly when combined with a forceful articulation of one position on that issue. Consider, for example, an argument for preserving ethnic tradition in which the speaker asserts that a nation is like a plant—it will wither and die if it has no roots. If one has not thought much about the value of ethnic tradition for national well-being, one may find even a simple statement of this sort to be compelling. It introduces an explicit model and asks us to think of the nation in terms of that model. We are likely to do so. As a result, we are likely to come to certain conclusions about nations (e.g., that preserving ethnic tradition is important for national well-being), conclusions that may not be very plausible and that may not even have occurred to us otherwise.

Of course, metaphors may be illuminating for much the same reasons. By orienting our associations in a particular way, they may foster the formulation of valid conclusions that would not otherwise have occurred to us. On the other hand, this sort of innovative thinking tends to occur only with highly novel metaphors, for obvious reasons. In most cases, national metaphors are not highly novel. Again, in general single metaphors tend to be part of recurring (thus non-novel) conceptual structures. For example, PEOPLE ARE PLANTS is the larger conceptual structure from which we specify such single metaphors as "Johnny really shot up like a weed." Those larger structures may be particularly constraining on our primed associations, thus particularly compelling for our inferences or our acceptance of inferences. In the case of nationalism, the problem is exacerbated by the fact that nationalist discourse tends to draw on a very limited set of source domains, producing a limited number of recurring conceptual structures.

To understand the nature of nationalist metaphors and to explore their consequences, then, we need to understand how they are structured in relation to their source domains. A first step toward achieving such an understanding is isolating those domains. To do this, it is helpful to return to our basic account of what constitutes a nation. That account identifies the properties that prime circuits from which people are likely to draw metaphors for the nation. As a result, it provides a framework for understanding recurrent patterns in nationalist metaphors.

As discussed in the opening chapter, our basic understanding of any identity category is defined by some inclusion criterion. In the case of nations, this criterion is formalized in international law. Of course, our intuitive sense of inclusion criteria for a given group may not be the same as the legal criteria. (Obviously, the intuitive sense is what bears on priming and the generation of metaphors.) However, the legal criteria do seem to capture our intuitions about citizenship. Specifically, Levi explains that the crucial issue in this area is what "represents a genuine link" between a person and a nation. There is no single, definitive criterion. Thus, "Birth in the state's territory (*ius soli*) or the parents' nationality (*ius sanguinis*) are not necessarily conclusive." However, "either is a very strong link to justify nationality." Moreover, "Under international law, marriage may give the individual the nationality of the spouse" (150).

The inclusion criteria for a national identity category, then, commonly involve one or both of these two domains—family and land. The connection with the land is unsurprising, for the nation is, in part, distinctively defined by a national territory. The family criterion may seem less expected. However, the family is the initial, most salient, most emotionally powerful, most functional, most opposable, and most enduring group for virtually everyone.[3] In consequence, the family is always a possible rival to any other identity group. One way of coopting the family is simply to incorporate it as the primary constituent unit of the larger in-group. Thus, the family is folded into ethnicity, race, religion—and nation. Indeed, it becomes a sort of guardian for the larger in-group, a crucial element in the defense of the in-group against out-groups and against internal hierarchical disruption. More positively, the family is the basic social unit of reproduction. Fundamentally, it reproduces the family itself (or the lineage of the

---

3. It is enduring for two reasons. First, even if disinherited, one is still the biological child of one's family. Second, one's familial ancestry necessarily extends back to the earliest humans. The same point cannot be made about other identity categories, such as the nation.

family). But, once incorporated into another group, such as the nation, the family serves as the primary unit for reproducing that group as well. In both ways, then, it is crucial for the nation.

In keeping with their roles in the definition (and practical operation) of national identity, land and family are two of the three crucial source domains for metaphors about the nation. Specifically, two of the most common forms of nationalist metaphor are homologies of the following form: (1) The citizen is to the nation as [metaphor] is to the family,[4] and (2) the citizen is to the nation as [metaphor] is to the land. In the former, the possible values for the variable are constrained in a straightforward way. The citizen is to the nation as some family member is to the family. We might first expect the possible values for the land variable to be more diverse. However, in this case, previously existing metaphorical structures come into play, most importantly the conceptual metaphor PEOPLE ARE PLANTS. The widespread use of this structure leads to the following, more fully specified homology: The citizen is to the nation as a plant is to the soil.

The majority of nationalist metaphors derive from these two domains. However, there is, as I mentioned, a third domain as well. Like the domain of the family, this is common across identity groups. Indeed, it even serves as a model for the family. The family may be the basic social group. However, it is not the basic human unit. The basic human unit or single, unified identity—thus a basic model for all human groups, including nations—is the individual person.[5]

The general idea that nationalism uses models drawn from the family and the person has been noted by some other authors. For example, Herzfeld writes that "the metonymic extension of 'those we know' to include a huge population is not confined to nation-states; they are not the only imagined communities. Perhaps people everywhere use the familiar building blocks of body, family, and kinship in order to make sense of larger entities" (5). However, Herzfeld's formulation here is a bit too narrow. When used as a source domain for modeling the nation, the person may be either a body or a mind. Thus, one might use the body as a model, saying that the father is "head" of the family, the police are the "arms" of the nation (cf. "the long arm of the law"), and so on. But one might equally say the nation is one spirit, sharing (national) interests or a common grief.

Almost all standard nationalist metaphors seem to derive from one

---

4. In general terms, this metaphor is fairly widely recognized (see, for example, Lakoff, *Don't*).

5. This, too, is fairly widely recognized in general terms (see Lakoff, *Don't*).

or another of these three domains. Most nationalists combine all three in their imagination of the nation. Consider, for example, the following case, discussed by Greenfeld: "The Russian national idea consisted in the following: The Nation was (1) defined as a collective individual, (2) formed by ethnic, primordial factors such as blood and soil, and (3) characterized by the enigmatic soul, or spirit" (261). The collective individual with an enigmatic soul draws on the person domain, while "blood" and "soil" refer to the kinship and land domains, respectively. Of course, many Russian nationalists no doubt believed that these claims were somehow literally true. Indeed, that tendency is common for nationalists from a range of countries. But that does not change the point. No matter how literal they imagine their claims to be, the modeling operates in the same way, and these are the crucial domains for that modeling.

In the remainder of the chapter, I will consider each of domains in turn.

THE SPIRIT OF THE PEOPLE AND THE CANCER IN THE BODY OF THE NATION

Modeling the group on the individual is probably the most fundamental form of metaphor, not only in nationalist discourse, but in the discourse of other identity groups as well. It is the basic way in which we come to imagine the unity of a diverse set of people. As such, the metaphorical structure, GROUPS ARE INDIVIDUALS, pervades our everyday speech. We speak of "groupthink" taking over in a committee meeting.[6] We refer to the "voice" of a society. We call a set of diverse legislators a "body." Moreover, this is not merely a matter of speech, but of thought and feeling as well. When we say that the committee members began to think as a group, we are trying to explain why certain errors or biases crept into their report, uncorrected by the diversity of individual opinions. When we refer to groupthink, we are also trying to communicate an emotional attitude.

In the case of nations, the first use of GROUPS ARE INDIVIDUALS is simply to give us a way of imagining this vast, diverse collectivity that

---

6. One could object that groupthink involves the group taking over individual thought and is thus opposed to individuals. That is true. But, to say that groupthink *models* the group on the individual or *metaphorizes* the group *as* an individual, is *not* to say that it supports individuals. Rather, it treats the group as a single individual—one person, with one brain, one set of beliefs, and so on. The implication is that the real individuals in the group are now only components of that encompassing individual. Thus, the group/real individual opposition is a part of the metaphorization of the group as an individual.

cannot possibly be experienced by anyone. As developed and particularized, it clearly has inferential and emotional functions in keeping with this imagination. For example, many national allegories share a common structure. This first of all involves a personification of the nation in one character. This character must choose between different possible spouses for his or her future. Those possible spouses commonly represent policy alternatives for the nation.

A good instance of this is Rabindranath Tagore's *The Home and the World*. This novel concerns a young woman, Bimala, and her husband, Nikhil. Nikhil has in the past tried to support the development of home industries in India. Currently, however, he is opposed to the increasing violence and communalism (Hindu-Muslim conflict) of the nationalist *swadeshi* movement for home industry. The third main character is a swadeshi activist, Sandip. Bimala is drawn to Sandip, not only politically, but personally. Thus, she is faced with the dilemma of choosing between Nikhil and Sandip. In the course of the novel, Bimala is analogized to the nation generally and to Bengal in particular. Nikhil and Sandip rather transparently represent different political options for the nation (and for Bengal). In keeping with this, the novel as a whole develops—indeed, narrativizes (elaborates into a story)—the GROUPS ARE INDIVIDUALS metaphor. It does this by way of the love triangle, allegorizing the society's choice of a political future. It also emotionally biases this choice by portraying the swadeshi activist as self-serving and dishonest and by making his selection illegitimate, since it would be adulterous.[7]

Similarly, in Derek Walcott's epic poem, *Omeros,* the character of Helen straightforwardly represents St. Lucia. She has two suitors—Achille and Hector. Achille is linked with the Afro-Caribbean rediscovery of African heritage. Hector, in contrast, is linked with Americanization. In the course of the poem, Helen's affections shift between the two men. Ultimately, Hector's craze for financial success proves literally self-destructive. When Hector dies, Helen returns to Achille. However, there is a complication here. Helen is pregnant and the father is uncertain. Pregnancy is a common metaphor for the future of the nation—unsurprisingly, as it is a common metaphor for the future generally. The poem leaves open the precise course of St. Lucia's future. However, it clearly suggests that, in Walcott's view, the right future is for St. Lucia to affirm African heritage. No matter what, that future will be the result (the "offspring") of both African tradition (Achille) and Americanization (Hector). But it should culturally affirm the former.

---

7. On Tagore's novel, see chapter 2 of my *Empire and Poetic Voice.*

Here, too, we see a narrativization of GROUPS ARE INDIVIDUALS (specifically, THE NATION IS A PERSON) by way of the love triangle plot, in this case extended to encompass pregnancy.[8]

A Marxist example of this general sort may be found in Peter Abrahams's *Mine Boy*. This work concerns Xuma, a black miner in South Africa. For a while, he is attracted to Eliza, a beautiful woman, but also a cultural mimeticist (i.e., someone who seeks to imitate the practices of the culturally dominant group—in this case, white people) and possessive individualist who thinks of herself as white. As he becomes increasingly aware of his national and class position, however, Xuma realizes that his future lies with the less glamorous, working-class character, Maisy, who is in touch with folk traditions. Abrahams's allegory involves the complex, allusive interweaving of particular historical conditions and events, political platforms, and individual leaders connected with debates over class solidarity and nationalism in South Africa (for discussion, see my "Allegories"). Nonetheless, the novel still takes up the GROUPS ARE INDIVIDUALS metaphor, narrativizing it in relation to a love triangle, which represents the possible future of the nation as mimeticist and driven by possessive individualism or as connected with folk traditions and motivated by solidarity for collective benefit.[9]

Of course, personification of the nation is not confined to love triangles or fictional works. Katherine Verdery brings together many common elaborations of this model when she explains that "nations are conceived—like individuals—as historical actors, having spirits or souls, missions, wills, geniuses; they have places of origin/birth (cradles, often, in the national myth) and lineages (usually *patri*lineages), as well as life cycles that include birth, periods of blossoming and decay, and fears of death; they have as their physical referent territories that are bounded like human bodies" (229).

There are three ways in which "individuals" may be understood, and thus three ways in which the GROUPS ARE INDIVIDUALS structure may be developed. First, individuals are spirits or souls. Second, individuals are bodies. Finally, individuals are persons, which is to say, a combination of body and spirit. It is commonly the case that nationalists invoke different aspects of the individual human source domain depending on the context or purpose of the metaphor.

---

8. On the national allegory in Walcott's poem, see chapter 5 of my *Empire and Poetic Voice*.

9. Another Marxist example, one from Ireland, may be found in Patrick Hogan's *Camps on the Hearthstone* (see Hogan, "Revolution").

Emphasis on the *spirit* is crucial when stressing, not only the oneness of the people, but their close relation to divinity. This is perhaps obvious in the case of monotheisms, such as Christianity and Islam. But the point applies equally to other traditions. For example, some Indian nationalists have drawn on Vedāntic metaphysics in this respect. Put rather simply, Vedāntism maintains that all souls are ultimately identical with God and that the appearance of differences among individual souls is merely illusory. Some Indian nationalists in effect posited an intermediate, national level between individual souls and the all-encompassing Absolute. For example, the important Indian nationalist leader, Bal Gangadhar Tilak, stated that "God and our nation are not separate, on the contrary, our nation is one of God's forms" (quoted in Stevenson 47). Stevenson explains the concept by reference to "the Advaita Vedanta system to which Tilak subscribed" (47).

Of course, spirit need not be treated in this transcendental way. Moreover, it need not be treated as absolutely uniform. We commonly see the human spirit as having attributes or components. These may be mapped onto the nation as well, preserving its unity but simultaneously isolating distinct functions (e.g., in the national hierarchy). For example, we may conceive of some politicians or social critics as the "conscience of the nation." Such organization or subdivision may draw on a more psychological version of this domain as well, referring to the national *mind*, rather than the national spirit. Here, nationalists may emphasize the ethics of the nation, instead of its divinity. Most obviously, the nation is likely to be endowed with particular ethical virtues, such as bravery, generosity, and compassion. Moreover, the enemy is likely to be characterized in terms of the opposites of these virtues—cowardice, greed, and cruelty. Nationalists may also look to the national mind for intellectual virtues of reasoning or imagination. In connection with this, Greenfeld explains that, for German nationalists, "German superiority was evident, first and foremost, in its thinkers, 'the German mind'" (366). This celebration of the lucidity of the in-group may be paired with a characterization of the enemy as inscrutable or insane. Extending the metaphor in a slightly different way, the national in-group may be viewed as mature or adult while the enemy is characterized as having a childlike intellect or suffering from senility. It has been widely observed that, during the period of modern European colonialism, children served as one common European model for Africans (see my *Culture* 136–38 and citations; see also Lakoff, *Don't* 11, 70, for current cases). The point applies equally to African national groups, who were considered not yet mature enough for self-government, which is to say, not yet mature enough to make life decisions for themselves. While the childhood model was used for perhaps every colony, some colonies were also interpreted in terms of senility. As Ashis Nandy discusses, this was a common way of understanding and justifying colonialism in India (see *Intimate* 17–18, and *Traditions* 39).

As the references to national virtues and vices suggest, it is also commonplace to draw on this metaphorical domain by making assertions about national *character*. Thus, we may believe that the French character is aristocratic; the Irish character is bibulous; the Spanish character is quick-tempered. Recently, I was speaking with a colleague who claimed Hegel's master/slave dialectic was very much in keeping with the German character. All such assertions involve stereotypes. They frequently involve severely prejudicial attitudes toward the national out-groups in question and may often enhance opposability. In each case, they are based on a particular form of modeling in which the national out-group is assimilated to a single individual with a particular character. Of course, we use the character model for our in-groups as well. Unsurprisingly, we are likely to attribute positive character traits to our in-group. On the other hand, in some cases, these positive traits are a matter of potential, rather than actuality. For example, an Indian nationalist might claim that Indians are spiritual people, but they have been diverted from spiritual goals by the possessive individualism of the West. Thus, they must make an effort to return to their natural character. This attribution of character traits to the in-group is bound up with the establishment of ideals and the homogenization of practical identity.

A predictable extension of the mental model involves assimilating national history to personal *memory*. Indeed, this connection has become so entrenched in our way of speaking and thinking that the idea of a national memory may seem literal. But it is not literal. History does not happen to one person. History does not even happen to a single nation. By assimilating national history to personal memory, one creates the sense that national history has intrinsic unity, that it is not merely a tendentious selection of past events designed to suit a contemporary purpose. Moreover, the model of history as memory is combined with the idea of a national character to produce a particular account of how history operates. There is an obvious sense in which each of us, individually, is the product of our innate tendencies combined with our experiences. Insofar as history is memory, the nation may be construed as having a national character that is the product of some initial propensities combined with a set of historical experiences. For example, in this view, the American character may be seen as beginning with an impulse toward freedom, which is then reshaped by such events as the arrival of the Puritans and the expansion to the West. But is it really the case that the individuals who vote in elections, the corporate executives who have such influence on those elections, the politicians who are elected and who make policy decisions, in any sense share this national character? They are certainly shaped by their own individual memories. But are they shaped by a collective, national memory? Of course, to some extent, national history may become personal memory through movies, television, education, and the like. (For example, I may be deeply affected by a portrayal of slavery.) But, outside this context—which applies to non-national history as well—it seems that there is no real basis for the assumption of a continuity of national memory. Yet this model has become so naturalized that almost all of us use it unreflectively. Put differently, in order for national memory per se to have any causal effects, it would have to be real. But just what would constitute a real national memory? It would have to be some sort of Jungian collective mental system. But there is no reason to believe that any such thing exists, or could exist. We are led to talk as if it exists simply because our use of this metaphor has become so naturalized.

Indeed, many writers extend the analogy, drawing on particular theories of memory. Consider, for example, Santayana's famous statement that "Those who cannot remember the past are condemned to repeat it" (284). The statement implicitly relies on a sort of Freudian account of memory. Not having worked through my Oedipal antagonism toward my father, I may repeat that antagonism with every authority figure I encounter. Similarly, if we as a nation do not self-consciously work through our traumatic memories of the past, they will continue in our unconscious and lead us to repeat them.[10] But, in fact, history does not operate this way. If something happened to some people one hundred years ago, that may or may not affect me. Indeed, in some cases, it may affect me only if I become aware of it. Consider, for example, the dissolution of Yugoslavia. In that case, it seems more appropriate to say that ethnic and religious conflicts were exacerbated by memory. The recollection of old communal grudges gave the subnational oppositions greater emotional force. Wachtel reports that, by the end of the 1960s, "the lower a person's level of education, the greater the chance that he or she would express integrationist views"

10. Of course, the account does not have to be literally psychoanalytic. The point is simply that it is of the same type. It presupposes that not remembering leads to compulsion, while remembering does not. Sometimes, that may be true. Often, however, it is not. Many people simply translate Santayana's statement into the commonplace that one should learn from one's mistakes. But that is not what the statement actually says.

(Wachtel 191). This suggests that, among other things, these grudges were not preserved popularly and spontaneously, but disseminated through literary and historical education. A similar point could be made about India. Recent attacks by Hindus on Muslims have been fostered in part by Hindu politicians' repeated invocation of the Muslim oppression of Hindus and desecration of Hindu temples centuries ago. Such oppression and desecration were not repressed memories, forcing ordinary people to act out their unconscious impulses and attack their neighbors. Rather, they were resentments fostered by contemporary political rhetoric.

In this context, it seems that Renan was closer to the mark when he drew on the same general metaphorical structure, but reached the opposite conclusion. Specifically, Renan wrote that "Forgetting . . . is a crucial factor in the creation of a nation, which is why progress in historical studies often constitutes a danger for nationality. Indeed, historical enquiry brings to light deeds of violence which took place at the origin of all political formations" (11). Similarly, Susanna Moodie wrote in 1853 that Irish Catholics and Irish Protestants should not "perpetuate the memory" of "an old national grievance" that led to "hatreds and animosities" (quoted in Trumpener 254).

Certainly, there are cases where Santayana is roughly correct. It routinely happens that societies do bad things, then enact laws to prevent those bad things from recurring. If we are not aware of the history of a certain law or practice, we may not recognize the purpose it serves. If we then change the law or practice, we may unwittingly lead the country back to the earlier harmful behaviors. For example, after the Vietnam War, the U.S. government tended to hesitate about committing troops to occupy a foreign country and the U.S. population tended to look with disfavor on suggestions of sending such troops. However, as people began to forget the horrors of that war, the general aversion to invasion declined. This ultimately allowed the invasions of Afghanistan and then Iraq. One could reasonably argue that U.S. occupation of these countries is, at least in some ways, a "reliving" of the occupation of Cambodia and South Vietnam. On the other hand, even here things are more complex than the metaphor suggests. For example, the "repetition" of Vietnam in Iraq is not a psychoanalytic acting-out or any similar compulsion (whether understood in Freudian terms or not). It is, rather, a parallel invasion based on political and economic interests. There are some ways in which Santayana's claim fits this situation. But the metaphor biases our thought about these situations, and may limit our analyses.[11]

---

11. Even in the case of Renan and Moodie, it tends to bias our judgment—for example,

This model is not confined to Santayana. It appears in a range of writings by political activists and commentators, as well as fictional works, where it is often extensively elaborated. This is particularly true in the treatment of national "traumas"—either traumas of suffering, where the national in-group was brutalized, or traumas of guilt, where the national in-group itself committed atrocities. Margaret Atwood's *Surfacing* is, in part, a story of Canada. The main character had an abortion and has repressed the memory. The story suggests that the European killing of the Native Americans is similarly repressed (see my "Identity" for discussion). Interestingly, the literary use of this idea need not be post-Freudian. Discussing William Godwin's 1817 novel, *Mandeville*, Katie Trumpener finds "the repressed trace memory of the 1641 Ulster Plantation Uprising" leading to a character's "mental collapse" (225; see also her discussion of John Galt's 1831 novel, *Bogle Corbet* on 287–88). As in *Surfacing*, the point bears on an individual character. However, its implications concern the nation as a whole.

Indeed, in Atwood and Godwin, we have examples of another common specification of the GROUPS ARE INDIVIDUALS structure. In this specification, violent subnational conflict is assimilated to mental conflict, even insanity. The most famous case of this sort is *King Lear*, where Lear's descent into madness parallels the descent of England into civil war. Another example of this is Bessie Head's *A Question of Power*. There, too, the main character suffers mental collapse. Her madness is inseparable from the oppressive racial divisions of South African society.[12] The same point could be made about Jean Rhys's *Wide Sargasso Sea*. The main character's mental disintegration reflects the racial and related colonial divisions that mark her society.[13] Speaking of Walter Scott, Trumpener writes that "the displacement of geopolitical struggle into mental conflict transforms public, political, and moral problems of power and of collective destiny into merely private neuroses, subjective mental states, and problems of emotional health" (189). She goes on to contrast some other writers with Scott. These authors "insist that the trauma of colonization can never be exhausted or recovered from. Instead they describe the neuroses . . . suffered in perpetuity by collective and individual 'national characters'" (247). For our purposes, the differences here are less important than the continuities, specifically the identity of the metaphorical source domain.

Finally, a somewhat different use of the metaphor of mind concerns the

---

by turning our attention to knowledge of history, rather than, say, current economic and political conditions.
12. For discussion, see my "Bessie Head's *A Question of Power*."
13. See chapter 3 of my *Colonialism and Cultural Identity*.

difference between sleeping and waking. Nationalists commonly analogize the state of a nation that has little nationalistic enthusiasm as "sleep." They then speak of the development of nationalist "consciousness" as a process of "awakening." For example, Hoffmann quotes writers on "the awakening of the German people into national consciousness" (119; my translation). Anderson explains that, "In Europe, the new nationalisms" of the nineteenth century "almost immediately began to imagine themselves as 'awakening from sleep'" (195).

In comparison with spirit metaphors, *body* metaphors seem to be associated more commonly with internal hierarchy. Generally, the body is one of the most important source domains for imagining authority, with the "head" being in charge of the various "limbs" and "organs." The "eyes" of the nation become the individuals who recognize and report sedition or treachery. The "arms" of the nation are those who enforce its policies. The nation's "central nervous system" may be some aspect of infrastructure, such as the communications system. Alternatively, it may be the set of administrators who keep the nation running. Indeed, the two uses are related, for the crucial part of infrastructure is precisely what allows these administrators to do their job. Thus, fear of a terrorist attack on the nation's "central nervous system" would be any attack that disrupts the ordinary operation of the country.

Outside of hierarchies per se, we invoke the heart of the nation when discussing its ideals. Similarly, we may also speak of national taste (usually the taste of a small fraction of the nation, as Bourdieu has argued) or of how the nation will have to "tighten its belt" during periods of decreased government expenditures, of how the nation has "grown fat" due to deficit spending, and so forth. The rhetorical effects of such metaphors are largely self-evident.

Some bodily metaphors bear on in-group/out-group relations. Thus, the "spine" of the nation is whatever makes it stand tall, rather than cowering in fright. If the nation does not have a large, well-equipped, and well-trained military, we may say that the nation has grown weak, or is out of shape. A particularly interesting aspect of the body metaphor is that it facilitates the emotion of disgust, since most of what we find disgusting is associated with the body. This introduction of disgust is most often recruited to characterize out-groups, especially as those out-groups may be understood as a threat to the bodily "health" of the nation. In these cases, the threat is often internal, the threat of disease. This use of the body metaphor tends to go along with a fascist or semifascist attempt to align the national category with other identity categories, such as religion or race. In this usage, those who are of the wrong religion or race are akin to a disease or parasite in the national body. They need to be removed. Examples from Nazi Germany are obvious and ubiquitous. However, this metaphor turns up in "respectable" outlets as well. For example, Chomsky cites an editorial in the *Washington Post* that, somewhat mixing its attitudes, refers to "the aggrieved Kurdish minority" as Turkey's "national cancer" (*New* 8). Sometimes the images are more graphic and the effect of disgust more straightforward. Anderson notes "that the brilliant, young, radical-nationalist [Hungarian] poet Sándor Petőfi (1823–1849) . . . on one occasion referred to the [non-Magyar] minorities as 'ulcers on the body of the motherland'" (103).

Not all uses of this model result from an effort to align national and other identity categories. Some are used to characterize groups that disturb legitimate national hierarchies or disrupt national unification (e.g., through fascist policies of alignment). For example, Rabindranath Tagore referred to dictatorships, such as those of Hitler and Mussolini, as "the worst form of cancer to which humanity is subject" (quoted in Das Gupta 45). Chomsky cites a *New York Times* article on "What It Would Take to Cleanse Serbia." "Cleanse" here means "purge," as when one purges the body with a cathartic. The goal, according to the article, is to "stamp out the disease" of "extreme Serb nationalism" (96). As this suggests, what is seen as rightful nationalist identification from one point of view is often seen as a sub- or transnational sickness from another point of view. This is most obvious in the case of revolutionary movements, such as those in some former European colonies. For example, Sicherman notes that even "moderate" settlers in Kenya saw the Kenyan anticolonial Mau Mau revolutionaries as "a subversive organization which is like a disease" (77, quoting one of those settlers).

This metaphor may be literalized as well. Thus, we find that, in anti-Semitic writings, Jews are not only characterized as a disease in the body of Germany, but are blamed for transporting diseases into Germany (see, for example, Gilman 96, 221). Bapsi Sidhwa represents similar ideas regarding the British in India. Thus, one character in her novel, *Cracking India*, attributes the spread of polio to the English (25–26) and another links the English with syphilis (70). The literal and metaphorical uses tend to reenforce one another, conceptually and emotionally. Both encourage a particularly sharp opposition between the nation and its disease-bearing/diseaselike enemy. The metaphor dehumanizes the out-group, permitting, indeed encouraging, the killing of that enemy, like the killing of bacteria or parasites. The literal connection adds urgency and apparent medical rationality to that behavior.

There are also more straightforward spatial and temporal mappings of the nation onto the human body. In the spatial mapping, the national territory is the body of the nation. This model is used most frequently when the national territory is not unified, but rather some part of the territory has been lost, thus (in one use of the metaphor) amputated. We find an example of this in Bapsi Sidhwa's novel about the partition of British India into India and Pakistan. The heroine has a nightmare that "men in uniforms quietly slice off a child's arm here, a leg there. . . . I feel no pain. Only an abysmal sense of loss—and a chilling horror that no one is concerned by what's happening" (31). Baxmann cites the example of Maurice Barrès who lamented the condition of "the body of France, from which Alsace-Lorraine was amputated" (354). She also cites the view of a German nationalist in 1930 that "The German people must form their political body, which is now mutilated." She explains that "The 'recovery' and 'regeneration' of the national body" have been central to "left-wing and right-wing political discourse" in both Germany and France (355; my translation).

Temporal mapping models the nation on the stages of life of a human body. The most obvious and most pervasive of these images is that of birth. From international law to film and literature, this metaphor is pervasive. Levi explains that "Once a state is born, it exists until its demise" (120). D. W. Griffiths's most famous film portrays *The Birth of a Nation.* Salman Rushdie's award-winning novel, *Midnight's Children,* allegorically parallels Saleem's birth with the beginning of Indian nationhood. A slight variation on this occurs in the notion that a newly empowered or successful nation has experienced a "second birth" or renaissance.

As the quotation from Levi suggests, the final stage of human life is also important in our understanding of the nation. Nations are not only born, but may die. Indeed, Levi has an entire section devoted to "The Death of States" (see 122). The idea of the death of a nation may be combined with its rebirth, as when Hindu nationalists see their nation as having died with the Muslim conquests, but as being reborn with a new, Hindu India. Indeed, the motif of national death and rebirth is common in postcolonization literature.

Abraham Lincoln's famous Gettysburg Address draws on this complex of metaphors in fascinating ways. The speech was, of course, delivered at a cemetery. Moreover, it was delivered during the Civil War, when there was a great deal of literal death and great concern about the death of the nation. Lincoln begins the speech with the famous statement that "our fathers brought forth . . . a new nation, conceived in Liberty." Lincoln extends the standard metaphors that parallel the history of the nation with the bodily life of the individual. First, he posits that the nation, like the individual, has parents—"our fathers." (This obviously leads us into the THE NATION IS A FAMILY structure, which overlaps with the THE NATION IS AN INDIVIDUAL structure on this point.) The nation is not only born, but it is "conceived" prior to being born.

Lincoln goes on to the issue of demise, questioning whether the nation will "long endure." He notes that the cemetery is being dedicated "as a final resting place for those who here gave their lives that that nation might live." Here the (metaphorical) life of the nation is established as parallel to, but far greater than, the (literal) lives of soldiers. Lincoln suggests that the nation will not die, since the deaths of its citizens give it life. The end of the speech is more explicit about this idea, stating that "government of the people, by the people, for the people, shall not perish from the earth." This concluding phrase suggests not only the eternity of the United States, but also America's salvationary role in bringing democracy to the world and guaranteeing the eternal life of democracy. In both ways, Lincoln is tacitly taking up and simultaneously negating the metaphor of bodily life. The nation is like a body in being born. But it is not like a body in that it will not die. The affirmation of immortality is particularly important in this context, for the division of the nation must have seemed a sort of national death—and, again, it was bound up with a great deal of literal death.

This mixed use of the stages of life model is possible because Lincoln tacitly joins the body metaphor with the spirit metaphor. Specifically, he affirms that "this nation, under God, shall have a new birth." This not only takes up the metaphor of bodily life, it spiritualizes the national "life." This "new birth" that is "under God" suggests both baptism and, even more important, resurrection. In both cases, the nation is not only alive, but sanctified. In this way, Lincoln effectively integrates the metaphor of the nation as individual spirit (which is undying and is connected with God, but is not precisely born) with the metaphor of the nation as individual body (which is born, but which dies). This prepares us for the subsequent assertion of national immortality and the suggestion of a salvationary role for the United States, making both more effective rhetorically.

Other variations on the model of the nation as a human body may be found, for example, in literary works where there is an abortion, miscarriage, or some other problem with birth or infancy. This abortion or miscarriage commonly represents the failed promise of the new nation. This may be followed by a second birth, which may represent a more genuine hope for the future. We see a case of this in Atwood's *Surfacing*. As we have already noted, the abortion appears to represent a founding national crime in which the original inhabitants of the place were killed. The second pregnancy, announced at the end of the novel, may hold out the possibility of national renewal, renewal that does not succumb to the cultural, political, and moral invasion of "the pervasive menace, the Americans" (226; note that Atwood systematically establishes opposability through this recurring characterization of the enemy—the United States being widely viewed as the major threat to a distinctive Canadian sense of identity).[14]

Another instance occurs in Moufida Tlatli's highly praised film, *The Silences of the Palace*. Most of the action of the film takes place during the Tunisian war for independence. The main character, Alia, is a sort of new Tunisia, just coming of age during this period of turmoil before decolonization. Indeed, the connection between Alia and Tunisia is indicated directly when an anticolonial militant sits with Alia beneath a map of Africa and compares her to the nation. He goes on to explain that she will become a singer. As such, she represents the voice of the people (an aspect of the nation as person metaphor). The new Tunisia, then, will not be subservient—like Alia's mother and the other women who kept "the silences of the palace" in the face of unjust domination. Rather, the new Tunisia will be free and will speak with its own, popular voice. In keeping with this, toward the end of the film, Alia defiantly sings a nationalist song at a public gathering. Simultaneously, her mother dies from an induced abortion. The abortion suggests that a new society will not be born from the old generation, the old Tunisia of servants and aristocrats. But, as it turns out, it will not be born from the new generation either, the new Tunisia of artists and revolutionaries. When the film moves to a time ten years later, after independence, the situation has not changed. Now, Alia characterizes her own life with the former revolutionary as a series of abortions. The new, independent nation has also failed to give birth to the promised society.

A further variation on these metaphorical structures may be found in Ngũgĩ wa Thiong'o's *Petals of Blood*, an allegorical novel about Kenya. In this novel, Wanja represents (roughly) the people and land of Kenya today. Like the people, she is seduced and betrayed by (a member of) the nascent capitalist class. The result of this false seduction is the birth of a child—in effect, independent Kenya—whom she throws into a latrine (291). For a long time, she tries to conceive again, thus to give birth to a new society,

---

14. Alternatively, this may not be Canadian national renewal, but supranational humanism. For example, the narrator hopes that this new child will be "the first true human" (230). As we will see in subsequent chapters, certain ways of developing nationalist stories involve a narrative and emotional logic that ultimately pushes beyond nationalism. *Surfacing* may be an instance of this sort.

but fails to do so. In the end, she finally conceives by joining with a former Mau Mau rebel. This suggests that the hope for a new Kenya lies in the union of the people with the radical activism of the revolutionary movement, not their union with the African bourgeoisie.

In a little-known, but very insightful essay, Walter Ong discusses the metaphorical assimilation of the nation to the human life cycle. He explains that "our tendency to represent a nation to ourselves as an individual human being who is born, lives and dies," our "tendency to consider the so-called 'life' of a nation by analogy with human life is all but overpowering" (85). Ong rightly points out that this is not a neutral matter. Viewing the nation as a living body tends to occlude the real lives of the real human beings who make up nations, and it tends to occlude the common humanity that links human beings across nations. Of course, what Ong does not point out is that this is one of the most important functions of this model. Without occluding both the real individuals and the transnational category of "human," the nation would not long endure.

The *person* source metaphor turns up perhaps most obviously in the development of national "mascots," personal representations of the nation—Uncle Sam, Dame France, Marianne, John Bull, Germania, Deutsche Michel, and so forth. However, it is used most extensively to specify the GROUPS ARE INDIVIDUALS structure when one's concern is deliberate and unified national action. In some cases, the metaphor focuses on government, subordinating the small persons of the nation to the big person of the state. For example, Greenfeld cites Adam Mueller, "the political philosopher of Romanticism *par excellence*" (346), who asserted that one should regard "the state as a great individual encompassing all the small individuals." Similarly, Ong cites Thomas Hobbes's idea of Leviathan. He refers particularly to illustrations "in which the state or Leviathan is pictured . . . as nothing more or less than an oversize man made up of an agglomerate of little men" (86).

In other cases, however, the metaphor concerns the people. For example, speaking of the United States in the eighteenth century, Greenfeld refers to Joseph Galloway's "view of a nation as a 'society animated by one soul, which directs all its motions, and makes all its members act after a constant and uniform manner, with a view to one and the same end, namely the public utility'" (410). (Note that this is not simply a spirit metaphor or a body metaphor. It concerns a spirit animating a body, thus a person.) The same metaphor is found across nations and periods. Greenfeld subsequently quotes Friedrich Schlegel to the same effect, as follows: "The concept of a nation requires that all its members should form as it were only one individual" (363). Referring again to Mueller, she writes that, when one recognizes this personal unity of the nation, "then one understands that human society cannot be conceived except as an august and complete personality" (347). Along the same lines, Hobsbawm quotes a German Imperial decree in which the Franco-Prussian war is "presented as the rising of the German people 'as one man'" ("Mass-Producing" 278). Malla reports that, "It is said that the Indian nation arose as one person against the British in India" (7). A related extension of the metaphor involves the analogizing of democracy to individual speech, as when we say that, through the recent election, "the people have spoken." The ideal here is well expressed by Baxmann, the people speaking "with 'one voice' as 'one man'" (359; my translation).

These cases are interesting for several reasons. Perhaps most significantly, the claim of complete national unity is patently untrue. In the case of India, for example, there was widespread opposition to British rule, but there were many different degrees of opposition. There was also indifference, and collaboration. In keeping with this, we would be highly suspicious of any election in which all the votes were cast for one candidate. Here as elsewhere, one could make the metaphor fit this diversity, as when we say that a person is ambivalent, that he or she engaged in the action, but without full commitment. However, the use of personification does encourage us in the direction of seeing the nation as engaged in singleminded action. It tends to deemphasize diversity of attitudes and actions, and is not, so to speak, welcoming of the idea of dissent.

Perhaps the most consequential use of the THE NATION IS A PERSON metaphor is to be found in international law, with its idea of nations as juridic persons. As Levi puts it, "Subjects of law are individuals (natural persons) or groups of individuals (juridic persons) directly recognized by that law as capable of having rights and duties and of acting with legal consequences." Juridic persons include corporations and states. He goes on to explain that, in international law, "states remain the only entities having the fullest measure of rights, duties, and the capacity to act legally" (64). Moreover, "as long as nationalism remains strong, states will try to retain their monopoly of subjectivity" (63).

ROOTS IN THE NATIONAL SOIL

Probably the most distinctive set of nationalist metaphors derives from the relation between the people and the land. However, these metaphors are also, in some ways, the thinnest. They are almost certainly the least diverse in their particularizations. Nonetheless, simply through repetition, they account for a large number of the particular uses of nationalist metaphors, and they certainly contribute to thought and feeling about nationalism.

The main use of the land as a source domain comes in enhancing opposability, primarily through polarization. It does this through a simple contrast between those who supposedly have their roots in the national soil—or, by extension, in the national culture—and those who do not. As the metaphor has developed, it also fosters a sense of durability, for the land is presumably timeless and the roots can be very deep, thus of long duration. Specifically, the most common use of this domain for nationalism relies on the general metaphorical structure, PEOPLE ARE PLANTS. It combines this with THE NATION IS THE LAND. The result is a homology—the relation of the people to their nation equals the relation of plants to land. There are three obvious implications of this. First, plants have their roots in the land. Thus, people have their proper place in the nation. Second, plants draw their nutrients from the land. Thus, people draw their life from the nation. Third, when they die, plants may contribute to the regeneration of the land. Thus, the death of citizens may contribute to the regeneration of the nation.

In each of these three cases, elements are drawn from the source domain that require further interpretation. In the first case, we find that roots suggest some long-term relation to the soil. In keeping with this, roots may be deep or shallow. The obvious correlate of roots is ancestry. If one has had many generations of ancestors in a given nation, then one has deep roots in the nation. Insofar as having deep roots is understood as involving greater belonging to a place or greater rights to a place, then someone with a longer ancestry in a place has greater belonging to that place and greater rights to that place. This may seem so obvious and so obviously true as to be banal. However, it is not banal. In fact, it is not at all self-evident that ancestry gives anyone a greater claim on a national place. Suppose Jones and Smith are both U.S. citizens and both were born and raised in the country. But Jones's parents immigrated to the United States, while Smith's great-great-grandparents did. Does this mean that Smith is somehow more American than Jones? The metaphor of roots encourages us to think that ancestry has such consequences for national belonging. However, it does not provide us with any rational reason to take up this view.

Of course, the metaphor of roots does not *force* us to think that greater ancestral connection entails greater national belonging. The metaphor may be used for very different purposes. For example, the land of the source domain may be connected, not to the national territory, but to the national culture. In this case, the analogy is, roughly, plant/land//person/national culture. This version of the metaphor does not celebrate people whose ancestors have lived in the national territory for a long time. Rather, it celebrates people who are deeply immersed in and committed to their national culture.

An interesting variation on the plant metaphor may be found in V. S. Naipaul's *The Mimic Men,* which treats Asians and Africans who have been born in the Caribbean due to a "New World transplantation" (118). This variation in effect combines the physical and cultural mappings of the model, deriving cultural rootlessness from ancestral rootlessness. Specifically, Naipaul portrays men and women whose cultural lives—including, for our purposes most importantly, their national politics—are unreal, mere mimicry, a sort of playacting in which "we each became our character" (196). In other words, they are men and women without real cultural roots. In part, this condition results from their ancestral displacement or *uprooting* from a physical place. One metaphorical image for this condition is a great uprooted tree, specifically one that floats in the water, like Indians and Africans crossing the ocean to the Caribbean: "on the beach I could see the stripped remains of a great tree, washed up, I had been told, months before, coming from heaven knows what island or continent, drifting on the ocean night and day for weeks, for months, for a year, until stranded on our island, on this desolate beach" (106).

Needless to say, this metaphorical structure—even as specified in complex, double mappings onto both culture and national territory—is not confined to works of literature. A professor of geography, B. S. Butola, describes the condition that results from "large scale transnational migrations," as follows: "nations are over populated by the people with no culture of their own and no roots. . . . Nations are increasingly being peopled by" inhabitants who are "rootless" and "live in a cultural vacuum and emotional void without any commitment to any thing that can match with national ethos, heritage, and ethics" (141).

Butola's use of the metaphor is obviously critical of migration and its results. But, here as elsewhere, the metaphor does not absolutely dictate one attitude or conclusion—even when understood as mapping the earth of the source domain onto the national territory of the target domain. The metaphor does seem intrinsically biased in that direction. However, when developed in the right way, the structure can be used to present a positive view of migration. For example, Bessie Head took up the (transplanted) Cape Gooseberry as a model for her own existence as an immigrant in

Botswana. The main character in *A Question of Power*, Elizabeth, grows the Cape Gooseberry; "eventually Elizabeth became known as 'Cape Gooseberry.'" The link could appear merely humorous, but the narrator explains that "a complete stranger like the Cape Gooseberry [which was not indigenous to the area] settled down and became a part of the village life" (153). Note that, in this context, the metaphor does not evaluate people on the basis of whether they have deep roots in the land/ancestral connections to the place. Rather, it evaluates the fit between a society and a given person, the degree to which the person flourishes and contributes to the well-being of the community. The implicit presumption of the model is that plants should be planted wherever they will thrive and benefit people and, likewise, people should be able to settle and "put down roots" wherever they will thrive and contribute to social life. This is a perfectly reasonable use of the metaphor. What is perhaps most interesting is that its consequences directly contradict those of the more standard uses of the model.[15]

It is only a short step from the metaphorical specifications we have been considering to the idea of hybridization. Writers such as Homi Bhabha have referred to people whose national culture is mixed as "hybrid" (see, for example, Bhabha 314). This, too, takes up the metaphor of people as plants and the nation as land. However, it suggests a third variation. In this case, the "native" plants have the roots. However, the immigrant, or the immigrant culture, is grafted onto a plant. The result is a combination of the two parent plants. In this case, too, the implication is most often that this should be done insofar as it allows people to thrive, or perhaps insofar as the product (i.e., the result of the grafting) is of value to the community, much as a hybrid fruit or vegetable may be of value. Bhabha is widely praised for developing a revolutionary theory of postcolonial culture. Whatever one thinks of Bhabha's account, however, it is not revolutionary in its sources. Fundamentally, it is a variation on standard nationalist metaphorical structures. (Of course, Bhabha is not alone in this. A point repeatedly stressed

---

15. One reader of this manuscript commented that some people might raise "a scientific question" bearing on "invasive species." If so, it indicates the degree to which the metaphor of people as plants has been naturalized and the extent to which it biases our thought against migration. The suggestion would be that some immigrant groups *really are* like plants that take over the land, choking out the native species. My point is simply that we may use the metaphor in different ways, selecting some aspects and discarding others. Thus, the metaphor itself does not *determine* whether we support or oppose migration, even if it does involve a bias toward the latter. The scientific discovery that some transplanted plants are "good" and others are "bad" simply offers one further possible use. (The person who made this comment seems to have had aggressive colonizers in mind. But the fact that this alters what metaphors we favor suggests the metaphors themselves are not determinative.)

by conceptual metaphor theorists is that even apparently radically innovative metaphors are most often instances of common metaphorical patterns. See, for example, Lakoff and Turner on literary metaphors.)

Turning to the second homology—that plants draw their nutrients from the land—one might reasonably ask about the national correlate for "nutrients" in this case. These nutrients are commonly taken to comprise anything in the culture that serves to sustain one physically, emotionally, or intellectually. This metaphor might have operated to suggest that the national culture should be developed in such a way as to provide the maximum growth for the individual citizens. For example, it might have been used to suggest the need for national health care. However, this usage seems rare, perhaps nonexistent. Rather, this homology is used most often to urge individual conformity to (putatively traditional) national culture. In this context, the metaphor suggests that, if one does not set down one's roots in a national culture, one will be deprived of the nutrients of such a culture. Thus, one will wither and die. Thus, if some citizens are socially afflicted and emotionally troubled, nationalists might invoke a lack of roots or a disconnection from roots to explain their condition. Again, the metaphor could be used just as easily to criticize the national culture. For example, it equally fits the view that the national culture has not provided proper nutrients to all these citizens, who are rooted in the nation simply by the fact of being citizens. However, the metaphor is not commonly used in this way. As a result, it is not a model that fosters improvement in national policies in order to increase human happiness. Rather, it is a model that fosters loyalty to national culture and commitment to its homogenized practices.[16]

A version of this metaphor turns up in a range of postcolonization narratives that present the dilemmas of "deracinated," which is to say uprooted, characters. For example, one character in Walcott's *Omeros*, Philoctete, combines several of the concerns we have been discussing. He suffers from a physical wound. But the physical wound is really an outward manifestation of an inner trauma, itself produced by historical conditions—specifically, the trauma of slavery. Philoctete recovers from his

---

16. As we have seen, many metaphors seem to bias usage in one direction or another. *Prima facie*, I do not see any reason why that would be the case here. I suspect, therefore, that the use of the metaphor is itself biased by views—prominently, the views of nationalist activists—that preexist the use of the metaphor. These views would include a disproportionate emphasis on the duties of citizens to the nation, rather than duties of the nation toward its citizens. However, it may also be connected with the broader cognitive salience of (concrete) individuals relative to the (abstract) nation. Thus, our focus in the metaphor is on people (CITIZENS ARE PLANTS IN THE SOIL OF THE NATION), not on the nation (as it would be in THE NATION IS THE SOIL IN WHICH CITIZENS GROW AS PLANTS).

physical and mental suffering only when he takes in the healing properties from an African root. It is only when he "reconnects" with his "African roots" that he is able to overcome the wound left by the ankle chains of slavery and the psychological trauma of colonial history (see 246–48).[17]

The third homology—that the death of some plants regenerates the land—obviously has the greatest bearing on self-sacrifice in war or revolution. The death of patriots nourishes the nation in the way that the death of plants nourishes the land. Moreover, this homology may be combined with ancillary information to produce new "blends" (to use Mark Turner's and Gilles Fauconnier's term). Most important, plants require not only fertile soil, but water. Linked by the ideas of fertility and generative capacity, the metaphor of rain may be combined with the metaphor of death to produce one common metaphor of "national martyrdom," that the blood of the martyrs will nourish the soil of the nation.[18] I take it that the implications of such metaphors—for thought, feeling, and action—are too obvious to require comment.

Sometimes, THE NATION IS THE LAND may be used on its own, without reference to PEOPLE ARE PLANTS. In these cases, the precise metaphor is often altered to enhance the value of the nation. A common version of this sort is THE NATION IS A GARDEN. Greenfeld cites an apt example—"France as a garden, an earthly paradise, *le jardin de France*" (102). On the other hand, if one's judgment of the nation is less positive, the metaphor may be altered in less flattering ways as well.

A noteworthy use of THE NATION IS THE LAND may be found in Wole Soyinka's early play, *The Swamp Dwellers* (first produced in 1958). A blind beggar tells the story of his homeland. It is a story about farming and drought. But it is also, implicitly, the story of a nation, specifically a nation after the end of colonial rule. (Soyinka is alluding in particular to the decolonization of Africa, begun in 1957 with the independence of

---

17. It is important to note that this is not an exclusionary vision, one that confines the nation to Africans. Indeed, one of the most striking and innovative aspects of the poem is that Walcott presents the rediscovery of African roots as curative for the main European character as well as the Afro-Caribbean characters (see my *Empire* 171–74)—suggesting once again the cognitive flexibility of the metaphor.

18. Sean O'Casey presents a variation on this in *The Plough and the Stars*. Drawing on Eucharistic imagery (a further "blend"), one character asserts that the "heart of the earth needed . . . the red wine of the battlefields," poured out "for love of country" (164). In another variant, the martyrs' blood is not rain, but seed planted in the soil. Lyons presents an example from the popular Irish novelist, Canon Sheehan—"the blood of the patriot will be the sacred seed from which alone can spring new forces, and fresh life, into a nation" (91). McHugh reports an instance from George Bernard Shaw—"the martyrs whose blood was the seed of the present Irish Free State" (361).

Ghana.) The beggar explains that "the land had lain barren for generations" (98), a metaphor for the colonized nation during the period of colonialism. However, at a certain point, "hope began to spring in the heart of everyone" when rain fell in abundance and kola trees and wild millet began to grow. Though "[t]he village had been long unused to farming," the people set to work. This is an extremely innovative and yet very straightforward use of the standard structure. Here, the work of self-government and nation building are analogized to farming the land (thus cultivating the nation). The colonial period kept people from this work. But, with national independence, they turned to it with vigor. Recapitulating the euphoric feelings of national unity that tend to accompany independence, he explains that, "This was the closest that we had ever felt to one another." But the locusts came and devoured whatever had grown. Then everything returned to the way it was before. There are few hints in this play as to the meaning of the locusts. But the great problem in the main story of the play is a corrupt leader. Judging from this and from Soyinka's other works, we may infer the meaning of the image. Soyinka, it seems, wishes to suggest that national independence did not secure communal well-being. The crops of the newly fertile land, which is to say the benefits of the newly independent nation, were devoured by a class of greedy parasites who did none of the work. As a result, the euphoria of independence quickly gave way to the feeling that nothing had really changed in the shift from colonial subordination to independence. Though based on one of the three standard structures of nationalist metaphor, Soyinka's narrative here greatly extends and complicates the specification of that metaphor. Moreover, Soyinka uses this specification to give emotional force to a complex, critical analysis of nationalism and particularly of national hierarchies.

CHILDREN OF THE FOUNDING FATHERS

In addition to the land, Soyinka refers to the feelings of the farmers. To indicate their great sense of unity, he says that they were a single "household" (99). This is an instance of our final source domain for nationalist metaphors—the family. For its emotional impact, and for its inferential effects, the domain of the family is almost certainly the most powerful of the three domains standardly used in modeling the nation.

THE NATION IS A FAMILY structure has several important functions. The first is to enhance affectivity. Especially when embedded in narratives, metaphors of this type may recall feelings one has toward parents or siblings and direct those feelings toward the nation. A second function is to enhance the sense of durability. Insofar as the nation extends back through ancestral generations, it has clearly endured in the past; insofar as it stretches forward through descendants, it promises to endure in the future. Third, this metaphor structure in effect coopts the defining trait of ethnic and racial categories. There may be an intense conflict between ethnic/racial categories, on the one hand, and the national category, on the other. Again, fascist and related nationalisms try to solve this problem by making ethnic/racial categories literally coincide with the national category, often by "cleansing" unwanted ethnic/racial groups.[19] Nationalisms that reject ethnic cleansing and other forms of literal alignment often respond to the same problem by metaphorically aligning national and ethnic/racial categories.

Instances of the familial metaphor are frequent and widespread. American nationalism posits "founding fathers" of the nation, as if we all have a common ancestry as Americans. A number of nationalisms make the nation itself into a mother or father, characterizing all citizens as brothers and sisters. The Irish nationalist Padraic Pearse asserted that, "The nation is the family in large" (quoted in ní Fhlathúin 163). Hobsbawm explains that the Don cossacks saw themselves as "sons of the holy Russian land" (despite the fact that their ancestral "origins were extremely mixed"; Hobsbawm *Nations* 65). Hoffmann quotes a German nationalist as saying, "We are one people of brothers" (120).

A number of good examples may be found in English political rhetoric during the Malvinas/Falkland Islands war. As Kevin Foster explains, "the family" served "as a symbol of the nation." It was important at this time that English people shared "the conviction that despite the traditional divisions of region, class, race and gender, the nation, like the family, is a naturally cohesive unit" (47). He gives an example, quoted from the BBC's *Nine O'Clock News:* "The Prime Minister said today that the courage and skill of the men in the Task Force had brought a new pride to this country. Mrs. Thatcher said it made us realise we are all really one family" (53). Here as elsewhere, the use of metaphor is connected with literal claims as well, in this case claims about the family, and related attempts to coopt the family as the elementary constituent of the nation. As Foster puts it, "The official, celebratory line on the conflict identified the family as a model

19. In fact, ethnic alignment is impossible. As Balibar puts it, "no national state has an ethnic basis," except via "a fictive ethnicity" (49). But this does not really make any difference. Ethnic cleansing is despicable whether the dominant group is genuinely ethnically homogenous or not.

social unit, a source of domestic harmony, communal coherence and an ideal of social organisation." In keeping with this, "official accounts made much use of the royals" as "a family that represents the nation, in itself a symbol of national unity and social solidarity" (57, citing Glasgow University Media Group 119). But Foster is careful to point out the relation of this propaganda to real families. Specifically, "The military's primary interest in the family . . . is centred on loosening its most basic ties, interposing itself between service personnel, their partners and children in order to nullify their potential threat to the good order of the fighting force" (61). The point is, of course, generalizable. The nation must supersede the family (or any other group) in cases of conflict. Insofar as nationalism cannot coopt familial ties, it must undermine them.

In nationalist developments of the familial metaphor, different components of the source domain—parents, children, siblings, and so forth—are often drawn out of the structure and elaborated on separately, sometimes developing their own characteristic uses. For example, the appeal to sibling relations may be used in any assertion of unity. However, it is commonly invoked in cases of acute internal division and is aimed at ending subnational conflicts. In keeping with this, it is not uncommon in nationalist narratives for two brothers to be fighting on different sides in a civil war. Liam O'Flaherty's famous story, "The Sniper," provides a good illustration. It concerns a soldier who engages in a battle with an enemy sniper during the Irish civil war. Only after killing the sniper does he realize that it was his brother. Stories of this sort recur in part because they are likely to be emotionally effective in opposing subnational divisions. The fracturing of the society is here assimilated to the fracturing of a family. The suggestion is usually that the national division is no less painful, immoral, and unnatural than the familial division. Anderson gives a good example from the United States. "A vast pedagogical industry," he explains, "works ceaselessly to oblige young Americans to remember/forget the hostilities of 1861–65 as a great 'civil' war between 'brothers' rather than between—as they briefly were—two sovereign nation-states" (201).

The NATION IS A FAMILY structure may also be used with a focus on parents or ancestors. An obvious case of this, already mentioned, is the American "Founding Fathers." Again, the founding fathers are metaphorical ancestors of all Americans. As such, they allow all Americans to share a (metaphorical) ancestry and thus to be one race, ethnicity, family. As Anderson puts it, "The son of an Italian immigrant to New York will find ancestors in the Pilgrim Fathers" (145). The general idea is by no means confined to the United States. Hobsbawm refers to a similar "cult of Founding Fathers" in "Latin American states" ("Mass-Producing" 272). The Malian epic hero Sundiata is hailed as "the father of Mali" (Niane 82). The Welsh national anthem celebrates Wales as the "Land of My Fathers" (Morgan 79). Needless to say, nationalists did not stop with merely mentioning these founding fathers. They often incorporated national ancestors into stories, usually heroic stories. In keeping with this, the Indian nationalist and novelist Bankimchandra Chattopadhyay insisted that it was crucial for Indians to learn about "the glorious deeds of their forefathers" (quoted in Chatterjee 76).

The emphasis on metaphorical fathers may be used to stress the brotherhood of the people. But it may also be used to reenforce the hierarchy within the nation (cf. Lakoff, *Don't* on the strict father model). This is commonly the case when the national leader is assimilated to a father or, less commonly, a mother. Such an assimilation operates both conceptually and emotionally. Conceptually, it suggests that the hierarchy of national authority is as necessary, benevolent, and natural as the hierarchy of authority in the family. This has more particular consequences as well. For example, parents do not have to explain all their decisions to their children. The children must simply assume that the parents have greater knowledge or wisdom, and have the well-being of the family in mind. The implications of this for national authority structures are obvious.

Emotionally, the family domain enhances the internal, national hierarchy by activating our feelings of filial respect and love, then directing these toward national leaders. We see this when a king is referred to as a father, or when a prime minister, such as Indira Gandhi, is viewed as a mother to the nation. In some cases, the metaphor becomes an explicit homology. For instance, in the great Ming dynasty novel, *Three Kingdoms*, a royal decree states that "in the human order the bond of father and son is foremost, and . . . in the social order the obligation between sovereign and servant is paramount" (Luo 66). Of course, a mere statement that the leader is our national father is unlikely to have emotional impact of any great significance. The metaphor needs to be developed. As elsewhere, the affective function of the metaphor is particularly likely to be strong when it is incorporated into narratives. On the other hand, even a brief reference to the supposedly parental qualities of a national leader does humanize him or her, and thus inclines us toward affective involvement in a way that abstract titles (e.g., "president" or "prime minister") may not.

As the preceding reference to "parental" qualities and the example of Indira Gandhi indicate, fathers are not the only precursors who define the nation. Mothers do so as well. However, it is less common for historical figures to serve as "mother of the nation." Indeed, we saw a striking case of this in Lincoln's Gettysburg Address, when he states that "our fathers brought forth . . . a new nation, conceived in Liberty." Here, Lincoln is referring to historical figures as fathers even as he attributes to them the maternal function of giving birth.

Foremothers do appear once in a while. For example, this use of the maternal metaphor, along with other aspects of the familial structure—and, indeed, the plant structure—are taken up in an interesting and complex way by Anne Hébert in *Le Premier Jardin,* a novel treating Québec. Her heroine is an actress who takes on the diverse roles of the nation and thus stands for that nation—or, more properly, the women of the nation. In keeping with this, she searches for "the mother that she never knew" among past "mothers of the country" (100; my translation here and below). The fact that she herself is orphaned (see 100–101) may suggest the absence of national "mothers" from official national histories. In the context of the familial metaphor, an absence of women from such histories is aptly assimilated to the loss of one's national mother. Utilizing both the family and plant models, Hébert elaborates on the metaphor of the foremother, writing of "the queen with a thousand names, the first flower, the first root," the original ancestor now "fragmented into a thousand fresh faces . . . in all her multiplied verdure, her womb fecund" (99). However, this use of the family metaphor remains rare—just as Hébert's treatment of lost national mothers would suggest.

On the other hand, mothers are often personifications of the nation. In these cases, rather than real people serving as metaphorical parents at some time in the past, we have the nation itself serving as a metaphorical parent for all the citizens. This personification can occur with fathers in the celebration of the fatherland. Sometimes, the two sorts of metaphorical fatherhood are even joined, as when Tsar Peter I was referred to as "the father of the Fatherland" (Greenfeld 196).[20] However, the personification of the nation as a parent seems to have more affective force when it is maternal (at least this is what the frequent emotional appeals to national motherhood suggest). Obvious instances include "Mother India," as in Mehboob Khan's famous melodrama, and the "Old Woman" who is Ireland as an aging mother (see, for example, Lyons 131), the old woman who was the topic of so much Irish nationalist literature (e.g., W. B. Yeats's *Cathleen ni Houlihan*). As Edna O'Brien puts it, "Countries are either mothers or

---

20. Eugene O'Connor has pointed out to me that the metaphor dates back at least to Roman times, when *Pater Patriae* (Father of the Fatherland) was applied to Julius Caesar, Augustus, and others.

fathers, and engender the emotional bristle secretly reserved for either sire. Ireland has always been a woman" (11). The influential nineteenth-century nationalist writer Bankimchandra Chattopadhyay proclaimed India, "The Mother that used to be, that is now, and that will be." He called on his fellow Indians to "Worship Mother Ind," for we are all "offspring of one mother . . . brothers all" (quoted in Abhijit Chowdhury 88–89). Uma Bharati, a Hindu nationalist in India, recently called on fellow Hindus to "console our crying motherland" (quoted in Nandy et al. 53). Greenfeld discusses the phenomenon in sixteenth-century France. "Contemporary authors," she writes, "constantly returned to this image of France—the mother, holding them [her children] at her nourishing breast. . . . Their patriotic concerns derived quite directly from this filial relation" (107). Subsequently, she cites Gérard François, the physician to Henri IV, on "offering" France "all the support that every child naturally owes his mother" (108; see also 240 for a Russian example). Wachtel cites a Yugoslav nationalist insisting that the religion of individual Yugoslavs is unimportant. What matters is that they are "all sons of the same mother" (103).

As these examples suggest, maternal metaphors take up the usual functions of the family structure. Thus, they may support internal hierarchy or oppose subnationalism. As to the former, Daniel explains that a "political state" may be "considered as the mother of a nation" (55), a conception that tacitly identifies the authority of the mother over her children with the authority of the state over the citizens or subjects. With respect to subnationalism, the metaphor is sometimes extended in clever ways to accommodate ethnic diversity or to establish a hierarchy of subnational groups. For example, Simón Bolívar made an attempt to reconcile literal ethnic differences in Latin America with metaphorical shared ancestry, stating that, "Born all of the same mother, our fathers [are] of different origins and blood" (quoted in Sommer 81). A nineteenth-century nationalist history from India extends the metaphor to adoption: "India is the true motherland only of" Hindus, and "only they have been born from her womb." Nonetheless, "the Muslims are not unrelated any longer. She has held them at her breast and reared them." Muslims are, then "her adopted children." As a result, there is now "a bond of brotherhood between Hindus and Muslims" who must "unite in taking care of our Mother." In keeping with the different status of natural and adopted children, however, "our leader" must be a Hindu (Bhudeb Mukhopadhyay, quoted in Chatterjee 111).

In other cases, the metaphor is extended into complex aspects of mother/child relations, often in combination with THE GROUP IS AN INDIVIDUAL structure. For example, Gonglah seeks to psychoanalyze subnational insurgency in Nagaland by reference to "the failure of relationship between the mother (India) and the child (Nagaland) due . . . to [the] deeply wounded psyche of the child and carelessness of the mother" (156). He goes on to say that the insurgency is fueled by "the carelessness of Mother India" (157). Along similar lines, Binayak Dutta reports that some Assamese complain that the government has given their state "stepmotherly treatment" (210) in extracting their resources and sending those resources elsewhere. Clearly, this metaphor uses the same familial domain, but it does so toward subnational ends. India, according to this model, is not the true mother of the Assamese, but a sort of usurper who will never treat the Assamese fairly.

In some instances, writers take up the metaphor to repudiate it. In Mohammed Dib's *La Grande Maison,* young Omar is faced with colonial propaganda that France is the national mother. He does not respond by asserting that Algeria is his national mother. Instead, he reflects simply that his mother is at home and that he does not have two mothers. Whether or not it is his nation, he thinks, it is not his mother. That identification is just a lie (20–21). In his novel *The Home and the World,* Rabindranath Tagore takes up the inflammatory use of this metaphor, criticizing the "hypnotic texts of patriotism" (36), prominently the slogan "Bande Mataram!"—"Hail Mother!" More important, the novel as a whole is designed to show the terrible consequences of thinking about the nation as a mother—for what violence is not justified in the name of defending one's mistreated mother, particularly in a culture where that mother (thus the nation) may be deified? For example, at one point Tagore has his heroine, Bimala, exclaim, "I would make my country a Person, and call her Mother, Goddess . . . for whom I would redden the earth with sacrificial offerings" (38).

We have seen that, drawing on the domain of family relations, the nation may be metaphorized in terms of fathers, mothers, and siblings. Our understanding of and response to the nation may also use the relation between lovers or spouses as a model. Thus, the South African poet Frank Chipasula wrote "A Love Poem for My Country" (Maja-Pearce 163) and the Nigerian poet Odia Ofeimun refers to "my land, my woman" (Maja-Pearce 186). Though usually used to express and inspire patriotic devotion, the metaphor may also be used more critically. The great Pakistani poet Faiz Ahmed Faiz drew on Arabic, Persian, and Urdu poetic traditions (particularly as manifest in the ghazal form) to portray Pakistan as a cruel beloved whose cruelty kills her lovers (see, for example, the poem "Spring Comes," 37). Stephens takes up the metaphor to make Ireland the abused wife of England: "We are a little country and you, a huge country, have persistently beaten us . . . you have never given Ireland any reason to love you, and you cannot claim her affection without hypocrisy or stupidity" (101–2).

One of the most common extensions of this metaphor assimilates attacks against the nation to rape. Examples are ubiquitous. To take one more or less at random, Frank Chipasula draws on this metaphor to express his obligations as a poet, writing in "Manifesto on *Ars Poetica*" that "I will address our raped land and expose her wounds" (quoted in Maja-Pearce 182). Trumpener discusses an example of this from eighteenth-century Ireland (135), while Buckley and Kenney treat the use of this metaphor in Northern Ireland (52–53, 65). Kennedy and Power point to the partially literal, partially metaphoric use of this image by Tamil rebels (22).

Some works combine and vary these metaphors in complex ways. In Yeats's *Cathleen ni Houlihan,* Ireland is both an aged, grandmotherly figure and a youthful beloved—though her relation to motherhood is not straightforward. At the start of the play, Cathleen is an old woman who has been deprived of her land by strangers (53), just as the national territory of Ireland has been taken over by the English. In the course of her life, she has had many lovers—allegorically, Ireland has had many lovers/patriots. She explains that "many a man has died for love of me" (54). Despite her age, she has never become a mother, thus never given birth to the new nation. At the end of the play, there is an uprising against foreign rule. But now, as Cathleen walks down the path, no one sees an old woman. There is only "a young girl" with "the walk of a queen" (57), suggesting the renewal of the ancient, enduring nation. That nation is now, once again, the beloved of the patriots, thus the young girl who can, perhaps, give birth to the new nation.

A final extension of the structure goes from people to places, modeling the nation on the house or home. In metaphors of this sort, the nation is analogized to the place where the family lives, where they form a family, feeling relaxed, free, and "at home." Anderson points out that "languages describe [the nation] . . . in the vocabulary of kinship (motherland, *Vaterland, patria*) or that of home" (143). He gives German and Indonesian examples, from among numerous possibilities. Indeed, in *Cathleen ni Houlihan,* Cathleen's dispossession is the result of there being "[t]oo many strangers in the house" (53).

These metaphors operate to enhance our sentimental attachment to the nation by associating feelings for our literal home with the nation or "homeland." (Again, this is most effective not in isolated statements, but in narratives.) They also help to guide our sense of who belongs in the nation, how and when someone should be allowed to enter, how long outsiders should be allowed to stay. For example, it makes perfect sense to have very tight border control if one's nation is one's home. After all, one can hardly allow anyone to just walk into one's house. Moreover, it makes sense that one should have very strict constraints on naturalized citizenship, just as one would have very strict constraints on who could move into one's house. The image may even suggest limits on privacy, depending on just what we consider appropriate for parental snooping. In this respect, it is probably fitting that the Bush administration referred to dangers from terrorism as "homeland security." Moreover, it is fitting that "homeland security" is the stated justification for the administration's attempt to expand surveillance. The implicit use of the structure THE NATION IS OUR HOME may have helped foster a sense that government observation of our computers, and so on, is justified in just the way that parental observation of children's computer files is (supposedly) justified.[21] The point may be clearer if we simply substitute a closely related metaphor. Imagine that, instead of viewing the nation as a home, we view it as a neighborhood. It seems clear that the implications of the metaphor are different on such issues as immigration and privacy. We do not in general feel that we can rigidly screen people who can move into the neighborhood. Nor do we feel that we can check our neighbors' computer files.

Though commonly used to enhance national identification, THE NATION IS OUR HOME metaphors, too, may be used more critically. For example, in Rushdie's *Midnight's Children,* the home transferred to Saleem's family at the moment of Indian independence clearly parallels the new nation—or, perhaps more properly, the state apparatus of the new nation. Rushdie cleverly explores the possible parallels, examining the ways in which aspects of the English house affect the behavior of the Indians who now live there. As it turns out, the new owners of the house/state "failed to notice" that the contents, organization, and routines of the house/state were "changing them" as they imitated English manners, interests, and customs (113)—including the regular observance of cocktail hours that leads Saleem's father into alcoholism. Trumpener explains that Walter Scott's novel *Guy Mannering* involves a parallel of this general, critical sort as well. Specifically, in this work, "Domestic mismanagement is repeatedly linked to imperial mismanagement" (188).

---

21. In general, I feel that parental snooping is wrong. The point here is simply that most people seem to believe it is fine. Insofar as they analogize governmental snooping to parental snooping, they are more likely to find the former acceptable as well.

MY COUNTRY 'TIS OF THEE

In order to understand the actual operation of these metaphorical structures, it is valuable to look in greater detail at the rhetoric of a popular patriotic text. An obvious choice for this would be a national anthem. However, the national anthem of the United States is tacitly embedded in a heroic plot and would be better analyzed in relation to narrative structure. "My Country 'Tis of Thee" has a status similar to that of "The Star Spangled Banner," and it is less narrowly emplotted (though it, too, is involved with heroic narrative in the third and fourth stanzas).

Perhaps the first thing to notice about the song is that it borrows its music from "God Save the King." In this way, it is directly paired with, and directly opposed to, English nationalism. This is not metaphorical. However, it is an aspect of the song that enhances opposability. This is furthered by the contrast in the lyrics between "My country" and "the King."

The song begins with a direct address to the nation, referring to it with the singular and familiar personal pronoun, "thee." This personifies the nation immediately, if unobtrusively. It also suggests intimacy and singularity. There are no doubt many reasons for the use of "thee," rather than "you." It may seem more elevated, more associated with high literature and ritual. It may help with the rhyme scheme. But one crucial aspect is that it cannot be plural. "You" would be ambiguous. It could refer to a single, personified country. But it could equally refer to all the many people who comprise the country. "Thee," in contrast, refers necessarily and solely to an individual.

The next line explains that the addressee is the "Sweet land of liberty." Several things are going on here. First, the emphasis on land is in keeping with the metaphor schema THE NATION IS THE LAND. However, this is developed in a peculiar way. It characterizes the land as "sweet." We commonly use this word to refer to foods or to personality traits ("Doe is so sweet") or to express affection (as in "my sweet"). All three apply in this case. The term suggests the fertility of the land in food production. It also suggests the kindness of a person. Since "sweet" is more commonly applied to women than to men, it may suggest that the nation is a mother or a beloved as well. It also expresses the poet's—and the singer's—affection for this (personified) nation. Finally, "liberty" contrasts with the rule of the king in the musical source. Thus, it serves to further opposability.

"Of thee I sing" repeats the personification. It also suggests the possibility of a romantic model since the beloved is almost certainly the primary "thee" about whom a poet is likely to sing. In addition, the line implicates not just the poet, but the singer—for example, me, if I am singing the song. (Contrast, "Of thee, I write my song.") Moreover, since the song is often sung by a group, the "I" may suggest that the entire group constitutes a single self.

The family metaphor enters overtly with "Land where my fathers died." The reference is clearly intended to connect all those singing the song with a familial heritage that is tied to the land. It does not matter that one may be an immigrant whose ancestors died in India or Ireland.[22] The subsequent line, "Land of the Pilgrims' pride," links the fathers who died with an enduring national history. Moreover, it celebrates the pilgrims for their pride, thus their refusal to submit to the conditions in England and their positive joy in the new land. It also implicitly identifies the speaker with these pilgrims, because most Americans are in fact immigrants or the descendants of immigrants—thus, loosely, pilgrims (i.e., people who made the pilgrimage to this land) or the descendants of pilgrims. The praise of "my country" included in the song further links the singers with the pilgrims by suggesting that the singers' relation to the land is also one of pride. Finally, there is a religious suggestion in the term "pilgrim," which is developed later in the song.

The first stanza ends with the lines "From every mountain side, / Let freedom ring!" "Freedom" here continues the opposition to autocratic rule, as celebrated in "God Save the King." This may seem anachronistic. However, it is a commonplace of the American national self-concept. We are the enemy of dictatorship. First, it was the English monarchy. More recently, it was the Soviet autocracy, then the religious authoritarianism of the Taliban and the dictatorship of Saddam Hussein. In this way, our self-understanding is inseparable from the idea that we spread freedom.

The second stanza begins with reference to the poet's and the singer's birth, addressing the nation as "My native country, thee." Here the suggestion is that we are the children of the nation. I take it that this encompasses all those who are singing the song and who accept the United States as their motherland, even if they were not literally born in the United States. However, it could also be understood as excluding new immigrants from the national community. This jarring ambiguity—which reflects a division in American nationalist ideology—may be one reason why singing of this song often stops with the first stanza. Even without thinking through the

---

22. I say that it is intended to encompass immigrants whose ancestors died elsewhere because otherwise the song would include only Native Americans, since "my fathers" refers to one's entire male ancestry. Of course, this does not mean that no one might try to use the verse to exclude, say, recent or non-European immigrants.

reasons, people may have felt that there is something not quite right in the second stanza, something not quite in keeping with the unifying purposes of communal song.

The second line explains that the nation is the "Land of the noble free." The phrase is intriguing. It in effect coopts the idea of aristocratic lineage for all people in the country. We are all "noble" and all "free." None of us is subject to a ruling family. We are all of the same, aristocratic ancestry.

The third line then shifts to the romantic version of the family metaphor. "Thy name I love." Initially, the line seems peculiar, especially given the rather awkward name of the United States of America. The line is designed to recall the lover's obsession with the beloved's name and his or her tendency to repeat it fondly. It also suggests that the speaker (thus all of us singing the song) loves the free union suggested in that name. In any case, the following lines go on to elaborate on this romantic link, enumerating the beloved's delightful features: "I love thy rocks and rills, / Thy woods and templed hills." "Templed" is an interesting term here. It suggests the temples of a person's head, thus a bodily metaphor for the mountains that rise above the rest of the land. But it also suggests that the hills have places of worship on them. "Temple" particularly points toward the ancient, Judaic heritage. This obviously gestures toward the association of the national in-group with God. The point is made clear in the closing lines, "My heart with rapture fills / Like that above." The singer feels the same sort of delight with the nation as he or she does with God. His or her patriotic rapture is directly comparable to religious devotion and the joy of union with God, "that [rapture] above."

The third and fourth stanzas develop this spiritual point, strengthening the link between America and God. Since this is more a matter of national emplotment, especially heroic national emplotment, I will not treat these stanzas. However, it is worth mentioning that they continue the personification of the nation and the land, even going so far as to call on the "rocks" of the national land to "break" their "silence" and sing "Sweet freedom's song." It also enhances opposability further by ending with an invocation of our only "King," who is "Great God." The contrast with England (and any subsequent autocratic societies) is obvious.

"My Country 'Tis of Thee" is, then, pervaded by standard nationalist metaphors. These metaphors serve nationalist purposes by enhancing salience, opposability, durability, affectivity, and, to a lesser extent—through its references to freedom and God—(perceived) functionality. The song is not at all unusual in doing this. In fact, it is typical of popular patriotic texts in this way. It also suggests a point of conflict in nationalist ideology regarding precisely who counts as a member of the nation. This sort of conflict is common, as we have seen. However, it does not always manifest itself in patriotic works, which are generally designed to smooth over disagreements.

In sum, nationalist discourse draws extensively on metaphors from three domains. It assimilates the nation to an individual soul, body, or person; it homologizes the relation between citizens and nations to the relation between plants and the land; and it models the nation on the family. These metaphorical structures are specified and extended in many ways. In some cases, the specifications and extensions may be critical of nationalism. Far more commonly, however, they operate to enhance nationalism—increasing our sense of the unity of the national identity group, sharpening our imagination of its polar difference from national out-groups, naturalizing the internal hierarchies that organize power and authority in our society, and so forth. Perhaps most important, these structures help to develop the motivational force of the national identity category and to orient its behavioral consequences.

On the other hand, the motivational force and behavioral consequences of the national identity category are developed far more fully by the extended trajectories of human emotion and action set out in narratives. Indeed, as I have repeatedly indicated, even non-narrative techniques of nationalization, whether monuments or metaphors, have their greatest effect by being integrated into stories—complex, causal sequences of non-ordinary, emotionally significant events and actions. This, then, leads us to what is perhaps the most complex and consequential part of nationalist thought and action—narrative structure or emplotment.

4

EMPLOTTING THE NATION

The Narrative Structures of Patriotism

IT HAS BEEN A COMMONPLACE since at least Homi Bhabha's famous collection that nation and narration are intertwined. Nationhood, everyone now seems to agree, is inseparable from storytelling. One problem with this claim is that it is often obscure. To take a prominent instance, it is not easy to say just how Bhabha himself conceives of the relation. For example, it is not clear how one might interpret such claims as, "Nations, like narratives . . . only fully realize their horizons in the mind's eye" (1). On the other hand, when writers do make clear what they have in mind, the result is often banal. Indeed, in these analyses, "narrative" often seems to encompass virtually every coherent causal sequence with human agents. Is it consequential that we do not have a sense of nationalism without a sense of causality and human action? A claim is consequential only if there is some competing theory that is contradicted by the claim. As far as I am aware there has never been a theory of nationalism that does not already acknowledge the importance of causal sequence and human action.

It does, of course, happen that writers on nation and narration consider stories in a narrower sense. But the implications of these studies are also unclear. For example, Monroe, Hankin, and van Vechten ask how Serbian identity came to displace all other possibilities and lead to murder in Yugoslavia. They go on to specify their quandary in narrative terms, asking, "What stories were in most frequent public circulation, and how might these have precipitated violence?" (439). It is undoubtedly true that our behavior is influenced by stories. But it is influenced by many things—including images, slogans, formal political arguments, ordinary conversations, scientific reports. The important theoretical issue is whether there is some nationalist function that is specific to narrative. Looking in another direction, Simon During sees narratives as producing models for behavior (144). This, too, is reasonable. But it involves no clear theoretical implications regarding narrative *per se*. Similar problems arise in studies treating narrative and other political topics. For example, the essays in Dennis Mumby's collection *Narrative and Social Control* help to explain such topics as the operation of conformity in the workplace and the social communication of racist belief. But they do not appear to have significant theoretical consequences for the relation between narrative as such (its particular forms, structural principles, etc.) and politics or social relations.

The problem I am pointing to has not gone unremarked. For instance, John Breuilly has outlined some main tendencies in narrative accounts of nationalism. He concludes his discussion by stating that "narrative must be theorized in order to provide an intelligible account of what is happening, in order for the reader to see why nationalism and nation-state formation (but not necessarily every nationalism and every conceivable nation-state formation) are such pervasive features of modernity" ("Approaches to Nationalism" 158).

And yet, there is, I believe, something extremely important in the narrative analysis of political issues. In other words, narrative is not only a matter of personal enjoyment and interest. It is deeply consequential for our social and political lives. In particular, nationalism is crucially linked with storytelling in a nontrivial sense. The development, organization, and specification of nationalist thought and action are bound up with narrative structure, both in its general or schematic form and in its most prototypical specifications. Moreover, in each case, the emplotment of nationalism is inseparable from our emotional response, thus our motivations for action. Indeed, I would go so far as to say that nationalism cannot be understood in separation from narrative, which itself cannot be understood in separation from our emotion systems.

In the following pages, I will overview the broad connections between narrative and nationalism in four sections. The first and longest section treats general narrative structure. In this section, I argue that human emotion systems generate distinctive features of narrative organization—narrative beginnings and endings, certain sorts of agent-oriented causal attribution, some broad patterns in the attentional selection and trajectory of emplotted events, and so forth. These features are not merely manifest in literature. The resulting narrative structure helps to guide the ways that we think about and respond to national identity. Since I cannot discuss all relevant aspects of nationalism, I will focus on one, arguably the most consequential of all nationalist actions and events—war. The second section briefly considers one component of narrative processing that bears importantly on nationalism—"development principles," the techniques that allow us to make general narrative structures into particular stories. Specifically, in this section, I consider two development principles that operate as techniques of nationalization, inhibiting subnationalism, fostering affectivity, and enhancing the sense of national durability. The third section outlines the three universal narrative prototypes, the standard narratives that are intermediate between general narrative structure and particular stories. The remaining chapters take up these prototypes, arguing that they serve to organize nationalist thought, feeling, and action in highly consequential ways. The final section of this chapter considers the theoretical issue of just how narrative prototypes operate to guide our emplotment of nationalism, which is to say, our narrative understanding of the nation and of our relation to it.

STORIES AND WARS

To explore the general features of emplotment and national conflict, it is useful to begin with a specific question about a specific case. For example, what gave rise to the recent war on terrorism? If you ask most Americans, I imagine you will be told "the terrorist attacks on September 11." What gave rise to the war in Afghanistan? Perhaps you will be told the same thing, or perhaps that the Taliban supported al Qaeda, the group responsible for September 11. What gave rise to the war in Iraq? Again, September 11 is a likely response, supplemented by Saddam Hussein's links with al Qaeda, and, of course, his weapons of mass destruction.

Beyond empirical issues of truth and falsity, several things are curious about the preceding questions and responses.[1] Perhaps most significantly,

---

1. Though curious, they are not at all unusual. Indeed, the same general features recur everywhere. See, for example, Angelova on Bulgarian, Serbian, and Romanian history textbooks (9).

they assume absolute and, in effect, singular origins for wars. This is curious, since it is not clear what this would mean in causal terms. Causal sequences do not begin from nothing. They are multiple and continuous. To say that the World Trade Center bombings gave rise to the recent wars is, implicitly, to suggest that these wars did not at all develop out of preceding U.S. policies. It also involves treating the bombings themselves as if they were uncaused. In fact, al Qaeda articulated several reasons for the bombings. Bin Laden argued that the United States has been responsible for numerous crimes against Muslims. These include the devastation of Iraq, the support of corrupt dictatorships in the Muslim world, and the underwriting of Israeli imperialism (see, for example, the interview by Hamid Mir). Consider Israel further. Supporters of bin Laden are likely to see Israeli imperialism as an absolute origin.[2] But Israeli policies derive from many sources, shaped by a continuous history. One element that went into the formation of Israel was, of course, the Holocaust. This too is not without a history, including the devastation of Germany during and after the First World War. In short, none of these cases really has a beginning. Any event results from the confluence of many earlier events. Nonetheless, we act as if there is an isolable point of origin.

I suspect that, as I was outlining these causal histories, some readers may have worried that I was justifying heinous acts. Indeed, opponents of the wars in Afghanistan and Iraq faced this objection repeatedly. But, of course, to say that a violent act has an historical explanation is not to say that it is justified. Indeed, that is part of the point. The continuity and complexity of history justify violent acts only in rare cases, and then only partially.

This leads us to a second curious feature of the preceding questions and answers. The assumption of an absolute and singular origin is widely taken to imply a particular moral evaluation. Specifically, in the case of destructive events, the initiating action is commonly taken to define who is morally culpable *for all subsequent events*. Thus, it assumes a sort of absolute moral culpability. This idea is strange.

First, it presupposes that the situation prior to the initiating act was just or at least normal (i.e., a form of moral ordinariness undisturbed by large

---

2. In "Road Map to Sustainable Ethnic Cleansing," Herman makes the same point about the Israeli side, explaining that, "since the occupation and ethnic cleansing are normalized and their results largely suppressed, and the violations of international law ignored, the propaganda system is able to make the causal force in the violence the suicide bombers, who seemingly came out of nowhere in an irrational assault on the peace loving Sharon and Israeli people."

injustices). We form our sense of moral normalcy in the same way that we form our sense of causal or any other sort of normalcy. Again, we form a prototype by weighted averaging over a set of instances. For example, we form our prototype for a bird by averaging over instances of birds. In the case of morality, we average different sets of perceived moral valence, forming prototypes of, roughly, "immoral behavior" (thus behavior that violates moral obligations) and "benevolent behavior" (thus behavior that exceeds moral obligations) for different contexts. We then judge negative or positive deviation from moral normalcy by reference to those prototypes. Following from this, a morally normal condition is simply a condition that does not trigger our prototypes for immorality.

More exactly, we do not evaluate most situations that we encounter because we see them as routine. As we will discuss more fully in the following section, we only ask why something is the case—thus raise the possibility of responding to and changing the situation—if it is in some way not routine. Put differently, judging a situation at all requires some sort of provocation. Once that provocation has occurred, we may engage in moral evaluation, particularly if the situation is aversive. To do this, we compare the causes of the situation to the relevant immorality prototypes.[3] If the causes fit an immorality prototype, that triggers our sense that changing the situation is morally obligatory. If they do not fit such a prototype, then no such obligation follows. Consider, for example, poverty. Our prototype for immorality regarding someone else's material well-being is probably something along the lines of robbery. Insofar as we isolate government or employer behavior as the cause of poverty, and insofar as this behavior appears similar to theft, we are likely to see it as immoral. Thus, we are likely to see actions to remedy poverty as morally obligatory. However, if we do not see such government or employer behavior as causing poverty or if we do not see that behavior as similar to theft, we will judge poverty to be morally normal. This is not to say that no moral issues arise in this context, for our benevolence prototypes enter at this point. Our prototype for benevolence regarding someone else's material well-being is probably something along the lines of giving money—in the case of strangers, donating to charity. In keeping with this, we are likely to see efforts to end poverty as benevolent (i.e., they will trigger prototypes for moral benevolence), though, again, not morally obligatory.[4]

---

3. I am leaving aside the issue of when and how we isolate causes. We will consider that in the next section.

4. As I have stressed, prototypes vary with context—our prototype for a dog in the context "Montana farm" is different from our prototype for a dog in the context "Manhattan

In the case of morality, prototype formation is almost certainly related to the triggering of emotion, as my reference to aversiveness suggests. As noted earlier, we have spontaneous empathic tendencies, derived in part from mirror systems in our brains. These tendencies help guide our moral judgments in the case of suffering (on empathy and the cognitive sources of moral development, see Blair and Prinz). For example, if we empathize with someone in poverty, we are much more likely to engage in moral evaluation of his or her condition initially. In addition, we may be more likely to assimilate the causes of that poverty to theft and more likely to see alleviation of poverty as morally obligatory. The emotions are, of course, crucial beyond their consequences for evaluation. Here as elsewhere, they provide the motivational force for action. We do not set out to maintain or change a situation based solely on abstract evaluation. We act only when we are moved to do so. We are moved specifically by emotion. As Zajonc explains, "cognitions of themselves are incapable of triggering an instrumental process, unless they first generate an emotion that mobilizes a motivational state capable of recruiting action" (47). Like other emotions, however, our empathic responses tend to decrease with habituation.[5]

Returning to the attribution of absolute moral culpability, we should note that this view has another peculiar feature. It presupposes that the (putatively) initiating act was a free and purely immoral choice, while the response was, in some sense, not free, but compelled by the initiating act.

---

apartment" (see Kahneman and Miller 140). The same point holds for prototypes of morality. In the case of poverty, it is certainly possible to have prototypes other than those just mentioned. This is, in part, a contextual matter as well. If we speak of poverty in the context of money, then the preceding prototypes are very likely. If we speak of poverty in the context of food, however, our prototypes shift. We may then see unequal division of food as prototypically immoral. This is likely to have different consequences for our moral evaluation of government policies and employer practices.

5. The cognitive tendencies just discussed help to explain why it is very easy for a society to drift toward repeated military aggression or toward other morally objectionable practices of corruption and cruelty. For example, when a practice such as torture is rigorously outlawed, we are unlikely to consider it morally normal. Indeed, torture is likely to be part of our prototype for immoral treatment of prisoners. Moreover, in these circumstances, we are more likely to experience empathic pain at the thought of someone subjected to torture. However, once a society begins to practice torture, people begin to shift their sense of moral normalcy. The averaging of their experiences alters their moral prototypes and they become emotionally habituated to the thought of the pain suffered by victims of, say, electrical shocks or near drowning. (On torture in the U.S. war on terrorism, see Hajjar and citations.) This is one reason why it is crucial to stop such practices (not only torture, but military aggression, violation of the laws of war, and so forth) early on. They very quickly become normalized, which makes them far more difficult to dislodge. Moreover, they are likely to have consequences throughout the social system (e.g., the habituation to the suffering of torture victims is likely to facilitate a much broader acceptance of cruelty).

Thus, the apparent immorality of the response does not taint the group responding, but accrues to the immorality of the initiating act. Consider again the idea that the bombings of September 11 gave rise to the war in Afghanistan. Someone who accepts this view is likely to assume that the pre-September 11 condition of, say, Iraq and Palestine was just or at least morally normal. They are also likely to assume that the September 11 bombings were a purely free and evil act, thus unaffected by preceding conditions. However, since the bombings were not just or morally normal, they compelled a violent response from the United States. In consequence, any suffering produced by the invasion of Afghanistan is to be blamed on al Qaeda and their allies, not on the government actually dropping the bombs.

Of course, the positing of a singular origin for grand events, the organization of causality by reference to blame (or praise), the intertwining of explanation and emotional response—these are not simply curious features. They are narrative features. They suggest that, in treating war, we do not engage in strict causal analysis. Rather, we tell stories. Stories certainly incorporate causal relations. But they do so in particular, cognitively biased ways. In technical terms, stories select, segment, and structure causal sequences. One important result of this is that stories involve, as Aristotle put it, a beginning, a middle, and an end. Aristotle's point seems trivial. But the feeling of triviality fades as soon as one recognizes that causality in the real world does not involve such components at all.[6] Stories only have a beginning, a middle, and an end because, when we tell stories or think in terms of stories, our minds pluck out causal sequences from the complex of events (selection); bound those sequences (segmentation); and bring them into comprehensible relations with one another (structuration).

Emotional Physics: How We Understand Causes

To understand stories, then, we need to consider causality, not in itself (as we do in natural science), but as it is spontaneously construed by the human

---

6. The general point has been recognized by a number of earlier authors. For example, Bennington remarks on "the faith in origins and ends which narration perpetuates" (132). Similarly, Breuilly notes that "the narrative form, with its assumption of a beginning, middle and end, could actually become an important component of the national movement" ("Approaches to Nationalism" 157). However, such observations are rarely developed into explanatory accounts, or even given a detailed descriptive treatment that would lay the groundwork for an explanatory account.

mind. As writers such as Ed Tan have suggested, our response to stories is animated, first of all, by interest. Only some aspects of the world excite our interest and thus draw our attentional focus. How does this occur? We have a set of prototypes that guide our judgments of and expectations about what we experience in ordinary life. We understand and evaluate the world, first of all, in terms of the normalcy defined by these prototypes. Commonly, our attentional focus is drawn to properties of events or situations that violate these prototypes. As Kahneman and Miller point out, we ask "a why question" when "a particular event is surprising," when there is "a contrast between an observation and a more normal [i.e., prototypical] alternative" (148; see also Frijda 272–73, 318, and 386 on attention to novelty or difference from expectation). We do not pay much attention if Jones is wearing a wristwatch on his wrist. We are more likely to take note if he is wearing one on his ankle. On the other hand, our interest in difference alone may fade quickly. Interest is intensified and sustained by emotional arousal. If someone is wearing an unusual tee shirt, I am likely to notice. But, without further emotional involvement, I am unlikely to keep the tee shirt active in working memory or to keep recalling it much past the initial perception. I am more likely to sustain interest, if I find the shirt funny, angering, or embarrassing. This results from the close relation between emotion and attention circuits in the brain (see Adolphs and Damasio 32–33).[7]

Emotional arousal not only sustains interest in one's environment. It focuses that interest. Specifically, emotional arousal stimulates our concern to isolate its cause. For example, if I feel fear, I need to understand just what has triggered the fear so that I can run away from it. It may seem that we just know what has caused an emotion. But this is not true. We need to infer the causes of our own emotions, more or less in the same way some third person would have to infer them (see Nisbett and Ross 226–27). As Frijda puts it, "One knows, generally, that one has an emotion; one does not always know why, and what exactly makes one have it; and if one does know, it is a construction, a hypothesis, like those one makes about the emotions of someone else" (464). In keeping with this, we are often mistaken in our attributions.

---

7. This relation is actually more complex than one might initially imagine. While emotion generally directs our attention toward relevant aspects of the environment or our bodies, there are conditions in which it might direct our attention away from such aspects. Simpson et al. present evidence in support of a model wherein "a situation that is evaluated as mildly threatening triggers the direction of attentional resources away from the stimulus." However, this diversion of attention is limited. As "the evaluated threat value of the stimulus increases, attention is directed back toward the stimulus" (692). This difference in attentional focus is parallel to the difference between mood repair and mood-congruent processing (see note 8).

There are many empirical studies of this phenomenon. For example, research indicates that our general emotional state will vary with such things as day of the week. However, we are likely to attribute our feelings to more perceptually and mnemonically salient objects. As Clore and Ortony explain, "people tend to experience their affective feelings as reactions to whatever happens to be in focus at the time" (27). As Zajonc expresses the point, "If the person is unable to specify either the origin or the target of affect he or she is experiencing, then this affect can attach itself to anything that is present at the moment" (48). Damasio cites research regarding "stimulation in a region of the left frontal lobe known as the supplementary motor area." As Damasio explains, the researchers "noted that electrical stimulation at a number of closely located sites consistently and exclusively evoked laughter." What is crucial for our purposes is that "the cause of the laughter was attributed to whichever object the patient was concentrating on at the time of the stimulation" (*Looking* 75).

Of course, this is not to say that our attributions are purely random. If I am sad, I am unlikely to blame my desk or the fact that my nose itches. Such extreme misattributions are not impossible. But clearly they are the exception rather than the rule. Two factors contribute crucially to constraining our causal attributions. Neither is a matter of abstract, rational inference. Rather, both are bound up with the operation of our emotion systems.

The first factor is perceptual. We have innate perceptual sensitivities to particular features of our environment—certain sounds, spatial relations, types of motion (or motion in general, as opposed to immobility), and so forth. These innate sensitivities are most often, perhaps always, potential emotion triggers or components of such emotion triggers. As Damasio explains, "we are wired to respond with an emotion, in preorganized fashion, when certain features of stimuli in the world or in our bodies are perceived" (*Descartes' Error* 131). Even when such features are not the cause of a given emotion, our innate sensitivity to these features gives them prominence in causal attribution.

The second factor is a matter of memories, specifically emotion-congruent memories, both episodic and semantic. When we experience anxiety in a current situation, that activates episodic memories of anxiety in earlier situations. As Oatley explains, "There is now substantial empirical evidence to indicate that when happy, happy memories come to mind, and when sad, sad memories come to mind" (*Best* 201).[8] As Bower puts

---

8. On some of the complexities of this, see Forgas, "Affect and Information" and Eich and Macaulay. There are circumstances when we engage in "mood repair" rather than mood-

it, when one "emotion is aroused ... activation will spread out along its connections, thus priming and bringing into readiness ... associated ideas and memories" (389). Common properties of the current and former situations (e.g., the presence of the same person) become prominent, defining likely candidates for causal attribution. A current experience also activates prototypes of emotion causation from semantic memory. These guide our causal attributions as well.

A common example is attributing one's emotional excitation to a romantic partner when the arousal in fact results from more diffuse somatic and environmental factors. As Gilbert and Wilson point out, citing empirical research on the topic, people "may mistakenly believe that a person is attractive when, in fact, their pounding pulse is being caused by the swaying of a suspension bridge" (183). A romantic partner is a likely candidate for causal attribution, and misattribution, for perceptual reasons (most obviously, the presence of emotion-triggering secondary sexual characteristics), memory-based reasons (due to personal recollections of romantic feelings in the past), and semantic reasons (as a romantic partner is a prototypical cause of emotional arousal).

The operation of our emotion systems, including their operation in causal attribution, is bound up with their evolutionary history. In recent years, cognitivists have emphasized the adaptive function of emotion. For example, Panksepp states that "brain emotive systems were designed through evolutionary selection to respond in prepared ways to certain environmental events" (Panksepp, *Affective Neuroscience* 123). A crucial adaptive function of emotion is that it usurps rational deliberation. For example, fear causes us to run rather than try to puzzle out our options, "lost in the byways of ... calculation" (Damasio, *Descartes' Error* 172), as a predator approaches. In order for emotion to have this adaptive function, it has to simplify. One important aspect of emotional simplification is valencing. It is a commonplace of emotion research that ambivalent inputs tend to cycle through our emotion circuits, producing a valenced output. The inputs may be partially anger-producing and partially fear-producing, but the output is likely to be anger (with a confrontation response) or fear (with a flight response), not some combination of the two. As Ito and Cacioppo put it, "The affect system has evolved to produce bipolar endpoints because they provide both clear bivalent action tendencies and harmonious and stable subjective experiences" (69). One aspect of this simplification (not widely

---

congruent processing. These cases do not bear on our present concerns as mood repair tends to divert us from causal attribution—or it follows the same general principles of causal attribution, but with a different emotional valence.

discussed as such) occurs in causal attribution. Just as inputs may bear on different emotions, they may derive from different causes. Just as outputs tend to reduce ambivalence, they tend to limit causal attributions as well. Elizabeth Anscombe, Nico Frijda, and others have drawn a useful distinction between the cause of an emotion and the object of an emotion (see Anscombe 16 and Frijda 190). The cause is what gives rise to an emotion. The object is something toward which we direct the emotion. In these terms, the cause of an emotion may be diffuse and ambivalent. However, the object of an emotion is likely to be singular and valenced. The point is obviously inseparable from the indirect nature of causal attribution.

Consider a hypothetical example. John has a range of experiences that include enough frustration to cycle through to, roughly, anger. Many of these experiences are miniscule irritations (e.g., his shoe pinches). The most perceptually and mnemonically salient aspect of John's environment, and one of the most semantically prototypical sources of frustration, is his spouse, Jane. As a result, John blames Jane for his anger. (As Tolstoy wrote, "it is difficult for a man who is dissatisfied not to reproach someone else, and someone, too, who is closest to him, with whatever he happens to be dissatisfied" [489].) This is largely true even when John is self-consciously aware that Jane is not in fact responsible for his frustration. Higher cortical processes allow John to understand that Jane is not the relevant cause. However, the emotion systems are distinct from these higher cortical systems. The latter may exert inhibitory control over the former, but they are not always fully successful (on the inhibitory operation of the cortex with respect to the largely subcortical emotion systems, see LeDoux and Phelps, *Emotional* 165). This may be due in part to the fact that strong emotions tend to usurp attentional focus. Thus, they tend to usurp the very aspects of the (cortical) working memory system (see LeDoux and Phelps, *Emotional* 277) that would otherwise inhibit the emotion systems. Weakness of inhibition seems particularly likely when there is no strong emotional support for the inhibition, which is to say when there is no countervailing emotion currently triggered by the object (e.g., if John has no strong emotion directing his attention toward affectionate, rather than angry memories of his wife or sustaining his cortical recollection of her innocence). Thus, there is no emotional impetus to seek other explanations.[9] Finally, in the context of strong emotions, it is almost impos-

---

9. Neurobiologically, this may be understood in terms of conflict monitoring in a "two-part system" (Ito et al. 198). First, the anterior cingulate cortex "monitors competition between processes that conflict during task performance" (Carter et al. 748). Second, "cognitive control" may be implemented "to reduce discrepancies" (Ito et al. 198). This account suggests

sible to inhibit one attribution for an extended period without substituting an alternative. John is not terribly likely to successfully inhibit blaming Jane if he simply thinks "It's not Jane's fault." Indeed, this keeps his attentional focus on Jane in the context of an angry mood that activates his anger-relevant memories, biases his interpretation of current interactions, and so forth. He is much more likely to inhibit this attribution if he thinks, "It's my boss's fault."

While the point may apply to any emotion, the situation is particularly extreme in the case of anger, which is, again, a crucial emotion for the mobilization of nationalist action in war and related forms of confrontational or aggressive nationalism. Eisenberg points out that, "People induced to feel anger also are likely to attribute responsibility or blame to others . . . which could increase the probability of aggressive behavior" (683–84). Indeed, Berkowitz explains, "It is customary for psychologists to interpret aversively generated aggression as being directed toward the lessening or elimination of the source of the noxious stimulation." However, Berkowitz's research indicates "that the goal of this reaction is frequently the injury of the attacked target" ("Towards" 19). Crucially, this holds even when it is clear that the object of the aggression is not the cause of the anger, as in some remarkable research done by Berkowitz and his colleagues (see 19). Moreover, citing animal studies, Berkowitz points out that "pain evidently created an impulse to aggression spurring *work in the interest of obtaining a victim*" (34; emphasis added). Insofar as the studies apply to humans as well, they suggest that, once we feel angry, we are likely to look for a target for our angry aggression. This takes us beyond spontaneous misattribution to a sort of willful misattribution. In other words, in the case of anger, we are actually motivated *not* to inhibit attributions that we know are false. Instead, we are motivated to act on them. When socially coordinated, then, even private feelings of pain and frustration may contribute quite powerfully to war.

Consider, for example, Americans who blame Saddam Hussein for the September 11 bombings, with the practical consequences this has for

---

that some sort of conflict must be present for the possibility of corrective processes to arise. Competing emotions with regard to a particular object would presumably produce such a conflict. The absence of such conflicting emotional inputs would, then, reduce the likelihood of corrective processes. Moreover, such processes are probably interrelated with attentional orientation and executive functions of working memory, perhaps via the dorsolateral prefrontal cortex. Kondo and colleagues have shown that "attention shifting for cognitive control" depends on the network linking the anterior cingulate cortex and the dorsolateral prefrontal cortex. Chein and Fiez cite research indicating that the dorsolateral prefrontal cortex "may contribute to domain-independent executive processes such as response inhibition and attentional selection."

supporting the invasion of Iraq. It is quite possible that many of them know that Hussein was not connected with the bombings. However, media coverage of governmental statements has repeatedly drawn their attentional focus to terrorist threats against the United States and toward Saddam Hussein. This has triggered anger (and fear) responses that are associated with Hussein and thus tend to usurp or limit attentional focus when Hussein is under consideration. Moreover, individual Americans' personal experiences of anger motivate them to seek a target for aggression. The motivation is not insignificant for, as Berkowitz points out, again citing animal research, "the inability to carry out the instigated aggression was physiologically harmful" ("Towards" 34). Finally, few Americans have any countervailing emotions that would draw attention to Hussein's innocence in these particular cases. As a result, inhibitory cognitive processes—processes that impede our emotional tendency to take Hussein as the object of anger—are unlikely to be triggered. Indeed, the victim-seeking that results from personal anger provides a motivation not to initiate or sustain such inhibitory processes.

In cases such as John and his spouse, as well as Saddam Hussein, misattribution is facilitated by another feature of our cognitive architecture. For a particular set of emotions, we tend to attribute causality to intentional agency. Speaking of cognition more generally, Boyer notes that, "It is part of our constant, everyday humdrum cognitive functioning that we interpret all sorts of cues in our environment, not just events but also the way things are, as the result of some agent's actions . . . our agency-detection systems are biased toward overdetection" (145). The point applies *a fortiori* to emotion. This sort of agency attribution is our default tendency for such emotions as anger, fear, gratitude, trust, and attachment. These emotions tend to orient our attention toward an agent, whom we are then inclined to blame or praise.

In keeping with this, as we discussed in chapter 2, a crucial aspect of both emotional response and causal attribution is our assumption that agents have a dispositional attitude toward us. For example, we fear certain animals and that fear is related to our view that they are disposed to eat us. Many emotional responses seem to rest in part on a preliminary, unselfconscious categorization of agents into benevolent and malevolent.[10] It is worth reviewing some aspects of such categorization in the present context. Again, we seem to have a bias toward categorization as malevolent, which may be overcome by familiarity.[11] The evolutionary advantage of

10. For further discussion, see my *The Mind and Its Stories*, 254–55.
11. As discussed earlier, the positive effect of mere familiarity is well attested in psycho-

this bias is obvious. There is a greater risk in underestimating threats than in underestimating opportunities for aid.

Evolutionary developments lead not only to a bias toward a default categorization of individual agents as malevolent. They also lead to a default categorization of groups. Negatively, this occurs when we recognize that certain groups, such as lions and snakes, are more malevolent or dangerous than our default. Positively, this occurs when we recognize that certain groups, such as sheep, are less malevolent or dangerous. The former allows for increased caution in critical situations. The latter facilitates the pursuit of opportunities in circumstances where a default presumption might have been overly inhibitory.

While this tendency seems largely unexceptionable in the cases of predatory animals and herbivores, it becomes much more problematic when applied to other people, particularly out-groups. The function of such categorization is the same in the case of out-groups as it is in the case of lions. However, in the case of lions, as well as snakes and sheep, the division is, first of all, a matter of species. That is obviously not the case with humans. We do not categorize unfamiliar people as benevolent or as malevolent based on identifying their species as human. In the case of humans, then, a subspecies distinction operates to perform an initial sorting into *prima facie* trustworthy and untrustworthy agents, potential enemies and potential friends. This is, of course, the fundamental division between in-groups and out-groups.

As this indicates, identity categories may very strongly bias our moral/causal attributions. As Herzfeld puts it, "ethnic and national terms are moral terms in that they imply a qualitative differentiation between insiders and outsiders"; indeed, conversely, "all moral value terms are to some extent negotiable markers for the lines of social or cultural inclusion and exclusion" (43). In some cases, the bias may be so strong that it resists the familiarity effect. Oatley reports a disturbing experiment in which subjects were shown photographs of people from different races. Their emotional responses to the pictures were monitored using neuroimaging. Oatley summarizes the results, explaining that the familiarity effect operated for whites with respect to white faces and blacks with respect to black faces, but not across races. As Oatley explains, "whereas the faces of one's

---

logical research (see, for example, Zajonc 35). This is most obviously explained by a categorization bias toward assumed malevolence (or, more generally, danger). If we see someone or something many times and he/she/it invariably proves innocuous, this tends to work against a malevolent or threatening categorization. If we assume an initial neutral categorization, the ameliorative effect of familiarity would be more difficult to explain.

own ethnic group become less threatening with repeated viewing, those of another group may remain threatening" (*Emotions* 73).

This suggests that the malevolence default operates at two levels—individual and collective. In the case of in-group members, only the individual default is in place. In other words, we distrust unfamiliar members of an in-group only as unfamiliar individuals. We do not distrust the group as a whole. Thus, our distrust of an unfamiliar in-group member is overcome by familiarity with him or her individually. However, in the case of out-group members, both defaults are in place. In other words, we distrust out-group members as unfamiliar individuals and as members of a malevolent group. Moreover, the group default appears to be more emotionally consequential at least in certain cases. As a result, overcoming the individual default through familiarity may not undermine our distrust of individual out-group members as long as our out-group categorization of those individuals remains strong.

In sum, our emotion systems tend to simplify causal attribution by reducing multiple causes to a single object, frequently a single agent. This tendency is particularly forceful in the case of anger, where our monitoring for causal misattribution may be more than usually ineffective. Our attributions are often guided by prior categorizations of agents as malevolent or benevolent. Those categorizations, in turn, frequently rely on highly robust, familiarity-resistant identity categories (along with associated prototypes—which, in this case, may be stereotypes).

Back to the Beginning

We can now give some explanatory account of story structure and our causally inadequate understanding of war. Our emotion systems lead us to think of causal sequences, not in terms of the complex, interacting systems of natural science, but in terms of stories. This is because our emotion systems create interest in and focus attention on nonordinary, perceptually and mnemonically salient objects that are prototypical for a particular emotion. We then tend to attribute causality to these salient objects. This simplifies causal attribution in precisely the way that natural science tries to avoid. (As Pascal Boyer explains, "scientific activity is quite 'unnatural' given our cognitive dispositions" [321].) The result of this is an inclination toward the projection of singular and absolute causal origins.

Simplification, in this case, is a form of selection. It combines with our tendency to segment and structure the causes of events in terms of benevolent or, more commonly, malevolent intentions. One result is the common generation of initial complications—early events that necessitate the development of the story—by the malevolent actions of some antagonist. We find this to some degree in all three cross-cultural narrative prototypes—romantic, heroic, and sacrificial tragicomedy. For example, in the standard romantic plot, the lovers are separated by an interfering parent. For our present purposes, the most important of these three prototypes is the heroic, for our emplotment of the nation generally, and of wars particularly, is first of all an emplotment in terms of the heroic prototype. That prototype manifests the malevolent initiating moment most starkly. Moreover, it does so through group-based categorization. Specifically, it sets out a malevolent attack by an out-group—usually an invasion by a foreign power—as the absolute and singular origin of the narrative conflict.

Beyond these matters, which bear directly on narrative beginnings, our cognitive dispositions have other consequences for our understanding of and our action regarding war as well. One such consequence is that we tend to experience our own emotionally guided (malevolent) response to the "initiating event" as compelled by the event, thus not morally blameworthy. This is particularly true when we have no attentional focus on the harmful consequences of our acts (e.g., enemy casualties that would trigger empathy). In contrast, we tend to see the (malevolent) actions of the out-group as deriving, not from prior events, but from dispositional group properties. Thus, their actions are immoral in themselves, and symptomatic of an underlying immorality of character. (This is, in effect, a version of our general tendency to see ourselves as responding to circumstances, while we see others as acting according to fixed character traits; see Holland et al. 222–24.)

A further result is that arguments against absolute and singular origins for conflict strike us as similar to the arguments of out-groups. Specifically, we tend to understand such arguments as positing a different origin for conflict, rather than as disputing origins per se. Due to the cognitive and affective constraints on our spontaneous causal understandings, we readily assimilate such arguments to justifications for the out-group actions. Simplifying somewhat, we might say that our spontaneous causal attributions give us two obvious alternatives—our own version of causal attribution and a parallel version offered by the out-group, a version in which we are dispositionally malevolent and engage in aggression that constitutes the absolute and singular origin of the conflict. If these are the two options, then any argument that is not of the former sort would seem to be of the latter sort. Of course, in many cases, attacks on antiwar arguments are duplicitous. Politicians know perfectly well that, for example, antiwar protestors are not supporters of Saddam Hussein. However, the point is that their objections to protestors can be broadly persuasive—despite their falsity and illogic—because of our cognitive propensities.

Finally, insofar as they involve strong emotions, our spontaneous attributions of causality may remain at least partially impervious to our knowledge about actual causal relations. In other words, our emotion systems may continue to spontaneously project a single, absolute, malevolent origin to conflict, even when higher cortical systems have inferred that this is not the case. I have suggested three possible reasons for this. (There are undoubtedly others as well.) First, our emotional responses may usurp working memory, thus the inferential processes that should inhibit our spontaneous causal attributions. Second, we often have no countervailing emotions that would turn us toward alternative analyses (e.g., we often have no positive feeling toward the individuals or groups we are blaming). This means that possible alternatives receive little attentional focus or elaboration even when they occur to us. Moreover, we do not have any particular motivation to seek such alternatives when they do not occur to us. The point holds most obviously in situations where we do not have to seek causes at all, as when the government tells us that the absolute and singular origin of a particular conflict was the unprovoked malevolent aggression of al Qaeda, the Taliban, and Saddam Hussein. Third, in the case of anger, our propensity toward victim-seeking actually motivates us to divert attention from anything that might qualify or defer our isolation of an object for that anger.

The Sense of an Ending

I have been speaking of beginnings. But similar points hold about endings as well. For example, as I write, I imagine that most Americans believe that the war in Afghanistan has ended. There was an evil regime allied with al Qaeda. We fought and defeated that regime. Now the country is free and peaceful. But, of course, that is not the actual situation. As Christian Parenti explains, "this country of 20–25 million inhabitants is an embryonic narco-mafia state, where politics rely on paramilitary networks engaged in everything from poppy farming, heroin processing and vote rigging to extortion and the commercial smuggling of commodities like electronics and auto parts. And while the Western pundit class applauds the recent Afghan elections, the people [in Afghanistan] suffer renewed exploitation at the hands of America's local partners" ("Who"; see also "Postcard" on the "wave of fraud and technical errors" that led to widespread denunciation of the Afghan elections as "illegitimate"). Scheer discusses the commonplace view that the war in Afghanistan has had a happy democratic outcome. He goes on to point out that "the bulk of the country is still run, de facto, by competing warlords dependent on the opium trade, which now accounts for 60 percent of the Afghan economy" ("Cultivating").[12]

Again, multiple and complex causal sequences precede any supposedly initiating event. Nothing is a true beginning. By the same token, multiple and complex causal sequences follow any supposedly concluding event—as the case of Afghanistan illustrates. Nothing is a true conclusion. Stories have endings. Social life does not. Here too, however, our emotion systems foster this emplotment. To say that the war in Afghanistan has ended is to say that there is no longer anything there to pay attention to, anything to trigger our emotional arousal and thus draw attentional focus.

To some extent, our shift in attentional focus is simply a matter of chance. As I write, the news media have not continued to report on Afghanistan to the degree that they did previously. But this is not a complete explanation. Most people seem to feel that the situation in Afghanistan has been resolved.[13] The mere absence of reporting could give rise to a sense that we just do not know what is happening; it could foster a feeling of incompleteness, rather than resolution. But our sense of an ending is much the same as our sense of a beginning. As we have seen, if there is nothing that inspires our emotional response, thus draws attentional focus, then there is, from our point of view, no event that has begun. There is, in other words, no cause. This is just as true at "the conclusion" of a sequence of events as it is at "the start" of a sequence of events. As soon as there is no longer anything that inspires or sustains our emotional response, the story is over. There are no new causes, in our subjective sense of causality, thus there are no new effects. In other words, once again, our primary relation to

---

12. Needless to say, these statements do not represent the entirety of the situation in Afghanistan. My point is not that the standard view of Afghanistan leaves out some peripheral phenomena or that Parenti and Scheer say every possible true thing that can be said about Afghanistan. My point is simply that research undertaken by these writers indicates that an accurate account of broad trends and general conditions in Afghanistan stands rather in contradiction with the standard view.

13. I realize, of course, that the situation in Afghanistan is volatile, and the tendencies of the news media are changeable. In consequence, one or the other may have changed very much by the time this book is in print. Unfortunately, I cannot predict the future and devise an example that will work better in a year or two, when the book is published—or for years after that when the book is read. I therefore can only ask that readers take the example to refer to the time of writing, rather than the time of reading.

causal sequences is defined by our emotion systems. Those systems cluster our causal inferences into finite sequences based on interest and emotional effect. Emotional effect is contrasted with normalcy. Causal sequences arise out of normalcy due to emotional change. Causal sequences dissolve back into normalcy when the emotion dissipates.

But just how does this dissolution into normalcy occur? Most often, it happens through the achievement of an aim. Specifically, the initiating emotional change gives rise to some aim (e.g., defeating the enemy in the war). This aim is simplified in precisely the manner that the causal attribution is simplified. Just as we tend to narrow praise or blame, isolating a single agent or a limited number of related agents, so too we tend to narrow our actional response. Indeed, there is a sort of double simplification in the case of actional response. First, there is the simplification regarding the object; then there is a further simplification regarding the action itself. More exactly, we may distinguish between the larger, functional purpose of our response to an emotionally arousing situation—a purpose of ending or (in the case of positive emotions) sustaining that situation—and the concrete goal that defines our practical action. In the case of fear, our functional purpose may be to end a current threat. Our concrete, practical action may simply be a matter of, say, leaving a dark alley, if the threat is a possible mugger; alternatively, it may be something more complex and difficult to achieve, such as getting tenure, if the threat is losing one's job. (As the second example makes clear, a concrete, practical action, in this sense, is not necessarily a spontaneous actional outcome.)

One result of this is that we may and often do form a clear idea of when an emotion episode—thus a causal sequence—is (or should be) complete. Jones feels anxiety. Perhaps it is the result of many factors. But he isolates job insecurity. He therefore plans to complete the work necessary to get tenure. The plan sets an end-point for the emotion episode (or, more accurately in this case, the recurring sequence of associated emotion episodes). Of course, in some cases, Jones will not feel the relief he expected to feel when he does get tenure. However, the crucial point is that the concrete goal provides a projected resolution to the trajectory of the emotion. As such, it defines a possible "end" to the causal sequence (as construed by his emotion systems). Put differently, it defines a possible story. Moreover, Jones is likely to believe that the earlier anxiety has ended—thus that the story has reached its conclusion—even when his anxiety returns. This is because he will probably attribute the post-tenure anxiety to a new cause. In other words, he will select, segment, and structure it into a distinct causal sequence. He will understand it as a new story. This is particularly likely if there is some period, however brief, in which he does not experience anxiety following the tenure decision. Given the episodic nature of emotion, this is almost certainly going to be the case.

The consequences for nationalism in general, and war in particular, are considerable, particularly when we understand the ways in which emotion-defined stories bear on such events as the September 11 bombings and the invasion of Afghanistan. The United States began by blaming al Qaeda as an absolute origin for the bombings. We blamed the Taliban as well, for giving governmental support to al Qaeda. This is a standard narrative pattern. Stories commonly involve not only heroes and enemies, but sidekicks, characters who aid the hero or the enemy. The character of the sidekick, too, is inseparable from our emotion systems and from our causal attributions based on those systems. Specifically, our tendency to form in-groups and out-groups on the flimsiest pretext extends to cases where we have isolated a particular antagonist. If my attentional focus is on the harm Doe has done to me, my inclination is to categorize all other agents in relation to that harm and its consequences. Specifically, my inclination is to view other people in terms of whether they are likely to help or hinder my pursuit of the goals that arise from my anger at that harm. During an anger episode, then, I am likely to evaluate everyone else in terms of whether they are "on my side" or "on Doe's side." I, in effect, form new in-groups and out-groups based on the central division resulting from the (simplified) causal attribution of the emotion and its (simplified) concrete goals. Moreover, these new, ad hoc group definitions may interact with more stable identity categories producing more fine-grained responses. For example, when other members of an important identity category do not take my side in an anger episode, I am likely to feel betrayed, even if they are merely neutral. This is, of course, one reason for the widespread feeling in the United States that France had betrayed us over Iraq. The case of the Taliban and al Qaeda was, of course, different from that of France. The Taliban fell into an identity category shared by al Qaeda (roughly, "militant Islamists"). This served to reenforce their categorization as part of the enemy out-group, and to intensify American feelings of anger toward them.[14]

But to get a sense of the narrative trajectory of the war (rather than its character types), we need to consider our emotional aims in the war. The

---

14. Peter Rabinowitz rightly pointed out to me that the Taliban had formerly fallen into the category of "anti-Soviet freedom fighters." It might seem that this would make the transition to an enemy out-group difficult. In fact, this is not much of an issue. The question would be—by September of 2001, for whom did the Taliban count as anti-Soviet freedom fighters? I suspect that, by that time, very, very few Americans thought of the Taliban in this way.

functional aim of most Americans in the invasion of Afghanistan was to end the danger from al Qaeda (an aim responding to fear) and to punish al Qaeda and their collaborators, which is to say, everyone "on their side" (an aim responding to anger).[15] Our concrete goal, however, was simply to destroy the Taliban-led state. We did that. Thus, our emotional story ended. The Taliban-led state is no longer there as a danger or as an object of anger. It does not matter if the successor regime is a gang of election-rigging heroin pushers. Our emotion systems organized our thought about and response to Afghanistan in such a way as to define a concrete resolution for the war. We reached that resolution, whatever happens to be going on in Afghanistan now. Note that this is true even if events in Afghanistan suggest that our functional aims have not been met by the achievement of our concrete goals. Of course, if news coverage insistently pointed out that our functional aims have not been met in Afghanistan, it is likely that most Americans would reassess the situation. Indeed, something of that sort is occurring in Iraq. But, as the case of Iraq shows, it takes a great deal—perhaps including significant numbers of American deaths—to undermine our sense of an ending when concrete goals have been achieved.

In sum, our sense of an ending, like our sense of a beginning, is inseparable from our emotional response to events and situations. It is, again, our emotion systems that determine which deviations from (prototype-defined) normalcy initiate our simplified isolation of causes. Our emotion systems also determine how those deviations fold back into normalcy by specifying concrete, practical goals. The achievement of these goals commonly (though not invariably) results in the dissipation of the motivating emotion (e.g., anger or fear), and a return to a sense of emotional normalcy. Again, that return to a sense of normalcy defines an ending for our emotion systems, thus a conclusion to our continued focusing of attention and our isolation of causal sequences. Even in cases where the emotion does not dissipate, we often understand the continuing emotion as a new emotion episode, deriving from a new cause. In short, our emotion systems lead us to select, segment, and structure the world in the form of stories. These stories include heroes, villains, and sidekicks; beginnings and endings; non-normal conditions provoking a pursuit of concrete goals, frustration of that pursuit, then achievement or abandonment of the goals, with a consequent return to normalcy. All this is defined and organized by feeling.

---

15. I say "most Americans" as it is not at all clear that these were the functional aims of the government. Those aims were much more complex, involving control of oil, establishing a right to invade enemy nations, and so forth; they may have had nothing to do with ending the danger from al Qaeda or punishing al Qaeda militants and their supporters.

But this is only, so to speak, part of the story. Our emplotment of nationalism and nationalistic events, such as war, is not merely broad and schematic. It involves levels of specificity as well. Indeed, the most consequential aspects of emplotment are not those of heroes and villains, beginnings and endings in general. Rather, the most consequential aspects are those of the standard character types and the standard beginnings and endings. For example, our simplified isolation of causes and our simplified imagination of goals do not arise from nowhere. They are most often specifications of prototypical openings and conclusions, which is to say, the openings and conclusions of our prototypical narratives (heroic, sacrificial, and romantic). Again, the general beginning for a narrative is an emotionally significant deviation from normalcy. Prototypical beginnings would include the following (for, in turn, heroic, sacrificial, and romantic narratives): (1) An invasion or other attack by a foreign country and/or a usurpation of political authority within the home society. (2) The violation of a divine or natural moral principle leading to social devastation. (3) Two people falling in love, but being kept apart by social hierarchies or antagonisms. I have already made some reference to these, as they turn up repeatedly in nationalist works. I will consider them in more detail below. Before going on to those prototypes, however, we need to consider one further constituent of narrative—development principles, the procedures that allow us to move from narrative generalities to narrative particulars.

DEVELOPMENT PRINCIPLES
Subnational Diversity and the Land

Individual narratives result not only from schemas and prototypes, but from techniques for particularizing and extending those schemas and prototypes. Put simply, when telling a story, we need some way of getting from the general structures to the particulars of the plot. I refer to these techniques as "development principles." There are, of course, many development principles. I would like to isolate two that have unusually significant nationalist functions. The first concerns characters. It consists in multiplying parallel characters of a certain type. The second treats the scene in which the story takes place. It maps out a particular geographical trajectory in the course of the narrative.

Though stories usually have one main character, they most often have a number of ancillary characters as well. In a heroic plot, we find a range of warriors; in a romantic plot, the love of the main couple may be mirrored in the less central stories of a second or even third couple. In the case of nationalist narratives, this multiplication is often used for anti-subnationalist ends. The risk of having a single hero is that the peculiarities of the hero could be taken in a subnationalistic way. The hero's region, ethnicity, or class may suggest to people from other regions, ethnicities, or classes that they do not share in the national heroic ideal. This problem can be overcome to some degree if subsidiary heroes come from different regions, ethnicities, and classes. We find cases of this ranging from Greek and Sanskrit epics[16] through a number of Shakespeare's plays to modern films.

Consider, for example, the *Iliad*. The Greek heroes represent a range of locations in Greece. Telamonian Ajax is from Salamis, in the central eastern part of Greece; Agamemnon, the leader, is from Mycenae, a central location; Diomedes represents Argos and Tiryns, south and west of Mycenae; Menelaus, of Sparta, takes us still further south and further west; Nestor brings us to Pylos, as far south as Sparta, but on the western coast; Odysseus is from Ithaca, an island off the west coast and well north of Pylos or even Mycenae (see the entries in Harvey for these characters; see also the map on 476). Another example may be found in the *Rāmāyaṇa* in which the heroes who fight with Rāma include two prominent figures from the region of the Narmadā River in west central India (Dhūmra and Jāmbavān; see Vālmīki, vol. 3, 65), two from the Kiṣkindhā forest in the southeast (Sugrīva and Hanumān; see the map in Mack 836), and an ally from the island of Laṅkā to the far south (Vibhīṣaṇa)—with Rāma and his brother themselves representing the northeast. The point applies not only to fictions, but to the emplotment of real events in history, news, and popular imagination. To take a small example, Maas quotes a French nationalist on how "the soldiers of 1870" had "hastened here from all corners of the land" (219; my translation).

Again, this strategy is not confined to regionalism. It may also operate against ethnic particularism, along with such variants as clan particularism in relevant societies. For instance, in the final episode of *The Epic of Son-Jara*, several figures are celebrated in addition to Son-Jara himself—the warrior Fa-Koli (from the Kantè line, and a defector from the enemy), the warrior Tura Magan (a Tarawere), and the loyal bard Doka the Cat (from

---

16. For present purposes, it does not matter whether these works had anything like a national function when they began to circulate. The fact that they have been taken up for nationalist purposes is all that is needed for this regional diversity to have a nationalist function. On the other hand, the existence of this development principle does suggest that there was something like a nationalist use of such works from the outset. Otherwise, it is difficult to explain the recurrence of this sort of character multiplication, a multiplication guided by regional and other identity-based differences.

the Kuyatè line). Along with Son-Jara (whose parents are from the Kònatè and Kòndè lines), these represent and unite a range of important, distinct lineage groups.

Of course, there is always a risk in this practice. Representing regional or other differences may have the effect of making those differences more salient. However, insofar as people are already aware of such differences, their exclusion from the work most often poses a greater risk.

Again, the second important development principle concerns scene—specifically, the land. I have emphasized the importance of the relation to the national land as one distinguishing feature of national identity. The most obvious way of engendering an emotionally consequential relation to the land is through actual travel, direct experience of the land. However, the same or even superior effects may be produced by the careful manipulation of a reader's relation to the land in literature, or of a viewer's relation to the land in film. The idea has been widely recognized by nationalists. For example, Trumpener explains that some nationalist "Irish and Scottish antiquaries" believed that "bardic performance binds the nation together" and "reanimates" the "national landscape" (xii). Literature and film foster affective attachment to the nation in part by creating a sense of familiarity, as discussed in chapter 2. But they do so also by associating the places with the reader's feelings for the hero and for the story. For example, the deep attachment some Joyceans feel for parts of Dublin is due entirely to the treatment of those places in *Ulysses*, largely their association with Bloom or Stephen.

One of the most common techniques of narrative development is the insertion of a journey, sending the hero on some quest or otherwise making him or her travel. This is routinely put to nationalist use when the hero proceeds on a tour of the national territory, passing through different regions that are united as part of a single, national story. In modern geographical terms, Rāma traces a path from northeast India, to the central west coast, then down to the southern tip, then across the water to Laṅkā (see the map of Rāma's route in Mack 836). If Rāma is not precisely the ruler of these areas, he does in effect establish his supremacy over them by defeating the "demons" he encounters or entering into alliances in which he is clearly the dominant partner. A similar point applies to the Tamil epic *Cilappatikāram*. As Peterson explains, "Like the journeys in . . . the *Rāmāyaṇa* [with respect to India more generally], the journeys of Kaṇṇaki and Kōvalaṉ [in the *Cilappatikāram*] trace a map of the Tamil land" (1249).

These national tours not only bind different regions together. When representing an ancient period—particularly in narratives that are themselves ancient—they also indicate that the national home and its territorial extent are enduring rather than ephemeral. An ancestral claim on the territory carries over—especially if it is bound up with a divine mandate, as is often the case. We see this clearly in the case of Rāma, an incarnation of God. A similar point holds for Israel and the story of King David (which we will consider in the next chapter). When David travels through Israel and Judah, he marks out a nation that many modern Israelis have seen as proper for their own contemporary state. Moreover, this ancestral linkage historicizes the land, and makes it resonant. By historicizing particular sites, the epic turns them into landmarks—thus places for visitation, places to which people might travel, which thus serve to render national categorial identity salient in a more concrete, active, nontextual way. Consider the epic of Son-Jara. One version of the poem urges the listener or reader to visit the landmarks of Mali, thus experiencing the geographical place, and recalling its history: "At Tigan you will find the forest dear to Sundiata. . . . Go to Ka-ba and you will see the clearing of Kouroukan Fougan, where the great assembly took place which gave Sundiata's empire its constitution," and so forth (Niane 83). Other instances of this sort include the putative birthplace of Rāma, a central point of conflict in contemporary Indian nationalist politics, or, in contemporary Israel/Palestine, the Temple Mount, the location of David's altar and Solomon's temple.

As the example of the Temple Mount suggests, one further function of national tours is the establishment of a national center. Often, the tour of the land is structured in such a way as to define a single geographical reference point. The nation is not toured as an undifferentiated and neutral geographical expanse. Rather, the national journey suggests a complex of geographical relations, often relations that point to a center. Jerusalem, particularly the Temple Mount, is, again, an obvious case, manifest, for example, in the physical orientation of Jewish prayer. As we will discuss in the next chapter, this centrality is developed in the crucial heroic narrative of David and Solomon. Another obvious instance is Mecca in the story of Muhammad—a heroic tragicomedy starting from the unjust denial of Muhammad's leadership through his exile to his triumphant return. (Though Islam obviously defines a religious identity, it has strong national elements as well, including a governing structure and a sense of in-group territory in the geographical division between *dar al-islam* and *dar al-harb,* the lands of Islam or submission and the lands of war.) Needless to say, Rome has this function in Virgil's *Aeneid,* and in the empire for which it was written. Ayodhyā takes this central place in the *Rāmāyaṇa,* and Hindu nationalists have sought to revive that function in the refashioning of Indian nationalism. Such a central focal point allows all the diverse regions of the country, all the people from around the nation, to imagine themselves in relation to a single place. It fosters national identification by allowing individuals to locate themselves relative to one another imaginatively, by orienting them all toward an enduring, ancestral center.

PROTOTYPICAL NARRATIVE STRUCTURES
Heroic, Romantic, and Sacrificial

In the foregoing sections, I spoke, first, of the most general narrative structures and, second, of some principles that guide the production of particular stories. But, as is so often the case, the cognitively crucial level is in between. It is the level of prototypes. Considerable research suggests that prototypes guide our semantic understanding generally. If I am told that there is a bird in the backyard or if I am asked to draw a bird, I imagine a prototypical bird—roughly a robin. I do not imagine an ostrich, even though a bare definition of "bird" might cover ostriches no less than robins. The same point holds for stories. There are stories that are prototypical, just as there are birds that are prototypical. When I set out to write a story, I begin with a story prototype, just as I begin with a bird prototype when I set out to draw a bird. One might expect that these prototypes would be very diverse, across and even within cultures. In fact, they are not diverse at all. As I stressed in the introduction, only three prototypes seem common, not merely in literature, but in the emplotment of nationalism. These prototypes particularize a more general schema (which is itself more particular than a minimal definition of "story" in terms of necessary and sufficient conditions). As discussed in the introduction, that schema involves a person pursuing a goal, with some sort of emotional distress because he or she lacks the goal; it also involves a series of non-normal events and actions in the initial establishment and subsequent pursuit of the goal, events and actions that are emotionally engaging for a reader or listener; finally, it involves the return of the events to normalcy, most often by the achievement of the goal, but in some cases (tragic cases) by the recognition that the goal is not achievable. The goals pursued by the protagonists are necessarily goals that the protagonists believe will contribute toward happiness. In their most extreme forms, they are conditions that the protagonists believe are key elements of living well. But happiness goals are like anything else; their most consequential semantic forms are prototypical. The point holds particularly for narratives that are designed for a broad public. The stories I tell my wife or that she tells me may be guided by our own individual and idiosyncratic goals. But for stories to appeal to a broader audience, the goals at issue should have broader appeal. Prototypical goals are precisely the goals that have broader appeal and that thereby define narrative prototypes.

In *The Mind and Its Stories*, I drew on both experimental studies and a wide range of canonical literature and orature from around the world to argue that there are three prototypical narrative structures generated by a few universal principles of human emotion. These are, once again, romantic, heroic, and sacrificial tragicomedy. These narrative prototypes develop out of cross-cultural prototypes for human happiness, specifically, prototypes for happiness in different contexts—personal, social, and physical. The prototypes define goals that the main characters pursue in the course of the prototypical narratives. The cross-cultural prototype for personal happiness is romantic union. Romantic union, then, is the goal of the romantic structure. Social happiness is more complex. It involves in-group domination over an out-group and individual authority within the in-group. Heroic tragicomedies develop out of these goals. Finally, the physical prototype for happiness is plenty, an abundance of what we need—particularly food and drink. The sacrificial structure takes up this prototype. I refer to the narrative prototypes as "tragicomedies" because, in their fully developed forms, they have positive resolutions, achieving their respective happiness prototypes, but they pass through a version of the corresponding prototypes for sorrow in the narrative middle.[17] Thus, the lovers are separated in the middle of the romantic plot, often with an implication that one of them has died; the rightful leader is deposed and the enemy comes to dominate the in-group in the middle of the heroic plot; and society is devastated by famine or epidemic disease in the middle of the sacrificial plot.

More exactly, the heroic plot, which is fundamental for nationalism, comprises two distinct and separable sequences. In the fullest version,

---

17. I have discussed the use of this term in *The Mind* (24n.3). I chose it to stress the standard structure of these works and their relation to tragedies (which, by this analysis, are roughly incomplete tragicomedies). I am not claiming that the standard structure is generically ambiguous (though this is often the case with heroic works, as we will see). Nor am I denying that there are such generically ambiguous works. I should also say that the audience need not experience the middle of the tragicomedy as sorrowful. The most prototypical versions of these structures incorporate the opposite of the relevant happiness goal into the middle in some form; for example, they may incorporate implications of one lover's death into the middle of the romantic plot. But they may do so in a way that the audience finds funny, if they know that the implications are false and that everything will turn out well in the end.

the legitimate leader of the in-group is removed from leadership by some usurper and exiled. While he or she is in exile, the home society is threatened by an enemy, commonly an invader. The exiled leader returns to defeat the enemy, often with divine aid. After routing the invading hordes, he or she is able to regain leadership. The result is the reaffirmation of the authority of the national leadership, the divinely guaranteed power of the nation, the inferiority of the national enemy, and the control of the national land.

However, there is a complication in this story. As I have been emphasizing, our categorization of people into "us" and "them" strongly biases our moral evaluations and emotional responses. Thus, in the course of the battle, we experience fear when the enemy attacks our side, not when our side attacks the enemy. However, our emotions are not entirely constrained by such categorizations. As already noted, we spontaneously empathize with suffering, especially the suffering of someone who poses no threat to us. In keeping with this, there is a peculiar twist in many heroic tragicomedies. Romantic and sacrificial tragicomedies commonly end with the achievement of the prototypical happiness goal. In heroic plots, however, there is often a sort of epilogue after the enemy has been defeated. Specifically, there is often a section in which the hero suffers remorse for the devastation he or she caused in prosecuting the war. This section appears to develop out of the spontaneous empathic identification that comes into play when the enemy is no longer dangerous (for further discussion, as well as instances, see chapter 4 of my *Mind*). The "epilogue of suffering," as I have called it, may serve to question nationalism and nationalist war, or it may show the moral scrupulousness of the national in-group, thus fostering further commitment to nationalism and war. In either case, however, it takes up what is perhaps the central emotional conflict in in-group/out-group divisions—that between categorization-based identification, with its inhibitions on empathy, and our spontaneous tendency toward compassion for those who are in pain.

The sacrificial structure begins with some communal sin. This is punished by communal devastation, often in the form of drought and famine or disease. The devastation may be reversed only through a communal sacrifice, often the sacrifice of a human life. This prototype is highly consequential for nationalism in cases where there is a widespread feeling of national devastation (e.g., after loss in warfare).

Finally, romantic tragicomedy begins with two people falling in love. However, some social conflict prevents their union. This conflict is commonly a matter of identity categories, such as race or class. It is usually enforced by a representative of the traditional social order, frequently a parent. In the fullest version, the blocking figures include not only social authorities, but also a rival. The lover is frequently exiled and the beloved is often imprisoned or otherwise confined. Especially during the period of the lover's exile, the rival may have some temporary success with the beloved. When developed separately, this section becomes a love triangle plot. In the complete, comic version, the lover is eventually able to return, defeat the rival, and be reunited with his beloved. One common use of the plot is to oppose subnational divisions (e.g., by race or class). However, the structure tends to oppose all forms of identity division. As a result, it may just as easily be taken up to oppose national divisions. Moreover, as we have noted, individual commitment to in-group hierarchies is in part a matter of trust and in part a matter of fear or coercion. The heroic plot usually stresses (and endorses) the trust. The romantic plot in effect stresses the coercion—which, of course, it opposes. As a result, it tends to express the resentment that people almost invariably feel toward social authority. Thus, the romantic plot may be taken up for antinationalist purposes in this respect as well.

It is important to note that each of these prototypes involves not only standard characters and events, but standard ethical preferences as well. The main heroic plot particularly celebrates martial virtues, such as courage and loyalty. It is based on what I have called an "ethics of defense" (see *Mind* 136–47), an ethics of supporting one's in-group in times of conflict. The epilogue of suffering tends to value virtues such as empathy and beneficence. It is bound up with an ethics of compassion (see 136–47), an ethics of sensitivity to human pain. The sacrificial plot turns our attention toward such virtues as self-discipline and self-abnegation. This prototype establishes an ethics of self-denial. It particularly condemns self-indulgence in food and sexuality, contrasting this with the moral ideal of sacrificing one's life. Finally, the romantic prototype tends to be concerned with the degree to which social prescriptions—including common moral ideas—should be allowed to restrict the behavior of individuals, particularly in the pursuit of pleasure. It values the virtues of tolerance—or, better, nonjudgmental liberality—and independence. Thus, the romantic plot tends to express an ethics of individual freedom or personal choice.

Though I have discussed this issue at length elsewhere, it is worth briefly reviewing the evidence. For reasons already discussed, we would expect prototypical narratives to treat agents pursuing prototypical eliciting conditions for happiness. The question, however, is—just what are these prototypical eliciting conditions? Are they the same across times and places, or do they differ? Clearly, there are differences in the precise stories that are told in different times and places and the precise goals people pursue. But do these different stories and goals manifest closely related or quite different prototypes?

Here, two lines of research suggest themselves. The first involves the isolation of happiness prototypes, preferably in cross-cultural studies outside of narrative art. The second involves the isolation of cross-cultural narrative patterns.

As to the former, different philosophical traditions have isolated something along the lines of prototypes for eliciting conditions of happiness, though using different terms. One obvious case is the ancient South Asian schema of the four goals of life—kāma, artha, mokṣa, and dharma. Dharma and mokṣa—duty or ethics and spiritual liberation—are not fundamental motivations, but, so to speak, secondary goals that inflect the basic goals of kāma and artha, so I will leave them aside here. This leaves kāma and artha as the basic or primary goals—in our terms, the fundamental prototypes for happiness. Kāma is pleasure, generally. However, in treatises on kāma, it is prototypically the pleasure of sexual union. Moreover, in literary works, it is prototypically a specific sort of sexual union—romantic union with one's beloved. Artha is material well-being, but in the treatises on artha (see, for example, the Kauṭilya or Nārāyaṇa), it is treated prototypically as a matter of power or authority.

This analysis by the ancient Indic writers is broadly in keeping with what one might expect from the European tradition. It suggests two prototypes for happiness in two distinct contexts—romantic/sexual union in the context of personal happiness; power or authority and prosperity in the context of social happiness. The former seems particularly clear in nonliterary, empirical studies. Consider research done by J. L. Freedman. Having surveyed 100,000 Americans, Freedman found that "love in marriage" is most closely associated with happiness (see Oatley, *Best* 361). Research by Conway and Bekerian on "Grief, Misery, Sadness" points toward both prototypes by highlighting their opposites. If happiness is romantic union, then sadness should be loss of a loved one, particularly a romantic beloved—precisely what Conway and Bekerian's research shows. If happiness is power or authority and prosperity, then sadness should be professional failure or impoverishment—a point also attested by their data. Indeed, almost all of their data point to one of these prototypes.

Work by Shaver, Schwartz, Kirson, and O'Connor also fits here. This work considers prototypes, emotion, and narrative. There are complications with their analyses, as they do not seem to maintain a consistent level of abstraction. For example, one of their categories is "Undesirable outcome" (1074), which seems to be at a level of abstraction above such categories as "Death of a loved one" and "Loss of a relationship" (1074; indeed, the second seems to be a case of the third which seems, in turn, to be a case of the first). But, insofar as they are concrete enough to count as prototypical, the categories they uncover are clearly in line with the preceding analysis. Thus, the eliciting conditions for sadness prominently include the two just mentioned, which are closely related to the prototype of happiness as romantic union. Other prototypes include "Discovering one is powerless" (1074), which is clearly related to the prototype of happiness as power. In relation to happiness itself, they isolate only three categories that are not overly abstract. These are "Receiving esteem, respect, praise," "Being accepted, belonging," and "Receiving love, liking, affection" (1075). The first is clearly connected with the prototype of happiness as power or authority. The third category is clearly related to the prototype of happiness as romantic union. The second category relates to both. Indeed, it relates to both in a way that bears on emplotment. Commonly, the conflicts that define the middle of a plot are resolved in such a way that the larger society comes together and there is an extension of acceptance and belonging in the end (e.g., through the reconciliation of parents and children in the romantic plot).

In short, we seem to have some good prima facie evidence for positing two happiness prototypes. The point is not confined to modern America and Europe. Clearly, there were no broad scientific surveys or controlled experimental studies of emotion in premodern societies. However, there are highly regarded discussions and widely accepted ideas—such as the ancient Indic isolation of goals—that provide converging evidence. For example, Chikamatsu, widely thought of as one of the two greatest dramatists of Japan, wrote that, "The only happiness in this broad world" is "True love to true love" (234). The celebrated Malian *Epic of Son-Jara* states that "All people . . . seek to be men of power" (Sisòkò, I. 1277–78). Euripides' Hecuba expresses both, lamenting the death of Astyanax: "if you had enjoyed youth and wedlock and the royal power that makes men gods, then you would have been happy" (200).

These literary references lead to the second line of research. In order to consider cross-cultural prototypes in narrative, I set out to read a wide range of highly esteemed works of verbal art in unrelated literary traditions. I took up highly esteemed works as it seemed that they were most likely to express common narrative and emotional tendencies in a given culture or period. One crucial feature of a prototype-based account of narratives is that it does not claim to cover all stories. Prototypes are not necessary and sufficient conditions. We can and do tell nonprototypical stories all the time. In keeping with this, we have idiosyncratic ideas of what will make us happy individually. In small circles of friends or family members, idiosyncratic narratives involving idiosyncratic (or relatively trivial) happiness goals may be of interest. However, as the audience for stories becomes broader, extending to an encompassing culture, those idiosyncrasies are weeded out. Put differently, if a story proves to be effective with a broader range of readers or auditors, then it is not merely idiosyncratic, but manifests properties of interest to and value for people outside an individual author's circle of intimates.

In reading a wide range of highly esteemed works of verbal art from the European, sub-Saharan African, Middle Eastern, South Asian, Chinese, Japanese, and other traditions, I repeatedly came upon two structures—romantic and heroic.[18] My research on these traditions strongly

---

18. Some of the works that I considered include the following. From the European tradition: *The Iliad*, Aeschylus' *Oresteia*, Sophocles' Oedipus plays, Euripides' *Trojan Women*, *The Bacchae*, and *Phoenissae*, poetry by Pindar, Sappho, Tyrtaios, and Kallinos, Virgil's *Aeneid*, Chariton's *Chaereas and Kallirrhoe*, works of Roman New Comedy (e.g., Terence's *The Mother-in-Law*), *The Song of Roland*, *Beowulf*, *Jerusalem Delivered*, the *Niebelunglied*, various plays by Shakespeare, Goethe's *Faust*, novels by Jane Austen, poetry by St. John of the Cross, Sidney, Spenser, Browning, Yeats's *The Countess Cathleen*, works by Kafka, Joyce's *Ulysses*, *Gone with the Wind*, Alain Robbe-Grillet's postmodern *La Jalousie*, and the *Star Wars* movies. From South and Southeast Asia: the *Mahābhārata*, various versions of the *Rāmāyaṇa*, Bhāsa's *Vision of Vāsavadattā*, Kālidāsa's *Abhijñānaśākuntalam*, Śūdraka's *Little Clay Cart*, Harṣadeva's *Ratnāvalī*, Bhavabhūti's *Uttararāmacarita*, Śaktibhadra's *Āścaryacūḍamaṇi*, Ilangô Adigal's *Shilappadikaram (Cilappatikāram)*, poems from Tamil and Sanskrit anthologies, Bilhaṇa's *Fantasies of a Love Thief*, Bihārī's *Satasaī*, Jayadeva's *Gītagovinda*, stories from the history of Kashmir, Kondh poetry, the Thai folk drama *Manohra*, Kamala Markandaya's *Nectar in a Sieve*, Santosh Sivan's *The Terrorist*. From China: the *Book of Songs*, Chêng's *The Soul of Ch'ien-Nü Leaves Her Body*, Ma Chih-yüan's *Autumn in Han Palace*, poetry by Wang Wei, Li Bo, Li Ch'ing-chao, and Du Fu, Kuan Han-ch'ing's *The Injustice Done to Tou Ngo*, Cao Xueqin and Gao E's *The Story of the Stone*, *Conversations from the States*, and *Three Kingdoms*. From the Middle East: the epic of *Gilgamesh*, *Genesis*, the *Song of Songs*, ancient Egyptian lyric poetry, works in the ghazal tradition, various psalms, Ferdowsi's *Shâhnâme*, Iranian ta'ziyeh dramas, Gurgānī's *Vīs and Rāmīn*, the *Sīrat 'Antar*, narratives from Muslim history, the *Book of Dede Korkut*, Niẓāmī's *Laylā and Majnūn*, various stories from *The Thousand and One Nights*, some Bedouin love poetry. From Japan: *The Tale of the Heike*, Lady Murasaki's *Tale of Genji*, several Nō dramas by Kan'ami and Zeami, several plays by Chikamatsu, Izaemon and Yūgiri's *Love Letter from the Licensed Quarter*, Namiki Sōsuke's *Chronicle of the Battle of Ichinotani*, the *Tale of Ise*, the *Tosa Diary*, works by Bashō, the *Kokinshū*, and a range of Ainu epics. From the Americas: Bororo and Arawak tales, poetry from the Abanaki, Sia, Pueblo, Hopi, Navajo, and Chippewa, the Mayan *Cuceb*, the Nahuatl/Aztec *Quetzalcoatl*, Luis Puenzo's *The Plague*. From sub-Saharan Africa: the *Mwindo* epic, various versions of the *Epic of Son-Jara*, the epic of Oziki, the epic of Da Monzon of Segou, poetry from the Bambara and Dinka, Amos Tutuola's *The Palm-Wine Drinkard*, plays by Wole Soyinka. From elsewhere:

supported the hypothesis that there are cross-cultural narrative prototypes. The recurrence of these narrative prototypes provided further evidence for the existence of two cross-cultural happiness prototypes. Conversely, the happiness prototypes helped to explain the cross-cultural prominence of the narrative prototypes. But there were several problems (as there should be in any developing research program). I will very briefly consider two here. First, the heroic structure was complex. Second, and more significantly, there were (as I have already noted) three narrative prototypes, rather than the two one would expect, given the two happiness prototypes.

From the initial prototypes, one might expect the heroic prototype to concern only individual power—thus the "usurpation/restoration" sequence in which a rightful ruler is displaced and reinstated. But this is not the only part of the heroic plot. Indeed, it is not even the most important part, which appears to be the threat/defense sequence, where the home society is endangered by an attack from an enemy. However, on reconsideration, this is not surprising. First, there are obvious reasons why the invasion of one's society by another society would be of general interest to readers. Second, the extensive research on in-group/out-group divisions suggests that our first concern for prestige and authority is probably group-based rather than individually based. Again, "when . . . subjects are asked to allocate rewards (or punishments) between ingroup and outgroup members, they do so in a manner that maximizes the differential between ingroup and outgroup even though this may reduce the absolute benefits to the experimental subjects" (Duckitt 68–69). Given this, one would expect the prototype of happiness as power and authority to be, first of all, a prototype of in-group power and authority, and only secondarily a prototype of individual power and authority. This is just what the literary cases suggest.

The issue of the third genre is somewhat more complicated. The goal in sacrificial narratives is twofold. First, there is health—basically a negative goal, since it amounts to not being ill or in pain. Second, and more positively, there is having plenty of food. This suggests a third context for happiness—physical—and a third happiness prototype, health and abundance. To a certain extent, this is simply a matter of dividing artha into power and authority, on the one hand, and prosperity, on the other. However, it is important that the prosperity at issue is prototypically connected with physical well-being in general and food in particular. Throughout

---

Trobriand Island poetry, Tikopia poetry, New Guinea poetry of the Kurelu, Aboriginal poetry of Australia.

human history, the avoidance of sickness and the acquisition of food have been the primary concerns of most people. In that way, one would expect them to define a happiness prototype. At the same time, it is unsurprising that these are less salient eliciting conditions for happiness among survey respondents who live amid supermarkets and receive modern health care. There is, however, some limited nonliterary research that fits with the literary data. For example, Harris, Olthof, Terwogt, and Hardman examined eliciting conditions for emotions as reported by European and Nepalese children. The Nepalese children more often brought up "anxieties" about agriculture and more commonly linked "foods" with "pleasure" (338). The researchers report two Nepalese statements regarding eliciting conditions for happiness. One is, "With good things to eat, people feel *happy*" (334; emphasis in original).

Finally, I supplemented this literary and survey-based data with work on human emotion systems. I did this by considering the ways in which these systems might serve to explain the prominence of the three emotion prototypes. Specifically, I treated systems for attachment and sexual desire (combined in the case of romantic love), hunger or the desire to eat, and anger, with its aggressive responses to inhibiting agents. (Note that, when successful, angry aggression leads to submission responses from those inhibiting agents.) I argued that these were the most likely emotion systems to produce positive happiness (however temporary or ambivalent), rather than the mere negative relief produced by, say, escaping an object of fear or avoiding an object of disgust. In consequence, they were the systems most likely to be salient in the formation of happiness prototypes. Thus, the research on emotion systems fits well with the other bodies of data and the preceding analyses of those data.

In sum, there appears to be significant converging evidence for the enduring, cross-cultural prominence of three happiness prototypes and three associated narrative structures.[19] In the remaining chapters, I will argue that nationalism is commonly emplotted in one of these three forms. That emplotment helps to specify our understanding, imagination, emotional response, ethical evaluation, and, most important, concrete actions with respect to the national in-group and national out-groups. As noted at

---

19. To avoid misunderstanding, I should reemphasize that I am not at all claiming it is impossible to tell stories with other structures (or to follow ethical principles other than those developed in these structures). We can tell other stories, and do so all the time. I am also not saying that individuals may not have different or more various prototypes. They may, and do. The point is that, over a range of people, these are the prototypes that recur, both within and across cultures. As such, they are the prototypes with the greatest social consequences.

the outset of this chapter, it has become a commonplace in recent years that nationalism is bound up with narration. The preceding analysis suggests that this is true in a profound sense. It is not simply that nationalism is enhanced by novels and movies. Rather, the way in which we think about the nation is inseparable from the ways in which our emotion systems guide our causal understanding into stories. It is the burden of the remaining chapters to further enrich our understanding of nation and narration by exploring the three fundamental narrative patterns as they operate to define three fundamental forms of nationalism.

NARRATIVE PROTOTYPES AS EXPLANATORY MENTAL STRUCTURES
A Note on Explicit and Implicit Emplotment

In the following chapters, I will consider a range of texts that, I argue, emplot nationalism by way of the universal narrative prototypes. The texts I consider may be divided into two categories: stories and nonstories. One might reasonably expect that a discussion of emplotment would treat only stories. However, my contention is that a wide range of thought and action, including a wide range of discourse, is guided by narrative structures. That guidance is most obvious in explicit stories. However, it is by no means confined to stories. Indeed, the preceding discussion suggests that, in ordinary life generally—whether we are telling stories or engaging in commentary, reasoning, or theorization—most of our complex and extended causal inferences are based on narrative modeling rather than on the abstraction of causal laws through inductive generalization. In keeping with this, we find tacit emplotment manifest in a sort of fragmented form in nonstories—political treatises, philosophical commentaries, and so on. Indeed, the most revealing and perhaps most socially consequential cases of emplotment are implicit rather than explicit, in part because those cases are not as readily open to self-conscious evaluation and inhibition. In other words, when we are unaware of the sources of our inferences, it is more difficult for us to be critical of those sources. For this reason, the following chapters concentrate on nonstories. I begin with two explicit stories—the biblical story of King David and the popular American movie *Independence Day*—straightforward heroic tragicomedies, which clearly manifest the fundamental form of national emplotment. These provide a basis from which the more complex analyses of emplotment-based nonstories may proceed.

Of course, this division is not absolute. There are mixtures; indeed, most cases are probably mixtures. Political treatises commonly include explicit stories while novels and plays include sections of reasoning. Moreover, there are intermediate cases. These are important as they often reveal the intertwining of emplotment and inference very clearly. A prominent instance of this sort is history. As Hayden White has emphasized, histories are emplotted. Moreover, they are more obviously emplotted than, say, metaphysical arguments or treatises on politics. Put simply, histories commonly concern agents pursuing goals through a series of non-normal events (e.g., wars, independence struggles, and so on). On the other hand, histories are not always as obviously emplotted as, say, fiction films. For example, they necessarily treat broad social trends in income distribution, voting preferences, and similar matters that at least appear to be a matter of data and explanatory inference alone. Lyric poems may present another transitional case, though one where the narrative contribution is perhaps less overt. I have argued in *The Mind and Its Stories* that lyric poems most often focus on moments of particular emotional intensity in larger narrative sequences ("plot junctures," as I call them, following Sanskrit narrative theory). Think, for example, of the number of poems that treat love in separation, or love in reunion, or the fall of someone in battle—all key (junctural) moments in prototypical narratives. On the other hand, these encompassing narratives are implicit.

Again, I begin the chapter on heroic emplotment with explicit stories. I have not included any explicit stories in the chapters on sacrificial or romantic emplotment. However, I begin both with intermediate cases—Hitler's *Mein Kampf* and Walt Whitman's *Song of Myself*. While Hitler's *Mein Kampf* is not solely historiography, it does include a good deal of that. *Song of Myself* is, of course, not a pure, isolated lyric poem. However, that only means that it includes more explicit, developed narrative sequences than is typical of lyric poetry.

Finally, collections of testimonies may be viewed as an intermediate case as well. On the one hand, they are made up of stories. However, these stories are necessarily to some degree personal. Thus, they are more likely to be idiosyncratic, less likely to be prototypical. In addition, they are necessarily to some degree fragmentary. Indeed, many of them are less appropriately characterized as full-fledged stories than as subnarrative incidents or episodes, focal moments that may suggest a larger story without spelling it out explicitly.[20] Moreover, they do not, in themselves, define a broader

---

20. Using the definitions of stories set out in the introduction, we may say that accounts

trajectory for the entire collection. That is presumably given by some other set of principles for selection and organization by the editors. These principles may or may not be story based. In other words, some sets of organizational principles will tend to create a story out of the incidents. Other sets of principles will not. I conclude chapter 5 with a discussion of tacit narrative organization in *The Winter Soldier Investigation,* a collection of testimonies regarding atrocities committed during the Vietnam War.

Though my analyses of implicit and explicit emplotments ultimately move in the same direction and toward the same goal, they face different, if complementary problems. Specifically, an analysis of emplotment in nonstories may seem forced or fanciful. An analysis of emplotment in stories may appear trivial. We may face both problems for the intermediate or transitional cases—the former in some parts, the latter in other parts. Put differently, an analysis of nonstories in terms of narrative prototypes must achieve the status of a *plausible explanation.* In other words, it must indicate how the narrative prototypes may have guided the premises, inferences, conclusions, foci of concern, rhetorical force, or other elements of the work that are not otherwise readily explained (e.g., by the author engaging in simple induction from uncontroversial data). An analysis of stories in terms of narrative prototypes must achieve the status of *reportable (or nontrivial) interpretation.* In other words, it must indicate how the prototypes reveal patterns, implications, or other nonovert meanings in the work. Obviously, explanation and interpretation are closely related processes. Indeed, generally, interpretations should include at least partial explanations. For example, if a cognitive prototype serves to reveal patterns in a work, then it should simultaneously explain those patterns. Similarly, explanations will often point toward nonobvious patterns in a work, thus fulfilling an interpretive function. (The main exception to this convergence of explanation and interpretation occurs when the interpretive method we are using is purely heuristic. In those cases, there should be some explanatory theory that indicates not only why the interpretive patterns are present, but also why the heuristic device reveals those patterns.)

But these are the ordinary tasks of explanation and interpretation. They are, in principle, no more difficult to achieve here than elsewhere.

---

of isolated combat atrocities—the particular concern here—rarely constitute full stories even in the minimal sense. This is because such accounts rarely emerge out of or return to something we would refer to as "normalcy" (except in an entirely context-relative way, with "normalcy" defined by, say, a certain combat mission on a certain day). Nonetheless, they often imply larger narratives—in this particular case, I will argue, narratives with the structure of the epilogue of suffering.

(Obviously, it is up to readers to determine whether or not I have succeeded in particular cases.) A more serious problem arises, however, when something beyond plausibility and reportability is demanded from theoretical analyses, as sometimes occurs in literary study. Specifically, there is a common view that interpretation should not only be reportable, but creative and even counterintuitive. Moreover, in this view, an analysis of nonstories should achieve not only plausible explanation, but creative and counterintuitive interpretation as well. It is important to respond to this view before continuing.

The "counterintuitive interpretation" criterion for evaluating theories, though commonplace among literary critics, is misguided. Specifically, one often hears something along the following lines voiced as an objection to a theory: "Well, we could have gotten these interpretations without the theory" (or "without any of the theoretical mumbo jumbo" or some other variant along the same lines). But this is simply not a reasonable objection to a theory. The problem with this is twofold. First, it assumes that the evidence for or against a theory is solely or primarily to be found in the interpretations it generates. Second, it assumes that this evidence supports a theory only or primarily if those interpretations are radically novel. As to the former, literary theories, like theories in any area, receive support from the convergence of evidence from many sources. A cognitive theory of narrative, for example, will receive support from the isolation of patterns across stories, from psychological research on cognitive structures, from findings in semantics, and so on. More important, the component of the evidence that derives from literature cannot be the result of radically novel or entirely counterintuitive interpretations—or, more precisely, interpretations that we could not get without the theory. On this second point, then, the common view has things precisely backwards. A theory may or may not generate radically new interpretations. However, insofar as a theory's interpretations cannot be generated except by assuming the theory, those interpretations cannot count as evidence for the theory. It would be circular to derive them from the theory, then count them as evidence for the theory. In other words, the only interpretations that can count in favor of a theory are interpretations that can be arrived at by other means.

Consider my account of narrative universals. Once I have isolated, say, sacrificial tragicomedy, I may be able to interpret (and explain) some works in surprising ways as covertly deriving from the sacrificial structure. In the extreme case, it may be that the structure is visible in a given work only through the theory. A sacrificial interpretation of that work may be valuable and valid. However, it cannot count as evidence for the theory, at least not as primary evidence. Rather, the primary narrative evidence for the theory has to come from works where we can recognize the sacrificial structure without presupposing the theory.[21] The primary evidence has to come from such narratives as the Christian story of the Fall and redemption of humankind. Even readers who reject the theory can acknowledge that this story involves a sin that displeases a deity, leading to general social punishment, requiring a sacrifice in reparation, and so on.

In short, we should not want theories that radically alter the way we interpret most narratives. Rather, we should want theories that are largely consistent with our extratheoretical understanding of narratives in a wide range of cases.

The point is perhaps clearer if we think of the physical sciences. Imagine that someone objected to the theory of universal gravitation along the following lines: "We already knew that objects fall to the ground when dropped. The theory predicts that objects fall to the ground when dropped. We want a theory that tells us something new about objects, that gives us a novel interpretation." I believe we would all recognize that this gets things backwards. We want a theory of gravitation that is consistent with things falling to the ground—and doing so at a particular rate that is ascertainable outside the theory. The same general point holds for narrative and other literary theories.

As this suggests, I would not consider it a significant objection to the preceding account if it turned out that my discussions of the story of King David and of *Independence Day* merely show the uncontroversial presence of the heroic structure. Indeed, this is particularly the case, given that the point of these analyses is to provide a basis for the subsequent treatments of less straightforward cases.

On the other hand, I too am a literary critic and I therefore hope, not only to provide evidence for the theory, but also (if secondarily) to reveal aspects of these works that we would not ordinarily notice. As I have already indicated, an interpretation is not reportable if it isolates only trivial or obvious patterns in a work. In consequence, an interpretive theory, however valid, may be of no great value if it delivers only unreportable interpretations. In the following pages, I do not aspire to reveal aspects of works that we "could not see without the theory." Again, that would render

---

21. This is not to say that the actual procedure of discovery has to occur without the theory. The theory may lead us to notice features of a number of works, and we may then count those features as evidence for the theory—as long as there are means of isolating the features without the theory. The point is that we can acknowledge those features without the theory, not necessarily that we actually did isolate them prior to the theory.

those interpretations irrelevant as evidence for the theory. I do, however, hope to reveal aspects of the works that have commonly escaped viewers and critics. My purpose in interpretation (and explanation), then, is (usually) not to say either "no" or "yes, but" to accepted basic understandings of works. It is, rather, to say "yes, and"—where the "and" includes both a reconfiguration of what has been accepted into a different frame (the one provided by narrative prototypes) and the drawing out of elements of texts that the accepted readings have not sufficiently attended to. The result is not a radical overturning of what we thought the texts were about but it is a substantial revision of how the texts work and what their readerly appeals are.[22]

Consider, for example, *Independence Day*. I will argue that, scene by scene, the film builds up a standard heroic emplotment of nationalism. This includes, for example, a unifying representation of ethnic and geographical diversity. Virtually no viewers of the film will fail to recognize that the film includes European American, Jewish American, and African American characters. In other words, if asked, they would no doubt say that there are such characters. However, they may not find this ethnic diversity salient (e.g., they may not remark on this feature if they are not asked). The same point could be made even more strongly for the geographical diversity of the film. More important, few viewers are likely to recognize that the systematic representation of ethnic groups—including interethnic friendships—and of different geographical regions is part of the unobtrusive nationalist operation of the film. Put differently, they may recognize that the president's Fourth of July speech has nationalist elements, probably even salient nationalist elements. However, they are unlikely to integrate these salient features of the film with nonsalient (but accessible) features of geographical diversity into the encompassing structure of nationalist heroic tragicomedy. Similarly, they can hardly miss the world leadership role of the United States in the coalition against the invading aliens. However, it is unlikely that they will recognize this as a particular American specification of the heroic emplotment, thus a standard and to some degree distinctive aspect of U.S. nationalism. An analysis of the film in terms of heroic emplotment does not create the basic textual properties (e.g., the ethnic diversity). In this way, it does not yield an interpretation that would be impossible to arrive at without the theory. However, it does make a wide range of such properties salient and it integrates these into an

---

22. I am indebted to Jim Phelan and Peter Rabinowitz for this formulation of my goals. On this issue, they expressed my aims better than I was able to do.

encompassing structure. In this way, it produces an interpretation that (insofar as it is successful and valid) broadens our understanding of the work.

Much the same points hold for the explanation of nonliterary and (overtly) non-narrative texts. Consider, for example, *Mein Kampf*. My account of this text does not seek to make it something radically different from what it seems to be. However, it does, I believe, explain some important features of the text—for example, its conclusions about Jews and communists. It may seem perverse to ask how it is that Hitler comes to reach his conclusions about Jews and communists. Ordinarily, we devote close interpretive and explanatory attention to authors who, we believe, have something to teach us. Needless to say, no decent person believes that Hitler has anything to teach us. But *the fact of* Hitler clearly does have something to teach us. The horror of Nazi Germany is something that we cannot ignore. It is in this context that it becomes important to ask how *Mein Kampf* reaches its conclusions. It is clear that it does not reach those conclusions based on the weight of evidence or the rigor of its reasoning. Yet the work was enormously successful, influencing many people and contributing to inconceivable cruelty and destruction. How could it possibly be the case that a badly argued book could have this sort of effect? My contention is that, among other factors, it had this effect because it is in fact deeply coherent, and coherent in a way that people can directly and unreflectively understand and respond to. However, its coherence is not argumentative, but narrative. That narrative coherence fits our cognitive predispositions well. This is not to say that the narrative structure itself leads to anti-Semitism, for example. It does not. However, prototype-based narrative organization may lead to anti-Semitism when that organization is specified in particular ways, in a social context where there is considerable anti-Semitism already, and in social circumstances that widely foster a type of emplotment that is amenable to identifying an "internal" national enemy. *Mein Kampf* took the sacrificial structure and specified it in such a way as to place Jews in a particular narrative role, a role that seemed to make them responsible for the national devastation that followed the First World War; it did this in a context where there was considerable anti-Semitism; and it did so in historical circumstances that fostered sacrificial emplotment of just this sort for a broad range of Germans. Obviously, this account does not explain everything. It does not explain the historical condition of Germany at the time; it does not explain the prior anti-Semitism; it does not even explain a wide range of features of Hitler's text (e.g., his attitude toward his father). However, it does provide a plausible account of how Hitler could come to think that he was actually presenting a case for his conclusions and how at least a certain set of readers could come to be convinced by this case (again, despite its argumentative inadequacy).

Parallel points apply to the other nonstory texts considered in the following chapters. For instance, contrary to common views, Gandhi's relation to violence was somewhat ambivalent, and at points his statements about violence and nonviolence are ambiguous. Moreover, he made statements about a range of issues (e.g., the relation between some natural disasters and the moral culpability of affected populations) that do not seem to derive logically from his ethical philosophy or political program. Given these problems, one is left to wonder at Gandhi's appeal as well. How could people become motivated by a political program that appears ambivalent on its central practical and ethical principle (of nonviolence) and that involves in some ways inscrutable causal sequences (e.g., that a belief in untouchability may lead to earthquakes)? The anomalous quality of Gandhi's statements disappears, however, once one comes to see them as guided, not by logic and evidence, but rather by an underlying sacrificial emplotment embedded within an interrupted heroic narrative. Moreover, the appeal of his work becomes much more readily comprehensible as well, since that work embodies one of our fundamental, shared structures for understanding, anticipating, and enacting or affecting causal sequences. Moreover, the social and political conditions of India at the time made that structure salient to an unusual degree for a broad range of people.

More briefly, we might note that Walt Whitman's *Song of Myself* has a number of curious features. One prominent instance is its evocation of a sort of pansexuality. We see this particularly in the array of forbidden sexualities he explores, explicitly or implicitly, prominently, including interracial marriage and even interracial homoeroticism. Just what are these doing in a poem that is, at least on the surface, a celebration of the nation? Surely at the time the United States was not a place where interracial homoeroticism was considered one's patriotic duty. Beyond this, Whitman's poem is nationalist, but it seems to move continually away from nationalism, drifting to a sort of universalism, before being pulled back to its nationalist concerns. How are we to understand this drift and rectification? My contention is that both points make perfect sense when we see the poem as an instance of romantic emplotment particularized in the context of a nation divided by subnational racial oppositions. Here, too, the explanation in terms of a standard form of emplotment helps to account for peculiarities of the work—peculiarities that are isolable without the theory. In addition, it helps to account for the poem's strong and enduring impact on readers, including its elevation to the status of a national epic.

Emma Goldman's work is not so much anomalous as diffuse. She is generally not seen as a systematic thinker and the topics covered in her writings seem diverse with no particular underlying pattern. On the other hand, readers of Goldman are likely to feel continuity in her thought, a consistency that is not the result of a well-articulated, fully developed political platform or the rigorously logical working out of the consequences of well-grounded philosophical principles. We might be inclined to refer to this unity vaguely as a matter of "voice" or "attitude," or even "personality." However, the unity of Goldman's work seems best understood by reference to a tacit romantic emplotment, the guidance of her concerns, arguments, analyses, and programs by a romantic narrative prototype. This helps to account for her appeal as well—obviously not in any way comparable to that of the other writers we are considering, but not insignificant.

Of the overtly non-narrative works considered in the following chapters, the speech by President George W. Bush is likely to be the one that many readers—at least many American readers—will find the most difficult *not* to understand. What I mean by this is that many readers are likely to feel that there is nothing interpretively problematic about Bush's speech. But, in fact, it is a highly anomalous speech. It is simply difficult to recognize the anomalies if the heroic narrative prototype is already active and guiding one's processing of information about global and domestic events. To take a simple example, for Bush, the September 11 events constituted an act of war. Of course, that is exactly what they are when incorporated into the threat/defense scenario of the heroic narrative. However, as a number of commentators pointed out, it makes more sense prima facie to see them as a terrible criminal act. Obviously, one is always free to argue that we should see them as an act of war rather than as a criminal act. But Bush did not do that. Rather, he simply assumed that they were an act of war. Moreover, he projected the prosecution of a war as the U.S. response to those events—not a criminal investigation, not an attempt to preserve (or restore) peace by developing more productive international relations, not any number of other possible responses. Again, one is always free to argue for one course of action over another. However, Bush did not do this. His speech proceeded as if there were no options other than war. Moreover, people widely accepted this. That widespread acceptance suggests that the non sequiturs and absence of alternative analyses in the speech are not a simple matter of, say, stupidity (a standard left-liberal response to Bush). Rather, they resulted from a widely accessible manner of thinking about the events of September 11 and possible responses to those events; they resulted from some model that was not alien to Bush's listeners. That model is the heroic narrative prototype. This prototype allows us to make explanatory sense of what Bush said, what he did not say, and, to some extent, why people responded positively to what he said. Finally, in this case too, social conditions made the heroic prototype particularly accessible and thus oriented people cognitively toward heroic emplotment even before Bush began his speech.

After Bush's speech, I briefly consider *The Winter Soldier Investigation* of the Vietnam Veterans Against the War. As already noted, this text records testimonies regarding atrocities committed in Vietnam. The soldiers who testified in these hearings were admirable, humane individuals who wished to put an end to the terrible human suffering caused by the war. I do not in any way wish to diminish the value of what they have done—any more than I wish to diminish the value of Whitman or Goldman. Indeed, these Vietnam Veterans are collectively one of the three heroes of this book, along with Whitman and, above all, Goldman. (After all, if I am right, then this book too must involve some elements of tacit emplotment—though, of course, I hope that it proceeds primarily by logic and evidence.) Nonetheless, like the works of Whitman and Goldman, *The Winter Soldier Investigation* has its own unexplained patterns. Most obviously, there is the issue of just why the editors selected these particular testimonies and organized them in this way. No doubt this is in part a matter of chance, idiosyncratic personal preference, the need for breadth of coverage, and so forth. However, once put in the context of the epilogue of suffering, at least certain aspects of the selection and structure begin to appear more systematic. Note that this would not be a matter of any self-conscious decision on the part of the editors. Rather, the prototypical structure—along with its associated emotional propensities—would simply tend to render some types of actions (e.g., the killing of individual children) and certain sorts of experience (e.g., seeing the face of a dead child) more salient; moreover, they would tend to produce a bias toward organizing the events in a certain way. We see instances of this general sort not only across testimonies (thus operating on editorial decisions), but within testimonies as well (thus operating on the storytellers' decisions). Unsurprisingly, these are imperfect instances, given the constraint of the narrative structure by actual events and the necessarily fragmentary nature of the individual testimonies. But they are recognizable instances nonetheless.

Another important aspect of this text, given our purposes, is its evident ambivalence about nationalism. Some of those involved in the investigation are opposed to nationalism; many simply leave it aside. But many clearly wish to affirm U.S. national identity—and even the U.S. position as the global leader of nations, the same position set forth in *Independence Day*. They wish to do this even as they are denouncing U.S. war crimes. At one level, this simply suggests a difference of opinion among the editors and among the witnesses giving testimony. However, it also fits very closely with the most common uses of the epilogue of suffering. On the one hand, an epilogue of suffering may serve to castigate the nation for its war crimes; on the other hand, it may serve to rehabilitate the nation, to reassert the legitimacy of the society and its leadership. Or, rather, it may serve to partially rehabilitate the nation, for the reassertion of national legitimacy is almost invariably ambivalent. It is rare for an epilogue to fully convince readers that there has been, or that there even could be, fully sufficient atonement for the crimes of war. In some cases, the superficial resolution that concludes the epilogue barely deflects our attention from an underlying sense of remorse bordering on despair. We find that ambivalence, too, in *The Winter Soldier Investigation*.[23]

In sum, the following interpretations and explanations serve first of all to provide evidence that we do routinely emplot nationalism and we do so most consistently in terms of the universal narrative prototypes. Our default mode of national emplotment is heroic. However, in particular conditions, we may shift to a sacrificial or romantic narrative, commonly embedding that sacrificial or romantic story within an ongoing if temporarily suspended heroic plot. (The primary exception to this comes from the romantic narrative, which tends to reapply from the subnational to the national level, thereby ultimately undermining heroic emplotment and, indeed, nationalism.) At the same time, the interpretations aim to make unremarked features of nationalist works salient and to help us recognize

23. This feeling is undoubtedly reenforced by the fact that the war was continuing at the time of the testimonies. In fact, for this reason, some readers have objected to the idea that *The Winter Soldier Investigation* could be organized by an epilogue of suffering at all, since the word "epilogue" suggests that the war is over. It is true that the term is somewhat misleading in this case. However, there really is no problem once one recognizes that this is an enduring prototypical structure that can guide our thought and action in a broad range of contexts, including the middle of a war. Indeed, some prominent instances of the epilogue occur in the middle of wars—an obvious case being that of the *Iliad*.

the organization of those features. In parallel with this, explanatory analyses take up and try to account for anomalous features of those works. Collectively, they suggest that prototypical narrative emplotment is central to the organization and orientation of nationalist ideology, to the acceptance of that ideology, and even to the enactment of that ideology,[24] generally and in the distinctive particularities of these consequential works.

24. Of course, the last point holds only to the extent that action is, in fact, produced by the ideology, rather than being produced by other factors and then merely rationalized by an appeal to ideology.

5

HEROIC NATIONALISM AND THE NECESSITY OF WAR FROM KING DAVID TO GEORGE W. BUSH

THE MAIN HEROIC PLOT involves, as we have seen, two components—a usurpation sequence and an external threat sequence, commonly a war story. The nationalistic functions of this narrative structure are self-evident. The usurpation sequence fosters an emotional commitment to the internal hierarchy of the national in-group. It creates an internal or secondary in-group/out-group division between loyalists and usurpers, with all that this entails evaluatively, emotionally, and so forth. It also links rebellion with social suffering, thus providing an aversive model for our imagination of political change. Conversely, narratives of this sort commonly identify the rule of the rightful leader as utopian, as marked by abundance of food, general health, general security, universal religious devotion, and so on. The threat/defense sequence no less obviously contributes to the saliency of the national category (through emphasis on threat to the group as such), its opposability (through coordinated battle against the enemy), its affectivity (through the many emotionally charged consequences of war), as well as our sense of its durability (through the nation's ultimate triumph) and our understanding of its functionality (after all, the entire conflict, with all its consequences, is a matter of nationality). The increases in our imagination of opposability, durability, and functionality are also bound up with the heroic narrative's strong reenforcement of the demonization of the enemy (both external and internal) and its concrete development of the divine election of the nation.

No less important, heroic narratives naturalize war. In other words, they take events that should be extraordinary and terrible and make them simultaneously ordinary and enticing. Greenfeld notes a view from early nineteenth-century Germany that is inseparable from heroic emplotment: "War was a good thing in itself. It was an ennobling, purifying rite which alone could assure true consciousness of nationality" (370). The emotional enticement is primarily a matter of the formation of heroes. The point is so obvious that it is easy to forget. Heroic narratives do not treat wars as a muddle of individual actions and reactions, partially coordinated, partially accidental. They treat war, and particularly victory, as the result of deliberate, brave, and celebrated (thus "glorious") actions by exceptional individuals. The point is not at all confined to fictions. For instance, the creation of heroes is stressed by Kevin Foster in connection with the Malvinas/Falkland Islands war (see, for example, 87). Speaking about nineteenth-century German nationalism, Maas comments that, "In the myth of the founding of the Reich, the dead soldiers would be martyrs for the unified nation. In recollection, the psychology of victory transfigured everything in the light of the national heroes" (217, my translation; see also Morgan 81, on Welsh national heroes). Of course, imagining heroes is inseparable from imagining enemies. As Eliot Weinberger explains, regarding the war in Iraq, "First, an Enemy is created by blatant lies that are endlessly repeated until the population believes them: in this case, that Iraq was linked to the attack on the World Trade Center, and that it possesses vast 'weapons of mass destruction' that threaten the world. Then, a War of Liberation, entirely portrayed by the mass media in terms of our Heroic Troops, with little or no imagery of casualties and devastation, and with morale-inspiring, scripted 'news' scenes—such as the toppling of the Saddam statue and the heroic 'rescue' of Private Lynch—worthy of soviet cinema."

The relation between nationalism and heroic tragicomedy has been recognized implicitly for some time. However, the recognition in these cases has not concerned narrative prototypes. Rather, it has concerned particular works or exempla.[1] It has also commonly been mischaracterized as

---

1. For example, Li refers to a mid-seventeenth-century work, *Shui-hu hou chuan,* that

a matter of epics, rather than heroic tragicomedies. (The crucial feature is not that the works are narratives in verse, but that they follow a particular narrative prototype.) There is, in fact, good reason for the focus on exempla. It has often been the case that nationalist movements have championed one or perhaps two heroic or at least partially heroic stories. Indeed, nationalism is shaped, in any given case, not only by the universal, prototypical structures and still broader universal schemas, but also by the more culturally and historically distinctive particularizations of those structures in paradigmatic exempla—often, though by no means always, epics. Thus, for example, Quint explains that, "In the Europe-wide quest for national origins and identity of the early nineteenth century, heroic poetry held a special allure. It could embody a pure state of national feeling because its martial subject not only invokes the patriotic unity of a people at war but also provides the mythic memories that can mobilize them" (353). As to particular paradigms, Quint cites the *Poema de Mio Cid* in Spain (353), *La Chanson de Roland* in France (356, 358), the Icelandic *Njalssaga* (353, 359), and other European works. The modern, nationalist use of celebrated heroic stories from the past is not confined to Europe. Non-European cases include Turkey, where national leader Kemal Ataturk's "cultural policy fueled interest" in *The Book of Dede Korkut* (a collection of primarily heroic narratives), so that it came to be "accepted as the national epic of the Turkish people" (Mack 1497); India, where the Bharatiya Janata Party used the *Rāmāyaṇa* to advance its Hindu nationalism; Mali, through the explicitly political versions of the Malian *Epic of Son Jara* (such as that of Fa-Digi Sisòkò, which celebrates the Malian prime minister, linking him with the great ancestral hero Son Jara; see 11.824–34), and through the use of a song from the epic for Mali's national anthem (see Durán xviii). Similarly, in Iran, the *Shâhnâme* has served to enhance commitment to the nation and to the internal hierarchy of the nation. As Vaziri explains, "It is fair to say that, when nationalism and national identity became concerns in the twentieth century, the *Shah-Nama* certainly served as the traditional folk source of such modern notions" (125). As Davis notes, "The Pahlavi kings who ruled Iran from 1925 until 1979 . . . assiduously promoted the study of Ferdowsi's poem" (xxxv; in contrast with Vaziri, Davis accepts

---

expresses "nationalist strivings." This work "uses the valiant exploits of the surviving bandit-heroes in fighting Chin invaders, defending the Sung dynasty . . . to express the hopes and anguish of Ming loyalism following the Manchu conquest of the Ming dynasty in 1644" (628). Without conceiving of it in these general terms, Li is referring here to the prototypical invasion/defense scenario of heroic tragicomedy, here recruited to standard nationalist purposes.

that the poem is at least "quasi-national" and exhibits "'nationalist' sentiment" [xxix]). An interesting manifestation of this bond between nationalism and particular, paradigmatic heroic tragicomedies may be found in the use of such works in thinking about battle or in giving courage and comfort to soldiers in battle and to nationalist revolutionaries (see, for example, Service iv, Quint 256, and Tagore, *Home* 139, for Chinese, European, and Indian examples[2]). Wachtel cites one Yugoslavian writer, referring to the primary national heroic tragicomedy of Yugoslavia: "[D]uring the course of the War of National Liberation, the verses of *The Mountain Wreath* sounded like a password on the lips of our fighters, and they could achieve their heroic feats" (144).

As I have already indicated, and as the preceding comments again suggest, heroic emplotment is the narrative form most fundamental to nationalism. Nationalist sacrificial and romantic stories are, in contrast, situationally specific deviations from that heroic emplotment. More exactly, prototypes do not arise and become dominant in a particular society in a particular period simply by accident. There are two principal ways in which one narrative prototype becomes dominant. Perhaps most obviously, different prototypes are triggered by different social conditions. Anything along the lines of an attack tends to trigger the heroic prototype; famine or military defeat may trigger the sacrificial structure. However, such historically particular triggers are not the primary source of the heroic prototype's dominance. In keeping with the usual operation of human cognition, the three prototypes are themselves hierarchized, with a default that may be overridden in specific circumstances. That default prototype for national emplotment is heroic.[3] In other words, everything else being equal, we tend to think of the nation in terms of a heroic narrative.[4] This is true for a simple reason. The heroic narrative derives from the two *social* happiness goals—authority and esteem of the in-group over out-groups and authority and esteem of a given individual within the in-group. When treating the national in-group and its hierarchy, the narrative prototype bearing on these social goals is necessarily fundamental. It is only when the heroic

---

2. In the case of Tagore, the revolutionary aptly carries "a small edition" of the relevant text along with "a little pistol" (139), suggesting a direct parallel between the two.

3. Similarly, our default prototype for a pet is a dog or a cat. It is only in particular circumstances that this default is overridden and we envision a goldfish or a parrot.

4. This is related to the common observation that nationalism is bound up with warfare. For example, as Balakrishnan explains, "For Weber, like Hegel, the modern state possesses a historical purpose and collective meaning because it organizes a community into a sovereign polity ready for war. It is during war that the nation is imagined as a community embodying ultimate values" ("National" 208).

structure is displaced that one of the other structures—otherwise usually confined to physical and personal contexts—comes into play. As a result, heroic emplotment is ubiquitous in nationalist thought and action.

On the other hand, heroic emplotment is not quite identical in all cases. Again, prototypes are the result of weighted averaging. Insofar as the familiar heroic stories in one nation differ from those in another, the prototypes held by the citizens of those nations will differ as well. Thus, we may refer, not only to heroic tragicomedy in general, but to the standard American or Israeli or Indian heroic tragicomedy. (I say "standard" as prototypes will differ, sometimes significantly, from person to person and group to group within a nation as well.) In India, particularly among Hindus, the *Rāmāyaṇa* is a paradigmatic heroic narrative. That is not true in, say, the United States. For this reason, certain features of the standard Indian heroic prototype may differ from those of the standard U.S. heroic prototype. For instance, the Indian prototype may stress abduction as a characteristic crime of the enemy, due to the central abduction of Sītā in the epic. (There is at least some suggestion of this in popular Indian film.) The cross-cultural features (e.g., demonization of the enemy, whether as Satan or as the *Rāmāyaṇa*'s Rāvaṇa) are almost always the most important, as they manifest human cognitive and emotive propensities most fully. Still, the national variations may be consequential as well.

As discussed in the preceding chapters, we may divide the most important forms of emplotment into explicit and implicit narratives. Some nationalist plots are explicitly articulated as stories. In other cases, nationalistic ideas are presented as the result of purely rational, objective, causal analysis—while, in fact, they are tacitly guided by an heroic structure.[5] In the case of explicit heroic plots, we may also distinguish between paradigmatic and popular or ephemeral narratives. Again, nationalists often champion one or perhaps two ancient heroic stories (often epic poems). These have long-term influence on nationalist thought and action. At the same time, nations continually generate heroic fictions that are particular to their current conditions. Collectively, these may have intense effects for shorter periods of time. In the remainder of this chapter, then, I consider one ancient, paradigmatic work; one current, popular fiction; and one implicit narrative from practical politics. Specifically, I begin with the biblical story of King David. This is a crucial paradigmatic narrative for Israeli nationalism, but it has also been influential throughout the Christian world,

---

5. As already noted, we find this in the formulation and statement of policies, in the writing of histories, and elsewhere. The point holds, for example, with respect to the historical work analyzed in chapters 4 and 5 of Chatterjee.

including the United States. I then turn to the blockbuster American film *Independence Day* (directed by Roland Emmerich), one of the twenty largest-grossing films of all time in the United States.[6] I conclude the treatment of the main heroic narrative with a tacit, and highly consequential emplotment—President George W. Bush's response to the bombings of September 11, 2001, as presented in his September 14 speech at the National Cathedral ("President's Remarks").

Again, after the main narrative sequence defining heroic tragicomedy, there is often an epilogue of suffering, a questioning of the values that motivated and (apparently) justified the battle along with the practices that brought victory. This epilogue is common in literature proper (prominent examples range from *Gilgamesh* to *The Iliad*, the *Mahābhārata*, the *Mwindo Epic*, and *The Tale of the Heike*). But, of course, it occurs in nonfiction also. I conclude this chapter with a brief examination of the epilogue of suffering in the emplotment of the Vietnam War. Specifically, I consider one of the most influential treatments of that war—the Winter Soldier Investigation into U.S. war crimes (an investigation that continues to have significant consequences for national thought and action in the United States, as shown by its prominence in discussions of John Kerry's candidacy for president in 2004).

EMPLOTTING PALESTINE
Israel, David, and the Amalekites

A few years ago, when flying back to New York from Tel Aviv, I picked up a copy of *Ha'aretz Magazine* (June 8, 2001). The first article in that issue, "Running out of time," by Arie Caspi, treats the al-Aqsa Intifada and the larger conflict between Israel and the Palestinians. In the course of the article, Caspi worries that Israel has squandered its reserve of Western guilt over the Holocaust, and is now back at the point where Jews began—or worse, for now some sectors in the West have come to identify sympathy for Jews as victims with support for Jews as oppressors. The point is significant in itself. But one particular aspect is important for our current purposes. Caspi speaks of a new "narrative [that] begins with Auschwitz and

---

6. As of May 2005; see http://www.the-movie-times.com (accessed May 2005). I should perhaps note that I have not chosen this film because I think it is somehow unique. Rather, I have chosen it because I take it to be fairly ordinary, though popular. Indeed, it would be counterproductive to take a unique film, since its very uniqueness would suggest that it probably does not tell us much about the society generally.

ends with the death of Mohammed Dura, the Palestinian boy shot and killed in front of the television at the beginning of the Al-Aqsa Intifada" (4). The fact that Caspi refers to this as a narrative may seem inconsequential. But it is not. Caspi's imagination of the position of Israel is a profoundly narrative imagination. The point becomes particularly apparent when Caspi begins to discuss the international evaluation of Israel and its relation to Palestinian public relations. Specifically, Caspi insists that non-Israelis are now much more likely to accept Palestinian views—including misinformation—"because the Western media now considers us the villain. And once you become the villain, you can be blamed for anything" (5).

The phrase "the villain" does not merely suggest criminal behavior on the part of Israel. It suggests a story in which "the hero" is a well-defined character, with particular heroic traits, and "the villain" is his or her opposite. We really can blame the villain of a story for anything, and we do. Once we learn that a particular character is the villain, we come to suspect that he or she is behind every terrible event in the story. Our attitude is a presumption of guilt, just as our attitude toward the hero is a presumption of innocence. In the real world, things do not work that way. In the real world, it is fairly rare to find heroes and villains. In a conflict between two groups, there is usually some genuine conflict of rights, there is usually some mix of motives on both sides, there is usually some cruelty and terror from both camps. It may be the case that one side has more justice in its cause than the other, that one side perpetrates more terror than the other—primarily because one side has more power. Currently, Israel is causing incomparably more pain to the Palestinians than the reverse—because Israel is incomparably more powerful.[7] But to imagine Israel—or,

---

7. We may divide this pain into pain caused by military action and pain that results from living conditions. As to the latter, one simply has to note some basic facts about life in the Palestinian territories and compare them with facts about life in Israel. For example, in a region where water is a crucial resource, Israel appropriates "80 percent of the water extracted from West Bank aquifers" (Chomsky, *Failed* 174). Clearly, Palestinians do not appropriate 80 percent of the water from any Israeli aquifers—presumably not because they are more generous. Or consider Gaza, which has "poverty rates at nearly eighty percent and unemployment at nearly forty percent" (Chomsky in Chomsky and Achcar 240, citing 2006 United Nations data). In contrast, the poverty rate in Israel in 2006 was 24.5 percent (Sinai) and the unemployment rate was 8.4 percent (according to Bank of Israel data; see http://www.bankisrael.gov.il/deptdata/mehkar/indic/eng_g04.htm [accessed November 10, 2007])—though even these statistics are misleading since, for example, 50 percent of Israeli Arabs live below the poverty line (Sinai). As to the pain of military action, according to official Israel Defense Forces figures, the proportion of Palestinians to Israelis killed at the start of the al-Aqsa Intifada was twenty to one (Chomsky, *Hegemony* 181; later the ratio dropped [185]). A revealing instance may be found in June 2006. At a time when Israeli jails held perhaps a thousand Palestinians without charges (thus people who were, in effect, kidnapped), Palestinians

worse, Jews—as "the villain" is to imagine that there is something deeper than this imbalance of power. For example, in most stories, we know that a victory for "the hero" would bring peace and justice. But who is the hero in the narrative suggested by Caspi?[8] Is it the Palestinian Authority? In narrative terms, perhaps. But in actual life it seems clear that Jews could expect no better treatment from the Palestinian Authority if the military situation were reversed—and even the situation of the Palestinians would remain fairly grim, as Amnesty International reports on the Palestinian Authority indicate (see the dozens of documents treating political imprisonment, torture, unfair trials, detention without charge or trial, etc., at www. amnesty. org).

In saying this, I am of course restating, in a particular context, what I argued more generally in the preceding chapter. I am presenting an instance of the ubiquitous emplotment of war, with its oversimplifying consequences. But, again, the emplotment of nationalism—and war—is not merely general. It involves genres, particularly heroic tragicomedy, and paradigms of those genres. The case of Israel and Palestine is no exception. In this case, a crucial paradigm is the story of King David, a story that has figured consequentially in the development of Israeli nationalism, including its relation to the Palestinians.[9]

Consider again the article in *Ha'aretz*. Caspi explains that "Israel's military might forced the Arab nations to accept its existence.... We felt omnipotent. The entitled underdog." This bears straightforwardly on the heroic plot. But how does it relate to the paradigm of David? The connection becomes clear in the next sentence: "We played at being... King David." Here, Caspi is taking up a specific element of this paradigmatic work, not merely its general heroic structure, but its particularization of that structure. More exactly, Caspi is alluding to a common metaphor for Israel's position as a small nation surrounded by much bigger, hostile

---

kidnapped an Israeli soldier. Israel responded with "bombing and shelling" in "acts of collective punishment," which Amnesty International condemned as "war crimes." Chomsky explains that "UN agencies... warned of a 'public health disaster' as a result of developments 'which have seen innocent civilians, including children, killed, [and] brought increased misery to hundreds of thousands of people" (in Chomsky and Achcar 239–40).

8. I should note that, despite Caspi's fears, this narrative is not widespread in the West—quite the contrary, in fact.

9. Since one reader has asked, I should stress that this is not the only story that has been important for Israeli nationalism. It is not possible to assimilate all nationalist emplotments (for Israel or any other nation) to a single paradigm. Nationalist emplotments are diverse, with many sources, outcomes, emotions, in-group/out-group structures, and so on. On the other hand, not all sources are of equal importance and influence. The story of King David has been one of the most consequential for Israeli nationalism.

countries—the metaphor of David and Goliath. The analogy is so widespread that Simha Flapan includes it as the sixth of seven "myths" about "the birth of Israel": "The tiny, newborn state of Israel faced the onslaught of the Arab armies as David faced Goliath: a numerically inferior, poorly armed people in danger of being overrun by a military giant" (187). Its use is by no means confined to 1948.[10]

When assimilating Israel to David in this way, one does several things. One associates Israel with an historical right to the place. At the same time, one associates the Arab world with power and threat. However vast Israeli weaponry might be, imagining Israel as David—a boy with no armor and only a slingshot for a weapon (1 Samuel 17: 39–40)—involves imagining the enemy as incomparably stronger and more dangerous. This simultaneously stresses God's support of the home nation, for that support allows the nation to defeat the enemy despite overwhelming odds. Finally, this assimilation is not merely a matter of personal understanding and imagination. It is politically consequential. To grasp the full extent of these connections, we need to consider that paradigmatic story itself in detail.[11]

David was the second king of the united Jewish people. He followed Saul and was succeeded by Solomon. After Solomon, the society divided into the two kingdoms of Israel and Judah. The story of David is a clear heroic tragicomedy, of the standard sort. Again, it is of great importance

---

10. Nor was it confined to Israel. For example, the 1967 war was often characterized in terms of David and Goliath, including by the United States (see Black). While most uses of this paradigm are straightforward, there are interesting variants in which Israel does not appear as David. Consider, for example, a recent interview with Irena Klepfisz, a Holocaust survivor and child of one of the heroes of the Warsaw Uprising. Her primary concern is for the Palestinians, for they are human beings suffering right now. But at the same time she is worried that Israel has taken "the wrong road to safety," explaining "I don't want the Jews in Israel to die" (Rothschild 29). One might wonder what raises this concern. For Klepfisz does not say that she does not want some Jews to be killed in terrorist attacks. She says that she does not want "the Jews in Israel to die," as if they are, as a group, assimilable to a single person and thus might die collectively. In part, this is, of course, a result of the Holocaust and the tendency of anyone—perhaps especially a Holocaust survivor—to assimilate any threat against Jews to that single overwhelming historical horror. But it is also due in part to an implicit emplotment of the Israel/Palestine conflict in terms of the paradigmatic heroic tragicomedy (and the associated use of the metaphor NATIONS ARE PERSONS). One need not engage in subtle hermeneutics to uncover this link. The entire interview is recounted under the rubric of the opening quote from Klepfisz, "Israel is not David in this case. It is Goliath" (27). If Israel is David, certain things follow. But if Israel is Goliath, then other things follow—for example, though Israel is overwhelmingly stronger than its opponents and currently defeats them with ease, it risks being killed by the tiny, stone-hurling Palestinians, as Goliath was killed by David.

11. We obviously need to consider the current conditions in detail, too. But that is beyond the scope of this study

for Israeli nationalism today. The centrality of this story is reflected in a range of things, from the Israeli flag[12] to the common insistence that Jerusalem is the capital of the Jewish people. Interestingly, Jerusalem is sometimes referred to as Israel's "eternal, undivided capital" (quoted in Said, "The End" 4). But the centering of Jewish nationalism in Jerusalem is no more eternal than any other nationalist centering. In fact, the unique position of Jerusalem begins with the reign of David and is established in the heroic narrative surrounding his reign.

The story of David begins in 1 Samuel, continues in 2 Samuel, and is completed in 1 Kings.[13] It is retold in Chronicles. I will begin with the

12. The Israeli national emblem, the star (or shield) of David, does not derive from the story (see Wigoder 618). But its resonance is clearly the result of its linkage with this story.

13. Just what marks this as one story rather than two or three? In fact, this is not really a significant issue. Any narrative discourse may be divided in several ways. We could consider Saul's conflict with the Amalekites as a story or we could consider the treatment of all the Kings as a story. It depends on our purposes. In this case, we are concerned with the operation of stories in nationalist emplotment. In that context, some stretch of discourse counts as a story if it functions as a cognitive structure for organizing nationalist thought and action. Here and elsewhere, that organization is most often defined by prototypes. In other words, the prototype picks out some sequence of events from the discourse as a story. For example, prototypical heroic organization commonly begins with usurpation and/or invasion, often prefaced by a limited amount of information that serves to contextualize the usurpation and/or invasion—without thereby suggesting an endlessly unfolding sequence of prior causes, such as we would find in reality. In the case of David, we have a prototypical structure with further additions and developments, as is commonly the case. Moreover, as I indicate below, the additions and developments are largely fragments of the prototype structure.

There is, of course, a further complication in this case, since the version in Chronicles differs in some respects from the version in 1 Samuel, 2 Samuel, and 1 Kings. For the most part, the versions are the same or compatible. As a cognitive structure, it is undoubtedly the case that the overlapping parts of the two versions and the parts that closely match the heroic prototype constitute the key features of a single paradigm, with far greater and more consistent effects than the contradictory parts or less prototypical episodes. On the other hand, in some circumstances, distinctive features of alternative or less prototypical versions may be strongly activated (for those who actually remember them). It would be valuable to examine those differences in the development of Israeli nationalism—across different nationalist writers and across different periods—to see how the different versions and different elements of those versions did or did not appear and how consequential they were when they did appear. However, that would be a project for a book devoted entirely to Israeli nationalism and the story of King David. My purpose here is simply to establish the basic biblical structures available for nationalist use. To that end, I treat the two versions, including all incidentals. In keeping with the likely cognitive organization of the story in most people's minds, I treat differences as versions of or alternatives for a single story, rather than separate stories. Put very simply, I have no reason to believe that people cognitively store and process the Solomon of Kings and the Solomon of Chronicles as different persons with their own separate stories. Insofar as they have encoded the differences at all, people presumably handle them in the usual way—the same way in which they handle contradictory information in the real world. For instance, if one person tells me that Smith was at the department meeting and another says that Smith was not, I do not form two separate ideas about two separate Smiths. Rather, former, then treat Chronicles on some specific points where the accounts differ. I will also extend the discussion to include the reign of Solomon. The story of Solomon is, in effect, the culmination of the story of David. (It is not uncommon for heroic plots to continue across two generations of rulers; sometimes, it may go even beyond two generations, though two generations may be stressed even in those cases.)

The first book of Samuel introduces the idea of the kingship of Israel. This change in governance is not without problems. Indeed, this text is remarkable for its ambivalence regarding kingship. Biblical scholars identify two distinct strains in the narrative—one supportive of the monarchy, the other opposed. This is one of the ways in which this narrative is more complex than one might initially expect, one of the ways in which even paradigm texts are often more equivocal than their later nationalistic advocates allow. In any case, the kingship is first established with Saul. However, Saul is soon rejected by God and David is chosen in his place. Though he is not deposed, this rejection by God establishes a situation in which Saul can take up the role of the usurper, though he was initially the rightful ruler.

The story of Saul stresses a number of national opponents. Of these, the Philistines are no doubt the most important. They constitute the exemplary enemies in this narrative. However, the Amalekites, too, have an important position, for Saul loses God's favor due to his behavior in the war against this group. Here, then, we have the usual two enemy out-groups, one of which is more fully demonized than the other. Specifically, God orders Saul to "kill man and woman, babe and suckling, ox and sheep, camel and donkey" of the Amalekites (1 Samuel 15: 3). However, Saul is rejected by God because he spares some of the animals as well as the Amalekite king. The nature of Saul's sin suggests that the Philistines fall into the category of enemies who should be dominated; indeed, they may even be allies, as we will see. The Amalekites, in contrast, are enemies so demonic—so antithetical to divine will—that they must be eliminated entirely (see also 15: 18).

The next episode brings us to the anointing of David for the kingship. From here, the narrative takes up David's heroism, and begins to establish

---

I have one set of ideas about a single Smith and that set of ideas includes two alternatives on this particular issue. On the other hand, these two versions of Smith may be connected with different evaluations of Smith by my two informants. Something along these lines is certainly the case with the different versions of the story of David and Solomon. As we will discuss, these different versions deal in quite different ways with important aspects of the heroic prototype.

him as an ideal to be emulated. This occurs most clearly in the renowned episode of David and Goliath. When everyone else is "dismayed and terrified" (17: 11) by Goliath, David agrees to fight him, though David is "only a boy" (17: 33) and does not even have armor. David defeats Goliath handily and, in consequence, the Israelites defeat the Philistines. The selflessness of David's act, his complete devotion to the well-being of the group, and his full protection by God are all common heroic characteristics with obvious consequences for national identity. What is distinctive about the story is the gross disproportion between David and Goliath. As we have seen, this aspect of the battle has been important in the metaphorization of Israel's situation in the modern Middle East.

Following this, Saul becomes "jealous" (18: 9) of David's success and his popularity with the people. Moreover, in connection with this, Saul is "seized" by "an evil spirit" (18: 10). As a result, he begins to make attempts on David's life. This variation on the usurpation sequence is fairly common in heroic works, with the current ruler attempting to kill his heir, often his own son (as in the *Mwindo Epic* or, with some variations, the "Bogach Khan Son of Dirse Khan" episode of the Turkish *Book of Dede Korkut*). This leads to David's exile, again a standard element in heroic plots.[14]

David's exile serves to take us on a tour of the land that covers its northern, southern, and eastern extremes, and to a lesser extent the western extreme as well. David's wanderings lead him to Ramah, north of the Sea of Galilee, through Aphek, also in the north, but west of Ramah, close to the Mediterranean—towns near the northern border of Israel today. He travels to En-dor and Jezreel, just north of what is now the West Bank. He moves through the region around Jerusalem, south to the area between Bethlehem and Hebron (all now in the West Bank), to En-gedi, on the bank of the Dead Sea, just within Israel, and to Gath, west of Hebron (in modern Israel). Finally, when he must flee to the land of the Philistines, he has occasion to travel south into the Negev in pursuit of the Amalekites. Though there is little sentimentalization of the land, it is delineated with almost cartographic precision. Interestingly, in this case, the exile among the Philistines does not have the usual function of contrasting with the national territory (e.g., by establishing the hero's feeling of alienation). Rather, David is quite at home in the Philistine territory, suggesting that this territory should be part of David's nation as well.

---

14. For example, in the *Rāmāyaṇa* of India, the current ruler operates as usurper by exiling his son and heir, just at the moment when that son is supposed to become king.

This tour does not lack contemporary relevance. David's journey maps out virtually the entire area claimed by proponents of "Greater Israel" (Reich and Goldberg 146), which encompasses "all of Palestine, including Judea and Samaria," thus including the West Bank (Reich and Goldberg 122, 215). The broader link between David and Israeli expansionism has been fairly explicit. For example, as Christopher Hitchens recounts, David Ben-Gurion referred to the "Anglo-French-Israeli attack on Egypt . . . as a campaign for 'the kingdom of David and Solomon'" ("Israel Shahak" 9).

David's exile also introduces us to David's wives. They, too, mark out the boundaries of the nation, for one is from the south (Abigail of Carmel) and one is from the north (Ahinoam of Jezreel). These two wives have another function as well, for David's kingdom was continually at risk of dividing into two halves—Israel (in the north) and Judah (in the south). Indeed, after the death of Solomon, it did just that. The fact that he draws one wife from the north and one from the south serves to dull regional subnationalism. Indeed, one could see the marriages here as an almost allegorical union of the north and the south with the one king, David.

The exile ends with a curious alteration of the standard structure. The Philistines do attack, and they defeat Saul. But David is not there to defend Israel. Indeed, it seems at one point that he is about to join forces with the Philistines against his own people. Instead, however, he ends up fighting, and defeating, the Amalekites. This may be related indirectly to a defense of Israel, for the Amalekites are, again, the great foes of Israel. Indeed, it turns out that the man who killed Saul was an Amalekite. Though this was evidently a mercy killing at Saul's request (or at least it is reported as such by the Amalekite), David has the man executed (see 2 Samuel 1: 5–16). This episode suggests a threat to the kingdom by the Amalekites, a threat defeated by David, if only after Saul is dead. Thus, it suggests the standard structure of the usurped hero's return from exile to defend the nation. However, to complicate matters further, this account directly contradicts an earlier account, according to which Saul kills himself (1 Samuel 31: 3–6). Perhaps the extant text is a combination of different versions, any one of which might make more sense on its own. In any case, the story tends to recapitulate the characterization of Amalekites as the unredeemable enemy, the enemy to be exterminated, as opposed to the Philistines, who should merely be defeated (and may even be used by God to defeat Israel, when Israel requires punishment).

The division, particularly the characterization of the Amalekites, is not without consequences for Israeli nationalist thought today. For example, Hitchens has noted that "state-sponsored Israeli rabbis . . . argue in public that the Palestinians ought to go the way of the Amalekites" ("Fallen Idols" 9). Similarly, Alexander Cockburn reports that "Nathan Lewin, a prominent DC attorney often tipped for a federal judgeship," has maintained "that the families of Palestinian suicide bombers should be executed." Cockburn goes on to say that "Lewin cites the biblical destruction of the tribe of Amalek as a precedent" (9).

Following the death of Saul, David becomes king of Judah. There is a period of civil conflict, from which David emerges as king of Israel and Judah. The period of conflict is due to David's rejection by Israel and the assumption of the throne of Israel by Ishbaal, the son of Saul. This is a second version of the usurpation story, now in a more standard form. The restoration of David as king of the united Judah and Israel is of course the restoration of divinely chosen rule. This unification, an overcoming of regional subnationalism, is obviously of central importance to the nationalist function of the story. Indeed, it is crucial to the paradigmatic status of David that he accomplished this.

After the kingdoms are unified, David's next task is their centralization, their orientation toward a capital that has no regional affiliation, and that can serve as a common focal point for the nation, both in politics and in religion. Thus, the next event after David's anointing as king of Israel (he had already been anointed king of Judah) is the conquest of Jerusalem. The sanctification of this national center is accomplished by the transportation of the Ark of the Covenant to the city (2 Samuel 6).

The remaining stories of David in 2 Samuel and 1 Kings present a series of loosely connected incidents, often involving fragments of the heroic plot (as with Absolom's usurpation and David's second exile). However, this part of the story does not have the same nationalistic value, except of course for the fact that David's many military triumphs are important for his standing as a leader who could advance the dominant position of the national in-group. The treatment of Solomon in this context is somewhat diffuse as well, though it is clear that David's work of sanctifying the national center, Jerusalem, is brought to completion by Solomon's building of the temple—the religious/national center within the center.

Interestingly, the reader does not have the sense that the rule of either monarch was particularly utopian. David's reign continues to be troubled, while Solomon's seems problematic due to continuing military conflicts, as well as the complaints that arise from Israel immediately after his death (1 Kings 12: 4). In this respect, Chronicles is closer to the canonical form of the heroic plot. In Chronicles, the reign of Solomon appears much more idyllic. Though Israel still complains after his death (2 Chronicles 10: 4), the general sense of his reign is one of peace, power, and prosperity for the kingdom. Thus, we are informed that, "For riches and for wisdom King Solomon outdid all the kings of the earth" and "All the kings of the earth sought audience of Solomon to hear the wisdom God had implanted in his heart" (2 Chronicles 9: 22–23). Indeed, "In Jerusalem the king made silver common as pebbles, and cedars plentiful as the sycamores of the Lowlands" (9: 27). More generally, "Yahweh brought Solomon's greatness to its height in the sight of all Israel, and gave him a reign of such splendor as none that had reigned over Israel before him had ever known" (1 Chronicles 29: 25). Thus, in this version, the story of David culminates in the utopian rule of his son and successor, Solomon.

There are other aspects of the Chronicles version that are relevant here, especially with respect to Solomon. The most important concerns the temple. Again, David establishes Jerusalem as the political and spiritual center of the nation, locating the government there and the Ark of the Covenant. However, it is Solomon who builds the temple, "the house of Yahweh in Jerusalem" (2 Chronicles 3: 1). Here in particular the heroic narrative of David culminates in the reign of Solomon. The building of the temple in effect absolutizes the centering of the nation in Jerusalem. Out of the entire world, Yahweh explains, "I chose Jerusalem for my name to make its home there" (2 Chronicles 6: 6). Within this home of Jerusalem, which is itself within the home of Israel/Judah, the temple is God's particular "dwelling" (6: 1). It is the "house built" so that God's "name might make its home" (6: 5). At the same time, the temple serves as a metaphor for the nation as a whole, taking up the common THE NATION IS A HOME metaphor. In keeping with this, the destruction and reconstruction of the temple are, symbolically, the destruction and reconstruction of the nation. Indeed, the destructions of the temple are crucial events in the destruction of the nation, crucial events in an historical heroic tragicomedy. The destruction of the first temple occurred at the time of the Babylonian conquest and exile. The destruction of the second temple occurred as part of the Roman defeat of the first Jewish uprising. The ritual prayer at the western wall, the remaining wall of the second temple, suggests (and fosters) the continuing centrality of the temple in modern Israeli nationalism. The different Jewish festivals relating to the first and second temple have the same function. Tishah B'Av, "the most important fast after Yom Kippur" (Pilkington 174), commemorates and laments the Babylonian destruction of the first temple and the Roman destruction of the second temple. Hanukah commemorates the rededication of the temple after its desecration by the Hellenizing ruler Antiochus, a rededication resulting from the nationalist/religious

Maccabean revolt (Pilkington 168–69). The conflict over the Temple Mount (or Haram al-Sharif) is unsurprising in this context. The Temple Mount, now the site of a Muslim shrine, is also the site of the temple of Solomon and the temple of Herod.

Despite what I said about Solomonic utopia, there is an important ambivalence that is part of this story as well. As we have noted, heroic plots often involve an epilogue of suffering, a period of anguish for the great hero, a second exile in which that hero is punished for the violence and cruelty of his or her heroism, so that he or she may return to the nation with greater wisdom. In this case, as told in 1 and 2 Chronicles, these two aspects of one leader—the violent warrior who crushes the enemy on his or her rise to power and the peaceful ruler who governs with wisdom and benevolence after he or she has achieved power—are split into two figures, David and Solomon. Indeed, in 1 Chronicles, the difference between these figures is related implicitly to David's military brutality. God explains to David that he cannot (as we might put it) culminate his own story, he cannot build the temple, because, as God puts it to him, "you have been a man of war and have shed blood" (28: 3). Thus, it remains for the relatively pacific Solomon to build the temple. The point is in significant contradiction with the story as told in 2 Samuel, where the reason David does not build the temple is that God does not require a temple: "I have never stayed in a house from the day I brought the Israelites out of Egypt until today, but have always led a wanderer's life in a tent. In all my journeying with the whole people of Israel, did I say to any one of the judges of Israel, whom I had appointed as shepherds of Israel my people: Why have you not built me a house of cedar?" (7: 6–7). Thus, 2 Samuel does not present any criticism of David's militarism. In connection with this, 1 Kings portrays Solomon himself as militaristic and violent. In Chronicles, however, we see the ambivalence that often goes along with nationalism in heroic plots, the sense that the violence of the in-group is wrong and that the ideal leader eschews that violence, even against out-groups.

Unfortunately, this part of the heroic plot appears to play almost no role in the nationalism of any country. The point is unsurprising. Such a pacific attitude is bound up with universalism and human empathy. Thus, it works strongly against nationalism. Indeed, in both 1 Kings and 2 Chronicles, Solomon is presented as universalistic, welcoming into the Temple "the foreigner too, not belonging to [the] people of Israel" (1 Kings 8: 41; 2 Chronicles 6: 32). This universalism is symbolized in his marriage practices. While David takes wives from the northern and southern regions of his nation, Solomon takes wives from around the world: "King Solomon loved many foreign women: not only Pharaoh's daughter but Moabites,

Edomites, Sidonians and Hittites" (1 Kings 11: 1). Indeed, in 1 Kings, the great fault of Solomon is that he opens the nation to religious diversity and establishes "pagan shrines . . . for his wives and for traders," as the *Jerusalem Bible* editors put it (435n.11c). In many ways, the rule of Solomon manifests the conflict between nationalistic particularism and a broader sense of human communality. In short, it incorporates supranationalist elements. That is clearly part of what makes his reign utopian in 2 Chronicles, but also part of what makes it a period of decline in 1 Kings. In the latter, it is precisely Solomon's cosmopolitanism, his acceptance of his wives' different religions and the building of shrines to their gods and goddesses, that leads Yahweh to punish Solomon and the nation by dividing the kingdom into Israel and Judah after Solomon's death (1 Kings 11: 11–13).

The obvious question here is what consequences all this has for contemporary national conflicts. The question applies to not only Israel and Palestine, but the entire Judeo-Christian world, for, again, biblical stories have been important for many European and American nationalisms. Indeed, they are perhaps particularly important for the United States, with its lack of ancient sagas and medieval epics. On the other hand, the story of David has the most direct bearing on Israeli nationalism—which itself has very significant consequences for the rest of the world.

Unlike a writer such as Stanley Fish, I do think that being aware of our prejudices can help to limit them (for discussion, see my *On Interpretation* 38–42). Awareness of the way the David story operates to shape and orient Israeli nationalism can contribute to an effective critical analysis of dominant Israeli ideology on this issue, at least for some Israelis. For example, this paradigmatic story provides one prominent structure for understanding and imagining Palestinians. As such, it tends to limit that understanding and imagining to two models—Philistines and Amalekites. In this context, thinking of Palestinians as Philistines becomes, in effect, the liberal position. One result is that a fuller humanization of Palestinians—an understanding of them as people like anyone else, as opposed to understanding them as the less dehumanized of two paradigmatic enemies—appears to be a form of extremism, perhaps even betrayal of the nation. At the same time, a virtually complete dehumanization of Palestinians (in their assimilation to Amalekites) enters all too easily into political discussion. Awareness of this skewing of the debate is at least a first step toward correcting it.

On the other hand, there are two problems with such a critical analysis. The first is that I have done only a small part of the ideological work here. There are other stories, metaphors, symbols, rituals that contribute to Israeli nationalism and its associated ideologies. Moreover, there is a parallel set of Arab stories, and so on. These prominently include the heroic tragicomedy of Muhammad, as recounted in the Qur'ān, a book orthodox Muslims take to be the final, complete, and encompassing revelation—identical with the book that rests by the side of Allāh Himself ("We have revealed the Koran.... It is a transcript of the eternal book in Our keeping" [43: 2–3]). There is no issue of metaphorically assimilating Jews to this or that out-group in the Qur'ān. Jews figure explicitly in the narrative, and in a way that is hardly promising for the future of Jewish/Arab relations. Specifically, the Qur'ān asserts that "God made a covenant with the Israelites.... But because they broke their covenant We laid on them Our curse.... You will ever find them deceitful" (5: 12–13). It goes on to adjure believers not to "take ... Jews ... for your friends" (5:51) and to insist that the Jews are, in a crucial way, the fullest enemy of the Muslim: "You will find that the most implacable of men in their enmity to the faithful are the Jews" (5:82).

The second problem is that this all concerns ideology. And ideology is secondary. Identity categories are bound up with real, material conflicts and no amount of ideological critique will, by itself, resolve those material conflicts—the limitations of land, the scarcity of water. Of course, I am not saying that ideological analysis is irrelevant. It remains important, particularly for those of us who do not have any personal interest in the ownership of land or the control of water. However, pointing out that there is a dehumanizing emplotment cannot change political conditions if material conflicts are not altered. One's hope, of course, is that ideological critique will contribute at least something to constructive work bearing on these material conflicts.

Caspi ends his article by worrying that, in Israel/Palestine, "No one 'learns his lesson.'" Thus, all attempts at military deterrence will lead to retribution, with the standard result of spiraling violence. He sees this as the result of "mythology" (5). The case is overstated. The violence is no doubt much more a matter of such practical issues as unemployment and water rights. Nonetheless, there is an ideological element here, and a narrative one, both suggested by Caspi's term *mythology*. If nothing else, the preceding discussion has, I hope, begun to clarify one component of that mythology on one side of the conflict.

INDEPENDENCE DAY
America Leads the World to Freedom

Again, the heroic emplotment of nationalism is not cultivated solely by classics, paradigmatic works of the past. It is cultivated by current, popular works as well. Indeed, in an age of mass media when relatively few people read Virgil and many people see many movies and television programs, it is almost certainly the case that those popular works are collectively more important than the ancient epics. Of course, no single work is likely to be crucial. However, some works are particularly close to the national prototype and popular enough for us to take them as fairly representative of the collective impact of popular media on nationalism.[15] *Independence Day* is a case in point. It is, as I have already noted, one of the largest grossing films ever in the United States.[16] It is also a work that adheres very closely to the universal heroic structure—while at the same time clearly manifesting the standard American version of that structure.

The main plot of *Independence Day* concerns an alien invasion of the Earth. After an initial loss, the Americans regroup and defeat the invaders. This is clearly the standard threat/defense sequence. There is, in addition, a very muted usurpation narrative—in this case, an inexplicit attempt to control the national leader, rather than explicitly taking over his role. Specifically, a repugnant secretary of defense tries to manipulate the president (e.g., through concealing crucial information) until the president realizes his perfidy and removes him from office. American particularity enters most strikingly with the fact that this is a global battle in which the United States leads the rest of the world to freedom—a standard element of specifically U.S. nationalism (see, for example, Wallerstein 123, on this aspect of American national ideology). In other words, the United States does not fight a local battle for its own freedom. Rather, it takes charge of a battle that benefits all nations. It has a "mission to redeem the world" (bound up with its "divinely ordained destiny"), as Weeks put it (144; quoted in Chomsky, *Failed States* 92). Moreover, in both the film and standard American ideology, the United States does this primarily through ingenuity—our national intellectual trait of practical intelligence or Yankee know-how—combined with the more standard heroic trait of selfless bravery.

15. This impact is a matter of forming our prototypes and linking those prototypes to nationalism. Again, as cognitive structures in individual people's minds, prototypes are formed by a sort of weighted averaging across instances. Thus, a film such as *Independence Day* will have different impacts on different people, depending on the precise set of national heroic narratives they have experienced to that point. The number of such narratives will affect the degree to which this film has an effect (e.g., it will probably have more of an effect on young viewers than on old viewers, other things being equal). But so will the precise nature of the cognitive structure formed by the prior experiences, the emotional effects of different components of that structure and of the film, current conditions that affect the salience of memories and the context-sensitive configuration of prototypes at that moment, and so on.
16. Again, the point here is not to say that *Independence Day* is itself strongly influential. Rather, the point is that films—including *Independence Day*—are, on the whole, strongly influential and that the popularity of *Independence Day* makes it an apt example to analyze.

In fact, the film develops nationalist concerns with such precision that it almost seems as if the filmmakers had an understanding of identity categorization comparable to that presented in the preceding chapters. The film begins with a date, July 2. If it was not clear already, this indicates that the Independence Day named in the title is July 4, the anniversary of the independence of the United States. On the other hand, it is important that the film is not called "The Fourth of July." "Independence Day" retains a generic sense, applicable to any "free" nation. This combines with its American particularity to suggest that the United States is the exemplar of global independence. The first shot in the film is the American flag on the moon. This has many implications. First, it once again indicates that this is a specifically American national film. It also suggests the territorial scope of the nation, extending beyond even the planet. After the flag, we see the associated plaque. The plaque explains that "MEN FROM THE PLANET EARTH FIRST SET FOOT UPON THE MOON." Viewers are well aware that the people who landed on the moon were American. Indeed, we see Richard Nixon's signature on the plaque. However, the plaque identifies those Americans as representatives and leaders of "THE PLANET EARTH." The rest of the plaque furthers the point, explaining that "WE CAME IN PEACE FOR ALL MANKIND."

Once the global—and even extraterrestrial—authority of the national in-group is established in this way, a shadow passes across the moon and we see the invading alien spaceship moving toward the Earth.

We cut from here to New Mexico, a space monitoring station. We first see a young East Asian man. He wakes his boss, an older white man. They are joined by a black man and a white woman. To some, this may seem like a politically correct inclusion of minorities. It may be. But it simultaneously results from a standard development principle that operates as a technique of nationalization. Specifically, the narrative brings together a range of characters from subnational identity groups in order to subsume the relevant subnational categories under the national category. The next scene takes us to Washington, D.C. In Washington, we first see the famous sculpture of U.S. soldiers raising the flag on Iwo Jima. The reference to the Second World War is crucial. There is a virtually universal sense that the Second World War was entirely justified on the part of the allies. As a result, the United States has tended to justify subsequent wars by claiming a close analogy with the Second World War. The filmmakers are clearly setting up a parallel with the Second World War in this fictional case as well.

We are soon introduced to President Whitmore, his name partially recalling our national poet, Whitman (perhaps fused with Mount Rushmore).

His cabinet is uniformly white. However, it does include one woman, Connie, who is arguably the most loyal and sensible member. More important, we learn that Whitmore was a pilot in the Gulf War (the first, of course, since the second had not yet occurred at the time of the film's making). The link suggests the continuity between this conflict and the conflict in Iraq, thus further particularizing the heroic tragicomedy, not only to the United States, but to a specific moment in U.S. history—perhaps unwittingly helping to prepare the way for the second gulf war.

The film continues with the tour of the national territory. Having covered the moon, New Mexico, and Washington, D.C., we now turn to New York. We are introduced to New York by the Statue of Liberty, with its visible inscription of July 4, 1776. Again, we are faced with the theme of the United States as the source of liberty. The inscription also suggests the durability of the nation, a property that will, of course, be important in what follows.

From here, we turn to a chess match in Central Park. Two characters are engaged in an intellectual form of warfare. We eventually learn that they are Jewish, a father and son. The son is aptly named "David." He wins the chess match. The scene suggests a number of things. First, it prepares us for the intellectual part of the war, the aspect of strategy and ingenuity. Second, it begins to point toward a connection between this David and the divinely chosen David of the Bible. Such a connection relates to the implication of divine preference for the United States. (In keeping with this, at the end of the film, just before he flies off to save the world from destruction, David gives his father a yarmulke and, it seems, a copy of the Torah.) Simultaneously, it suggests that the martial victories of King David are now recapitulated by the intellectual victories of the American David. Finally, it brings Jewish Americans into the film's treatment of national unity across potential ethnic subnationalisms.

This incorporation of subnational identity groups is continued when David goes to work and meets his associate. It seems likely that we are supposed to assume that this associate is gay. This is not explicit. However, the character is given a series of stereotypically gay mannerisms and is played by the well-known gay rights activist Harvey Fierstein. This, too, serves to defuse a potential threat of subnational divisiveness.

It is almost as if the filmmakers were given a list of subnational groups to include, for the next scene takes us to a trailer park in California. This obviously extends the geographical survey of the nation. It also extends the integration of subnational groups. Up to now, the characters have had no identifiable class background. They are all vaguely middle class. Here, we have a widely ridiculed, lower economic class—"trailer trash." In this case, the film doubles up on subnational groups, as we see a group of dark children and hear Spanish being spoken. Russell, the main character in this group, may not be Hispanic himself. However, his children (e.g., his oldest son, Miguel), are clearly Hispanic. Russell is himself a Vietnam veteran and an alcoholic. The connection with Vietnam serves to establish a continuity in American militarism from Vietnam through the Gulf War to the present conflict. Since he is impoverished and addicted, it also suggests the mistreatment of Vietnam veterans. That mistreatment is, of course, commonly blamed not on the people who sent them to war but on the peace movement that worked to bring them home. In any case, we later discover that Russell is abused by his neighbors. This is literally due to his idea that he was abducted by aliens. However, it clearly suggests the stereotype of the abused and discarded national hero, specified in this case to the "hero" of Vietnam.

The alien ship now begins to send out smaller pods that will travel to the major cities of the world. The first glimpse we get of this is in the Northern Desert in Iraq. This again suggests the crucial importance of Iraq for American "national defense."

As the alien ships seem to pose a danger, we find that the sinister secretary of defense wants to run, while the brave general and president insist that they will stay while others are moved to a secure location. The general asks Whitmore what will happen if the aliens turn hostile. Whitmore introduces the crucial element of divine election, responding, "Then God help us."

Here, having seen the general pattern of integrating subnational groups, we may wonder why blacks have been so underrepresented. The film would have a serious flaw in serving national integration if it did not include an African American among the heroic warriors. Thus, a black family is introduced. The man is wearing dog tags, so we identify him immediately as a soldier. Though on leave, he has to report immediately to his base, due to the crisis. Though his girlfriend, Jasmine, is angry, he shows no hesitation in his commitment to duty.

We return to Washington, this time introduced by the Lincoln memorial—in part, perhaps, to suggest the emancipation of the slaves, thus a moment of important national division and reconciliation. We are also introduced to the president's young daughter, who parallels Jasmine's young son, and we learn that the president's wife is away, just as Jasmine's boyfriend is going away. The parallelism serves to connect these seemingly very different (American) families, thereby partially occluding subnational differences.

At this point, the shadows of the pods pass over the Washington Monument, the Statue of Liberty, and so forth, suggesting the threat to our traditions and our freedoms. In between, we see the pictures on the president's table. There are, of course, pictures of his wife and daughter. However, more important, there are pictures of the president with the Dalai Lama and with the Pope, suggesting the close connection between his temporal authority and the authority of God.

We now return to David. Like the president and the general, he refuses to run and hide. Having isolated the signals sent by the mother ship to its pods, he manages to interpret the message. Specifically, he learns that the signals are cycling down to zero. He realizes that zero is the point when the ships will attack. It is never quite clear why a countdown necessarily means destruction. David does, of course, turn out to be right. But the obscurity of the inference is important. It suggests that it is necessary for us to have faith in military expertise, even when the arguments do not seem compelling. The point is illustrated as David tries to communicate his discovery to his ex-wife, Connie. Connie initially hangs up on him. David shows persistence and ingenuity. As a result, he is able to communicate his "findings" to the president. However, due to Connie's skepticism, the president, David, the general—all the main heroes of the film—are almost killed. They manage to escape just in the nick of time. The message (or at least one message) is clear—we must trust the inferences of our experts when they point to the malevolence of out-groups.[17] (This is, of course, just what the American public did during the lead-up to the Gulf War.)

The point is enhanced by the fact that, in Los Angeles, a group of (presumably liberal) crazies is trying to welcome the aliens while in Washington the despicable peaceniks are out with signs demanding that we not make first contact through a military attack. Again, the film is specifying the heroic structure in ways particular to the contemporary United States. We often find some obstacle to the prosecution of the war in heroic plots. Here, the obstacle is not, say, the self-indulgence of the great hero (as it is, for example, in the *Iliad* or the *Shâhnâme*). Rather, the obstacle is members of the in-group who do not recognize the malevolence of the out-group, members of the in-group who are inadequately nationally iden-

---

17. Peter Rabinowitz has rightly pointed out to me that it is common in films of this sort for the character who should be trusted to be the one who is least trusted initially. This is a narratively important point and extends back at least to the biblical prophets who go unheeded, Cassandra, and so on. I suspect that this figure results primarily from the emotional intensification of narrative. The tragic outcome is rendered all the more painful by the fact that we could have known and averted it. As *Independence Day* shows, the discounted prophet role may be effectively taken up in heroic nationalist narratives by a character whose distrust of the out-group is particularly extreme.

tified. Indeed, these are, in effect, the film's version of traitors. However, they are themselves naïve, not malevolent traitors. That is made clear when the crazies in Los Angeles turn out to be the first ones annihilated by the aliens. Clearly those calling for peace and friendship with the enemy are both profoundly mistaken and profoundly dangerous—even to themselves. At this point, the only hope seems to be that mentioned by a newscaster just before the fatal attack: "God help us all." In other words, the only hope appears to be divine preference.

It is now July 3. The initial attack has occurred. The Statue of Liberty is face down in the water. Liberty itself is profoundly endangered. The president compares the present crisis to the Gulf War. Now the retaliation, the self-defense begins. Our African American hero, Captain Hiller, is at his military base. The United States will launch a counterattack. The planes take off. The great battle scene will begin. But it is a slaughter. The Americans do not have a chance. They are, in effect, facing a mighty Goliath. Only Hiller survives, killing one of the aliens through his remarkable ingenuity. Specifically, he uses his parachute to blind the pursuing pilot (who is evidently not using anything like radar). Hiller then ejects before crashing into a wall. The blinded alien crashes. However, it survives and exits the pod, only to be knocked senseless by a crushing blow from Hiller's fist, in good epical fashion. Unsurprisingly, the alien is slimy and has many tentacles. It is made to be as disgusting as possible, thus foreclosing any possibilities for empathy.

As Captain Hiller is outwitting this alien, other alien ships are destroying his military base in a scene that seems designed to recall the attack on Pearl Harbor. Here again, the film is both invoking and reenforcing the use of the Second World War as the paradigm of U.S. military action. Obviously, fictional space aliens are the culprits in this film. However, films such as this encourage us to model real contemporary events on such a fiction—and on the historical events of the Second World War. They create a context in which it is easier to see, for example, the September 11 bombings as an invasion, thus the initiation of a war/the beginning of a heroic plot, rather than, say, a criminal act.

While this is going on, the president learns that many years ago the United States had actually captured three such aliens. The secretary of defense had kept this secret—a form of usurpation, since he was in effect running part of the government without the knowledge of the president. Subsequently, the film cuts among several story lines. Jasmine and her son survive the attack, find a truck with the keys, then drive around picking up other survivors, including the First Lady. Hiller has bundled the alien up in his umbrella and is dragging it across the desert when he meets a caravan of trailers escaping the devastation. The caravan prominently displays an American flag. It includes Russell. Hiller explains that he saw a base when he was flying over. The caravan then proceeds to that base, which happens to be the ultrasecret location of the captured ship and aliens.

The president, his staff, and David are now at this ultrasecret location, Area 51, in Nevada. They are trying to figure out what to do—especially since the captured aliens have been dead for fifty years and are now evidently preserved in formaldehyde. Fortunately, the caravan arrives with the fresh alien. Through peculiar means, the alien manages to communicate with the humans. Whitmore says that the humans wish to negotiate a peace. This follows the usual ideological principle that our national group is peace-loving and resorts to war only when forced by the enemy. The malevolent alien replies, "No peace." Whitmore asks, "What is it you want us to do?" It replies, "Die." This is a representation of pure out-group malevolence. The president manages to learn that this species is like locusts. They simply consume all the resources of a planet, then move on.

The unspeakable vileness and inhumanity of the alien, and the absolute nature of the threat, prepare the audience for the president's decision: "Nuke 'em. Let's nuke the bastards." Here the in-group determines to use its ultimate weapon. When this, too, does not work, the situation seems hopeless.

At this point, romantic concerns enter briefly, both comic and tragic. Hiller steals a helicopter to rescue Jasmine and the First Lady. (He cleverly guesses where they will be.) He brings them to Area 51. He and Jasmine are eventually married there. But the president's wife has been too badly injured and dies. Thus, July 3 ends in a moment of both national and personal sorrow.

As July 4 begins, David suddenly realizes that he can use the captured alien pod to upload a virus that will lower the enemy's shields. As a result, the aliens will be defenseless and we will be able to defeat them. The secretary of defense objects to the plan and the president finally realizes that he is a pernicious influence on the government. Now the president fully takes charge, first roughing up the weasely secretary, then firing him. This ends the very limited usurpation/restoration sequence. He agrees to David's plan. It is, we may infer, only through David that America will defeat this foreign Goliath.

Before initiating the attack, the president contacts allies throughout the world, forming the sort of coalition of the willing celebrated later by George W. Bush. First, we see British soldiers in Iraq hearing about the coalition. This once again suggests the importance of Iraq for American national interests. It also suggests the particular closeness of Britain to the United States. Immediately following this, we turn to Israel, probably the most loyal American ally. A third sequence takes us to Russia and a fourth to Japan. Russia and Japan are, I believe, chosen to indicate that old conflicts have been overcome and every free nation in the world now recognizes that freedom can be maintained only by following the leadership of the United States.

American pilots gather at Area 51—including Russell, who has been recruited to join the force. The president gives a speech in which he makes explicit some of the distinctive themes of U.S. nationalism. Tacitly recalling the moon plaque we saw at the outset, he explains that we must be "united" as "mankind" in "fighting for our freedom." He connects this with the date, going on to say that the Fourth of July is not just America's, but the world's Independence Day. The point may seem to be very egalitarian and global. But it is not. The United States is clearly the leader in the global coalition. It initiates the cooperation. It gives the instructions. It also faces the mother ship of the aliens, thus taking on the most crucial and formidable part of the fighting. To say that the Fourth of July is the world's Independence Day is to say that the freedom of the United States is what allows and even defines the freedom of the world. Again, this is a standard part of U.S. nationalist ideology and its specification of universal national structures, including the heroic narrative.[18]

After a rocky start, Hiller and David set off in the captured pod as the pilots go to fight. Fortunately, Hiller is such an expert warrior that he can fly even this alien craft with enormous skill. They enter the alien mother ship and dock. David easily links his laptop to the alien mainframe and uploads the virus. As a result, our bombs work against the alien ships. But this is not solely the result of ingenuity. We learn that, deep in the underground confines of Area 51, David's father has gathered a group of people to pray. He is wearing his yarmulke and saying prayers in Hebrew. Perhaps the absurd compatibility of David's laptop and the alien mainframe is the result of divine intervention.

Despite all this, the battle is going badly. American weapons are not enough to destroy the great disk that hovers over Area 51. The disk is opening up to fire its death ray, the same weapon that destroyed Los Angeles. Russell is the last hope of the world. He has only one missile. It won't

---

18. We saw a version of this specification in the Gettysburg Address. When Lincoln asserts that "government of the people, by the people, for the people, shall not perish from the earth," he tacitly identifies the existence of the United States with the existence of democracy on "the earth."

fire. He realizes that he can fly up into the disk, destroying it along with himself. What follows is, in part, a standard scene of self-sacrifice for the good of the nation. Russell radios back, "Tell my children I love them very much." Laughing in the face of death and mocking the aliens, he flies into the belly of the beast. Thus, he becomes a suicide bomber—though I suspect that few viewers recognize this fact, in part because our prototype for a suicide bomber is so different. His self-sacrifice destroys the disk. It is a case of pure, selfless devotion to the nation, in a standard heroic tragicomic episode. It is also another case of ingenuity, thus it is particularly American as well. As the disk explodes, the high command sees that the strategy is generalizable. The United States now can tell the rest of the world "how to bring those sons of bitches down."

Hiller and David are still inside the mother ship. They try to leave, but with no success. It seems that they, too, have no choice but to become suicide bombers. They fire their weapons. Fortunately, this manages to dislodge their pod, allowing them to escape before the explosion They fly through the ship, barely squeezing out before it is destroyed. The explosion kills literally millions of aliens. One must assume that these millions include countless children and civilians.[19] Nonetheless, it is only a cause for celebration. There is no epilogue of suffering in this film.

We now have another series of global scenes, showing the results of American leadership in freeing the world. We begin with a group of African tribal people brandishing spears and celebrating the fall of an alien disk. Since the Africans have only spears, we can infer that they did not destroy the disk themselves. Evidently this was the result of the destruction of the mother ship. I assume the move to Africa is an attempt to undermine black/white subnational divisions in the United States. First, the aliens are defeated by the cooperation of an African American and a (Jewish) European American; then, we see that Africans are themselves freed by America (not enslaved, as they were formerly). From here, we move to Egypt, arguably the major U.S. ally in the Muslim Middle East (along with Saudi Arabia). Finally, we see Australia, another important ally and a part of the larger English-speaking world. The film ends with the reunion of the main characters and their celebration of this Fourth of July.

---

19. Peter Rabinowitz has pointed out to me that the film does not show us any women and children. This is an important point. As already noted, it does give us the information that this is a nomadic civilization, moving from planet to planet. Thus, we must assume that the ships include the entire range of society. But it does not make the women and children or male civilians salient. The film does not encourage our indifference to the murder of enemy civilians by exposing and celebrating it. Rather, the film does this by showing us mass killing, but occluding the presence of noncombatants, a standard technique in real warfare.

The film has gone through, and extensively elaborated, the invasion/defense sequence of the heroic plot, specifying it in ways that are distinctively American. It has given us a survey of the national territory. It has brought together heroes from various subnational groups, joining them in common nationalist identification. It has rendered the national category more salient and emotionally powerful, connecting it with pride, anger, and awe. It has represented the nation as enduring, opposable, and highly functional. It has also reenforced the rightness of the hierarchy of authority in the United States. It has suggested the divine election of the nation as well as links between the national hierarchy and that divine election. Finally, it has done this in such a way as to represent the United States, not as an antagonist of other nations in the world, but rather as their natural leader and the source of their own freedom. It ends with a reference to fireworks, the traditional way of celebrating the Fourth of July, and a shot of what are evidently the alien pods streaming down from the sky, plummeting toward destruction. The final scene then turns the devastation of war into an object of aesthetic delight—not unlike what national poets and popular storytellers do in creating heroic tragicomedies.

PRESIDENT GEORGE W. BUSH AND SEPTEMBER 11

In many ways, *Independence Day* could be seen as preparing the way for the recent invasion of Iraq. To some very limited extent, I suppose, it did. However, most of the continuities between the film and subsequent historical events are the result of the universal principles of nationalism and heroic tragicomedy, on the one hand, and the standard specification of those principles in U.S. nationalism, on the other. Thus, the continuities are not a matter of the influence of this particular film. Rather, they are evidence of broader patterns—some universal, some national—that bear on both the film and the invasion. These more encompassing patterns are visible in Bush's speeches after the bombings of September 11, perhaps most clearly in the September 14 "Remarks" that incorporate and extend his briefer statements from the preceding three days. Because it manifests these patterns, this speech is valuable beyond what it tells us about Bush's thoughts at that moment. It is important for understanding the development of U.S. policy in subsequent years, including the invasions of Afghanistan and Iraq. For our purposes, the crucial point is that, like *Independence Day*, the analyses it puts forth and the policies it announces are tacitly organized by a heroic narrative—specifically, a heroic narrative particularized in the standard American ways.

September 14, 2001, was declared a National Day of Prayer and Remembrance for the victims of the September 11th bombings. Only three days after the event, President Bush's speech already shows a clear heroic emplotment of the bombings. The speech begins by stating that "we" are in "the middle hour of our grief." The phrasing is interesting from a narrative perspective. It is almost Aristotelian in suggesting a sequence of beginning, middle, and end. The beginning of the narrative, and thus the beginning of "our" grief, was of course the bombings. The end will be the resolution of our grief.[20] Though it is not clear yet, that resolution will come in our defeat of the enemy. Though brief, the passage is resonant. First, by tacitly starting the emplotment of events with the bombings, it indicates that there is an absolute, punctual beginning to the story. Bush's opening statement, then, already suggests what will become clear later on—that there is no prior story, nothing that explains the bombings. In contrast, the wars that will follow September 11 are implicitly characterized as an outcome, an end, the conclusion of a story. If we bomb Afghanistan, that is not the beginning of a story; that is not an unprovoked attack comparable to the September 11 bombings. Rather, our bombings are the end of the story, or of one part of the story that will lead to an ending. The September 11 bombings clearly had a series of precedents, as we discussed in chapter 4. However, those are set aside in this emplotment.

In the second sentence, Bush refers to "our nation's sorrow" and our concern "for the missing and the dead, and for those who love them." Note that this first of all defines a particular category for identification—the nation. Moreover, it links the personal, lived suffering of people who lost friends and family members with that identity category. The implication is that all Americans have been harmed in just the way those immediate victims have been harmed. The connection is crucial, for it bears directly on the affectivity of the national category, and on its specification in terms of "our" (national) response. If we are all harmed by the bombings, then we should all feel fear or anger. Moreover, if the pain of September 11 is the pain of a nation, then one should expect a national reaction. The obvious form of a national reaction is military. One can see this more clearly by imagining the difference it would have made if Bush construed the event in sub- or transnational terms. Suppose, for example, he had referred to

---

20. The phrase may mean either "the middle time, which is one of grief" or "the middle of our time of grieving." Either interpretation fits my analysis. By the first interpretation, the next hour is the one when we have overcome our grief. By the second interpretation, the next hour is the final stage of grief, prior to its resolution. In both cases, there was normalcy, then a trigger of grief, followed by grief (now), to be followed by resolution and overcoming of grief.

"the sorrow experienced in New York" or "this great human sorrow." If we were to sympathize with all New Yorkers as the ones affected by this attack, we would probably not think primarily of a military response. Similarly, if we thought of the group harmed as humans, we would probably not think of attacking another nation. In both cases, we might, instead, imagine policing and/or judicial responses.

To some extent, these points imply the narrative ending. Again, the middle of our tragicomedy is "grief." Given this, how do we reach the ending, the happy resolution? If the grief is national, thus social, then presumably we can achieve the happy resolution by achieving the prototype of social happiness—domination of the out-group, specifically the devastation of the group that engaged in the bombings. Clearly, this orients us toward war. The point is clearer if we do not follow Bush's national generalization of the grief, but think of the victims primarily as the people whose lives were actually affected—those whose friends or relatives were killed, those who were injured or whose homes were destroyed, those whose businesses were ruined, and so forth. In this case, we would be more immediately inclined to offer financial support, medical services, job programs, counseling, or other sorts of human comfort. Here, too, we may be more likely to think of the bombings themselves as criminal acts, requiring some sort of law-enforcement response. War might not even occur to us as a way of responding to this grief.

In the third sentence of the speech, Bush introduces supernatural causality, thus the issue of divine preference. He explains that Americans have "come before God to pray." The point is enhanced by Bush's decision to deliver the speech in the National Cathedral. It clearly serves to align the nation with divinity, for if God approved of the bombings, there would be no point in appealing to him.[21] Moreover, it suggests that the outcome of this developing narrative will indeed be comic—though, again, it can be comic only for the nation, not for those whose parents or children or husband or wife died.

Though very little is explicit in the opening paragraph, Bush has prepared us for a construal of the September 11 events as the tragic beginning of a national heroic tragicomedy. This becomes explicit in the second paragraph. "On Tuesday, our country was attacked with deliberate and massive cruelty." The phrasing is, in a way, brilliant. The reference to the day of the week begins to suggest the utter normalcy from which the narrative

---

21. Of course, one might ask God's forgiveness for whatever inspired His wrath. But that is obviously not what Bush has in mind.

emerges—again, the normalcy that tells us there was no preceding story. The rest of the sentence asserts that this was not any narrative beginning, but specifically the beginning of the threat/defense sequence of heroic tragicomedy. Again, it was not New York, or symbols of commerce and militarism (the World Trade Center and the Pentagon), or even a group of particular, innocent individuals that was attacked. Nor was it humanity, or principles of international law. Rather, it was "our country." Moreover, the attack was deliberate and massively cruel. "Deliberate" here is crucial. One of the key differences between "us" and "them" concerns the killing of innocents. If we kill innocent people, it is unintentional. If they kill innocent people, it is deliberate. By this distinction, hundreds of thousands of innocents killed by U.S. policies in Iraq simply do not count. We did not kill them on purpose. In contrast, the three thousand people killed on September 11 do count, because the killing was intentional. In fact, it is very difficult to explain this distinction. The U.S. government knew that hundreds of thousands of people would die in Iraq if certain sanctions were imposed. It went ahead and imposed the sanctions. The leaders of al Qaeda knew that thousands of people would die in New York if the towers were bombed. They went ahead and organized the bombing. U.S. government officials could say that they did not want to kill those people. If the Iraqi government had simply behaved differently, they would have ended the sanctions. By the same token, al Qaeda could say that they would have aborted their bombing plans if the U.S. government had behaved differently—if it had ended the sanctions in Iraq and supported a genuine solution to the Israel/Palestine conflict. But, of course, it is part of the emplotment, and part of the in-group/out-group division, that the actions of the out-group are malevolent while ours are not. The intentional harm of innocents is part of that malevolence.

The point is obviously reiterated in the idea of "cruelty." The out-group is driven by an actual desire to harm us. It is not merely animated by the normal desires and ambitions that motivate everyone. Members of the out-group enjoy our pain. That, too, is part of their malevolence. We, of course, are cruelty-free, for we are benevolent. We attack only when provoked, when endangered by the cruelty of the enemy.

The qualification "massive" is in some ways peculiar. Certainly as a crime, the bombing of the towers was massive. But, in terms of war, few people would consider it massive at all. At least according to some estimates, the United States subsequently killed more than three thousand civilians in three months in Afghanistan (One estimate, in January 2002, put the number around four thousand [see Szabo]). Virtually no one seems to have considered this an atrocity, or anything terribly serious. Again, this may be because four thousand civilian casualties do not seem massive in the context of war. But the whole point of the speech is that the September 11 bombers were engaging in war, not simple crime.[22]

In fact, the significance of "massive" is never fully clarified in the speech. It is only after the invasion of Iraq that the meaning is evident. Bush prepared Americans for that invasion by invoking "weapons of mass destruction." The crucial point in this early speech is that the enemy has massive powers that can cause massive destruction. One common development of heroic emplotment involves enhancing the power of the out-group, for that makes the story more tense, and the comic outcome more powerful. It suggests the true heroism of the national in-group. Moreover, if the enemy is not seen as adequately powerful, there is a risk that we may come to feel empathy with their sufferings. Bush does not go so far as to imply that we are David facing Goliath. But the suggestions of the word "massive" here—like those of the putative weapons of mass destruction in Iraq—are a less drastic version of the same basic idea.

In the next sentence, Bush reenforces the national/heroic emplotment of the bombings by his reference to "images of fire and ashes, and bent steel." Though perfectly accurate, the phrasing is designed to prime associations with images of devastating aerial bombardment in times of war. What is crucial here is selecting and organizing information about this complex event so that the event is narratively comprehensible, and points us (narratively) toward certain goals. In this case, the selection and organization are a function of the opening of the threat/defense sequence in the heroic plot, and the goal is, of course, "defensive" war.

The third paragraph continues the imagery of war as it refers, not to those who died or were injured, but to "the list of casualties," a phrase with clearly military resonances. The following sentence refers to the people themselves, "men and women who began their day at a desk or in an

---

22. Of course, there is the fact that the three thousand victims of the September 11 bombings were all killed in a day, not in the course of three months. But I find it hard to see how killing four thousand innocent people becomes morally acceptable if the killing is simply spread out over a few months, rather than confined to a single day. There is also the issue of deliberate versus accidental killing. But, again, it is not quite right to say that civilian casualties in war are accidents in the morally exculpatory sense. When a government decides to bomb another country, the officials who make the decision know that there will be civilian casualties. They choose to engage in the bombardment anyway. Given that such casualties are foreseeable, they form part of one's decision to act and thus part of one's moral responsibility. If I decide to race my car through a crowded marketplace, I can be fairly sure that I will kill people. The fact that I would prefer not to kill anyone does not make me innocent of the deaths that I cause.

airport." The point is to foreground the normalcy of these people's lives before the bombings. And that is right. These people were not involved in a causal sequence that led up to the bombings (except in the banal sense that we are all to some degree involved in the actions of our government). Thus, in their case, and in the case of their relatives and friends, the bombings were an absolute narrative beginning (and, in another way, an absolute ending). But the speech serves to obscure the difference between the absoluteness of the beginning in these individual cases and the (beginningless) history that preceded the bombings at the national level. In this way, the speech repeats the elision performed by al Qaeda, who punished three thousand innocent people for the crimes of a government (which itself repeated the earlier U.S. elision when U.S. sanctions punished hundreds of thousands of Iraqi children for the actions of Saddam Hussein).

The paragraph ends with a reminder of some of the most heart-wrenching moments of the bombing, when husbands called their wives or mothers called their children just before they died. But the speech uses these terribly painful, personal moments to communicate a nationalist and heroic narrative. First, in emphasizing that the men and women called "home" (rather than, say, "relatives" "loved ones"), Bush's phrasing may recall the link between home and homeland—a connection exploited soon after this speech in the institution of the Department of Homeland Security. Second, and more important, Bush tells us that these calls home communicated two messages. One was "I love you." The other was "be brave." The latter is particularly important for our purposes. Obviously, if a dying man calls his wife and says "be brave," he means that she should not give in to despair, that she should not be overwhelmed by the personal loss. But by invoking the concept of bravery, Bush links the dying wish of those who were killed with the heroic imperative that the nation, the "home" or "homeland," should be courageous in the military sense.

The last point is taken up in the next paragraph, where Bush names two categories of those who died in the bombings. The first category is "passengers who defied their murderers." Clearly, these were genuinely brave people, and they did something admirable in trying to retake the plane. However, this is most obviously human bravery, bravery in attempting to save lives. I find it hard to imagine that these people would have behaved differently if the hijacking was a matter of some personal vendetta by a lunatic (e.g., a rival to the architect who designed the towers). Yet, the entire speech contextualizes this act as a specifically national response to an enemy attack. This is even clearer when Bush turns to the second group, a group that is presumably parallel to the first. This is the group of "men and women who wore the uniform of the United States, and died at their posts." Though very few of the "casualties" on September 11 were U.S. military personnel, Bush to some degree connects all the deaths with military deaths, thus reenforcing the link between the bombing and battle.

The following paragraph adds a third group, "rescuers." Again, these were genuinely brave people. They should certainly be honored. But this is protective bravery. Even in the context of warfare, it is the bravery of the medic working his or her way across the battlefield to help the wounded. It is not the bravery of the soldier, crossing the battlefield in order to kill the enemy. Moreover, it is not clear that the rescuers acted bravely due to a categorial identification as American. It is at least possible that they died performing a human act, trying to save fellow human beings. But Bush says that, when we read the names of these men and women, "many Americans will weep." It is crucial that he says Americans. It is not people with empathy or people with moral sense who will weep. It is Americans.

The next paragraph addresses the families and friends of those who have died, assuring them that "you are not alone." One certainly cannot object to the act of trying to comfort the bereaved. However, there are many ways in which one could feel and assert such sympathy. Again, Bush does not assert that they are not alone because of human feeling. He suggests, rather, that they are not alone because all Americans are, in some sense, the bereaved family, because those who died were not, first of all, husbands, wives, children, parents, friends—they were, first of all, Americans.

The following paragraph begins by referring to Americans' understanding of the events. This reenforces the sense that the victims' families are not alone precisely because all Americans share this trauma. The second sentence in the paragraph again brings us to the heroic emplotment. Bush says that "our responsibility to history is . . . to answer these attacks and rid the world of evil." Answering the attacks is precisely following out the heroic plot. Identifying the out-group as evil is, of course, part of that plot. The rather grandiose claim about "our responsibility" to "rid the world of evil" is not so universal. It is, rather, bound up with the distinctive nationalism of the United States. It has been a crucial part of American self-definition that all history leads toward freedom and that (as I have stressed) our nation leads all other nations toward that freedom. Thus, what at first seemed like a very personal loss—the death of these particular people—is in fact a challenge to the historic role of the United States. That historic role is, of course, bound up with divine election. Indeed, it is messianic.

The United States will not merely defeat lawless attackers. Like Christ during his Second coming at the time of the apocalypse, the United States will actually do away with everything on earth that is evil.

In the following paragraph, Bush returns to the main heroic theme, "War has been waged against us." He goes on to denounce this, somewhat redundantly, as involving "stealth and deceit and murder." The crucial point here is that the enemy is not what he appears to be. His stealth and deceit suggest that we should guard ourselves against any empathy with him. Indeed, in the context of the speech as a whole, there is some suggestion that the enemy is not only satanically evil, but Satan himself, the Great Deceiver.

Bush goes on to make a statement about the American national character, implicitly using the standard metaphor of the nation as a person and drawing on the standard characterization of the in-group as benevolent. "This nation," he claims, "is peaceful." In keeping with standard in-group/out-group oppositions, we only wish to live harmoniously with everyone. But there is a potential problem with such benevolence. Nice guys, as they say, finish last. Thus, Bush adds that we are, however, "fierce when stirred to anger." "Fierce" is an interesting choice. It suggests a sort of animal-like force and lethalness. When attacked, we are unrestrained and deadly. Put differently, once the heroic plot begins, we fight with full heroic energy. The explicit invocation of anger is important as well. Bush has dwelled on the sorrow of the event. But sorrow is not a mobilizing emotion. Here, he begins to point toward anger as the most appropriate and productive response to the bombings.

Following this, Bush returns to the opening of the heroic plot, asserting that the enemy began this "conflict" (again, note how different it would be to say that someone committed this crime, rather than that "others" began this "conflict"). He then looks ahead to the conclusion of the narrative. Speaking more like the author of a story than the president of a nation, he claims portentously that, "It will end in a way, and at an hour, of our choosing." The beginning of the heroic tragicomedy is always in the hands of the enemy. But how can anyone possibly predict that his or her in-group will be able to choose the precise resolution, the turn from tragedy to comedy? The assertion, I think, relies on the assumption of divine providence, which is, again, important in the heroic plot generally and crucial in Bush's particularization of that plot. Bush in effect explains his certainty in the following paragraph, where he once again invokes prayer. Prayer is, presumably, the most important means by which we will be able to choose the ending of this conflict.

Bush goes on to state that "Our purpose as a nation is firm," though we suffer "wounds." Here, again, he employs the metaphor schema THE NATION IS A PERSON. He transfers the individual bravery mentioned in the preceding paragraphs to a collective firmness of purpose here. It is clear by now that this purpose is military. Of course, at this point, no one knows what the object of our military attack might be. But that is secondary. The only crucial thing is that the heroic, military response will begin; the only crucial thing is that we will fight. The reference to "wounds" here is particularly significant. This metaphorization translates the deaths of individual people into nonfatal harm experienced by the nation as a whole/ the nation as a person. Among other things, this extends the idea that all Americans suffer because of the bombings (as it is our collective body that is wounded). It also fits with the appeal to the active, militant emotion of anger (as a response to these wounds), rather than the passive emotion of grief.

Of course, while firmness of purpose is a necessary condition for final triumph, it is not a sufficient condition. Rather, we need the help of God, His active supernatural support for His chosen nation. Thus, Bush quotes a woman in St. Patrick's Cathedral: "I prayed to God to give us a sign that He is still here." It is interesting that the transcript on the White House website capitalizes the first letter of "He." When heard, the statement could mean that the woman was looking for a husband, father, or son who was missing. However, as written, it means that the woman wondered if God was still present "here." Even this is ambiguous. There are several places she could mean by "here," including New York or the world as a whole. But the suggestion of Bush's speech is that "here" is America, the nation. This woman's personal question, then, comes to suggest a grand, national question—whether or not we remain the chosen people, the divine country.

In the immediately following paragraph, Bush takes up the issue of "God's signs," explaining that they are difficult to identify. However, he asserts confidently that our prayers "are known and heard, and understood." Bush's complete confidence in God's understanding suggests a special relation to the deity—which is, of course, what we would expect for the leader of the divinely preferred nation. It is precisely this divine relation that validates the national hierarchy—a hierarchy that was uncertain in Bush's case due to the way in which he was declared winner of the 2000 election after losing the popular vote and possibly losing the electoral vote as well. Bush continues to discuss prayer, noting that it gives us "strength." It is not accidental that he invokes strength, a martial virtue. After all, prayer, if it can change our qualities and condition, could equally give us humility, honesty, compassion—or even peace. More important, Bush ends his paean to prayer with an invocation of hierarchy, and specifically the hierarchy of authority (not, say, a hierarchy of Christian love). The culminating prayers he discusses are "prayers that yield our will to a will greater than our own." Bush takes up the importance of a strict hierarchy in authority, a hierarchy that is inseparable from divine authority. He implies his own special relation to God. He tacitly urges Americans to surrender their will to God. It is not difficult to infer what relation Americans should have to Bush's administration as well—a relation of trust, fear, and awe in which citizens give up their "will to a will greater than [their] own." That relation subsequently came to be codified in legislation such as the USA PATRIOT Act.

The next paragraph takes up the idea that the world "created" by God "is of moral design." This is an indirect statement of the view that the world is ultimately just and that the good will triumph. Since we all know at this point that the national in-group, America, is "the good guy," the implication is that we will triumph. Specifically, we will triumph because we are chosen by God, and we are chosen by God because we are moral.

The very idea of a "moral design" is a narrative idea. One almost wonders if Bush's speechwriters had been reading Aristotle, who referred to a noncausal organizing principle in narrative, "design," which is most often a sort of moral reequilibration. Aristotle's example concerns a murderer who is in turn killed when he is crushed by a statue representing his victim (see Aristotle 39). In the following sentence, Bush continues the implicit reference to narrative. As if he had read my account of tragicomedy, he explains that "tragedy" is "only for a time." Of course, he could not really say that "comedy" follows. He substitutes "Goodness" as what will always return. The choice makes perfect sense. The happy ending is, in this view, only for the good—which is to say, us. Of course, the obvious difficulty here is the group of actual victims. They are useful for establishing the tragedy, but something of a problem for asserting the ultimate comedy. It is far from clear that the lives of the bereaved, or of those who lost their jobs, will end in "goodness." Thus, Bush concludes the paragraph with the rather vague claim that the people who died and the people who mourn are "held" by God. But even here the point is not that God will somehow restore them individually. By saying that God is holding these victims, Bush is primarily indicating, once again, that God is on our side.

Bush goes on to make the almost incomprehensible assertion that "adversity introduces us to ourselves." The following sentences make clear that he is returning to THE NATION IS A PERSON schema. Now, he explicitly addresses "our national character." He says, "we have been reminded . . . that our fellow Americans are generous and kind, resourceful and brave," citing, for example, "blood donors." While "resourceful" may be a virtue of distinctive importance for American nationalism—a version of Yankee ingenuity—the others are universal. The reasons for the reemphasis on bravery are too obvious to require elaboration, as are the reasons for the example of "blood donors," with their obvious bearing on war.[23] "Generous" and "kind" may seem more peculiar until one realizes that Bush is construing the benevolent acts that followed the bombings as benevolent acts within a national in-group. Generosity and kindness are not human virtues in this context. For example, they are not virtues when addressed to the enemy. They are, rather, a crucial part of mutual benevolence within the national in-group, that is, mutual benevolence among "our fellow Americans."

Following this, Bush gives moving examples of what I would be inclined to call human compassion. However, in this context, they stand as examples of a specifically American character that is brave, resourceful, and so on. They are also examples of self-sacrifice—the precise virtue that one wants in the ideal soldier. Indeed, in the context of the speech, every example cited by Bush may be seen as having resonances of war. Thus, cognitively, every example probably does have such resonances for many listeners, even if they are not self-consciously aware of it.[24] One man stays with a quadriplegic. A priest gives someone last rites. Two people carry a disabled stranger down sixty-eight floors. Several men drive all night to deliver skin grafts. With only slight variations, each of these cases could have occurred on a battlefield. Indeed, they sound almost as if they were taken from war movies. One soldier stays with his buddy who cannot walk. A priest remains on the battlefield to give a soldier last rites. Two soldiers carry a third through a stretch of dangerous territory. Several soldiers drive all night to bring skin grafts to a medical unit near the front. In each case,

---

23. Of course, I am not claiming that, in a neutral context, people's first association with blood donors would be with war. I am merely pointing out that war is undoubtedly linked cognitively with loss of blood and the need for blood. The entire speech "primes" or gives extra activation to all war-related associations. In that context, donating blood is likely to activate links with war more fully. Put differently, given the operation of ordinary cognitive processes, we would expect a blood donors/war link to be enhanced by the militaristic associations activated throughout the rest of the speech and, in turn, to contribute to those associations.

24. Our brains allow considerable breadth in the activation of associations. These associations then help to guide our subsequent thought and feeling, whether or not we are aware of them—indeed, perhaps particularly when we are not aware of them.

the examples contribute to the transition from personal miseries and personal acts of compassion to the larger national story of war.[25]

Bush then explains what is going on in all these cases. These acts are not the result of broad human feeling. They do not follow from the spontaneous compassion that is produced by human empathic capacities and inclinations. Rather, they are examples of "Americans show[ing] a deep commitment to one another, and an abiding love for our country." He then invokes Franklin Roosevelt, implicitly recalling the bombing of Pearl Harbor and the American entry into the Second World War. This, too, helps to emplot the event as part of an heroic tragicomedy by connecting it with a salient exemplum, a clear instance of enemy invasion, military response, and decisive American victory. Specifically, referring to the patriotic acts of rescue and aid listed above (again, they were not, in Bush's account, human, compassionate acts, but specifically nationalistic acts), he cites Roosevelt on the "courage of national unity."

Through this citation, Bush returns to the theme of bravery ("courage"). But a new aspect of the heroic plot, and of nationalism more generally, makes its appearance as well. This is subnationalism. Here, Bush takes the idea that national identity should subsume all rival identities. In keeping with the general American ideology of optimism, he does not appeal for such unity. He simply asserts it. Specifically, he goes on to state that there is "a unity of every faith, and every background." Thus, religious, racial, ethnic, and class categories are all implicitly subordinated to the national category. Again, this is not a goal that we seek; it is part of our national character—if one that is enhanced by the bombings. Indeed, the bombings have "joined together political parties in both houses of Congress." There is, then, no disagreement. To be American is, by the nature of the American character, to agree. Our unity is perfect. We all agree, across race, class, religion—even across political affiliations. Indeed, we all agree that we agree. But what is it that we all agree with? The speech leaves us with no other answer but—war. We agree with the idea that the bombings were an act of war. We agree with the plan to make a "fierce" military response to the bombings. Anyone who does not agree, anyone who dissents from

25. Peter Rabinowitz has pointed out that I may be giving Bush—or his speech writers—too much credit in suggesting that this transition is a matter of the way they selected examples. Catastrophes generally—floods, earthquakes, terrorist attacks, battles, anything that involves swift and widespread physical harm and death—require many of the same sorts of response. In that way, Bush's task in selecting examples was not that difficult. All that he had to do was to provide a cognitive context in which associations with war would be primed. In such a context, most instances of emergency relief would probably have resonances related to war or even narrative parallels in war.

this view, is simply not American. To be American is to agree. Those who do not agree take up a standard character role in heroic tragicomedy—the role of the traitor.

From here, Bush turns to the sorts of public ceremonies that serve to make the national category salient. He begins with "services of prayer and candlelight vigils." It is important that both are religious (necessarily in the first case, commonly in the second). This reenforces the nation's special relation to God. It is no less important that these ceremonies are nonsectarian. Prayer services at the time tended to be explicitly "interfaith." They were not necessarily nationalistic. However, it is clear that Bush is categorizing them as nationalistic. He is taking them up implicitly as instances of unity across potential subnational divisions. The nationalization of the prayer services and vigils is made clear by the third practice cited by Bush—displaying the American flag. One could imagine a response to the bombings whereby many people put up peace signs to oppose violence, or wore black armbands as a sign of mourning, or even displayed images of firefighters or the towers. But Americans saw the bombings in nationalist terms, thus displaying American flags. In part, this preceded Bush's statements, due to the ubiquity of nationalization discussed in the preceding chapters. However, this tendency probably would have dwindled on its own. It was sustained and intensified by Bush's emplotment of the events and a range of governmental actions and pronouncements.

Bush goes on to describe the attitude with which people displayed the flag—"in pride." The choice of pride is important. It is precisely the attitude one is supposed to have regarding the in-group. Indeed, it defines in-group bias. Moreover, in this case, it also enhances the sense that the bombings had no precedent other than the malevolence of the out-group. Taking pride in one's group works against self-examination or any even-handed attempt to understand the background of these events. Self-criticism is the opposite of pride. If I am critical of my behavior, then I am not proud of it. Moreover, if someone else is critical of my behavior, then my pride directly opposes that criticism. It is a commonplace of American ideology that any criticisms from abroad are the result of jealousy. Europeans do not have a reasoned opinion about our foreign policy, our environmental policy, or anything else. They just criticize us because they are jealous. Similarly, the malevolent bombers were not responding to anything we had done. They were simply acting out of gratuitous cruelty. Moreover, speaking of pride in this context fosters the idea that pride is not justified primarily by what one does as an individual. Rather, it is justified by what one is, in the sense of what national category defines one's identity. Americans should feel proud not because they personally opposed or inhibited acts of cruelty or aided people who were suffering. They should feel proud precisely because they are American. Thus, they display the American flag with pride—pride simply that they are part of the in-group signaled by that flag.

The paragraph ends with a remarkable twist. A central part of the American specification of national character is rugged individualism. Our rejection of monarchy and our institution of democracy are bound up with a sense that Americans will not take orders. We refuse to be bossed around. A crucial part of our pride is that we follow our own paths; we buck the trends. Indeed, this is one reason why we are (in this view) the rightful leaders of the world, directing all other nations toward freedom. Thus, Bush concludes that our flags "wave in defiance." Obviously, the bombing of the towers was a heinous act. But it was the act of people who resorted to this sort of attack precisely because they have no power over us. In this part of the speech, Bush implicitly identifies the bombers with tyrants who falsely claim authority over us. Thus, in keeping with the usual heroic plot, we must rebel against this false authority; we must be defiant of these invaders/usurpers. Of course, we must simultaneously remain loyal to the true authority, the authority designated by God. In short, there is nothing genuinely defiant in Bush's ideal American. That ideal American is loyal and devoted to the national hierarchy. We have already seen that Bush urges us to give up our will to the will of God, a will implicitly manifest in the decisions of our national leaders (prominently, Bush himself). Thus, the speech does not characterize Americans (i.e., true or genuine Americans) as defiant generally, nor does it adjure them to be defiant generally. Rather, it affirms that Americans are defiant only against the out-group. This is, of course, a standard part of in-group conformity. However, Bush's framing of the issue suggests that anyone who does not accept the internal hierarchy of the nation is not defiant, but rather is conforming to the dictates of the enemy. The result is that, in the terms of this speech, dissent is not only treachery; it does not even count as dissent. Moreover, Bush's emphasis on defiance not only coopts American individualism for conformism. It also effectively urges anger and belligerence, both of which are central to the heroic plot and to Bush's subsequent policies. Indeed, angry and belligerent defiance of the invaders/usurpers is crucial to the development of the heroic plot.

At this point, Bush takes up THE NATION IS A FAMILY schema, asserting that our "unity is a kinship." He shifts to THE NATION IS A PERSON, saying that our unity is "a steadfast resolve to prevail against our enemies."

After the reference to "defiance," this is particularly striking. It is entirely clear that we are to "defy" the enemy, but maintain the strictest form of unity with our nation in thought and action.

From here, Bush turns briefly to the view that the United States is the leader of the free world, or indeed of the entire world. Just as the U.S. government is at the head of a hierarchy that defines internal American unity, the nation as a whole is at the head of a hierarchy that defines world unity. But what is the out-group for this in-group? Terrorism, which is to say, pure and unmotivated malevolence, what we might call "pure out-groupness." Terrorism is always the beginning of a story, just as our wars are always the middle and end of a story. Terrorism is never a response to prior incidents or policies, just as our wars are never unprovoked or unjustified. Thus, as if recalling the scene of global coalition from *Independence Day*, Bush explains that "unity against terror is now extending across the world." However, this brief reference to the United States as an international leader is not elaborated on—a point that is unsurprising, given the subsequent development of Bush's foreign policy. Following this, Bush takes up the issue of who the enemies are and why there are terrorists.

Clearly, the bombings have to be explained in some way. However, within the prototypical nationalist/heroic narrative structure, they cannot be explained by anything that we did. Again, that is what makes the bombings into the beginning of the story. Thus, the origin must simply be out-group malevolence. This is transcendentalized and dehumanized in cross-culturally standard ways. But it is also specified in terms particular to U.S. nationalism. Again, the United States is, in one common ideological characterization, the initiator and guarantor of the freedom of the entire world, thus of human freedom generally. In consequence, anyone who wishes to attack human freedom is likely to attack the United States. In keeping with this, Bush characterizes the enemies of the United States as the "enemies of human freedom." Their Satanic character is suggested by the scope of their antagonism (all humanity) and their eternity (they arise in "every generation"). They have attacked us "because we are freedom's home and defender." The precise phrasing here is significant. The term "home" takes up the standard familial metaphor. In context, it calls to mind more particular nonmetaphorical images as well—the homes of families affected by the bombings, homes deprived of parents, spouses, children. But, here too, Bush extends these particular, human homes to the national homeland, tacitly coopting individual pain for the affirmation of group identity and, beyond that, the policies of the group leadership. The reference to the United States as "defender" reenforces the military aspect of

Bush's account, particularly its relation to the invasion/defense sequence of the heroic plot. The final sentence of the paragraph identifies the enduring, historical character of our defense of freedom by appeal to the standard THE NATION IS A FAMILY schema. Specifically, Bush explains that this defense was "the commitment of our fathers." That commitment, he says, is our "calling." The use of a term with religious associations is, of course, not accidental.

Those religious associations are taken up in the final paragraphs, which immediately follow. First, Bush reminds us that this is a "national day of prayer." Both the word "national" and the word "prayer" are crucial. He goes on to specify the nature of the prayer: "We ask almighty God to watch over our nation." The choice of "almighty" as an epithet is, of course, not accidental (contrast, say, "merciful," "all-loving," "all-embracing"). "Almighty" suggests that God should watch over our nation in a way that asserts His might, thus in a way that secures our victory. At this point, Bush returns to the actual suffering of the bereaved, at last indicating how their suffering may be resolved—through the "life to come." This leads Bush to an apocalyptic conclusion, where he explains that "neither death nor life, nor angels nor principalities nor powers . . . can separate us from God's love." The sequence does not make much sense. (Who raised the issue of principalities—an order of spiritual beings superior to archangels—separating us from God's love?) However, it suggests the most catastrophic events. Perhaps we are to understand that the "angels" are fallen, thus not angels at all, but devils. Perhaps the powers are those of the demonic Adversary himself. In any case, the suggestions of apocalyptic events recall the bombings. The implication seems to be that whatever chaos and devastation may rain down on humankind, we—that is, Americans and all those who follow our leadership—will always be protected by God. Bush then explains that God will "bless the souls of the departed." This idea, too, is bound up with war and nationalism. Specifically, the statement suggests the national version of martyrdom—for it is not a point of general Christian doctrine that being killed by a criminal act guarantees salvation for one's soul. It is, rather, a point of national ideology that someone killed in the service of the nation is a sort of martyr. Finally, God will give the bereaved "comfort," and, we pray, "always guide our country." The last point tells us almost explicitly that the ultimate leader of the nation is God, operating through the national hierarchy. By praying that he will "always guide our country," we imply that He has guided our country in the past and does guide our country currently. If God has guided our country in the past and does guide our country currently, this in turn suggests that the decisions of the national leadership are and have been inspired by God. Moreover, the prayer for divine guidance in the future suggests that the national leadership will continue to be divinely inspired, for the prayer itself shows that they are devoted to following God's will.

Bush ends with a prayer, "God bless America." Though the phrase sounds innocuously pious, it is more than clear by this point that such a blessing constitutes divine support for military victory, the devastation of a demonic enemy. That alone will turn the story begun by the September 11 bombings into a full heroic tragicomedy.

THE EPILOGUE OF SUFFERING AND THE VIETNAM VETERANS AGAINST THE WAR

The outcome of Bush's emplotment of the September 11 bombings was the War on Terror and the two more concrete wars on Afghanistan and Iraq. The killings of innocents have been extensive. Again, in Iraq alone, there were over one hundred thousand excess deaths by November 2004 (see Roberts et al.). These are precisely the type of events that one would expect to generate an epilogue of suffering. In fact, there are signs that this is occurring—prominently in the "Winter Soldier: Iraq and Afghanistan" hearings organized by Iraq Veterans Against the War (IVAW). In these hearings, "US veterans of Iraq and Afghanistan, as well as Iraqi and Afghan survivors" provided "first hand accounts of their experiences" of the occupations (Nichols 5; see also the website of IVAW, http://ivaw.org/wintersoldier). The title of the hearings refers to what is probably the most significant formalization of an epilogue of suffering in U.S. history—the 1971 Winter Soldier Investigation. This hearing brought together Vietnam veterans and some others who had witnessed atrocities in Vietnam. It provided a forum for them to testify about the crimes they had witnessed. The impact of this investigation is suggested by the fact that it was a crucial issue in the 2004 presidential campaign; over thirty years after John Kerry testified at these hearings, self-proclaimed patriots continued to see him as a traitor. These hearings are now serving as a model for understanding and evaluating U.S. policies and practices in Iraq and Afghanistan. In the remainder of this chapter, I will consider the tacit narrative structure of this exemplary investigation.

To a great extent, the speakers' testimonies at the 1971 Winter Soldier Investigation were responses to their own experiences, articulations of their own moral judgments, and expressions of their own feelings of spontaneous human empathy with the victims. Similarly, the editors' selection for the published version was largely based on a desire to represent both the magnitude and the extent of criminal activities. However, as I have been arguing, we do not define and evaluate the broad trajectories of our actions in terms of strict causal analysis and the rational application of abstract moral standards. Rather, we emplot our projects, most commonly through the universal narrative structures. This is no less true in the case of the epilogue of suffering, though in this case, the plot is itself more limited.

In outline, the narrative structure is the following. The hero begins the war with a strong sense of commitment and with anger against the perfidious acts of the enemy. In the course of battle, however, he becomes involved in the killing of innocents—paradigmatically, a very young boy. The innocents often remind the hero of his own family. Filled with remorse, the hero goes through a period of isolation and atonement before he is able to return to society and take up his rightful place. Examples, involving different variations, range from Gilgamesh to Mwindo (of the Nyanga epic), from the story of Kumagae in the Japanese *Tale of Heike* to that of Yudhiṣṭhira in the Sanskrit *Mahābhārata*.[26]

In most nationally celebrated heroic tragicomedies, the epilogue of suffering operates to establish the ultimate goodness of the national in-group.[27] It indicates that we may commit errors in the prosecution of war, but we pay for them—we experience remorse; we undergo penance. Again, we are the benevolent ones and thus deeply unlike the malevolent enemy. In this way, the epilogue of suffering commonly allows us to reaffirm the heroic narrative.

However, there is always a tension in this development of the epilogue. It shows how moral we are, how willing to admit to and suffer for our mistakes. But, at the same time, it foregrounds the crimes of war, the wrongful killing. Indeed, it suggests something about war generally, and about our justifications for war. It suggests that war cannot avoid "mistakes." Thus, we know, any time we enter a war, that innocents will be killed. Next time, we cannot pretend that only the wicked will suffer and the guiltless will be

---

26. See chapter 4 of my *The Mind and Its Stories* for a discussion of these and other examples.

27. I take it to be obvious that the Winter Soldier Investigation is not nationally celebrated. Thus, my comments here are not intended to apply to that investigation or the text that came out of it. There is a nationalist and militarist strain in the text. But there is also a very strong antinationalist and antimilitarist strain. Indeed, even mainstream epilogues are to some degree ambivalent. That ambivalence is even more pronounced in a nonmainstream work, such as the Winter Soldier Investigation.

spared. Worse still, the epilogue indicates that we commit the same crimes as the enemy. When the enemy kills an innocent person, we view it as justification for our war-making, even if it is a retrospective justification, for this crime shows us the perfidy of the enemy. But the epilogue emphasizes the fact that we too kill innocents. In these ways, the epilogue always threatens to undermine the heroic enterprise.

In the United States, there was a name for our collective sense that the heroic national narrative had been undermined—The Vietnam Syndrome. (Note how the name takes up the metaphor of the nation as a human mind, implying that pacifism is a disease and that national belligerence is a state of health.) The Winter Soldier Investigation contributed to this "syndrome," which is the primary reason why prowar segments of the nation revile it along with all those who took part in it. One effect of the September 11 bombings—or, rather, one effect of what became the standard construal of those bombings—was to put an end to that syndrome by triggering the threat/defense sequence from the heroic plot.

The fact that the investigation was published by the Vietnam Veterans Against the War (VVAW) is already significant. The epilogue of suffering is not a matter of external investigators, foreign reporters, philosophers such as Bertrand Russell, activists such as Noam Chomsky. It is crucial that the testimonies came from the soldiers themselves. The power of the epilogue derives from the fact that it is the heroes who question what they have done. Indeed, this is why one aim of prowar activists has been to convince us that any opposition to a given war is an opposition to the troops. The accusation is almost incoherent. Suppose Jones says that soldiers should be sent to fight in Iraq and Smith says they should not. What sense does it make to claim that Jones is "supporting" the troops (by putting them in combat where they may be killed) while Smith is "opposing" the troops (by saying that they should not be put in combat)? But the reasonableness of the assertion is irrelevant. The crucial rhetorical point is to create a sense that there is a complete division between the "heroes" of the war and the opponents of the war. The crucial point is to foreclose the possibility of an epilogue of suffering (though, obviously, prowar activists would not put it this way). In relation to this, any troops who do question the war can only be understood as traitors to their comrades. (This characterization was clear in the campaign against John Kerry.)

The volume begins with a poem that refers to the killing of families. It is interesting that it begins with "would-be-fathers," which is to say, young boys who are not yet fathers. This suggests the cross-cultural paradigm of the heroic crime—the killing of a young boy. It goes on to add a parallel paradigmatic war crime—rape of young girls—through its reference to "daughters spread-eagled" (Vietnam Veterans v). The image of the family here is crucial. Again, our own nation is repeatedly assimilated to a family. In the epilogue of suffering, the hero commonly sees a reflection of his or her own son or daughter in the innocent person he or she kills. Alternatively, the hero recalls this victim's parents. Either way, the scene evokes family ties without distinction between in-group and out-group. For example, in the Japanese *Tale of the Heike,* when Kumagae is about to kill Atsumori, he connects the boy with his own son and imagines the grief of Atsumori's father (317). This leads to his own remorse, as represented in Zeami's renowned drama, *Atsumori*. The function of these familial connections is to enhance our sense of empathy. This use of family relations is not a matter of extending the metaphor of the family to the in-group in the usual nationalist manner. Rather, this invocation of family leads us to recognize that literal family relations are the same everywhere, in all groups, including the national enemy.

Interestingly, this poetic call to empathy for the enemy is followed by an epigraph from Tom Paine. The epigraph explains the title of the investigation. Paine refers to some soldiers as "summer soldiers." These are the equivalent of fair weather friends. They support the nation only in the good times. But they leave their post when the difficult fighting begins. The winter soldier, then, is the true hero, the true patriot, who does not abandon the fight when it is difficult. The suggestion is that those who are now testifying are the true patriots. In this way, the published text of the investigation manifests the usual ambivalence of the epilogue. On the one hand, it appears to condemn national war. On the other hand, it reasserts the national heroic plot by affirming the patriotism of the remorseful heroes—indeed, affirming even their commitment as soldiers.

The preface to the volume returns us to the first, broadly critical view. Specifically, Al Hubbard, the executive secretary of VVAW and author of the opening poem, stresses and condemns the dehumanization of the enemy. He insists that this dehumanization enables the commission of war crimes, as does our national conviction "that we are good and most other countries are inherently evil" (xiv). Hubbard overstates the case here. Americans, like everyone who accepts a heroic emplotment of conflict, tend to see the national in-group as good and the national enemy as evil. They are mostly indifferent to everyone else. But Hubbard does indicate precisely what happens with heroic emplotment: it focuses our attention on a binary opposition and identifies the enemy with evil. In this way, he tacitly takes up the critique of heroic emplotment.

The opening statement by Lt. William Crandell, however, restores the ambivalence, partially reasserting the heroic narrative. Crandell explains that, "In the bleak winter of 1776," many summer recruits went home. But "the winter soldiers . . . stayed after they had served their time" (1). The parallel is suggestive. The winter soldiers of 1776 stayed to fight. In other words, they maintained their commitment to the heroic narrative. Insofar as the Vietnam veterans are comparable to the winter soldiers, Crandell implies, nothing in their testimonies undermines a commitment to the military or to warfare. Indeed, he suggests that, in testifying, they are continuing their duty as soldiers (not as, say, human beings or general moral agents). Crandell goes on to distinguish between the normal conduct of war and the commission of war crimes. The distinction is entirely reasonable. Yet it has the effect of securing the national heroic narrative for the future. The problem, this suggests, is not a matter of the heroic emplotment per se. It is, rather, a matter of the way the heroic narrative has been instantiated in this particular case. He goes on to say that, "We are here to bear witness not against America, but against those policymakers who are perverting America" (3). The phrasing of the alternatives is important. It leaves out the possibility that the soldiers might be testifying against nationalism and heroic emplotment generally. It isolates this particular war, so that the testimonies imply nothing larger. Indeed, at the conclusion of his opening statement, Crandell explicitly presents the testimonies, not as questioning heroic emplotment, but as allowing it. The problem with the current war is precisely that it makes us "a little troubled" about the military "uniform." That uniform should be "one of our prides," for it is "acquainted with honor" and "familiar with great deeds and noble." We should "revere it." The same point holds for "our flag," which should be "worshiped" and should wave "in far lands" (3). This divinization of the in-group is, of course, at the root of the us/them dichotomy decried by Hubbard. Crandell, then, is taking up the nationalist and heroic use of the epilogue, reasserting in-group identity and heroic emplotment. He even goes so far as to affirm American global hegemony, asserting that the American flag should wave "in far lands."

The following 160 pages of testimony give instance after instance of soldiers beginning the war with enthusiastic commitment, before they become involved in the killing of innocents, thus the sorts of crime that trigger the epilogue of suffering. This involvement is repeatedly followed by the soldier's isolation, then return to society through the atonement brought about by this investigation itself.[28] For example, one sergeant

---

28. The testimonies also involve critical references to some of the central techniques of

explains that he was so fired up about fighting for his nation that he would have killed his own mother (157). But, once he arrived in Vietnam, his zeal "lasted for about one day. When I got there and saw the shit being beat out of a few children, you know. And from there on, it was all downhill and, man, like I was a great American" (158). There are numerous variations on this story throughout the book. Many, like this one, involve children. There is no point in going through all of them. However, it is worth noting the text's first instance of deliberate killing of an innocent individualized person, a person with whom one should have empathic identification. It is the paradigmatic case of a young boy—or rather, in this case, two young boys: "there were two little boys playing on a dike and one sergeant just took his M-16 and shot one boy.... The other boy tried to run ... when this other guy ... shot this other little boy.... The little boy was like lying on the ground kicking, so he shot him again to make sure he was dead" (9).

A crucial part of the testimonies is the way in which they repeatedly emphasize empathy—not only ours, but that of the soldiers, the heroes trained to dehumanize the enemy. That empathy is, of course, precisely what triggers the epilogue of suffering. The murders of innocents seem brutal. They are brutal. The testimonies indicate again and again that many soldiers treated the Vietnamese as animals. But even the most hardened of the killers cannot entirely suppress his sense of human identification. Given the operation of the human brain, this is unsurprising. As Boyer explains, "the experience of other people's pain, as handled by the brain's dedicated systems, to some extent overlaps with that of one's own pain" (105). Again, that is why there is an epilogue of suffering, manifest in these hearings. Part of this empathy is simply the result of seeing the human face, seeing its expression of pain and, as a result, experiencing that pain empathically.[29] That experience changes the way we emplot the surrounding events. This is brought out both horrifically and movingly in one testimony. The speaker explains that he came upon "a tiny little form, that of a child, lying out in the field with straw over its face. It had been clubbed to death." After seeing the corpse, he learns that "the Marine that clubbed the child to death didn't really want to look at the child's face, so he put straw over it before he clubbed it" (30).

---

heroic emplotment, as one would expect. Most obviously, the dehumanization of the enemy is emphasized in the testimonies. The recruitment of religion to the national military cause also recurs. For example, one chaplain is reported to have advised soldiers to "do unto others before they do unto you" (8).

29. See Plantinga and citations on empathic experience and facial expression; see also Boyer 104–5, on imagination, imitation, and the brain.

Though the cases just recounted refer to other soldiers, it is important that the testimonies are not merely a matter of third-person observations, thus guilt by complicity. The witnesses repeatedly treat their own actions, their direct culpability. For example, referring to the officer blamed for the My Lai massacre, one speaker tells us, "It isn't just Lieutenant Calley. I was involved" (12). One soldier recounts the practice of firing into a village, even when there was no fire coming from the village. He recalls a particular attack of this sort. When his unit stopped firing, "there was a big silence, and all of a sudden, just babies crying." He goes on to explain, "you know, it just—everytime I hear a baby cry right now, I—that comes back to me" (24). Another soldier describes the way in which he and others tried to suppress empathic feelings. Again, the story concerns a young boy. In a game, this soldier and his companions used the blast from a helicopter to blow the child back into the road. He was killed by a passing truck. The soldier explains that "our first reaction was, I guess, you would call normal . . . horror, pain." But he stopped the feeling immediately and began laughing, joking (40). Yet, even when suppressed, the human feeling was still there. Later, it haunted the soldiers.

This personal involvement, the associated shift from enthusiastic commitment to disillusion, even horror, and the subsequent sense of isolation and remorse define the narrative structure of the epilogue of suffering. But they do not complete that structure. The final resolution remains. In this case, the testimony itself is the culminating moment of the soldiers' penance, the moment of somber wisdom, and the formal (though not always real) end of their isolation. One soldier explains, "The reason I came down here was because I've been living with this thing for two and a half years" (27). Another imagines that his victims, like Jesus, pray for him. He describes the napalming of a village, then explains that he and his fellow soldiers entered the village "after the fires burned down." He saw "an old man on a cot, burned to death with his hands stiff in rigor mortis reaching for the sky as if in prayer or supplication forgiving us for what we had done" (31). He then takes up the familial parallelism that is so common in epilogues of suffering. He sees a group of dead children and recalls that it is his mother's birthday. As a result, "I somehow seemed to feel that these were her children" (31). This is very much in keeping with the prototypical resolution of the epilogue, which is often spiritual, familial, or both. Consider, for example, Zeami's famous play treating the resolution of Kumagae's epilogue of suffering. Driven by remorse for killing Atsumori in battle, Kumagae wanders as a monk until he meets the ghost of Atsumori. For a moment, it seems that Atsumori will kill Kumagae. But suddenly they both achieve salvation and "they shall be re-born together / On one lotus-seat" (Zeami 712).

Needless to say, things do not always work out so well in life as in fiction. Reality sometimes inhibits our ability to emplot events with a happy ending. The final testimony in the book is given by a lieutenant. He explains, "I'm here because, like, I have nightmares about things that happened to me and my friends. I'm here because my conscience will not let me forget what I want to forget" (163–64).

The closing statement of the book tries to resolve these feelings, in a sense, collectively, just as the (fictional) epilogue resolves them individually in the somber wisdom of the hero and his return to society. M/Sgt. Don Duncan explains that "I don't want anybody here to carry away a feeling of guilt with them" (171). He recalls his own period of isolation. Five years earlier he had "testified to many of the things that have been testified to here." But for him that was not a return to society, an end to exile. Rather, as a result of that testimony, he "was very lonely." Only this investigation at last ends the isolation, the hero's separation from society that defines the penultimate part of the epilogue of suffering. Duncan says that "I'm not lonely any more" (172). He indicates that this should be true for others who testified as well. One hopes his declaration was not overly optimistic.

This nearly concludes the book. But something else does follow. Unlike Crandell, Duncan does not seem to be interested in rehabilitating the heroic narrative. Indeed, he states that "We have to stop producing veterans" (172). The way to stop producing veterans is, of course, to stop producing wars. This view is, indeed, much closer to that implied by the witnesses in the preceding pages. Despite the heroic implications of the opening statement, the testimonies almost inexorably point toward a questioning of all nationalism and war. For example, one sergeant describes the brutal treatment of a Vietnamese woman, then explains, "We were conditioned to believe that this was for the good of the nation, the good of our country, and anything we did was okay" (14). Reading statements such as this, it is difficult not to see nationalism and its heroic emplotments as fundamentally inhumane. It is difficult to believe that the epilogue of suffering in any way justifies future stories of heroism and war.

6

SACRIFICIAL NATIONALISM AND ITS VICTIMS

Sin and Death in Germany and India

THE SECOND OF OUR three universal narrative prototypes is sacrificial tragicomedy. In this structure, the in-group is suffering some sort of devastation—prototypically, drought and famine (or, less often, epidemic disease). The devastation so exceeds our usual experience that it requires some sort of moral explanation. The alignment of values in the heroic plot sets God on our side as His special people. Devastation suggests that we have been abandoned by God. Specifically, divine punishment is visited upon a group for sin committed either collectively or by some individual who is representative of the group as a whole (e.g., in being an ancestor or a leader of the group). Most commonly, the punishments of famine and epidemic disease are associated with sins of eating and/or sexuality. In keeping with this, the primary virtues of the sacrificial plot—after self-sacrifice—are self-denial in food and sex (just as the primary virtues in the heroic plot are loyalty, obedience, and bravery). In the fullest version of the sacrificial narrative, the sin was prompted by some out-group tempter, usually identified with the spiritual opposite of God (e.g., Satan). Since the devastation is a form of moral retribution for a communal sin, the way to regain divine preference, and thus restore normality, is to do penance for that sin. This penance is invariably a matter of sacrifice. Most often, someone must die to prevent the death of the entire community. The story of the Fall of humankind through Adam and Eve, then our eventual salvation through the sacrifice of Jesus, is an obvious case of this sort of plot.

But what determines the identity of the victim? There are two ways in which this may be approached. In one, the sacrifice is itself a retribution and an attempt to rid society of the guilty parties. Someone is sacrificed because he or she has sinned. The guilty parties include one or more members of the in-group and tempters from some out-group. Either may be the primary sacrificial victims. However, this version invariably emphasizes that the origin of the guilt is in the acts of out-group tempters, who are commonly associated with demonic evil. This is the attitude associated with "religious terrorism," at least in the interpretation of Jessica Stern, who argues that the purpose of such terrorism is "to purify the world of . . . corrupting influences" (xix). In its most extreme form, the entire out-group may be seen as guilty and thus the sacrificial narrative may lead to genocide. I have sometimes referred to this as the "secularized" version of the sacrificial plot, since it imitates normal processes of law in claiming to find and punish the guilty parties. However, it is perhaps better referred to as "purgative," for it is still based on ideas of spiritual causality (not quotidian physical or psychological causality) and it shows little concern for due process, reasonable determination of guilt, or anything else we associate with a system of justice. This version in effect seeks to end devastation by sacrificing the enemy who destroyed the home society from within and the collaborators who allowed that destruction. As we will see, this is the prototype that guided Nazism.

The second approach to sacrifice is precisely the opposite. In this version, members of the in-group cannot atone for their guilt by sacrificing members of the out-group. After all, if God has withdrawn from our side, divine punishment is aimed at us, not at our enemy. Penance must be performed by the home society itself. (This is consistent with versions of the sacrificial plot in which the tempter is actually associated with God—as when, in Yoruba belief, Èṣù tempts humans into sin in order to provoke the need for some compensatory sacrificial offering [see Awolalu 29].) There are two ways in which this is likely to be developed. In one, the sacrificial victim is an innocent member of the in-group, a pure soul untainted by sin. The other common variant requires that everyone in the in-group—or some representative selection from the in-group—atone for the sin. Most often, the two variants are interwoven, with the self-sacrifice of one or more innocents complementing the broader self-punishment of the home society. We might refer to this type generally as the "penitential" sacrificial plot.

This division of the sacrificial plot should not be taken to suggest that the tempter is irrelevant to the penitential version. Indeed, both types of sacrificial plot tend to share the view that the tempter should not be part of the national society, though this is not usually stressed in the penitential version. In nationalist uses of the sacrificial prototype, the difference in attitudes toward the tempter is often at least in part a matter of the degree to which the tempter out-group has become integrated into or pervades the home society. In the case of colonial India, the British, commonly cast in the tempter role (implicitly or explicitly), were likely to leave following Indian independence. In this way, exclusion was not a special problem beyond independence. In contrast, fascist movements tend to focus on groups that, to some degree, pervade the population.

Having just distinguished these varieties, I have to note immediately that they are often combined, both in explicit stories and in implicit, nationalistic uses. Sacrificial narratives do tend to stress one form of sacrifice. However, that emphasis need not be exclusive. For example, in a particular story, the only way to purge society of the tempter may involve the death of some innocent in-group member. Though a story of this sort is oriented toward a purgative sacrifice, it includes the sacrifice of an innocent victim.

As I have already emphasized, the heroic prototype is the default form for emplotting nationalism. In conditions where heroic triumph is impossible—most obviously, conditions of devastating defeat and foreign domination—the sacrificial plot may be triggered. This is all the more likely when the group has experienced such prototypical sacrificial conditions as famine. Nonetheless, even in these cases, the heroic plot remains the national standard. It can be taken up whenever circumstances alter appropriately. Moreover, the heroic prototype, so to speak, interferes with the sacrificial plot, altering its development or specification. This is an ordinary cognitive phenomenon. It is often the case that different prototypes affect our response to individuals or to situations. For example, if I meet a cognitive scientist and learn that he or she is also a ballet dancer, my prototype for a ballet dancer may displace certain aspects of my prototype of a cognitive scientist. This sort of interference is a prominent feature of the nationalist operation of sacrificial narratives.

Since the sacrificial plot has its greatest force in defeated and hungry nations, the United States does not provide prominent examples.[1] Striking cases are to be found in former European colonies, such as Ireland and India. The sacrificial plot played an important role in the anticolonial movements of both nations—anticolonial movements that have been highly influential. But to focus solely on India or Ireland would be misleading. The sacrificial plot is not at all confined to colonies. Nazi Germany provides an example from a powerful European country. I will therefore draw one example from German Nazism and one from colonial India.

Hitler's version of sacrificial nationalism is almost entirely purgative. Indeed, the Holocaust itself was inseparable from the sacrificial emplotment of German nationalism found in the works of Nazi writers and elsewhere in German culture after the First World War.[2] In connection with this, I will consider the sacrificial emplotment of nationalism found in Hitler's *Mein Kampf,* the most horribly consequential theorization of nationalism in human history.

In contrast Mohandas ("Mahatma") Gandhi is perhaps the political leader who represented the pure collective self-punishment approach most thoroughly. He may also be the national leader whose approach to nationalism contrasts most obviously with that of Hitler. Moreover, his paradigm for sacrifice was found, not first of all in Christian tradition (which invariably inflects Western versions of sacrificial nationalism), but in Hinduism. For all three reasons, it is useful to examine Gandhi's thought in this

---

1. This is not to say that the prototype is entirely absent from American nationalism. It turns up, but in somewhat peripheral areas. For example, this emplotment is found in much Christian nationalism. As Goldberg explains, many Christian nationalists believe that God became "angry" with the United States, largely because of sexual sins. As a result, He "began to withdraw his favor" so that "In the last decades of the twentieth century, the forces of darkness threatened to turn America into Sodom" (7). In keeping with this, Goldberg stresses the parallels between Christian nationalism and Nazism.

2. For example, it is clear in a film such as Murnau's *Nosferatu* (see my "Narrative Universals, Nationalism"). It is worth noting here that there is an interesting contrast between purgative sacrificial narratives such as this and such post-Nazi sacrificial narratives as Gerhard Lamprecht's 1946 *Somewhere in Berlin.* The latter emphasizes devastation and specifically hunger after the recent war. Perhaps most important, one young boy tries to relieve the hunger of a returning soldier. He initially fails. However, he later tumbles to his death from a shattered building. His death inspires the other young boys to try to change things, and the film ends with the small society being renewed through cooperative work. The film fairly clearly presents this as a microcosm of the larger society, advocating national cooperative renewal in keeping with East German socialist policy. In this case, the cooperative renewal is crucially enabled by the sacrifice of an innocent (and not through the purgation of an internal enemy).

context—not only for his differences from other sacrificial nationalists, but for his similarities as well, similarities that we may fail to understand, or even to notice, without recognizing their relation to sacrificial emplotment.[3]

PURGING THE SEDUCER
Hitler's *Kampf*

As just mentioned, the most destructively consequential sacrificial emplotment of nationalism was undoubtedly that of German fascism.[4] It contributed to two of the most horrible events of world history—the Second World War and the genocide of European Jews. Though the scale of the terror remains unimaginable, this sort of dual result is broadly what one might have expected. World War II was a military struggle—among other things, a response to the Treaty of Versailles and an attempt to join all Germans in a single nation. It was, in effect, the continuation of a suspended heroic narrative. The Holocaust was an attempt of unprecedented magnitude and cruelty to purge the home society of a particular internal "enemy."[5] For our purposes, there is one obvious work to consider as exemplary, for German fascism had a central text—Adolf Hitler's *Mein Kampf* or *My Battle*.[6] The book is remarkable for our purposes as it directly expresses many of the concerns we have been addressing. It not only manifests a sacrificial narrative, but takes up the alignment of conflicting identity categories and develops standard metaphors of national unity. *Mein Kampf* is an enormous work (over one thousand pages in the English translation). In order to make the discussion more manageable, I will concentrate on the first of the

---

3. Both examples are clearly drawn from the modern period. For a detailed analysis of a premodern instance, in this case from China, see my "Narrative Universals, National Sacrifice."

4. Consider, for example, the prosecution of the Second World War. As Evans explains, "There is plenty of evidence that the deep-seated identification of a majority of Germans with the nation—their nationalism, in a word—was more important than anything else in maintaining their commitment to the war effort." In connection with this, Evans stresses "the cult of self-sacrifice . . . in the interests of nation and race" (28).

5. Obviously, there are many horrible instances of genocide, for example, that of Native Americans. My point in writing "unprecedented" is not to rank the suffering of oppressed groups. However—though I am not an expert on, say, the genocide of Native Americans—my sense is that these other horrific cases are not, for the most part, aptly characterized as "an attempt to purge the home society of an internal 'enemy.'"

6. There has been considerable psychological discussion of Hitler (see, for example, chapter 13 of Fromm for a psychoanalytic approach). However, little or none of this work has been cognitive, nor has it taken up the topic of emplotment.

two volumes. More exactly, I will begin by outlining some of Hitler's main arguments and motifs. I will then go on to treat the work in somewhat more detail, proceeding chapter by chapter.

The book begins as a sort of autobiography. The early sections are most significant for treating Hitler's youthful concern over the separation of German communities in different states. He explains how he joined the pan-Germanists in lamenting the division of the "German race" and worried that non-Germans—especially Eastern Europeans—were coming to dominate Germans in countries such as Austria. In short, the opening sets up Hitler's approach to national identity. National identity should be aligned with "racial" or ethnic identity. All members of a particular ethnic group should be in one state. One might expect that he would advocate the converse of this as well—one state for one people, therefore one people for one state. Thus, one might expect him to advocate the expulsion of all other ethnic groups from a German state. Hitler is, of course, concerned with expulsion. But this concern is not general. It is focused on a single group, Jews. The narrowness of this concern partially fits the details of his argument, as we will see. But, more important for our purposes, it fits the sacrificial narrative. Hitler clearly places Jews in the role of tempter, the role of the out-group that seduces the in-group to destructive sin. In the sacrificial structure, it is specifically the tempter that must be expelled from the society.

After articulating his pan-Germanism (and considering a few other topics, such as deference to authority), Hitler goes on to his main concern, the First World War. In keeping with the general pattern, his treatment of the default mode of nationalism—the heroic—gives way to a sacrificial emplotment with the German defeat and the end of the war. In connection with this, Hitler spends a good deal of time treating a central concern of all sacrificial narratives—the Fall, the moment of sin that brought on collective misery. It is important to note that this misery prominently included hunger. As Schivelbusch points out, "the Allied food blockade" resulted in a "starving home front" with "numbers of [civilians] dead" that "bore comparison" to the numbers of combatants killed (235). The hunger, of course, preceded the loss of the war, thus the crucial moment of transition from the "normal" pursuit of national domination to a condition of hopeless devastation. In terms of strict causal analysis, this may seem to make it irrelevant to a sacrificial emplotment. But it fits cognitively. For many Germans, the experience of collective hunger almost certainly served to prime the sacrificial prototype, thus a narratively organized sense of sin, punishment, and the need for salvation through social penance in sacrifice.

It thus contributed importantly to the cognitive organization of subsequent events through that sacrificial structure.

Hitler directly blames the final loss of the war and the devastation of Germany on the behavior of the German people. Many of them gave up on the war. They failed in the national defense component of the heroic narrative. Indeed, there was even a usurpation—the 1918 revolution. In Hitler's account, then, the First World War formed a sort of truncated heroic tragicomedy. The usurpation and invasion occurred, but the restoration of the true leader and defeat of the enemy did not come. Hitler clearly envisioned such a restoration through his own role as national leader or Führer. In connection with this (and in keeping with the heroic prototype), he envisioned a defeat of the enemy in a subsequent war under his leadership. But before this victory could occur, something else was necessary—or, rather, two things were necessary. First, Germans must have an unwavering willingness to sacrifice themselves for the good of the group. Second, there must be a complete elimination of the seductive enemy.

More exactly, in Hitler's analysis, the great German sin—the sin that devastated nationalism—was internationalism, a form of identification reaching across national and racial divisions (most obviously in connection with class). Thus, the seductive enemy was not, say, France or England. It was not a rival national group. Rather, it was a specifically *international* group. The obvious candidate here was Communism, which explicitly advocated international proletarian solidarity against nationalism. Hitler spends a good deal of time denouncing Communism. However, in Hitler's explanatory scheme, all political, economic, and other social developments must ultimately be understood in terms of race. For him, race is the underlying determinant of all social life, much as political economy is the ultimate determinant in Marxism or divine providence is the ultimate determinant in some forms of Christianity. As he puts it toward the middle of *Mein Kampf,* "All world historical events . . . are only the expression of the races' instinct of self-preservation" (406). Thus, for Hitler, Communism, as an ideology or a social movement, could not be the ultimate cause, the final explanation of any social development, including the devastation of Germany following the First World War. Even Communism required a further explanation—specifically, a racial explanation. To account for an internationalist political movement, then, Hitler turned to an international "race"—Jews. Jews, he claims, were the ultimate source of the devastation of Germany.

In short, at the time when, in Hitler's view, Germany should have expanded to encompass all "racial" Germans, it collapsed. It was humiliated, further fragmented, and impoverished because Germans lost their nationalistic commitment. They lost this commitment, he believed, because they were seduced by internationalists. The seduction was promulgated primarily by an international race, not by mere adherents of an internationalist ideology (though the two were, of course, related). That race was, again, the Jews. (I am not saying that Hitler arrived at his anti-Semitism through this chain of reasoning, however faulty. The genesis of Hitler's thoughts and feelings are no doubt much more complex. In part, the reasoning derived from and justified a prior anti-Semitism; in part, it extended that anti-Semitism. The point is simply that these are the ideas that face us in *Mein Kampf*, whatever their personal, psychological origin.)

As we would expect, we find Hitler specifying and developing the sacrificial narrative through the same racialist principles he used to interpret nationhood (and history). The same fundamental biologism governs his choice of metaphors for the nation as well. These metaphors, in turn, further guide his analysis of and response to the national situation, and his specification of the sacrificial prototype, prominently including his response to the tempter figures.

Though Hitler does sometimes use metaphors of plants or homes, his most common metaphor for the nation/race is the human body. The German people form a single body, which clearly should have a single home/state. It should also have a single head, the national leader. Perhaps most important, the tempter is typically viewed as an enemy that has entered the nation and wrought destruction from within. When the nation is assimilated to a human body, the alien invading that body is very likely to be assimilated to a parasite, a virus, a cancer—something that should not be in the body and that must be killed or cut out.

The body metaphor also contributes to the respecification of the standard sacrificial concern with sexual sin. Though the metaphor applies to the nation as a whole, it necessarily primes a concern with the literal bodies of citizens, just as the metaphor of disease primes a concern with actual disease. In other words, the operation of certain models for the nation tends to foster concern for the literal sources of those metaphors. Hitler's near obsession with syphilis fits here in an obvious way. Indeed, in Hitler's analysis, syphilis was an incidental cause of the great Fall of 1918. Moreover, it too is ultimately blamed on Jews.

Finally, and also in keeping with his biologism, it is worth noting that Hitler brings a sort of scientific or pseudoscientific discourse into his analysis as well. While many nationalists (e.g., Gandhi or, in Ireland, Pádraic Pearse) further specified their sacrificial ideas in religious terms, Hitler tended to rely on scientific idioms. In connection with this, supernatural causality is much less clear in *Mein Kampf* than it is in most sacrificial emplotments of the nation. Hitler clearly isolates national sin and national devastation resulting from that sin. However, he does not usually treat the devastation as a punishment per se. Rather, he tends to represent it as the scientifically predictable outcome of the sin, in the way that illness is the scientifically predictable outcome of unhealthy practices. Of course, Hitler does not present scientific support for his claims. Insofar as they are accepted by readers, these claims operate, not logically and empirically, but narratively and metaphorically. In other words, the rhetorical force of Hitler's assertions derives from their conformity to and specification of emotionally compelling narrative prototypes and associated metaphors, crucially the sacrificial prototype.

Before turning to the first chapter, it is important to note that the book is dedicated to sixteen men who were executed. Though sacrificial themes do not appear until later, the broadly sacrificial orientation of the book is indicated by this opening dedication. The men were killed, Hitler insists, because of their "true belief in the resurrection of their people" (xiii *altered;* xxix[7]). In only a few words, Hitler manages to call up the entire sacrificial plot. Moreover, he implicitly relies on his standard metaphor of the nation as a human body. Germany, like a human body, is dead and must be resurrected. The resurrection will come from sacrifice—the sacrifice of not only these men, but of others in the "movement" as well. Thus, after listing their names, he explains that these "martyrs" or, literally, "blood witnesses," may serve to "light" the way for those who come after (xiii; xxix).

Hitler also uses the list to criticize implicitly the assertion of class identities—and thus the assertion of subnational class oppositions—that went along with internationalism. Specifically, he includes the occupations of the men. Four were salesmen or merchants; three were bank employees; three were engineers; one was a cavalry officer; one was a county court councilor; one was a headwaiter; one was a hat maker; one was a locksmith; one was a servant. All these are brought together, unified across their economic positions, by their national identity. He also gives the ages of the men. By showing the range, from under twenty to over fifty, he suggests the cross-generational unity of German national identity as well.

---

7. Here and below, when a citation of Hitler includes two page numbers, separated by a semicolon, the first refers to the English translation and the second to the German. If only one page number is given, it refers to the English translation, unless otherwise indicated.

These representations of diversity are parallel to the joining of warriors from different regions in standard heroic plots.

The cross-generational unity of the German race/nation bears at least indirectly on the opening chapters of *Mein Kampf*, where Hitler treats his own rebellious youth. These sections are curious in that they present a picture of young Hitler as fractious, as impatient with authority. In terms of his own personality, this fits well with his subsequent desire to dominate others. However, it does not seem at first to fit his argument, which ultimately insists on deference to the Leader. But, again, the structure here is a matter of narrative rather than logic. Specifically, the opening sections rely to a great extent on a romantic emplotment. This turns, in subsequent chapters, to a sacrificial emplotment—and, at certain points, to a more overt heroic emplotment—as conditions and topics change.[8]

The first chapter is entitled "In the Parental Home" (3 *altered;* 1). It concerns Hitler's youth, thus the time at home with his parents. But this title also refers to a standard nationalist metaphor that assimilates one's nation to one's home, and particularly one's parental or ancestral home. Again, this is not Hitler's preferred metaphor. However, he does make use of it now and again. The metaphorical significance is signaled in the opening paragraph, where Hitler explains that he was born on the border between Germany and Austria and that the "reunion" of these two states is his "life's work" (3 *altered;* 1). Later, Hitler uses the metaphor overtly when he refers to the entire people's longing to return to the "paternal home" (18; 11). He also draws on the related, familial metaphors, referring to the "fatherland" and the "mother tongue" (see, for example, 15; 9).

The sacrificial narrative appears on the opening page as well, when Hitler asserts that "from the tears of war there grows the daily bread for generations to come" (3). The phrase clearly conjoins the heroic and sacrificial plots, just as one would expect in a nationalist context. The tears of war are the tears shed for "our" soldiers who have died (i.e., Hitler is presumably not concerned with the sufferings of the enemy). Their deaths constitute the sacrifice needed for the provision of food (the prototypical

---

8. As I have been arguing, a single narrative prototype often dominates the thought and action of an individual activist and of a group during a particular period. Thus, we find Hitler and his government relying primarily on a sacrificial prototype (with the usual underlying heroic structure). However, everyone has all three universal narrative prototypes, and other prototypes as well. These prototypes are likely to turn up and have consequences in particular contexts. Thus, in the case of Hitler, the separation of Germans in different nations triggers the romantic prototype, even though the sacrificial prototype generally dominated his emplotment of nationalism. Put differently, to say that one prototype is dominant for a given activist or group is not to say that it is absolute and all encompassing.

happiness goal for the sacrificial narrative). Moreover, the phrase he uses for food, "daily bread" ("tägliche Brot" 1) alludes to the "Lord's Prayer." This has several functions. First, it signals the Christian—thus both sacrificial and non-Jewish—provenance of the idea. Second, it calls to mind the single, beneficent deity, the Father who gives the daily bread, perhaps associated with the national Leader who commands the army. Finally, it implicitly points toward the following line in the prayer, "and forgive us our trespasses," a crucial theme in the sacrificial narratives.

Again, the opening is largely romantic in orientation, with Germans who live outside Germany, like separated lovers, "dreaming" and "longing" (15) for union with the Reich. However, sacrificial concerns become prominent after the deaths of Hitler's parents at the end of chapter 1. Specifically, the second chapter begins with Hitler's own experience of penury and, in particular, hunger—which, he says, was "pitiless" and "never left me" (29). More important, he stresses the generality of this condition. Thus, he repeatedly emphasizes how the unemployed man "loiters about hungrily" (36), "going hungry in times of need" (37). In these cases, "hunger . . . overthrows every resolve"; "hunger conjures up . . . visions of a life of abundance"; after "meager" meals on some days, "lean days" follow, days "spent in hunger" (37).

These are, of course, the sorts of experience that are likely to incline someone toward sacrificial emplotment, not only of his or her own life, but of nationalism. This is true especially insofar as one explains hunger in nationalist terms—which is, of course, what Hitler does. For him, the problem was the result of not living in the "parental home" of a united Germany. In connection with this, Hitler emphasizes literal homelessness. Thus, he speaks about the "homeless" unemployed who slept in "the mud of the canals" (33); he explains that, in the most brutal season, winter, it was often "hard . . . if not impossible" to find "a new home" (35). He goes on to talk about how people "often" became "homeless" (36). He explains that, in general, unskilled workers experienced "dreadful" misery over "housing." Even those who had places to stay frequently found themselves in "sinister pictures of dirt and repugnant filth" (38). Though asserted literally, these statements clearly have metaphorical resonance as well. They refer implicitly to the German people exiled from the parental home of the Reich.

Hitler actually makes a quite reasonable argument that these conditions should not be eliminated by patronizing generosity from the wealthy. The condition of the homeless and hungry should be ameliorated by the return of their social and economic rights (34). Unfortunately, this reasonableness is not sustained. Hitler's idea of those social and economic rights was, first, a matter of a return to the paternal home, which is to say, a union of all Germans in one state, and, second, an elimination of what caused the loss of these rights. Here, the body metaphor becomes consequential. Hitler's solution to these problems is "the ruthless resolution to destroy the incurable social tumors" (39). On the next page, he takes up the soil/plant metaphor to similar ends, explaining that a race must "brutally . . . pull up the weeds" (40).

The reasons for Hitler's insistence on improving the conditions of the impoverished become clear over the following pages. His concerns are not humanistic, but nationalistic. Specifically, he indicates that the poor tend to understand themselves individualistically or as members of a class, rather than as part of a nation. For them, the nation is represented by the wealthy—precisely the people who seem to prosper at the expense of the poor. The proper response to this is improving the conditions of the poor so that they can join with the bourgeoisie, sharing a sense of national unity.

He goes on to denounce socialists who foster class identification, thus division within the nation and internationalism in foreign relations. Returning to metaphors of the body—but altering them slightly, in anticipation of his subsequent concern with syphilis—he refers to the Social Democratic Party as "a pestilential whore" (52). Like the tumors and the weeds mentioned earlier, this disease-bearing prostitute must be eliminated if Germany is to survive.

In the course of this chapter, Hitler repeatedly discusses nationalism in terms of love (see 44, 55, 56). But the chapter is more directly guided by sacrificial emplotment. Indeed, in keeping with his representation of Social Democracy as a prostitute, he characterizes Social Democrats as "seducers." He views their urging of class identification and internationalism as "seductions" (59). Here, we find the standard sacrificial interpretation of the enemy as tempter.

But, of course, for Hitler, this is only part of the story. He goes on to claim that one can understand Social Democracy only if one understands "Jewry" (66). Again, race must be the ultimate cause of all social phenomena in Hitler's view. Here, Hitler insists that he was a strong supporter of the Jews until the weight of evidence (not presented in this book, of course) forced him to realize the truth. To explain this "truth," he returns to his standard models. Any "filth or shamelessness" of "cultural life" is like a "tumor"; "cutting open such a tumor," one invariably finds "a little Jew . . . like a maggot in a rotting corpse" (75 *altered;* 61). Returning to the metaphor of the prostitute, he then goes on to link Jews with prostitution and "the white slave traffic" (78).

The chapter culminates in a repetition of the sacrificial themes, but this time regarding Jews rather than Social Democrats. Hitler asserts that "the Jew was no German"; rather, the Jews were "the seducers of our people." He then explains that it is "possible to save the great masses, but only after the greatest sacrifices" (80). He repeats the accusation that Jews are seducers, linking their seduction with the devil ("*teuflischen*" 67)—a standard part of the characterization of the seducer.

The chapter ends with a brief invocation of the heroic plot. Hitler claims that Jews are in the process of conquering all the nations of the world. Thus, Jews pose a danger not only to Germans, but to all humankind—an intensified version of the heroic threat scenario. He also insists that his fight against "the Jews" is "fighting for the Lord's work" (84), thus taking up the alignment of national and religious values as well as the divine election of the national in-group.

In the third chapter, Hitler begins with the issue of ethnic conflict in the multiethnic state of Austria. He goes on to antidemocratic arguments. These are certainly consistent with the strict hierarchization of both sacrificial and heroic narratives. But authoritarianism is not distinctive of these structures, and one need not invoke them in explaining Hitler's views here. The chapter has some heroic elements, especially in its repeated condemnation of cowardice (see 105, 123), its advocacy of courage (132), its stress on "tough fighting strength" (128), and so forth. However, this advocacy of martial virtues is linked with an emphasis on "sacrifice" (128, 131, 132). This combination prepares the reader for the discussion of the military campaigns of World War I as well as the sacrifice-requiring devastation that followed. This is particularly clear when he condemns the pan-German movement for having "lost the force to oppose a catastrophic destiny with the defiance of martyrdom" (135).

Just as the preceding chapter opposed class divisions in the nation, this chapter opposes religious divisions within the nation. Specifically, Hitler treats the possibility of Catholics being German nationalists. He insists on this point, opposing those who wish to align German nationality with religious confession. This advocacy of religious tolerance makes sense, given his fundamental principle that biological race (thus not class or religion) is the determinative factor in social explanation and national definition.

In an interesting passage, Hitler argues that the leader must make it seem that there is one great enemy of the nation. If, in fact, there are numerous enemies, the leader should nonetheless present them as if they were one enemy (152–53). This raises the question of whether Hitler actually believed his racialist account or merely adopted it as an effective way of polarizing in-group/out-group divisions. In any case, his reduction of all enemies to one—the Jews—does have the effect of maximizing oppositionality for the national identity category. Again, one obstacle to elevating the national categorial identity above others is that its force is diffused by multiple oppositions. The potential for such diffusion was clear in the case of Germany, which could be understood in opposition to France, England, the United States, and other nations, as distinct out-groups. Hitler sweeps all these aside with the insistence that there is only one crucial out-group, Jews.

The conclusion of this chapter returns to the romantic structure, as it reemphasizes the importance of uniting the separated Austrian Germans with Germany. Thus, Hitler explains that—like a lover far from his beloved—though he was in Austria, his "heart dwelt somewhere else" (160). He represents his feelings for Germany as "secret wishes and secret love." He speaks of how the "wish of [his] heart" would be "fulfilled" in the "union" of Germany and German Austria. He expresses "the intensity of such a longing." The reason for this sudden shift back to the romantic structure is straightforward. He is leaving Austria for Germany. His personal separation ends with this chapter.

The fourth chapter takes up the central sacrificial concern with food, thus the issue of "feeding" the nation and the "impending danger of hunger" (168). It considers how agricultural production could be increased to avoid "hunger" (172) and the possibility of "famine" (173). As one would expect, Hitler treats the topic in a superficially scientific way, arguing that increases in population require increases in available land, thus conquest. In subsequent years, Nazi policy did indeed involve considerable attention to food and the elimination of hunger, in connection with conquest. Thus, during the war, "foodstuffs were seized in vast quantities from the granaries of the Ukraine to feed the population at home"; similar policies were followed in Greece, and there were plans along these lines for Russia, as "food supplies at home constantly needed to be replenished from abroad" (Evans 26). Hitler's advocacy of conquest here leads in an obvious way to heroic motifs, and Hitler does stress "heroic virtues" (197) in this chapter. But the focus on hunger and famine is, of course, bound up with sacrifice. Unsurprisingly, then, Hitler emphasizes sacrifice as well. Thus, he celebrates "the individual's willingness to sacrifice itself" (197) and "the sacrifice of the personal existence" to preserve the group (198). He even goes so far as to claim that "the forces forming or otherwise preserving a State . . . can be summed up with one single characterization: the individual's ability and willingness to sacrifice himself for the community" (199–200).

The chapter ends with the heroic structure once again. Hitler asserts that "heroic virtues" characterize "Aryan States" (in contrast with the "cunning" that characterizes "Jewish colonies of parasites"; 200–201). Yet, in looking at recent German history, he finds a growth of pacifism and a loss of martial commitment. He then returns to the metaphor of the body, asking how the "German people's political instincts" could "become so morbid"; how "the national body" could be inflicted with "poisonous ulcers"; how "a continuous flow of poison" could run through the "blood vessels of this one-time heroic body," leading to "paralysis" (201). These questions prepare for the following chapter, which treats the great war.

Over the next three chapters, Hitler tells the story of the heroism shown by German soldiers in the First World War, their bravery in prosecuting battle after battle "against a force superior in number and weapons" (215)—a standard heroic motif, as we have seen. He insists that Germany was not at all responsible for the outbreak of the war; it was entirely the fault of Germany's enemies (236). Here, too, his account is fully in keeping with the usual heroic structure. But, rather than the expected victory, earned (in Hitler's view) by the German troops, the whole enterprise was undermined by a sort of usurpation: "at the moment when the German divisions received their last instructions for the great attack, the general strike broke out in Germany" (257). This did not finish the heroic narrative, but instead put Germany in a position of devastation. Hitler's subsequent program involves ending the usurpation through the establishment of the proper leader (i.e., himself) and ending the devastation through sacrifice (especially the elimination of the putative seducers), then taking up the interrupted war and marching to victory.

In these chapters, in keeping with the sacrificial emplotment, Hitler does not fail to bring up hunger. For example, he says that "distress was very great everywhere" in Berlin; "The city of millions suffered hunger" (249). In keeping with this, the eighth chapter, which (along with the ninth) considers Hitler's early political activities, turns again to "the possible bases of a feeding of the German people" (281), his "fight" to secure "nourishment" for the people (288–89).

Chapter 10 brings us at last to the main concern of the book—the causes of the devastation of Germany, its "fall" (302), as he calls it, drawing on the body metaphor ("the fall of a body" [302]) and alluding to the central sacrificial narrative of Christianity. In discussing the topic, Hitler elaborates on the bodily metaphor, referring to "the cure of an illness" and the necessity of finding the cause of that illness. In keeping with this, Hitler rejects the Marxist idea that "economy" is crucial, insisting instead that "factors of blood and race" are most important. (Hitler mentions "political" and "ethical-moral" factors as important as well. But, by the end of the analysis, he makes it clear that race is the definitive, fundamental factor.)

The first thing Hitler feels he has to establish is that the collapse of Germany was not due to a military defeat, but was "a consequence of other causes" (307). The crucial point here is that these other causes involve a fault on the part of the in-group. Thus, the devastation is the result of sin. Though Hitler often tries to recast his sacrificial narrative in plausibly scientific terms, toward the beginning of this chapter, he sets out the issue straightforwardly in terms of ethical causality (i.e., a causality of sin and punishment for sin): "the military defeat of the German people is not an undeserved catastrophe, but rather a deserved punishment by eternal retribution" (309). He goes on to contend that the "bottomless lying of Jewry and its Marxist fighting organization" (312) seduced the people. Hitler imputes to Jews what later came to be called the "big lie" technique, a central Nazi propaganda device, exemplified perfectly by Hitler's statements about Jews. Specifically, Hitler claims that Jews were able to seduce people because "the great masses of a people may be more corrupt in the bottom of their hearts than they will be consciously and intentionally bad, therefore with the primitive simplicity of their minds they will more easily fall victims to a great lie than to a small one" (313).

By this point, readers will not be surprised to find that Hitler almost immediately turns to the metaphor of "national bodies" and their "diseases" (314). Once again, he insists that one must isolate the "causes" of the illness, the "contagious matter" in the "nation's body" (314). He develops the metaphor in a peculiar way, saying that a particular problem arises when "an absolutely noxious poison" has been in the body too long. At a certain point, one no longer recognizes that it is "alien," and instead "tolerates it" (315). This takes us to Hitler's concern that Jews have become integrated into German society. Thus, they are difficult to recognize, difficult to distinguish and resist in their seductions, difficult to remove. As I have discussed in *The Culture of Conformism,* this sense of the out-group's dangerous invisibility is regularly bound up with the assimilation of the out-group to Satan and with policies of expulsion and extermination (thus, in the terms of the present study, policies of nonelective alignment). The connection of this with purgative sacrificial emplotment should be clear.

The following section recurs to the issue of "daily bread" (315, 316). The image is, again, appropriate for sacrificial emplotment because of its emphasis on the basic necessity of food and its allusion to the Lord's Prayer with its reference to "our sins." This section also indicates what the first sin of the German people was—a sin denounced by Jesus himself. Specifically, "money became the god whom now everybody had to serve and to worship" (316). Along with this, the "hero" declined and the "Jew banker" rose (318). Hitler develops the point by drawing on a common motif from heroic tragicomedy. He sees one sign of social decline in the replacement of true heroes by fawning courtiers. The true heroes gave honest, critical advice to the monarch (see 323–24). With their replacement by bankers, that bravely disinterested honesty is lost. He goes on to discuss the importance of being willing to die for one's master (327)—in this context, a heroic virtue, which had declined in Germany.

Hitler returns to the topic of food (330), opposing it to poison (330, 335), specifically, the "terrible poisoning of the health of the national body" (336). This allows Hitler to discuss the next cause of national decline—syphilis. Indeed, it turns out that syphilis is a part of the same complex, for syphilis results from "the mammonization of our mating impulse" in prostitution (337). It therefore takes part in the elevation of money to the status of God, characterized by Hitler as the "Judaization of our spiritual life" (337). He even goes so far as to say that the children produced by mammonized love are not "vigorous children of natural feeling"—presumably the children who would develop into valiant heroes. Rather, the children of the money worshipers and prostitutes are "miserable specimens of financial expedience" (337; this reasoning may suggest one source of Nazi views on the disabled).

On the other hand, however bound up with monetary considerations, the source of syphilis is a sexual sin—a widespread sexual sin of just the sort one expects to find in a sacrificial narrative. Hitler goes on to maintain that the struggle against syphilis is crucial to the future of the nation (339, 341). It will require "sacrificial measures . . . enormous sacrifices" (342).

But syphilis cannot be considered a true cause of the fall. In keeping with his racialist principles, Hitler maintains that "the illness of the body is here only the result of an illness of moral, social, and racial instincts" (349). The last are, of course, the most important in his scheme.

The following pages speak of various sorts of degeneration, emphasizing again "the service of money" and asserting directly that this service undermines "heroism" (364). He maintains that the Reichstag "sinned" in relation to the army (373), specifically in "the defense of the fatherland"

(375). Again, the two key narrative structures are intertwined. The cause of the fall in Hitler's sacrificial narrative is precisely what interrupts the heroic tragicomedy in the (tragic) middle. In this case, the sins were individualism (378), one of the great dangers facing in-group solidarity at all times, and internationalism—thus forms of sub- and supranational allegiance. Individualism was, in effect, a form of usurpation as it concerned political self-advancement and "the way towards the minister's seat" (378). In contrast with those who were seduced into these sins, the army, Hitler insists, retained its heroic "value" (383), taught "courage in a time" of "cowardice" (384), rejected the common commitment to one's "own 'ego'" (384), and repudiated international "fraternity" (385). In other words, the army was the source of heroic ethics, and the enemy of threats against national identity, both supranational (class solidarity) and subnational/usurping (egoism). Finally, the army was the one weapon in the fight for the "nourishment" of Germany (386). In short, the army alone did not sin.

Up to this point, Hitler has been addressing superficial reasons for the fall. At the end of this chapter, he announces that the "deepest and the ultimate cause" of the "ruin" was a matter of race, particularly a lack of attention to race "and its importance for the historical development of the people" (388). This leads to the culminating chapter of the first volume, the chapter treating nation and race.

Hitler begins this chapter with a sort of evolutionary view, insisting that Nature tends to "breed life . . . towards a higher level" (390). But in some instances this tendency is blocked by perverse interbreeding of species. This interbreeding includes that of races, which results in a "lowering" of the "higher race" along with "physical and mental regression" and, of course, "illness." Once more, despite the general attempt to give his claims a scientific presentation, Hitler returns to ethical causality. Miscegenation, he claims, is "nothing less than sinning against the will of the Eternal Creator. This action, then, is also rewarded as a sin" (392). Here, the seduction by the alien tempter is extended from a seduction in belief (i.e., a seduction toward internationalism), then a seduction through prostitution, to a seduction into "interbreeding." Later, in discussing colonial conquest, he returns to the same idea. He explains that the conquerors eventually "mix with the subjected inhabitants," thereby ending "their own existence." He goes on to invoke the Judeo-Christian paradigm of the sacrificial prototype. Specifically, he comments on the colonizer's loss of existence through miscegenation, stating that "the fall of man in Paradise has always been followed by expulsion from it" (400). The same image recurs a few pages later, when Hitler writes that "The Aryan gave up the purity of his blood" and thus "also lost his place in the Paradise" (406).

Unsurprisingly, Hitler turns from this discussion of sin to a discussion of sacrifice. He begins by speaking of the parents' "readiness to sacrifice . . . themselves" for their children, connecting this with their work seeking "food . . . for the young ones" (407). In the context of sacrificial narratives, the conjunction is clearly appropriate. Hitler goes on to celebrate the "will to sacrifice" (407) over against the concern with one's "own ego" (408). He discusses "giving up one's life for the existence of the community" as the "fulfillment of duty" (410) and explains that the triumph of "egoism" in a nation has the result that "people fall . . . out of heaven into hell" (412). By this point, the ethical causality is so obvious that it does not require comment.

At this stage in his argument, Hitler is faced with the problem of explaining just how Jews are to blame if Germans become egoistic. He solves the problem by sharply opposing Jews and Aryans in terms of self-sacrifice. The "will to sacrifice . . . his own life for others, is most powerfully developed in the Aryan" (408). In contrast, Jews are entirely individualistic (414). The seduction of the Aryan by the Jew is thus, in part, a seduction into "Jewish" individualism. (The point is made explicit only in the second volume; see 591.)

From this point, Hitler returns to body metaphors. He characterizes "the Jew" as "a *parasite* in the body of other peoples" (419), a "bacillus" that kills the "host people" from within (420), a "plague" (426), a "blood-sucker" who practices usury (426) and who takes the "blood" of the Aryan race. In collaborating with these foreign seducers, "German monarchs . . . sold themselves to the Devil" (428). This linking of Jews with devils is repeated in the subsequent pages (441, 447, 448). Hitler also elaborates on the ways in which Jews putatively defile the racial purity of Aryans—through rape, as well as prostitution, the importing of Africans, and so forth (448–49).

Hitler concludes the chapter with a restatement of his basic thesis, that the devastation of Germany was the result of "the non-recognition of the race problem and especially of the Jewish danger" (451). It was, in other words, an unwitting collaboration with "the internal enemy" (454). This resulted in a "sin against the will of eternal Providence" (452).

But what is one to do now? How was one to reverse the situation?

In the course of the chapter, Hitler suggests some responses to the devastation caused by the people's sin. Most significantly, he refers to "making the acquisition of soil legally impossible" for Jews (427), which is to say, excluding them from the national territory—just what the sacrificial narrative appears to require for the seducer. However, his development of the body metaphors and his account of miscegenation indicate that this is not a sufficient response. The final chapter of the first volume and the bulk of the second volume treat the development of the Nazi party, clearly intended as the solution to the problem, the way of achieving "the resurrection of our people" (500). But the current chapter ends with indications of the "final solution," indications that follow directly from Hitler's particular development of the sacrificial narrative.

First, continuing with the body metaphor, Hitler refers to "the various political doctrines which doctored about the German national body." These treated only "the symptomatic forms of our general sickness, but passed blindly by the germ" (453). The implication here is clearly that the Nazi party will treat the true cause, the "germ" that has been isolated in the preceding pages. Insofar as the Satanic seducer is understood as this germ, there is, of course, only one "solution." Though unnamed here, it is precisely the policy followed by the Nazis when they came to power—extermination. As Hitler puts it in the final chapter, the "international poisoners" of the German people must be "extirpated" (469).

But what of the other side? This is clearly a purgative version of the sacrificial narrative. Nonetheless, there are indications throughout that the in-group must sacrifice itself as well as the seducer. For example, the reader is prepared for this by Hitler's emphasis on the Aryan's innate capacity for self-sacrifice in service of the group. The penultimate section of the chapter ends with a suggestion of such self-sacrifice and its consequences. Referring to "the peoples oppressed by the Jew," Hitler writes that "With the death of the victim this peoples' vampire"—thus, the (Jewish) bloodsucker who causes their death—"will also die" (451). In short, the text suggests that the extermination of the seducer and the self-sacrifice of the victim must and will be combined to reverse the fall, thereby restoring and "resurrecting" Germany.

The chapter ends with a Nazi slogan, "One German State of the German Nation" (455 *altered;* 362). This is the alignment of state and "race" that will result, first, from the extermination of the tempter and national self-sacrifice, then from the completion of the heroic plot, which had been interrupted by temptation, sin, and punishment.

Through these chapters, then, the sacrificial structure is firmly established. Specified through bodily metaphors and Hitler's fundamental explanatory principle—racial determination of all historical events—it has helped to shape the interpretation of history given in the book. Moreover, it has helped to suggest particular actions as a response to that history—with terrible results, too well known to require reiteration.

GANDHI, FASTING, AND THE HEROISM OF COLLECTIVE SELF-SACRIFICE

Around the time I was writing the preceding analysis of *Mein Kampf*, I attended a talk by the influential political and cognitive literary critic, Elaine Scarry. Scarry mentioned that Gandhi had once made the following remark: "Among the many misdeeds of the British Rule in India, history will look upon the Act depriving a whole nation of arms as the blackest" (*Autobiography* 446). The worst thing the British did to India was to deprive Indians of weapons. I was distressed to hear this and felt that Scarry must be misrepresenting Gandhi. After all, even if he said such a thing, it seemed wildly inconsistent with his trademark advocacy of *ahiṃsā* or nonviolence. But I was teaching Gandhi that semester as well and, as I read more of his work and as I thought more about his life and practice, I realized that Scarry was right. This statement was not entirely anomalous or decontextualized. Moreover, this was not the only strangeness in Gandhi's thought and work; it was not the only point that seemed difficult to integrate into an understanding of his politics.

Consider, for example, his obsession with chastity.[9] Perhaps the strangest manifestation of this were his "brahmacharya experiments," in which, in his late seventies, he slept naked with young women—most often his assistant, Manu—in order to test his ability to avoid sexual arousal (see Judith Brown 377–78). At least at the conscious level, his motivations for sleeping with Manu seem to have been antisexual, rather than sexual. Thus, in defending the practice, he affirmed the value of becoming a "eunuch," not through surgery, but through "prayer" (Wolpert, *Gandhi's* 229). Moreover, he seems to have believed that this practice would have beneficial social consequences. As Wolpert explains, "He appears to have hoped that sleeping naked with Manu, without arousing in himself the slightest sexual desire, might help him to douse raging fires of communal hatred in the ocean of India" (228). Related to this, there was his obsession with diet, his

---

9. Again, chastity is one of the primary virtues associated with the sacrificial narrative. In keeping with this, a virtual obsession with chastity is shared by some sacrificially oriented groups. Consider, for example, the Liberation Tigers of Tamil Elam (LTTE), which pioneered suicide bombing. They forbid their members from having sex before the age of 25 (for women) or 28 (for men), and punish adultery by execution (Kennedy and Power 23).

concern about what foods contribute to lust and what foods have a cooling effect on the passions.

Of course, these are personal matters. Many political leaders have had peculiar sexual attitudes and many have had a complex relation to food. But, in Gandhi's case, these did not remain private. They pervaded his political life also, as his political use of fasting shows. Or consider his Satyagraha Ashram, established to embody the principles of Indian independence (see Judith Brown 100). Members of the ashram had to take six vows (see Wolpert, *Gandhi's* 84). Four have obvious bearing on social order and/or the struggle against colonialism: Truth, nonviolence, nonstealing, and nonpossession. The others, however, are less clearly relevant. These were "celibacy (even for married couples) and self-denial over food" (Judith Brown 100).

Then, there was his apparent superstition, at least what many people would consider superstition. Gandhi objected to scriptures when their claims were "opposed to trained reason" (quoted in Jordens 91). Yet he often made claims that would seem to stand against most views of "trained reason." We have already seen an instance of this in his peculiar contention that sleeping naked with young women would help end Hindu-Muslim violence. A claim such as this may seem to be a self-justifying pretense. But it is consistent with his proclamations on a range of other matters. For example, thinking of this sort was one basis of a well-known conflict between Gandhi and Rabindranath Tagore. As Ashis Nandy explains, the "best known of the controversies between Tagore and Gandhi centered around the Bihar earthquake of 1936, which killed thousands. Gandhi declared that the natural disaster was a punishment for the sin of untouchability" (280n.9; see also Das Gupta 45).

Gandhi was one of the most influential and effective political leaders of the modern period. He was a man of great intelligence and great practical ability. What, then, are we to make of the points just mentioned? Considered in reference to Gandhi himself, are they merely personal quirks, irrelevant to the larger structure of his political thought and action? Again, they seem to have been worked into that political thought and action too thoroughly to be dismissed in this way. Considered in reference to Gandhi's followers and his general success, are they mere incidentals that had no impact on the masses? This, too, seems implausible, given their pervasiveness in Gandhi's public discourse and his political practices.

As is no doubt already obvious, these apparent anomalies in Gandhi's statements and activities are not mere incidentals. Rather, they show us something about the way Gandhi thought through nationalism. They also suggest part of the reason why his statements and activities resonated with ordinary people. Specifically, they show us that Gandhi's politics manifest an implicit sacrificial tragicomedy, in its collective self-punishment version.[10]

To discuss this, it is helpful to focus on a single text. But the choice is not simple. Though constantly busy with his political work, Gandhi was nonetheless a prolific writer. His collected writings, published by the government of India, sum to ninety fat volumes. Clearly, it makes no sense to try to cover even a representative portion of this. The question is—what would constitute an appropriate selection? An ideal work would be extended, but not too diffuse. It would treat his central concerns in a way that may be generalized to a range of political activities and connected to the thought and feelings of his followers. Indeed, we would not want a work that was private to Gandhi, but a work that had an impact on the people who made the independence movement—for, after all, it is that impact that makes Gandhi significant. For these purposes, no work could be superior to Gandhi's commentary on the *Bhagavad Gītā*, initially delivered as a series of public lectures at his Satyagraha Ashram between February 24 and November 27, 1926. As I have already noted, Gandhi established the ashram on the basis of his principles for Indian independence. As Judith Brown puts it, through this ashram, Gandhi "tried to create an environment . . . where people could grow into servants of God and thus into servants of India" (199).

The *Bhagavad Gītā* was (and is) one of the most important works of Hindu scripture. It was particularly important among anticolonial authors, and some had already written about the book in a nationalist context—most notably Bal Gangadhar Tilak, "the greatest leader of the extremist wing of the Indian nationalist movement, which advocated militant overthrow of the British" (Minor 8; on Tilak's commentary on the *Gītā*, see Stevenson). It was a familiar and revered text for Gandhi's Hindu followers outside a nationalistic context as well. Moreover, it was a work that was specially important to Gandhi himself. As Jordens explains, "No book was more central to Gandhi's life and thought than the *Bhagavad Gita*. He constantly referred to it as his 'spiritual dictionary'" (88). He brought this enthusiasm to his followers as well. "Communal recitation of the *Gita* was a regular

10. Like Hitler, Gandhi has been examined psychologically, and his nationalism has been treated by historians and political scientists. As with Hitler, the psychological approaches tend to be psychoanalytic, not cognitive, and the treatments of his nationalism do not touch on narrative. The most influential psychoanalytic treatment is that of Erikson. Useful mainstream accounts of his nationalism may be found in Wolpert (*Gandhi's*) and Judith Brown.

feature of life in his ashrams; in fact it was the principal religious ritual" (88). Indeed, Gandhi went so far as to argue that "schools should incorporate the study of the *Gita* into their curriculums" (90).

In this section, then, I shall focus on Gandhi's lectures on this important scripture. However, before going on to this, we need to consider some of the cultural background that Gandhi brought to his reading of this text—in other words, some of what went into his cultural specification of the sacrificial emplotment of nationalism. In developing the sacrificial prototype, Gandhi drew particularly on Hindu ethical theory, the theory of dharma or duty.

National Dharma and Violence: Cultural Backgrounds to Gandhism

Traditional Hindu ethical theory divides ethical duties or dharmas into a number of broad categories. The largest or most encompassing division in Hindu ethical theory is between *swadharma* or self-dharma, the dharma that is particular to one as an individual, and *sādhāraṇadharma*, universal dharma that applies to everyone. Swadharma includes several subcategories, such as "stage of life" dharma (e.g., the obligations of a student are not the same as those of a "householder" or family man/woman). Perhaps the most important of these subcategories is *varṇadharma* or caste dharma, the duty that goes along with one's caste. For example, a priest has the duty of performing rituals. Two sets of caste duties are particularly important for Gandhi—the dharma of the lowest caste, śūdras or servants, and the dharma of what might be called the political class, the kṣatriyas or warriors/rulers.

In effect, Gandhi generalized the duties of both śūdras and kṣatriyas to the entire population. In both cases, this gave rise to difficulties. Śūdras were supposed to serve the upper castes. But, if everyone is a servant, whom might they serve? This problem is easily solved in a nationalist context, for they are clearly supposed to serve the nation. Indeed, even within the traditional caste system, śūdras' lives of service may be seen as a sort of ongoing self-sacrifice for the good of the society. In that way, there is a loose connection between this śūdradharma and sacrificial narratives. Had Gandhi stopped with the generalization of śūdradharma, then we might also expect him to repudiate caste, leveling everyone down to śūdras, eliminating the very idea of upper castes. In fact, Gandhi did no such thing. Rather, he strongly affirmed the importance of caste, as we will see. This is in some ways unsurprising, if one keeps in mind the strict hierarchical ethics of both the heroic and sacrificial plots.

The generalization of kṣatriyadharma created other, less easily resolved difficulties. The "kṣatriyazation" of nationalism—its transformation into a "warrior" movement—was advocated, explicitly or implicitly, by many Hindu nationalist leaders at the time. It was bound up with militarism and with what Ashis Nandy refers to as "impotent" violence, "such as the immensely courageous but ineffective terrorism of Bengal, Maharashtra and Panjab." As Nandy explains, "Many nineteenth-century Indian movements of social, religious and political reform . . . tried to make Kṣatriyahood the . . . nearly exclusive indicator of authentic Indianness" (*Intimate* 7; on kṣatriyazing developments in Hinduism, developments that are inseparable from Indian acceptance of European colonialist ideas, see 24). The problem here is that kṣatriyadharma is the dharma of violence, the dharma of warfare. Specifically, it is the duty of warriors/rulers to protect the nation against threats and to keep order in society. In other words, kṣatriyadharma is the dharma of the heroic prototype. But, of course, Gandhi is most renowned for his advocacy of and strict adherence to nonviolence. This would seem to place him at the opposite pole from anything having to do with kṣatriyadharma.

This apparent conflict is not new with Gandhi. It has one important source in Hindu ethical ideas themselves. Specifically, in addition to varṇadharma, the other main source of Gandhi's ethical development of nationalism was sādhāraṇadharma or universal dharma. The two primary components of universal dharma are ahiṃsā (nonviolence) and truth (cf. O'Flaherty 96). As is well known, these were the two main pillars of Gandhi's political thought and activism. Moreover, they are directly opposed to the violence and often deceitful tactical strategies that operate in kṣatriyadharma. The point is obvious not only from a contemporary perspective. The conflict of universal dharma with self-dharma has been clear from early on in Hindu tradition. The opposition between sādhāraṇadharma and kṣatriyadharma has been recognized as particularly sharp.

Indeed, conflict in dharma is precisely what frames the *Bhagavad Gītā*, which is no doubt one reason it was so important for Gandhi. Specifically, the *Gītā* is a section of a long heroic epic, the *Mahābhārata*. In this epic, two families of cousins—the Pāṇḍavas (the "good guys," at least superficially) and the Kauravas (the "bad guys")—are about to engage in a war over their kingdom. Arjuna, one of the Pāṇḍavas, is ready to begin the battle. But suddenly he hesitates. He feels that it is a violation of his familial dharma to kill his cousins. His charioteer is Kṛṣṇa, an incarnation of the savior god, Viṣṇu. Kṛṣṇa responds to Arjuna's doubts by presenting a detailed treatment of metaphysics and ethics, the final conclusion of which is that Arjuna must follow his kṣatriyadharma over all other dharmas.

Whatever one thinks of Kṛṣṇa's argument, it would still seem not to solve Gandhi's problem, since the issue addressed by Kṛṣṇa is not specifically that of universal dharma. Nor did Kṛṣṇa establish ahiṃsā as the foundation of his politics. This is precisely where the sacrificial narrative comes in. Gandhi can value and even generalize kṣatriyadharma on the assumption that successful warfare is impossible in current circumstances. In that context, the generalization of kṣatriyadharma becomes a matter of generalizing defense of one's nation and its structure through whatever means are likely to succeed. In a collective self-punishment narrative, those means are a matter of general and ongoing self-sacrifice. But how does ahiṃsā enter here? Again, in the collective self-punishment version, the out-group is irrelevant. Their supremacy is merely the byproduct of one's own sin. The penance for that sin must be entirely one's own. A rigorous form of self-punishment would strictly avoid pushing the blame onto the out-group and punishing them. Gandhi's insistence on ahiṃsā is, I believe, a development of this sacrificial idea through the Hindu notion of universal dharma. To affirm kṣatriyadharma and nonviolence is, then, simply to take up a rigorous form of the collective self-punishment version of the sacrificial narrative. But, at the same time, this sacrificial emplotment does not entirely abandon the heroic emplotment that is so intimately bound up with kṣatriyadharma. Specifically, Gandhi's sacrificial emplotment asserts a way of defending the nation in a context where the default heroic narrative cannot be pursued. Once again, in nationalism, the sacrificial narrative presupposes the heroic structure. Nationalists repudiate the heroic structure when they see victory as impossible—which returns us again to Gandhi's idea that the worst thing the British did to Indians was to disarm them.

Starving for Freedom:
Understanding Gandhi Understanding War

Again, Kṛṣṇa's task in the *Bhagavad Gītā* is to convince Arjuna that his dharma requires him to participate in a violent war. Given the usual understanding of Gandhi, one might expect him to begin his commentary with a strong statement against the militaristic conclusions of the book. In fact, Gandhi begins by apparently diverting the entire issue of real war.

Specifically, he claims to interpret the *Mahābhārata* battle as an inner or spiritual conflict between impulses toward dharma and impulses toward adharma (the violation or opposite of duty). In connection with this, he indicates that the Kauravas are "evil" and the Pāṇḍavas are "good" (95).[11] Of course, such a polarization of values is just what one would expect from a heroic emplotment of this conflict. This already begins to suggest the presence of a heroic model. The relation of Gandhi's interpretation to the heroic prototype, and the relation of both to his own nationalistic commitments, become clearer when, two pages later, he directly connects the Kauravas with the British colonial government (97). Indeed, here it becomes impossible to take seriously the idea that Gandhi is interpreting the *Gītā* as an allegory for struggles within an individual soul. He is, in fact, reading it as a text that bears directly on nationalism, on the colonial status of India and the aspirations of its people for political liberation. Given the historical context in which the talks were delivered, and given Gandhi's own political career, most listeners would have tacitly understood this political context even without such an explicit connection.

Gandhi goes on to say that he will "leave aside" the issue of violence (95), hardly what one would expect. Moreover, he admits directly that the *Gītā* does not "prohibit physical fighting" (96). This apparent indifference to the issue of violence suggests that ahiṃsā is not the fundamental principle of his politics. However strongly held, Gandhi's advocacy of nonviolence appears to have rested on some other principle. Perhaps this is the principle enunciated in Gandhi's 1929 work on the *Gītā*. There, he asserts that "The author of the Mahabharata has not established the necessity of physical warfare; on the contrary he has proved its futility" (*CW* XLI 93). In this case, Gandhi's objection to violence is not moral, but practical. Warfare fails; it is futile—precisely the view one would expect to lie behind a sacrificial nationalism. The notion echoes a passage in Gandhi's widely influential *Hind Swaraj* of 1909. There, Gandhi draws on the usual heroic alignment of spiritual and moral values, characterizing the conflict between the British colonial government and the Indian people as a conflict between "the Kingdom of Satan" and the "Kingdom of God." He goes on to explain that Indians who take up "modern methods of violence to drive out the English . . . are following a suicidal policy" (*CW* X 189).

Returning to our main text (Gandhi's 1926 commentary on the *Gītā*), we find that his apparent acceptance of war in principle, if not in practice,

---

11. Unless otherwise noted, citations of Gandhi refer to Discourses on the "Gita," *Collected Works* XXXII, 94–376.

is not confined to a few ambiguous statements at the outset. The first chapter ends with what certainly seems to be an advocacy of kṣatriyadharma and war, at least in certain cases. Specifically, Gandhi concludes that "Arjuna . . . had no choice but to fight" (101).

Before continuing on to chapter 2, it is important to remark on one other passage in the opening chapter. When discussing the parallel between the Kauravas and the British, Gandhi also treats several characters who were fundamentally good and thus who should have been on the side of the Pāṇḍavas, but who joined the Kauravas. These characters, he argues, are parallel to the Indians who have given their support to the British. He concludes that evil cannot succeed on its own. Rather, it requires the cooperation of good men and women (see 97). Here, we see the fundamental characteristic of the sacrificial sin. We have been devastated by the out-group, but the out-group succeeded only because of the sin of the in-group, their error in accepting the seductions of the out-group.

Again, this view could develop in different ways, emphasizing the guilt of the enemy or that of the home society. Gandhi chose the latter. The departure of the English, who filled the tempter role here, remained crucial, as the slogan "Quit India" indicates. Nonetheless, Gandhi's focus was on the in-group and the version of the sacrificial narrative that guided his work was consistent with that focus. In keeping with this, early in the second chapter, Gandhi explains that "If one must kill, one should kill one's own people first" (103).

This hint of sacrificial concerns does not mean that Gandhi has left aside the heroic narrative. In fact, the second chapter elaborates on and generalizes Gandhi's conclusion that it was necessary for Arjuna to take up arms and fight the battle. For instance, he explains that if one's enemies "deserve to be killed, they ought to be killed; and one must not hesitate even if the entire world were likely to be destroyed in consequence" (106). More generally, "A Kshatriya has no duty higher than that of fighting in a righteous war" (116).

The *Gītā* stresses that Arjuna's hesitation on the battlefield is the result of attachment—for example, his attachment to the people he would have to attack and possibly kill. Gandhi takes the extreme stand of the heroic narrative on this, insisting that, "Should it become necessary to cut off, with a sword, one's father's head, one must do so if one has a sword and is a Kshatriya" (103). In keeping with this, Gandhi stresses the importance of eliminating egoistic attachment. Indeed, this is precisely what makes violence morally acceptable: "If a person remains unconcerned with defeat or victory . . . he commits no sin in fighting" (116).

Gandhi elaborates on the changes in attitude and emotion that result from ending egoistic attachment. Given common views on Gandhi's politics, one might expect these changes to be a matter of fostering, say, peace and empathy. In fact, he says nothing of the sort. He could be speaking either to a warrior or to a sacrificial victim when he explains that detachment should lead to "submission" (105) and the elimination of "fear" (108). Just after this, he urges that we should behave mechanically, allowing Kṛṣṇa to act through us as his instruments. This is, of course, the same Kṛṣṇa who, in the *Gītā,* is arguing that Arjuna should begin the massively destructive *Mahābhārata* war.

Gandhi goes on to indicate that we not only need to rid ourselves of egoistic attachments and to have faith in God. We also need to "have faith" in the "spinning-wheel movement" (121). The instance is specific, but the implication is general. Gandhi is suggesting that the abandonment of egoistic attachment should be accompanied by a commitment to nationalistic activity—including a pragmatic commitment to the success of that activity. In "Anasaktiyoga," he perhaps makes the point more clearly. There, he insists that one must renounce the fruit of one's actions, but one should absolutely not be indifferent to the results of one's actions (*CW* XLI 97). At first, this may seem contradictory. However, the point is that, like a soldier or a sacrificial victim, one must renounce any individual gain, but one must be fully committed to achieving the goals of one's actions, for the goals benefit the entire group.

As the preceding discussion indicates, the early passages of Gandhi's commentary are oriented more toward heroic than toward sacrificial narratives. There are, however, a few suggestions that the heroic emplotment is merely background to the sacrificial narrative. We have already noted one good instance of this, when Gandhi says, "If one must kill, one should kill one's own people first" (103). The comment makes perfect sense in a sacrificial context, but would otherwise appear obscure. Subsequently, Gandhi makes a more directly sacrificial comment when he remarks that "We shall breathe life into the Ashram [a sort of synecdoche for India] by laying down our own lives" (110). He also alludes to the Judeo-Christian myth of the Fall, the first part of the paradigmatic Christian sacrificial narrative. Specifically, Gandhi says that we must renounce the fruit of our work because God has ordered us not to "pluck a fruit from the garden" (124).

More significant, Gandhi goes on to discuss at length a verse that refers to someone who fasts. (The English version misleadingly translates the Sanskrit *nirāhārasya* [see Sargeant 144] as "starves his senses" [131]). It is not clear from the verse whether Kṛṣṇa is or is not a proponent of fasting. It is clear that, in Kṛṣṇa's view, fasting is an inadequate or insufficient spiritual practice, since it eliminates experience of sense objects without eliminating the taste for those objects. The taste is eliminated only by the experience of "the Supreme." Gandhi, however, sees Kṛṣṇa as stating that we should fast, that it is a crucial part of striving to experience the Supreme. Though this is a possible meaning of the passage, Gandhi's interpretation is clearly influenced by his prior conceptions—specifically, the narrative prototype through which he is implicitly structuring his ideas about nationalism. Thus, Gandhi says that fasting should help free us from desire and should wither our appetite. He even represents the enlightened person as one who is indifferent as to "whether he eats or does not eat" (132). The ethics of self-deprivation, specifically self-deprivation of food—thus one important part of the ethics of the sacrificial narrative—could hardly be clearer. Gandhi connects self-indulgence in food with sexual self-indulgence as well, thereby interrelating the two most standard sins of the sacrificial narrative. In commenting on the immediately preceding verses, Gandhi had introduced the issue of food, though it had no evident bearing on the verses then being explicated. He stated that one should not eat too much, explaining that "a boy who eats till he is full cannot preserve celibacy" (130).

Gandhi develops the discussion of fasting to some rather extreme conclusions. Once egoistic attachment vanishes—a liberation to which fasting contributes powerfully—then, he tells us, "the body" will "cease to exist" (136). Indeed, if we find it impossible to control our senses "we should give up food altogether" (131). One should even be willing "to stake one's all and perish" in a fast (135). While not literally urging suicide, Gandhi's orientation in these passages is clearly moving in the direction of suicide. The discussion is perhaps influenced by Jain self-starvation or *sallekhana,* a religious practice aimed at spiritual purification and liberation in death (for a discussion of this practice, see Dundas 155–56). In any case, this is just the sort of idea one would expect to find in a writer relying on sacrificial emplotment.

The connection between fasting and nationalist sacrificial emplotment becomes more explicit in the concluding pages of the chapter. Gandhi discusses "the ideal for the Satyagraha Ashram," thus the ideal, not only for spiritual achievement, but for political activism on behalf of India. This ideal is precisely the ideal he has been discussing, the ideal of those who "eat sparingly" (143), the ideal of those who take on "voluntary suffering" (142n.4). More significant, Gandhi refers to the activism and ultimate success of the nationalist movement in clearly sacrificial narrative terms.

Skeptics, he explains, claim that "we cannot win liberty by keeping fasts." But, Gandhi affirms, "we shall get" liberty by those fasts (142). On the next page, he repeats the point, claiming that "we can achieve self-realization through fasting and spinning" and that "self-realization necessarily implies swaraj" (143), that is, national independence.

In connection with this emphasis on fasting, it is important to recall that hunger was a pressing issue in India. Moreover, the extent and intensity of hunger were bound up with the political condition of the nation. On the relation of famine in India to British colonialism, consider two brief examples. In 1879, when Gandhi was a child, the viceroy removed import duties on British cotton, "despite India's desperate need for more revenue in a year of widespread famine" (Wolpert, *New* 248). In 1895, when Gandhi was a young man, famine began to spread "to virtually all of the Deccan." This was a result in part of monsoon failures, but it was equally a result of "grossly inflated home charges [that] had consumed all of India's grain surplus" (Wolpert, *New* 267). In an analysis of colonialism and hunger written in Gandhi's own time, Dutt argues that, under the colonial practices of British rule, "any nation on earth would suffer from . . . recurring famines" (vol. I, xvi). Thus, here too the sacrificial emplotment of nationalism is bound up, not only with a sense of military despair but with a history of widespread hunger as well.

The chapter ends with a return to hints of suicide with the assertion—again, good advice to a soldier or a sacrificial victim—that "our bodily existence is not a thing to be cherished" (146).

The third chapter takes up the theme of service, thus shifting away from kṣatriyadharma to śūdradharma. In keeping with this, there is a corresponding shift from talk about war to talk about sacrifice. The theme is broached first in the introduction to the chapter. There is a brief return to the heroic when he comments that "There can be no hypocrisy in ceaselessly fighting the enemy who holds us in his grip" (149). But the following page takes up sacrifice (*yajña*) and the theme is developed through the rest of the chapter. Perhaps the most important assertion comes right at the outset. Gandhi gives a perfect statement of the collective self-punishment version of the sacrificial plot when he writes that "it is not a true sacrifice in which we kill other creatures" (153).[12] This is, of course, a perfectly logical point, and one that radically separates self-punitive sacrificial emplotment from its purgative counterpart.

---

12. This particular sentence refers to animal sacrifices. But the encompassing paragraph refers to the killing of humans. Thus, the general principle is clearly meant to apply to all other creatures, not merely animals.

Later, in a remarkable passage, Gandhi indicates his acceptance of moral causality and he does so in connection with drought and famine. He begins with a quotation from the *Gītā:* "From food springs all life, from rain is born food; from sacrifice comes rain" (160). He then says that "there would be no rains if people did not perform *yajna* [sacrifice]" (160). He goes on to discuss earthquakes, maintaining that "If a nation is sunk in sin and God wants to save it, He might send an earthquake with that aim" (165). He ends this part of the discussion by considering the possibility of rain having a "connection . . . with whether we lead sinful or virtuous lives" (167).

In the course of this chapter, Gandhi recapitulates some of the themes we have already treated—restricted eating (169), the necessity of Arjuna fighting the battle (172–73), acting without fear (178), and so on. He stresses the importance of sexual abstinence as well, even establishing as an ideal the "man who has made himself a eunuch" (150). In keeping with the underlying heroic structure, he in effect supports violence, in part by equivocating on the term *violence*, when he claims that "Violence does not consist in the act of cutting off someone's head; it consists in the motive behind the act" (179). At one point, he returns to the topic of making oneself into an instrument or tool. Interestingly, he uses the image of a spinning wheel. Given the nationalistic associations of that piece of equipment, the image suggests that one should be like a tool, not only for God, but for the nationalist movement as well. He also repeats the connections among sacrificial self-denial, self-realization, and political independence.

Toward the end of the chapter, Gandhi turns from issues of food and sacrifice to sexuality. In a pun, he directly opposes the rule of kāma or sexual pleasure to the rule of Rāma (184–85). Rāma is, like Kṛṣṇa, an incarnation of Viṣṇu. The perfection of his rule is proverbial and "the rule of Rāma" is widely used to refer to the ideal society. Gandhi's pun, then, not only associates sexuality with sin, but opposes such sin to social well-being—once again, a standard theme in sacrificial thought. Following this, he identifies the "baser . . . impulses" as "demoniac" (186).

The main sacrificial themes are all present at this point, and the rest of the book more or less recapitulates these points. This fits with Gandhi's own assessment of the *Gītā* itself—specifically, that, after the early chapters, "Krishna had nothing further to add" (quoted in Jordens 94). It is nonetheless worth following out some variations and extensions of these themes.

Early in the fourth chapter, Gandhi returns to moral causality, when he explains that he was eager to undertake "penance" that would put an end to Hindu/Muslim conflict (190). He extends the point a few pages later, maintaining that, when adharmic behavior spreads throughout society, some people begin to practice austerities and through their self-mortification "generate goodness in the world" (193). This is, of course, the positive side of moral causality and the culmination of the sacrificial plot. While sin leads to communal devastation, self-sacrifice leads to communal well-being.

Subsequently, Gandhi turns again to sacrifice and the relation of sacrifice to self-denial. He particularly stresses chastity, thus reintroducing the antisexual theme. He even goes so far as to claim that "It is not natural for human beings to violate *brahmacharya*" (210; brahmacharya is sexual abstinence in devotion to study). He implicitly addresses suicide when he refers to how someone may become "desperate" in his or her struggle against desire, especially sexual desire, and undertake "an indefinite fast" in order "to stop all organs from functioning" (214). (Being a prudent political organizer, he does go on to mention "the *yajna* of money," which may be performed by people who wish to "let their wealth be shared by others" [214].) Toward the end of the chapter, he returns to the topic of food, saying that animals live by food, but "Man does not live by bread alone." Rather, humans live by performing sacrifice (219). Gandhi links the performance of sacrifice with nationalism two sentences later by referring to the spinning wheel, a central symbol of Indian nationalism and a central part of Gandhi's nationalist program.

Chapter 5 opens with a long meditation on eating. Gandhi presents this as if it were a comment on the opening verse of the fifth chapter of the *Gītā*. But there is only the most general connection between the two. It seems clear that Gandhi has brought to the text his own presuppositions about the centrality of food to self-discipline, presuppositions that are bound up with the sacrificial prototype. Unsurprisingly, he argues that one must detach oneself from eating, eat only as if one were performing a sacrifice, and so on (222). He subsequently connects this with the self-punitive theme, though in a much more positive way than is common. Specifically, he explains that, if one must choose between giving food to an enemy and to a friend, one must give food to the enemy (231). This is the positive correlate of the self-punitive sacrificial injunction that one's in-group must sacrifice from itself, not punish the out-group.

Chapter 6 continues the theme of food. Gandhi has to deal with a passage from the *Gītā* in which Kṛṣṇa says that one must neither eat too much nor fast too much (243). This seems to be perfectly reasonable advice. But it does not entirely fit the sacrificial approach adopted by Gandhi in the rest of the work. Gandhi begins by accepting Kṛṣṇa's statement. But he then immediately denies it, urging his audience to undertake ascetical practices. He tells them, "you should not spare yourself any harshness in striving for self-purification" (244). Indeed, he explicitly brings up suicide here. Speaking of a person "who, however hard he tries, cannot acquire control over his senses," Gandhi says, "let such a person certainly undertake long fasts, even if his body should perish in consequence" (243).

Toward the end of the chapter, Gandhi takes up the theme of obedience to God, here in a way that relates it directly to the submerged heroic plot. Specifically, he refers to the dutiful devotee as "a soldier in God's army" (252). The image may initially seem odd, given Gandhi's emphasis on such matters as fasting. But in the broader context, it suggests once again that the nationalistic sacrificial narrative presupposes a nationalistic heroic narrative.

Chapter 7 stresses the relation between national and individual suffering, a crucial link in sacrificial emplotment. In connection with this, chapter 8 lays particular stress on individual liberation. Most significantly for our purposes, in discussing this topic, Gandhi uses imagery that bears on the independence struggle. For example, he compares ordinary life to "one long imprisonment" (270). Thus, sacrifice is what releases one from imprisonment—presumably both individual and national.

More important, this chapter returns to the topic of moral causality, which Gandhi accepts unequivocally. Thus, he writes that "If we get a disease, we should believe that we ourselves are the cause of it." He goes on to say that we should "believe that our illness is the result of our sins" (265). Though he is apparently speaking of individuals with medical conditions, the relation to collective suffering is clear. In a fascinating passage, Gandhi connects this directly with, of all things, fear. "If we have any fear whatever in our heart," he claims, "that too is a form of evil and we suffer from many serious diseases because of it" (265). It is as if a sort of cowardice in battle is the sin of the nation, the sin that has made the heroic solution impossible and requires a sacrificial solution. Gandhi goes on to link this to suicide as well. Specifically, he argues that anyone who has "overcome his evil desires . . . will refuse to be cured" by physicians. Rather, he will insist that "when the evil in him has disappeared, he will be all right." Gandhi concludes, "If, as a result of this attitude, he dies, he will welcome death" (266).

Chapter 9 takes up a corollary of the identity between ātman (the individual soul) and brahman (the ultimate spiritual reality), an identity affirmed in certain schools of Hindu philosophy. This corollary is the ultimate unity of good and evil. Gandhi, following traditional Hindu principles, explains that God must encompass not only all good, but all evil as well (282). In consequence, we should not view "even the most wicked of men as wicked" (285). In the first chapter, Gandhi had separated good and evil rather clearly. He linked evil with the Kauravas and the British government. Correlatively, he linked good with the Pāṇḍavas and, by implication, the Indian nationalists. That was tacitly within the context of the heroic prototype. Having shifted to the sacrificial prototype, the issue of wickedness changes. It is now important to set aside ideas about British evil, because here the nation needs a sacrifice. As we have already seen, for Gandhi, a "true" sacrifice is not a sacrifice of others. Rather, it is a sacrifice of ourselves. As such, it is not based on identifying others as the source of evil. Rather, it is based on a recognition of our own sinfulness.

Here, one might wonder about the precise relation between the heroic emplotment that seemed to characterize Gandhi's discussion at the outset and the sacrificial emplotment that appears prominent at this point. Unsurprisingly, it is the cross-culturally standard relation. Specifically, Gandhi writes that "Knowing that there is no limit to the power of God, we should submit to violence if anyone attacks us, without offering violence in return." This seems to be a matter of pure ethical principle. But, in fact, it is a barely concealed expression of despair over the possibility of military victory. In the next sentence, Gandhi tells his audience, "If we attempt to resist Him with violence, God will humble our pride" (292). In case this still seems to be a matter of general principle, one need only recognize that Gandhi's claim cannot possibly apply to both sides. The clear implication is that the enemies who attack "us" (i.e., India) will win if we try to engage in a war. Gandhi does not say that God will humble the pride of both the attackers and the people attacked. He does not say that the pride of the British will be humbled in a battle. Logically, the point does not seem to make much sense. But, once again, it makes perfect narrative sense. We have sinned. Thus, we need to make amends, not fight a war that we will certainly lose. Here, we see the basic principle of the shift from the heroic to the sacrificial plot—not only in Gandhi's thought, but generally. The heroic plot assumes that God is on our side. The sacrificial plot assumes that, however special we are to God, He has (temporarily) withdrawn His support due to our sin.

Chapter 11 treats Gandhi's decision not to flee a predicted flood (see 295). He allows other people to leave, but he does not undertake an evacuation. The practice here is a concrete illustration of his acceptance of moral causality. Fleeing the projected flood would, presumably, be even worse than accepting medicine when one is sick. It would seem that one should rather work on purifying oneself so that the flood is not necessitated by one's inner evil. Unsurprisingly, at this point, Gandhi's first advice to his followers is that they should observe restraint in eating, that they should not eat "to gratify your palate" (295).

Chapter 12 emphasizes nonviolence, but it does so in a peculiar way, a way that is more consistent with warfare than one might initially imagine. Specifically, Gandhi adjures his followers to free themselves "from all thoughts of violence" (302). Prima facie, it seems that nothing could be more opposed to violence and warfare. But, in fact, it is precisely this absence of violent thoughts that allows Arjuna to engage in the battle. By freeing himself from all *thoughts* of violence, he frees himself from attachment to violence. He is thereby able to fulfill his kṣatriyadharma with purity. Once again, Gandhi's stance against violence is more consistent with the narrative presuppositions of sacrificial narrative than with the pure logic of moral imperatives. In keeping with this, the chapter ends with another affirmation of caste dharma: "All of us have our appointed tasks, as Brahmins or Kshatriyas, Vaisyas or Sudras. Anyone who does his work without hope of reward and in a disinterested spirit is a *bhakta* [devotee] of God" (305). It is important to note in this context that the specific form of attachment decried in the *Gītā* is attachment that *inhibits* acting violently; it is the attachment that initially leads Arjuna to set down his weapons and refuse to fight.

Chapter 13 in effect takes up the sorts of argument that the priest might make to the a sacrificial victim.[13] This is unsurprising, as all Indians are potential sacrificial victims in a collective self-punishment version of the sacrificial narrative. Indeed, some of Gandhi's statements hardly make sense outside that context. For example, what is one to make of the notion that a person who realizes some basic principles of nonattachment necessarily "starts with the thought, 'I am sin'" (307)—not "I have sinned" or "I do sin," but "I am sin"? The only one who "is" sin is the sacrificial victim, for one of the standard functions of the scapegoat is to represent all the sins of the community. For example, in some Yoruba ceremonies, the scapegoat carries the sins out of the community by being driven into the bush (see, for example, the ritual represented in Soyinka's *The Strong Breed*). In other cases, the scapegoat may be killed in a symbolic destruction of the sins he or she represents. In any event, it seems to be only in the context of

13. On arguments of this sort, consider, for example, the Kondh, one of the "tribal" peoples of India, who practiced human sacrifice into the nineteenth century. In the Kondh ritual, the priest would try to convince the sacrificial victim of the necessity of the sacrificial death (see Mahapatra xix–xx).

sacrificial narrative that one can reasonably think of oneself as being sin. Indeed, Gandhi immediately connects this idea that "I am sin" with moral causality, asking "Why is it, we should ask ourselves, that we are afflicted with all manner of diseases?" (307).

Gandhi goes on to make some metaphysical sense of the idea that "I am sin" by maintaining that egoism is the source of sin. As a consequence of this, "There is no sin where there is no consciousness of the 'I'" (310). What is interesting here is the ambiguity of the statement. Selfless detachment—precisely what one desires in a soldier or sacrificial victim—presumably results in this absence of ego-consciousness and ends one's selfish, thus sinful behavior. However, the absence of ego-consciousness, and the absence of sinful behavior, are produced even more fully by death, the end and goal of the scapegoat.

Gandhi concludes the chapter by connecting the theme of egoism with moral causality. A person who is "free from egotism . . . does not suffer because of old age and disease" (313). Indeed, such a person turns out to be the perfect sacrificial victim, for he "is not attached to his son or wife or home" (313). At the same time, such a person is a perfect soldier—recall that Arjuna's hesitation before the war was an aversion to harming his own relatives.

The fourteenth chapter reiterates many of these ideas, stressing three "virtues." One is "sincerity." This seems to bear more on political leadership and the danger of hypocrisy than any issues we have been considering. However, the other virtues fit the present account nicely. Outside a discussion of heroic and sacrificial narrative, one might expect Gandhi's prime virtues to be, say, compassion and generosity or something of that sort. Instead, he names "fearlessness" and "humility" (320). Fearlessness is the most obviously crucial virtue for both the soldier and the sacrificial victim. But it must be conjoined with humility, for humility is what guarantees obedience to one's superiors. Pride, in this context, is almost as grievous a fault as cowardice.

Chapter 15 further extends some of the preceding points. In keeping with the idea that the sacrificial narrative presupposes an underlying heroic narrative, Gandhi suggestively refers to "the weapon of non-cooperation" (322). More significant, he explains that the perfectly detached person is one who is "not fear-struck but serene at the moment of death" (323)—in effect, a description of the perfect sacrificial victim.

Chapter 16 plunges us back into moral causality. Toward the beginning of the chapter, Gandhi tells his audience, "I would ask every person who suffered from a disease if he was free from attachments and aversions" (327). He goes on to make the link between sexual sin and communal suffering more explicit, stating that "Sexual indulgence necessarily leads to death" (328). He explains that the point is not merely individual, but has broad, social consequences. "If people gave themselves up to [sexual indulgence], God's rule in the world would end and Satan's prevail." In contrast, chastity "leads to immortality" (327).

In chapter 17, he connects sexual sin with food and fasting. Specifically, he explains that the eating of sweets is not conducive to chastity. He then urges his followers to eat "bitter, sour and saltish foods" instead (333). The chapter ends with a repetition of Gandhi's advocacy of extreme selflessness. Speaking once again as if he is addressing a sacrificial victim, he urges his listeners to think of themselves as "ciphers" (336).

The eighteenth chapter reiterates many of the main sacrificial themes. For example, in keeping with a pattern we have come to expect at this point, he takes up a series of verses that treat a range of topics, such as meditation, solitude, restraint in speech, and so forth. One item in this list bears on diet. Gandhi virtually ignores everything on the list except diet. He discusses at length the importance of limiting one's intake of food. In a particularly striking passage, he criticizes himself bitterly for having eaten a date that very day (346).

Gandhi ends this chapter by affirming that Arjuna is right to take up his weapons again and fight. He writes that "he who has pure knowledge and the necessary energy to act upon it, that is, has taken up a bow and arrow, will never depart from the path of morality" (350). The passage seems odd if we take Gandhi to be advocating nonviolence as a foundational moral principle. But it makes perfect sense when we understand his advocacy of nonviolence as deriving from a sacrificial emplotment of anticolonial nationalism and when we recall that this sacrificial emplotment is merely a conditional deviation from an underlying default mode of heroic emplotment.

The Conclusion goes over some of the main themes more systematically. Toward the beginning, Gandhi again takes up the issue of violence, treating it in a manner consistent with the sacrificial narrative. Thus, he claims that "violence committed for the sake of *yajna* [sacrifice] is not violence" and he allows for forms of violence that do not involve "the intention . . . to give pain" (353). The second point suggests the usual defensive stance of the home society in heroic emplotments. It is, after all, only the invader who intends to give pain. Our side is engaged in self-defense and merely wishes to end the unprovoked attack from the enemy. When we give pain, it is an unfortunate side effect of self-protection.

In the following pages, Gandhi pays particular attention to hierarchy, in a manner directly recalling the military discipline of the heroic plot and its valorization of obedience. Gandhi's ideal person "will not even think what his duty is." How, then, will such a person act? Will he or she be filled with spontaneous compassion or driven by a repulsion toward violence? No. Such a person will act "only as directed by others" (354). Here, Gandhi considers the difference between Protestants and Catholics. He explains that the Pope may be immoral. In consequence, a Protestant would urge Christians not to follow the corrupt Pope, following instead their own conscience. But Gandhi opts for following the orders of the spiritual leader. Following one's own conscience is not consistent with living as a "cipher" (355). It may no longer come as a surprise that when living as a cipher and following the direction of one's spiritual leader, one's acts are, by definition, nonviolent (354–55). In a revealing metaphor, which he had already used in an earlier talk, Gandhi explains that, when we do something as sacrifice, we "enlist ourselves as soldiers in God's army" (355). He goes on to explain that, if we have no ego-involvement in what we do, then "even the most dreadful-seeming act may be regarded as an act of ahimsa" (356). He subsequently connects this with varṇadharma, caste dharma. He insists once again that swadharma—a person's own dharma, which includes caste dharma—should not be violated. He explains that "Our duty is what society assigns to us" and the "definition" of swadharma is that "one must do the work assigned to one by one's superior" (369). This is true even for work that "smells of violence" (370). The Conclusion does, however, include a brief reference to the futility of warfare (360), in keeping with the sacrificial preference of the lectures as a whole.

In short, the final section of Gandhi's commentary not only recapitulates the sacrificial themes, but reemphasizes the close connection between a sacrificial politics and a heroic politics. Indeed, in keeping with an analysis in terms of narrative prototypes, it indicates that, to alter von Clausewitz's famous phrase, sacrifice is the continuation of war by other means.

Before concluding, it is worth remarking briefly on a case of Gandhi's practical activism. Gandhi's satyagraha campaign against the regulations governing salt provides a perfect illustration. As Wolpert points out, this was "Gandhi's most famous and difficult struggle against" the British empire (*Gandhi's* 144). Judith Brown explains that, after Gandhi's death, Jawaharlal Nehru considered it the "episode which best recalled the nature and impact" of Gandhi's work (237). Less than four years after the lectures we have been considering, Gandhi set aside many oppressive British laws and practices to focus on one that concerned food—the regulation of salt. (Recall that Gandhi found salty foods less objectionable than sweet foods, on the grounds that they are more conducive to chastity [333].) Brown explains that he announced the campaign against these regulations at the Satyagraha Ashram, stating that "he and a column of satyagrahis would march from the ashram, carrying copies of the *Gita*" (236). In discussing the campaign, he made direct reference to the hunger that triggers sacrificial narratives, maintaining that the salt regulations "reach even the starving millions" (quoted in Wolpert, *Gandhi's* 143). The campaign involved the sorts of suicidal self-sacrifice that are definitive of the sacrificial narrative and that require the reduction of the self to a cipher. But it did so in a manner that is reminiscent of a war. For example, before the campaign, Gandhi explained that they "may have to see . . . hundreds and thousands being done to death during the campaign" (quoted in Wolpert, *Gandhi's* 147)—a comment that one might expect more before a battle than before a sacrifice. Subsequently, he said that "My heart now is as hard as stone. I am . . . ready to sacrifice thousands and hundreds of thousands of men if necessary" (148). When people did die, he implicitly revealed the reliance of a nationalistic sacrificial narrative on a nationalistic heroic narrative. For example, when two young men were killed, Gandhi "congratulated their parents 'for the finished sacrifices of their sons,'" going on to explain that "A warrior's death is never a matter for sorrow" (149). The culmination of this campaign was reached at Dharasana on May 21, 1930, when a group of Gandhi's followers marched to "the giant salt depot protected by armed constables and helmeted British police officers" (151). In one of the most famous events of the Indian independence struggle, the marchers offered no resistance, not even raising their arms in self-protection as the police cracked their skulls. As one protestor collapsed, another would march into the vacated space, showing no fear during this "brutal massacre of innocents" (151), this perfect, self-punitive sacrificial offering.

In this chapter, I hope to have shown something about Hitler and Gandhi. Specifically, I hope to have shown the internal consistency of their thought and action, even at those points where it seems contradictory. This is not the consistency of strict normative principles and inferential logic. It is, rather, the consistency of a sacrificial narrative prototype, embedded in a (frustrated) heroic prototype, and specified through cultural principles. For example, Gandhi's apparent inconsistency on the issue of military strength, his strange statements about an earthquake as punishment for sin, his technique of fasting, and a range of other seemingly disparate ideas and tactics all fit together in this context. In short, I hope to have increased our understanding of these political figures.

At the same time, I hope to have explained something about the success of these figures. Hitler and Gandhi had mass, nationalist followings. Needless to say, different individuals were attracted by different aspects of their thought and action. But to some extent, the many elements that made up their political programs and strategies must have resonated fairly widely. In both cases, this resonance derived, at least in part, from the universal narrative prototypes on which they drew. Moreover, in both cases, those prototypes and their specific relation to one another were triggered by a particular history, a history marked by hunger and inseparable from a sense of military despair. In this way, I hope that the analysis contributes to our understanding of these nationalist movements.

Finally, I hope to have advanced our knowledge about this profoundly important form of nationalism, beyond these particular cases. Specifically, I hope to have demonstrated that nationalist activists and ordinary people regularly emplot nationalism in terms of the sacrificial prototype. They commonly do this in the context of a national history marked by salient instances of famine or faminelike hunger. Even more important, sacrificial emplotment becomes dominant among activists and ordinary people in conditions of social devastation and military despair, thus despair over successful heroic emplotment, with its comic conclusion aided by divine preference. Despite that despair, this emplotment does not entirely repudiate the heroic prototype. Rather, politicians and citizens continue to draw on heroic narrative as an underlying or default structure. In connection with this, I hope to have clarified the two opposed versions of sacrificial emplotment—purgative and penitential—which are themselves fostered in part by particular historical conditions. In each of these versions, and in their combination, sacrificial emplotment is highly consequential, not only for the expression of nationalism in fiction, but, far more important, for nationalist thought and action in real, worldly politics. Indeed, within the past century, specifications of the sacrificial prototype have helped transform the lives, and have contributed to the terrible deaths, of millions of people around the world.

7

ROMANTIC LOVE AND THE END OF NATIONALISM
Walt Whitman and Emma Goldman

ROMANTIC TRAGICOMEDY STARTS with two people falling in love. For some social reason, they are unable to be united. This social inhibition is usually enforced by representatives of traditional social order, frequently parents. A rival is often included among the blocking characters as well. One lover is often exiled, while the other is often imprisoned. When the lovers are separated, the rival may have some temporary success. However, in the complete, comic version, the lover returns (perhaps through the good offices of some helper figure, or through some accomplishment when away). He is reunited with his beloved, frequently after defeating the rival. The final reunion of the lovers may also involve a larger familial reunion or reconciliation as well. This is most often a reconciliation of the lovers with their parents. In some cases, however, the lovers may have a child. In this case, the final reunion of the lovers brings them together with their children as well.

The nationalist implications of heroic and sacrificial plots are straightforward. This is less true of the romantic plot. Indeed, the romantic plot seems to operate directly against one aspect of the heroic plot and thus against the corresponding nationalistic ideas. The usurpation/restoration sequence in heroic stories serves to reaffirm social hierarchy. In contrast, the union of the lovers, in most cases, directly contradicts the social hierarchy of the in-group. The authority of parents or community leaders is overthrown for the preferences of the children. Moreover, the reasons for the separation of the lovers often have to do with identity categories, such as class, caste, ethnicity—or even nationality. If the separation is due to nationality, then the romantic plot is likely to work against the other component of the heroic plot as well. While the heroic plot sets the national in-group against the national out-group in military conflict, the romantic plot may join the two national groups together, challenging the entire idea of national divisions. On the other hand, if the separation is due to some subnational division—class, caste, ethnicity, religion—then the romantic plot may operate in a nationalistic way. Specifically, the celebration of the lovers' union suggests the importance of uniting those subnational groups. Indeed, the romantic emplotment of nationalism is particularly likely to arise and have broad influence during periods of subnational division (just as sacrificial plots are particularly likely to arise and have broad influence during periods of national devastation and military despair). In this case, the rejection of internal hierarchy is likely to be the rejection of a false or usurping leadership, a leadership that promotes national division rather than national unification.

The result of all this is that romantic emplotment tends to operate in one of two ways. On the one hand, it constitutes the most intense opposition to subnational divisions, including the divisions enforced by purgative sacrificial narratives. In this form, it often underlies liberal varieties of nationalism.[1] This use of romantic tragicomedy is suggested by Doris Sommer's work on Latin America and, in a more complex way, by Katie Trumpener's analyses of British colonial narratives (see 133–37, 141, 146, 148, 329–32). For example, Sommer writes that "Latin American romances are inevitably stories of star-crossed lovers who represent particular regions, races, parties, or economic interests which should naturally come together" (75). Moreover, she points out that the pattern is not confined to the Americas.

---

1. Of course, this model need not lead to liberalism. For example, we saw a variation on this general use of romantic emplotment in Hitler's treatment of Germans outside Germany. In that case, the "subnational" divisions were not a matter of regions or races, but of states. Hitler's program for unifying that putatively divided nation was hardly liberal. On the other hand, Hitler's case seems unusual. The general tendency of this model is toward a broadly inclusive politics that is starkly opposed to purgative nationalism.

Specifically, she explains that "As in Latin America, European foundational fictions sought to overcome political and historical fragmentation through love" (84).[2]

But, again, this is only one use of romantic tragicomedy. Romantic tragicomedy simultaneously constitutes the most intense opposition to national in-group/out-group divisions. Thus, it underlies certain forms of internationalism. More generally, the impulses of romantic tragicomedy are almost invariably against hierarchy, against group categorization, against in-group/out-group divisions, and in favor of individual freedom and choice. As such, this prototype almost always pushes against nationalism and against orders of social authority, even in those cases where the focus is on subnational reconciliation. Consider, for example, Mani Ratnam's celebrated film, *Bombay*. A Hindu and a Muslim fall in love. They marry in defiance of their parents' bigotry and lead a happy, indeed joyous family life. But Hindu/Muslim riots—ignited by the inflammatory speeches of illegitimate national leaders—almost lead to the death of their children. The parents save their children by bravely facing the rioters and appealing to their common identity as Indians. The film concludes with Hindus and Muslims ending the riots and joining hands in national unity. The film clearly involves a romantic emplotment of nationalism. It directly celebrates the nation in doing so. Yet, at the same time, it is clear that our sympathy with the couple and their children would be no different if the Hindu were Indian and the Muslim were Pakistani and if their children were nearly killed in war between nations rather than in riots within a nation. Moreover, if these leaders are illegitimate because they undermine the human relations of ordinary people through the enforcement of subnational identity categories, other leaders should be illegitimate because they undermine the human relations of ordinary people through the enforcement of national identity categories.

In short, there are both nationalist and antinationalist uses of the romantic plot.[3] However, even the nationalist uses commonly have antin-

---

2. A recent European example may be found in Margarethe von Trotta's 1995 film, *The Promise*. It treats two lovers, Sophie and Konrad, separated by the construction of the Berlin wall. Their longing for union parallels and exemplifies the longing of East and West Germany. Their reunion occurs when the separation of East and West Germany ends.

3. There is actually a third common use of this structure as well, a use that is not precisely nationalist or antinationalist. Specifically, literary works often employ the romantic plot allegorically in treating nationalism. A remarkably frequent form of this allegory involves the love triangle. In this version, the beloved (male or female) represents the nation and the two rivals represent different possible futures for the nation. It is up to the nation to choose one or the other. Commonly, the author strongly prefers one rival (i.e., one possible future for

ationalist implications, which may be more or less overt. Put differently, the prototype is not easily confined to a narrowly nationalistic use. It structures events and orients our sympathy for characters in such a way as to resist in-group/out-group divisions, including national divisions, and their associated social hierarchies. In the following pages, then, I will consider one nationalist, though ultimately somewhat ambiguous case of romantic emplotment, and one antinationalist case. There are many straightforward instances of nationalist literary works that involve romantic emplotment. Some of these have been discussed at length by other writers, as I have just noted. For that reason, I will consider a less straightforward case, a work in which the romantic emplotment operates more covertly—thus a transitional case in which the analysis of that plot is potentially more illuminating. Walt Whitman's *Leaves of Grass* is perhaps the closest thing the United States has to a national epic. Specifically, "Song of Myself" is widely recognized as a powerful statement of American national self-definition. Though it involves some localized elements of the heroic plot, it is primarily romantic. Indeed, it has all the characteristic elements of the romantic plot. But Whitman eschews overt narrative connections. Thus, the larger emplotment of the poem's nationalist politics is not at first obvious. It becomes clear only when interpreted in light of the romantic prototype.

In keeping with the antinationalist tendency of romantic emplotment, Whitman's nationalism continually spills over into universalism or nonnational globalism. Some other writers have taken up this nonnational globalism more thoroughly and explicitly. I will conclude with a look at a nonliterary and (apparently) nonnarrative case in which romantic emplotment leads to an overtly internationalist and antiauthoritarian politics—Emma Goldman's Anarchism. These two writers allow us to return to the United States, treating another strand of American thought, one very different from that of *Independence Day* and President Bush, but also (if to

---

the nation) and the point of the work is to urge his or her readers to adopt that choice for the nation's future. I briefly outlined three cases of this sort—from Rabindranath Tagore, Derek Walcott, and Peter Abrahams—in chapter 3. Other cases would include sections of Salman Rushdie's *Midnight's Children* and Ngũgĩ wa Thiong'o's *Petals of Blood*.

I leave this use of the romantic prototype aside here as such allegory is confined to explicit, fictional stories. In other words, in these cases, the romantic plot has definite literary consequences. But it is not clear that it has any practical, real-world consequences (beyond the straightforward rhetorical consequences of associating a particular national policy or practice with a character we like and a rival policy or practice with a character we do not like). Moreover, it is a formal use of the structure, for it does not involve any particular view of nationalism or policy for the nation. Virtually any positions may be associated with the lovers.

a lesser degree) different from that of the Vietnam Veterans Against the War.

WALT WHITMAN
Romance, Race, and the Pansexual Nation

As is well known, the first title of "Song of Myself" was "Poem of Walt Whitman, an American." Whitman changed this to "Song of Myself" after the second edition of *Leaves of Grass.* The history of the title is suggestive, for it indicates how we are to understand the "self" of the poem—the self is, first of all, an American.[4] In other words, the self being sung in the poem is the self defined by the national category. (Contrast, say, "Poem of Walt Whitman, a Man.") Even without the first title, the point would be clear from the poem, which catalogues the various people and places that comprise the "self" of the poem's speaker. That "self" is clearly America. The poem begins "I celebrate myself, and sing myself," this is not mere personal narcissism, but the celebration and singing of the nation, a specification of the standard metaphorical model, THE NATION IS A PERSON. When he says that "every atom belonging to me as good belongs to you" (1. 3), he is not speaking nonsense, but referring to the shared "self" of Americans.

Of course, without "an American" in the title, this shared self could simply be shared humanity or even shared life. Indeed, the poem develops in this direction, passing beyond the nation to larger aggregates, following the universalizing impulse of romantic emplotment. But the link with America in particular becomes clear quickly. "My tongue," thus both his linguistic idiom and the actual organ that (we might imagine) sings this song, is "form'd from this soil, this air." His speech is not, then, English, but American, the product of just this physical place, and the air breathed in and out by all the other American speakers. Moreover, "every atom of my blood" (1. 6) derives from this soil and air as well. Taking up another

---

4. Of course, the fact that Whitman removed the phrase is important also. It may suggest an ambivalence about the strict categorial identification of the self as an American. As Peter Rabinowitz pointed out to me, the removal could be taken to "suggest that [Whitman] felt the first title was too nationalistic." I completely agree with this point. As will become clear by the end of this section, I believe that Whitman's poem begins with a nationalist orientation, but is continually moving away from nationalism toward internationalism. Such ambivalence or shifting between stressing and downplaying the category of "American" is, then, just what we would expect, given the internationalist impulse of romantic emplotment and Whitman's particular development of that emplotment.

standard nationalist metaphor, THE NATION IS A FAMILY, he asserts that his ancestry, his "blood," is American. What we share with the speaker, "every atom," becomes by association "every atom of . . . blood," thus kinship. The self's national identity encompasses or substitutes for ethnic identity. Whitman goes on to reject divisive belief systems as well, putting "Creeds and schools in abeyance" (1. 10). In the course of the poem, Whitman repeatedly repudiates organized religions.

These few opening lines set out Whitman's nationalist ideas clearly. The United States faced several threats to national identification. One was a continued sense of unity with England. This is a transnational, language-based identification. Whitman deals with this through the affirmation of an American language, "form'd from this soil." Indeed, part of the influence of Whitman's poetry, and "Song of Myself" in particular, derives from his practical development of American English as a poetic idiom. A second danger was ethnic division, both sub- and transnational. He deals with this in the usual way of affirming a metaphorical familial/ethnic connectedness—shared blood—of Americans. A third possible conflict was religious, which was again sub- and transnational. His response in this case, a response very much in keeping with that of America's "founding fathers," was to reject the validity of religious categories. (On the attitude of the founding fathers toward organized religion, see Allen.)

But Whitman knows perfectly well that other divisions threaten American unity. Indeed, those are the difficult ones. Language, ethnicity, and religion were relatively limited in their divisive impact. The risk in these cases was less that national unity would end, that a national categorial identification would be lost, than that it would be weakened by other—primarily transnational—identifications. In contrast, both regional and racial identifications threatened to end the nation as such through sharp subnational conflicts. Indeed, those two forms of subnational identification were inseparably intertwined. Citizens of the slaveholding states increasingly identified themselves regionally rather than nationally. This identification was bound up with their racial identification. Both identifications were enhanced in the usual ways. Within the national context, slaveholding had become highly salient, functional, affective, and oppositional. (Obviously, it had been salient, functional, affective, and oppositional in other contexts—for example, plantation life—from the outset.) One point of conflict concerned just how enduring it would be.

This situation of internal division fostered romantic emplotment in the usual way. In Whitman's case, however, that emplotment was complicated by a number of factors. First, his primary metaphorical schema for the

United States was THE NATION IS A PERSON. Thus, he sought to model the nation (metaphorically) on a person and (narratively) on the union of lovers. This creates some obvious difficulties. Whitman solves these difficulties in part simply by accepting imagistic contradictions. Indeed, he affirms the necessity of contradiction toward the end of the poem, when he writes, "Do I contradict myself? / Very well then I contradict myself, (I am large, I contain multitudes.)" (11. 1324–26). This is not a celebration of illogic, but an acknowledgment that no single image or statement can encompass the diverse ideas and attitudes found in a nation. America is large. It contains multitudes. These multitudes do not always agree. In fact, they probably never fully agree. On the other hand, Whitman was seeking to enhance the sense of unity as well. His poem does not set out to fragment Americans, quite the contrary. A combination of these images—America is one; America is not one, but a division that seeks union—helps to suggest this complexity in a way that is unifying without being reductive or what Bakhtinians would call "monological."

Perhaps more important, he shifts among different levels of "self" in the course of the poem. At times, "myself" is the overarching nation. At times, however, "myself" is the poet celebrating the nation—not simply Whitman as a biographical person, but Whitman as a sort of principle of agency that could be any American, anyone who sings about America, as the lover sings about the beloved. Put differently, "myself" is at times the nation as a whole and at other times those individuals that comprise the nation. In the terminology of ancient Indian thought, which is as apt for Whitman as for Gandhi, it is both the ātman and brahman; it is both the individual soul and the Absolute—here, a sort of national Absolute—that is ultimately not different from the individual soul.[5] Of course, the romantic emplotment bears primarily on "myself" as an individual. It is this poet, singing of America, who would be separated from his beloved by national disunion.

But there is a further complication here. The subnational threat Whitman faced was not a simple regional division for which he could imagine a straightforward, healing union. Many such divisions may be imaginatively reconciled by joining lovers from each side. But uniting a white northerner and a white southerner would not have resolved the dilemma. It would have left out the black population. It would have healed the regional split while exacerbating the racial opposition. Whitman had no inclination to do this.

---

5. For a discussion of Whitman's relation to Indian philosophical thought, specifically Vedāntism, see Chari.

However, a simple union of black and white would not have worked either. This would have deepened the cleft between the north and the south.

Whitman's primary strategy for dealing with these problems was to generalize the sexual union, extending it everywhere.[6] The poem becomes, in a sense, pansexual[7] (or, as James Miller puts it, "omnisexual" [see chapter 6 of his *Leaves of Grass*][8]). By encompassing all Americans in a sort of sexual ambiance, Whitman partially avoids the problem of choosing blacks over southern whites or vice versa. He also partially reconciles his collective and individualistic uses of "myself."

On the other hand, the generalization of sexual union is not entirely even-handed. Specifically, there is nothing in the poem that suggests a particular union of the poem's "self" with southern whites. Whitman does mute his criticism of southern whites. This has led some interpreters to criticize him for not being adequately antiracist (see, for example, Simpson). However, it seems clear that this is a necessary result of his nationalist purposes. He cannot strive to unify the nation while vilifying most people in one region of the nation. Moreover, he makes clear that one is an American whether one is good or bad. To cultivate national unity, national acceptance of a national categorial identification, is not the same thing as claiming that all members of the nation live up to national ideals. In any case, he does not draw from his pansexual America a particular sexual union of northern and southern whites. He does, however, suggest the sexual union of whites and blacks. In this way, he takes up more fully the romantic solution to racial division. At the same time, he tempers this by suggesting sexual unions among regionless whites and by partially occluding the sexual aspects of the black-white union.

After all this, there is still one further complicating factor—Whitman's own sexuality.[9] When he imagined romantic union, he most powerfully imagined the union of men. Moreover, this imagination was closely related

6. This is not to say that Whitman recognized the problems self-consciously and set out to resolve them by extending sexuality in this way. In certain cases, he was no doubt self-consciously aware of problems and solutions. In general, however, it seems more likely that he had a looser sense that some ways of singing America were not quite right, while others were more consistent with his ideas and feelings.

7. A range of critics have stressed the importance of sexuality in Whitman's poetry. See, for example, Pollak for a recent, extended exploration of this topic.

8. I prefer pansexual as it avoids associations with omnivore and related words, suggesting instead such ideas as pantheism and thus Whitman's "sacralization of sexuality," as Ostriker put it (104).

9. Needless to say, the importance of Whitman's sexual orientation has not gone unremarked by critics. For an analysis of Whitman and his work, focusing on homosexuality, see Schmidgall.

to his imagination of national union. As Justin Kaplan put it, "manly love" was, for Whitman, "the ultimate democracy of the heart" (233). But he could only suggest that sexuality indirectly in the poem. He could not state it overtly. Thus, beyond the complications of specifying the romantic plot in a conciliatory manner, Whitman faced the necessity of concealing that plot insofar as it pointed not only toward miscegenation, but toward homosexuality as well.[10] In combination with his need to encompass all divided groups, this further helped to foster the pervasive sexualization we witness in the poem. Specifically, pansexualization, by encompassing everyone, necessarily joins forbidden partners—blacks and whites, men and men. But, by the fact that it encompasses everyone, pansexualization does not make those forbidden unions salient.

In the second canto, Whitman introduces his pansexual relation to America. Moreover, he introduces a recurring image for that relation—immersion in water. The image is apt in its encompassing sensuality. Whitman's sexuality engulfs the body of the nation as water engulfs the body of the swimmer. Specifically, he refers to the "atmosphere" (1. 17), which appears to be ambient American nature, the physical space of the nation that is, once again, so important for national identification. He explains that "I am in love with" this atmosphere (1. 18). This explicitly introduces the romantic motif. The self seeks romantic union with the national place. As a result, "I will go to the bank . . . and become undisguised and naked, / I am mad for it to be in contact with me" (11. 19–20). Even when he is not in the water, water serves as a model for his relation to America. For example, just as his body is immersed in the waves, his "voice [is] loos'd to the eddies of the wind" (1. 25). The eddying movement is tacitly carried over to the next line and sexualized in the reference to the circling embrace of lovers—"A few light kisses, a few embraces, a reaching around of arms" (1. 26).

The third stanza expands on the motif of sexual union, explicitly generalizing it—and implicitly contrasting it with religious accounts of creation, thus with the divisive identity categories of religion. Whitman rejects "talk of the beginning or the end" (1. 39). He substitutes his pansexual understanding of life: "Urge and urge and urge, / Always the procreant urge of the world" (11. 44–45)—what we share, "substance and increase, always sex" (1. 46). (The antireligious point becomes clearer when he asserts that

---

10. Indeed, it seems that he concealed the homosexuality even from himself. As, for example, Railton has noted, Whitman apparently "could never bring himself to acknowledge that his attraction to men was sexual." Railton concludes that Whitman "was seriously repressed" (15).

there "will never be . . . any more heaven or hell than there is now" [ll. 42–43].) In keeping with the familial model for nationhood, Whitman is stressing procreation. But this is not to say that the urge need always be procreative in order to be affirmative, creative, and unifying. Later in the canto, Whitman speaks of his "hugging and loving bed-fellow" who "sleeps at my side through the night, and withdraws at the peep of the day with stealthy tread" (1. 60). Though the image is ambiguous, "fellow" points more toward a man than a woman, and the image of the lover sneaking away from his beloved's bed at dawn at least suggests some socially unacceptable liaison. Moreover, the 1855 version of the poem identified the "bed-fellow" as "God," not a goddess or an unsexed "divine being."

The suggested homosexuality of this scene is, of course, first of all a function of Whitman's own feelings. It is also a matter of his embracing diverse outcaste groups, as Nussbaum has stressed. But it derives perhaps most importantly from Whitman's attempt to combine romantic union with an affirmation of absolute national identity, an absolute identity well-represented by the all-encompassing being of God. Again, it is a sort of national version of ātman and brahman in spiritual realization. It is a union that is simultaneously a recognition of sameness. In this sense, the divine bedfellow and "myself" are one and the same. It is fitting that they have the same sex.

D. H. Lawrence famously criticized Whitman for "Myself monomania" (182; see Simpson 171 for a recent development of Lawrence's objections). He connected this with Whitman's celebration of "manly love" (176–78). But Lawrence's criticism begins by understanding Whitman, "Myself," as a necessarily limited individual outside the poem and, so to speak, outside the nation. I take it that the direction of Whitman's affirmation is the precise opposite. The point is not to begin with "Myself" as a distinct, uncategorized individual and to assert that everything else is an instance of me (including my sexual partner). The point is to begin with the (national) collective and to recognize an identity across the seeming diversity. The national category becomes the most important identifier for me when I recognize that the nation is myself—and not myself merely as an abstract idea, but as a feeling, a drive. Thus, in the third canto, Whitman does speak of "the procreant urge" (1. 45), but when he explains that urge, he refers to something else: "always sex, / Always a knit of *identity*" (ll. 46–47; italics added). Again, in the romantic emplotment of nationalism, the ultimate aim is precisely that union, that making one and identical. We see this later in the canto when Whitman takes up his image of fluid pansexuality again. "I . . . go bathe," he tells us, "and admire myself" (1. 56). Here, we see another function of the water image. When the water is still, it reflects back the image of the speaker, like a mirror. It shows him his own self. As such, what he sees must be identical with what he is. Indeed, that is the point of saying that "myself" is America. Again, they are one and the same—and they are a self intermingled with itself, like eddying currents. Thus, the "hugging . . . bed-fellow" reaches his arms around like the river or the watery wind of canto 2. When he departs, he leaves "white towels" (l. 61), what he used following the embrace of water and the reflection on the still surface.

The converse of this theme is taken up in canto 4 when Whitman locates himself in the ward, then the city, then the nation (l. 67), making the nation the highest and most encompassing category by which he defines himself. He speaks of a series of difficulties, beginning with the "indifference of some man or woman I love" (l. 70). He concludes with "Battles, the horrors of fratricidal war, the fever of doubtful news, the fitful event" (l. 72). The relation between the two is clear. The fratricidal war is also alienation in love. But Whitman responds to these romantic and personal divisions by tacitly assuming the voice of the nation (recall, here, the opening of the poem "what I assume you shall assume" [1. 2]). In that voice he tells us that these things "come . . . and go," but "they are not the Me myself" (ll. 73–74). What "I am," he explains, is "unitary" (ll. 75–76).

The fifth canto takes up the antiauthoritarian attitude that is part and parcel of the romantic plot, and thus contrary to the heroic plot. It begins by explaining that "the other I am must not abase itself to you, / And you must not be abased to the other" (l. 82). All those particular people that comprise the nation must be equal. None must be subordinated, for they are all one. Whitman repeats this idea at various points in the poem.

The sixth canto considers the physicality of the national land. Whitman focuses particularly on the grass—an apt image for, like a nation, it is a collective entity named in a singular noun, but composed of individual leaves, all rooted in the one soil. He then takes up the crucial subnational divisions, stressing unity once again. The grass, he explains, sprouts equally in all "zones"—which, this suggests, cannot be separated off arbitrarily from one another, but are necessarily continuous from north to south (see l. 109). Most important, it grows "among black folks as among white" (l. 108). It is appropriate that the encompassing volume, *Leaves of Grass*, takes up this image as a guiding metaphor for Whitman's entire project.

The seventh canto again manifests the pansexuality that characterizes the nationalism of the poem. Specifically, Whitman explains that "I am the mate and companion of people" (l. 137)—"mate" here meaning not only "companion" (which would make the phrase repetitive), but also sexual partner. He, as a representative of all individuals, is united with the nation, the people, in both comradeship and all-encompassing sexuality. Together, they are a union. Recurring tacitly to the image of water and bathing, he calls out to his readers, "Undrape!" Implicitly recognizing the sexuality of the call, he reassures us "you are not guilty to me" (1. 145). Like water or the eddying air or lover's arms he spoke of earlier, he too—the sexually encompassing nation—is "around" and "cannot be shaken away" (1. 147).

In my view, the poem reaches a sort of culmination in the following cantos, particularly cantos 10 through 13. Here the romantic emplotment becomes clearer. In connection with this, we understand more fully the purposes of Whitman's national pansexuality and the associated water imagery. To interpret this section, it is useful to begin, not with canto 10, but with canto 11, for in this canto the sexuality is most overt. Understanding canto 11 gives us a better sense of just what is going on in the preceding and following cantos.

In canto 11, a young woman "by the rise of the bank" (1. 202) watches twenty-eight young men bathe by the shore. She delights in watching the "Little streams [that] pass'd over their bodies" (1. 211). Whitman goes on to explain that "An unseen hand also pass'd over their bodies, / It descended trembling from their temples and ribs" (11. 212–13). Martha Nussbaum has argued persuasively that this unseen hand is not only the hand of the woman, but the hand of Whitman as well (667).[11] At the very least, it parallels a scene from the following canto, where the speaker introduces "Blacksmiths with grimed and hairy chests," explaining, "I follow their movements, / The lithe sheer of their waists plays even with their massive arms" (11. 219, 221–22). Here, Whitman's delighted and sensual gaze recalls that of the young woman, implicitly connecting the two. More important, the unseen hand is not only that of the poet but that of all the agents he represents, all Americans who, in reading the poem, share the gaze of the young woman in another instance of the poem's generalization of sexuality. Finally, the scene provides a sexual context for the more extended descriptions that precede and follow, descriptions that contribute importantly to the romantic emplotment of the nation as a unity across lines of forbidden love—crucially, interracial love, including interracial homosexual love.

---

11. Nussbaum also discusses the degree to which this section of the poem affirms female sexual desire against patriarchal repression (669–70). Indeed, Nussbaum stresses the anti-patriarchal elements of the poem, as have other writers (see, for example, Ostriker). These elements, too, are clearly bound up with romantic emplotment. We will see this connection again in the case of Goldman.

Now we may return to canto 10, which begins this intensely sexualized section of the poem. The speaker witnesses "the marriage of the trapper," a white man. He continues, "the bride was a red girl." The redness is her salient racial marker. "Her father and his friends" attend the ceremony wearing moccasins. The trapper holds the hand of his bride, whose "coarse straight locks descended upon her voluptuous limbs" (ll. 185–86, 188). Whitman introduces interracial romantic union through Native Americans. This eases the reader into the topic as European–Native American unions are not so wholly tabooed as European-African ones. This is, of course, inseparable from the fact that, for European Americans, the subnational category of "Native American" (or "Indian") is far less functional, affective, salient, and oppositional than the category "African American" (or "black").

The next stanza of the canto turns to precisely the union of European American and African American. Whitman explains that a "runaway slave came to my house" (l. 189). What follows is not explicitly homoerotic. However, Nussbaum has argued forcefully that the relationship of these men is indeed sexual. She explains that this is suggested by the language of the passage and its parallels with preceding and following stanzas. Expanding on Nussbaum's insights, we may note that the scene in some ways takes up where the marriage ends. We do not see the trapper take the "red girl" into his home. But we do see Whitman take the escaped slave into his kitchen. At this point, Whitman "brought water and fill'd a tub for his sweated body." This is the image of immersion in water that Whitman so closely links with sexual union. The suggestion is furthered when he explains that he "gave [the runaway] a room that enter'd from my own" (ll. 193–94). Their intimacy is such that Whitman "had him sit next to me at table" (l. 198). This most obviously means that they did not sit separately; they were not racially segregated at meals. But it also indicates that they did not sit across from one another. Rather, they sat in nearer physical proximity, like new lovers who do not wish to be physically separated even by the width of a table.

These stanzas suggest that, when Whitman envisions the reconciliation of the nation, its union, he envisions the marriage of the trapper and the "red girl," the shared bathing, sleeping, and eating of the poet and the runaway slave. He imagines a forbidden romantic union across lines of subnational division.

The tenth canto ends with this oblique story of the slave. The eleventh comprises the story of the twenty-eight bathers and their lusty observer. The twelfth canto recounts Whitman's own sexually tinged observation of the blacksmiths. This observation is, again, parallel to that of the young woman with the bathers. It is significant for the poem's romantic nationalism for it suggests a union of different economic classes. More important, the thirteenth canto introduces us to "The negro that drives the long dray of the stone-yard." Whitman dwells on this figure "steady and tall," noting how "His blue shirt exposes his ample neck and breast and loosens over his hip-band." He admires "the black of his polish'd and perfect limbs." He concludes, "I behold the picturesque giant and love him" (11. 226–27, 229–30). The statement may seem to be a simple expression of Platonic admiration. In context, however, it seems clear that it is more. That "more" has nationalist resonances. Here again, Whitman has suggested the romantic emplotment of national unity. He does not dwell on the fact that such love is forbidden, in the way that most romantic stories do. There is no need for such an emphasis here. Such social intolerance is all too obvious—as are its effects on national unity.

The fifteenth canto takes up the motif of interracial sexual union to treat the mixing of different races and ethnicities as a distinctively positive American trait. Whitman refers to the "groups of newly-come immigrants" who "cover the wharf or levee," pairing these with the African slaves who "hoe in the sugar-field" and the "overseer" (11. 285–86)—all immigrants. More important, he refers to a "half-breed" and a "quadroon girl" (11. 282, 278). Having affirmed American unity in the opening cantos, Whitman now turns to the diversity of America. Having made Americans a metaphorical family, he now acknowledges their literal ethnic variety. Having tied Americans to the land, he now recognizes that they have immigrated to the land. Most significant, however, having tacitly acknowledged their racial divisions, he now indicates that the sexual union of races is not only metaphorical, but literal as well—and, indeed, metaphorical at a second level, for in a sense all Americans become such quadroons and half-breeds, part of a nation that is itself mixed in race. Despite the criticisms of Simpson (see 186–87) and others, this section does not pass over the crimes of racism, when the "quadroon girl" is "sold at the auction-stand" (1. 278). Yes, Whitman does tacitly appeal to white identification with a girl who is three-quarters white. But that identification only encourages whites to imagine themselves in the position of the slave girl. It only helps to make us all aware that all our "blood" mingles together, for we are all one nation—a quadroon nation that is itself only in part white.

Unsurprisingly, the canto concludes with sexual union: "The old husband sleeps by his wife and the young husband sleeps by his wife" (1. 326). They are without race and without region. Or they are every race and every region, as well as every class. At the end of this canto, unity emerges once more from diversity. Indeed, it is at this point that the speaker explains the name of the poem: "of these one and all I weave the song of myself" (1. 329). Again, that self is the nation.

Whitman makes the preceding points more explicitly in the sixteenth canto, where he names the United States "the Nation of many nations" (1. 334). Here, in affirming the oneness of all Americans, he simultaneously acknowledges a prior range of origins, albeit a range of origins that must be superseded in the new "Nation." Capitalizing "Nation" suggests that the United States is a higher principle, a greater and fuller unity than the smaller bonds it encompasses. That higher unity is, implicitly, romantic. The smaller bonds are precisely what must be loosened or even undone in the promiscuous sexuality of "National" union.

The first subnational division Whitman names is regional. Of regions, the first distinction he makes, and then denies, is the one based on slaveholding. The speaker affirms his self, thus America, to be "A Southerner soon as a Northerner" (1. 335). He then names his state affiliations—Connecticut, Kentucky, Louisiana, Georgia, Indiana, Wisconsin, Ohio, and so forth. Following regions, he turns to race, class, and religion, explaining, "Of every hue and caste am I, of every rank and religion" (1. 346). Here, too, it may seem that he is passing over the injustices of slavery. But he is not. He is, rather, setting out to overcome all subnational divisions, all categorial identities other than that of the nation. This crucially includes the affirmation of national identity that would align it with racial and ethnic identity. That is why he is of every hue or race. That is why the quadroon girl can suggest America itself. That is why the poet, speaking as America, can say "I resist any thing better than my own diversity" (1. 349). He is resisting any form of alignment nationalism by articulating an American sense of national self as encompassing all races, ethnicities, religions, and so forth.

Whitman's assertion of national unity that encompasses diversity, is not only a rationally considered repudiation of alignment nationalism and, of course, subnationalism. It is, again, an instance of romantic emplotment as well. Romantic stories are routinely about union across opposed identities. The separation of the lovers is the result of social division—the separation of classes, castes, ethnic groups, tribes, rival families. The romantic plot pushes invariably toward an affirmation of oneness across socially defined differences. I have been suggesting that the patterns we find in Whitman's work—the opposition to subnational divisions and categorial identifications, the affirmation of unity across social distinctions, the sexualization of this unity as a physical union—are not accidental. It is not mere chance that Whitman interweaves interracial marriage and eroticism with his poetic work to overcome subnational division with union. Rather, it is the manifestation of an underlying structure, a structure that guides his imagination of agents, relations, actions, events, identities—specifically, the romantic structure.

Indeed, as I have already pointed out, the emotional and conceptual logic of romantic emplotment is so opposed to categorial identification and so favorable to union that romance almost invariably pushes beyond the nation as well. In keeping with this, Whitman turns from the affirmation of national identity to the affirmation of a broader unity. The following canto begins with the admission that "These are really the thoughts of all men in all ages and lands" (1. 355). The crucial word in this sentence is "lands." Here, Whitman is extending this same affirmation of unity to all nations. Indeed, he ends the canto by tacitly denying nationhood itself. He takes up once again the image of the grass, the grass that is continuous across the regions of the United States. Now it is universal. "This is the grass that grows wherever the land is and the water is," he tells us; "This is the common air that bathes the globe" (11. 359–60)—the sexually encompassing bath now embraces not the nation, but the entire world.

I cannot discuss the whole poem in this detail. However, it is important to remark on some striking features of what follows. The eighteenth canto introduces the topic of battle, speaking of victors and vanquished. But Whitman asserts that he will celebrate the vanquished. In other words, he introduces heroic emplotment to reject or undermine it. This and the following cantos are, in part, self-consciously antiheroic in their rejection of hierarchies of social authority as well, including the hierarchies sanctioned by religion (a crucial part of the heroic plot, as we have seen). Thus, he asks, "Why should I pray? why should I venerate and be ceremonious?" (1. 398). He insists that no social subjugation is right, claiming that "Whoever degrades another degrades me" (1. 503). He praises animals because "Not one kneels to another" (1. 690). In direct opposition to the usurpation part of the heroic plot, he will "beat the gong of revolt" (1. 496).

Unsurprisingly, throughout this antiheroic section, Whitman repeatedly recalls the romantic and sexual. He "give[s] the sign of democracy" by allowing "long dumb voices" to speak (11. 506, 508)—not the voices of the heroic victors, but the voices of the vanquished. Crucially, these are "Voices of sexes and lusts" (1. 517). The "Prodigal" shares with him "unspeakable passionate love" (11. 446–47). The image of water returns: "You sea! I resign myself to you. . . . I undress. . . . Dash me with amorous wet" (11. 448, 451, 453). Later, "Picking out here one that I love," Whitman goes "with him on brotherly terms" (1. 700). The image seems innocuous enough. But immediately following this, he refers to the "gigantic beauty of a stallion, fresh and responsive to my caresses" (1. 701). The reader cannot help but recall the "negro" with his horses, a "picturesque giant" (11. 225, 230) whom the speaker loved in canto 13. Whitman "embrace[s]" the stallion with his heels (1. 705) and "His well-built limbs tremble with pleasure" (1. 706). The description fits a horse. But at the same time it allows the expression of "forbidden voices, / Voices of sexes and lusts . . . /Voices indecent by me . . . transfigur'd" (11. 516–18). Here, once again, we have the unity of the nation. And, once again, it is not the unity of battle, of heroism. Rather, it is a sexual union across forbidden lines.

Despite all this, a curious thing happens in the thirty-third canto. Whitman suddenly shifts toward the heroic mode ("Do I contradict myself? Very well then I contradict myself" [1324–25]). He speaks of "the dense-starr'd flag . . . borne at the head of the regiments" (1. 747). He goes on to discuss "some great battle-field" (1. 813). In canto 34, he recounts the conflict at Goliad. He tells of John Paul Jones in 35. He seems suddenly to embrace the heroic emplotment of nationalism. But in canto 36, he recounts the aftermath. It is a paradigmatic epilogue of suffering. As the victorious American "captain . . . coldly giv[es] his orders," Whitman points to "the corpse of the child that serv'd in the cabin" (11. 932–33). It is the standard image of the innocent youth that dies in battle and triggers remorse. The devastation is multiplied. There are only "two or three officers yet fit for duty" (1. 936). They are surrounded by "Formless stacks of bodies and bodies by themselves, dabs of flesh upon the masts and spars" (1. 937). The speaker now suffers the remorse that follows the enthusiasm of war. "I am possess'd," he tells us, "I . . . Embody all presences outlaw'd or suffering / See myself in prison shaped like another man" (11. 396–98), presumably a man who, a short time earlier, was the enemy. Thus, he undermines the glorious fantasy of belligerence found in the heroic narrative (specifically in the threat/defense sequence). He goes on to challenge the internal hierarchy (thus the usurpation/restoration sequence) as well, explaining that "Not a mutineer walks handcuff'd to jail but I am handcuff'd to him and walk by his side" (1. 952).

After this brief detour into heroic narrative and the epilogue of suffering, Whitman returns to romantic emplotment for the remainder of the poem, though with some differences. The thirty-ninth canto in a sense brings us back to the marriage of the trapper and the "red girl." It also takes up the image of water and the pansexuality of the opening. However, it changes the girl to a man, and it complicates that sexuality. The canto begins by introducing "The friendly and flowing savage" (1. 976). The term "flowing" suggests the ambient sexuality that has served as a model for national unity in earlier parts of the poem. Whitman then brings up the crux of ideological opposition between Europeans and Native Americans (as well as Africans)—"civilization." Whitman asks "Is he waiting for civilization, or past it and mastering it?" (1. 977). The usual European view would be that the savage desires civilization, or rejects it, or is blissfully unaware of it. But Whitman suggests that the Native American may in fact have gone on to another stage, surpassing European practices. This admiration for the Native American is simultaneously an affront to European biases and an affirmation of a common view of America—that we distinguish ourselves in part by an incorporation of the wisdom of the natives. In the next stanza, the "flowing savage" comes to represent all of America as Whitman names all the places from which he might have come—Iowa, Oregon, California, "the Mississippi country" (1. 979), and so forth. The sexuality follows. "Wherever he goes," Whitman tells us, "men and women accept and desire him." Moreover, "They desire that he should like them, touch them, speak to them, stay with them" (11. 981–82). Again, the union of the nation is an interracial sexual and romantic union—in this case a union that is both hetero- and homosexual, as well as one that crosses all regions of the country.

The fortieth canto continues the idea. Whitman addresses the earth as "old top-knot" (1. 990), a term of familiarity, referring to a Native American.[12] He continues, "Man or woman, I might tell how I like you, but cannot . . . might tell that pining I have, that pulse of my nights and days" (1. 991). The point is once more the same narrative point—the longing of America is Whitman's longing for union across racial lines, a romantic and sexual union.[13] Subsequently, he refers to the "cotton-field drudge" (1. 1003), suggesting the slaves. He tells us, "On his right cheek I put the family kiss" (1. 1004)—the kiss of a brother, or the kiss of a husband or wife. Either way, THE NATION IS A FAMILY. Subsequent cantos stress the ubiquity of national sexual union. His "lovers" form a crowd. They are everywhere—"streets and public halls . . . rocks of the river . . . flowerbeds, vines, tangled underbrush." They come to him "naked . . . at night . . .

---

12. See Bradley et al. 1762n.8.
13. The longing is not by any means unique to Whitman. Leslie Fiedler has argued influentially that a sort of interracial, homosexual—if also "innocent" (12)—marriage is one of the most important and most definitive motifs of American literature.

Bussing my body with soft balsamic busses, / Noiselessly passing handfuls out of their hearts and giving them to be mine" (11. 1172–76, 1178–79). In themselves, these are, of course, isolated moments with only limited narrative content. But why do they occur here, what are their source and function? It could be a matter of mere chance that he links this sexual and romantic union—and its associated repudiation of racial, regional, religious, and other identities—with the unity of the nation. Or there could be some cognitive reason for the continual recurrence of these images of love, particularly forbidden love across identity categories, and the connection of these images with a specifically antihierarchical nationalism. Again, it seems extremely unlikely that this very clear pattern in Whitman's poem is the result of chance. It is, rather, explicable by reference to an underlying cognitive structure, a standard structure for emplotting actions and events, including those that bear on nationalism—romantic tragicomedy.

But here, again, at the end of the poem, the romantic structure pushes Whitman toward something beyond the nation. In a typically romantic scene, he leads his beloved "upon a knoll, / My left hand hooking you round the waist." But his beloved is not at all typical—"each man and each woman." As he holds these countless lovers "My right hand points to landscapes." Here, one might expect that it points to landscapes of the nation, of the northern and southern regions that he wishes to unite in the nation, of all (and only) the states of the Union. But that is not where he points. Rather, his right hand directs us to "landscapes of continents" (11. 1207–9). In the fiftieth canto, he further extends this connection between universalism and sexuality. He speaks of something "in me" that he cannot name. He speaks of being "Wrench'd and sweaty" first. But "calm and cool then my body becomes." Afterward, "I sleep" (11. 1309–11). This inner "it" that is "without name" (1. 1312) is the force that drives his sexual desire, that makes his act "Wrench'd and sweaty," then turns his body "calm and cool" before sleep. It is, he explains "union" (1. 1318), but it is not the Union of his particular nation. Rather it is even "more than the earth" (1. 1314).

Though not developed extensively in the course of the poem, this global humanism—or even biologism, uniting and celebrating all life—is a sort of telos for the implicit narrative trajectory of the poem. However national Whitman's orientation was initially, his romantic emplotment of the nation pushed inexorably beyond the nation.

In a sense, Whitman's use of the romantic plot ends where that of Emma Goldman begins.

EMMA GOLDMAN
Romance Against Nationalism

Emma Goldman did not write novels or make movies. However, her political thought was pervaded by the romantic structure. Indeed, her concern with romance was explicit, for she treated romantic love as an important political topic—just as one would expect from her adoption of romantic emplotment. More exactly, Goldman imagined politics through a romantic narrative prototype because she imagined happiness, first of all, as romantic union. Romantic union is, again, the happiness prototype that generates romantic tragicomedy, just as the happiness prototype of social domination generates heroic tragicomedy.

Romantic modeling has, at best, an uneasy relation with the heroic emplotment that is fundamental for nationalism. As a result, writers drawing on the romantic prototype often repudiate the heroic structure—and nationalism along with it. We find this to some extent in Whitman. But that repudiation is much more thorough, explicit, and extensive in Goldman. It is perhaps most obvious in her opposition to national war, thus the threat/defense sequence that serves to rationalize national war. But it extends to the usurpation sequence as well. Indeed, she understands tyranny in terms of romantic oppression, not heroic usurpation. Thus, she claims that the results of "our present social structure" are "broken hearts and crushed lives" (440–41)—in short, romantic tragedies. In keeping with this, she does not criticize a particular "usurping" social hierarchy in order to affirm the importance of loyalty and obedience to a "true" (or divinely mandated) hierarchy. Rather, she broadly denies the authority of social hierarchies to inhibit the free choice and personal happiness of ordinary individuals. Perhaps most important, she rejects the very foundation of heroic emplotment, the standard social prototype for happiness. In "Was My Life Worth Living?," Goldman brings up "What is generally regarded as success—acquisition of wealth, the capture of power or social prestige"—in other words, the happiness goals that structure heroic tragicomedy. She comments that "I consider [these] the most dismal failures" (443).

Goldman did not write extended treatises comparable to, say, Gandhi's commentary on the *Bhagavad Gītā* or Hitler's *Mein Kampf.* Her political views are expressed largely in short essays and speeches. I will concentrate on her broad statement of her principles in "What I Believe." The essay is divided into seven sections, which briefly treat topics broached elsewhere in her work. I will bring in other essays as they bear on the particular points developed in those sections.

Property

In the first section of her essay, Goldman is concerned primarily with the private ownership of the means of production. This leads to exploitation of workers, who toil to produce "mountains of wealth for others" (50). Of course, this analysis—which she shares with most socialists—does not presuppose a romantic emplotment. Yet, from the outset, there are suggestions that she is tacitly drawing on a model of romantic union to understand social relations generally. Readers of Goldman's other writings are likely to sense in this section a tacit parallel between forced labor and forced marriage. Economic necessity drives people to pile up wealth for others, placing them in a "humiliating and degrading situation" (50). This is precisely the problem for women in marriage. Marriage, she argues elsewhere, is something into which women are coerced, by either parental (especially paternal) authority or economic need. At this point, the woman becomes, precisely, the *property* of the husband—after she has, in effect, been the property of her parents (again, particularly her father). Put differently, labor today is like marriage today. The latter is out of keeping with the prototype of happiness as (freely chosen) romantic union. As Goldman makes clear in, for example, "Marriage and Love," the opposite of romantic union is economically motivated sex—either that found in a prudent marriage or that found in prostitution. In both cases, the woman has sold herself. Similarly, a worker "must sell his labor" in order to survive. Moreover, all these forms of selling oneself are "humiliating and degrading" (50).

Goldman contrasts the humiliating and degrading work forced on most people today with the possibility for truly fulfilling work that is, she maintains, offered by Anarchism—the comic conclusion of a social tragicomedy. Goldman implicitly understands this fulfilling work in terms of romantic union. Thus, she explains that the nature of a person's work should be determined by his or her "latent qualities and innate disposition" (50). The description fits marriage better than labor. Latent qualities are just what romantic union should develop. Disposition is just what leads someone to prefer one mate over another. Put differently, one might have expected work to be determined by one's manifest skills (not latent qualities) along with individual and social needs (rather than one's dispositions). I am not saying that Goldman was wrong to put things the way she did. But there are many possible ways of characterizing work that is not humiliating and degrading. Goldman's precise selection seems to have been guided, in part, by a tacit romantic model.

The romantic model becomes clearer when Goldman turns from production to consumption. She maintains that one's consumption should be based on "one's physical and mental appreciations and . . . soul cravings" (50). Goldman was opposing mindless consumerism long before others saw this as a problem. But, here too, one might have expected a statement referring to genuine needs and, beyond that, objects of real enjoyment. Instead, she chooses an idiom that reveals what her ideal model is—again, romantic union. A consumer does not choose a new commodity on the basis of "physical and mental appreciations." Physical and mental appreciations apply to another person, a person one desires and admires—paradigmatically, in romantic love. Similarly, even in the ideal society, one would rarely buy objects (e.g., a new table, a jacket) on the basis of one's "soul cravings."[14] That is how one chooses a spouse—or, rather, that is how one chooses a spouse in a romantic plot when one is not constrained by economic necessity.

Finally, Goldman makes a general statement about her ideal society, the society promised by Anarchism, a society "based on voluntary co-operation of productive groups" (50). The vision is general, and certainly need not be based on the romantic model. However, in context, it is reminiscent of the productive group formed by the lovers who have resisted social authority in order to enter into a voluntary (rather than a coerced) union. Moreover, in Goldman's view, groups of both sorts are unions of equals and thus a matter of cooperation, not subordination.

Other essays make these points more directly. As I have noted, in "Marriage and Love" Goldman stresses the "practical" way in which people approach marriage. She laments that "The time when Romeo and Juliet risked the wrath of their fathers for love . . . is no more" (208). Rather, a woman makes her marriage decision my asking "Can the man make a living? Can he support a wife?" Directly contrasting romantic love with consumerism, she bemoans the fact that a young woman's "dreams are not of moonlight and kisses" but of "shopping tours." The result is "soul-poverty and sordidness" (208). Subsequently, she links the paternal authority that stifles women in coerced marriages with "that other paternal arrangement—capitalism" (210). In this way, she interprets, and condemns, the evils of capitalism directly in terms of the evils of the blocking characters in romantic tragicomedy.

Most important, in "Marriage and Love" Goldman makes clear just

---

14. Of course, one might employ a sort of ironic hyperbole, saying that one has soul cravings for slacks, when of course one has only consumerist envy. But there is no reason to believe that Goldman is being ironically hyperbolic here.

what her utopia is, the utopia suggested in her reference to voluntary cooperation. It is not a life of wealth or power. It is, rather, "a beautiful life." Spelling out her prototype for happiness, she explains that "love in freedom is the only condition of a beautiful life" (213). Indeed, her economic program here appears as a mere means to the fostering of love in freedom. In this essay, it is clear that prosperity is not an end in itself. Prosperity is a way of ending the economic coercion of marriage. Thus, Goldman writes that "High on a throne," a person "is yet poor and desolate, if love passes him by. And if it stays, the poorest hovel is radiant with warmth, with life and color." But, she explains, "love is free" and "it can dwell in no other atmosphere" than freedom (211). Part of that freedom is economic.

Government

As I have emphasized, the romantic prototype almost invariably involves the condemnation of hierarchical social authority. In political thought, that condemnation is often generalized from intimate, familial units to the national structure of social authority, which is to say, government. (This generalization is facilitated by the fact that the hierarchy of authority in the family commonly serves as a model for thinking about national government, as we have seen.) Such antigovernment politics are precisely what we find in Goldman. Indeed, Goldman goes so far as to maintain that "whatever is fine and beautiful in the human expresses and asserts itself in spite of government, and not because of it" (51). Again, Goldman does not celebrate, for example, "whatever is proud and courageous in human accomplishment," as one might expect from a heroic emplotment. Rather, she phrases her ideal in romantic terms, in terms of beauty and expressiveness. With slight rephrasing, the comment could be applied to stories in which the lovers defy paternal authority, as in the case of Romeo and Juliet who "risked the wrath of their fathers for love" (208): What is fine and beautiful in Romeo and Juliet expresses and asserts itself in spite of parental governance, and not because of it.

But the opposition to government is not solely a generalization of the romantic antagonism toward paternal authority. It is also part of a systematic opposition to the heroic emplotment of social relations. Here, too, the heroic narrative is the default assumption for social thought. However, this does not mean Goldman accepts the heroic emplotment. Rather, it means that she must address it and oppose it, for its hierarchies and antagonisms are pervasive and incompatible with her romantic ideals. Specifically, her opposition to government is an opposition to the presuppositions of the usurpation/restoration sequence of the heroic plot; it is an opposition to the idea that there is a right order to society and that some members of society are or should be superior to others. (She turns to the other part of heroic emplotment, the threat/defense sequence, in the following section, which treats militarism.)

These points are reenforced in many of Goldman's essays. In "Anarchism: What It Really Stands For," Goldman explains how Anarchism allows the expression of beauty: "In destroying government . . . Anarchism proposes to rescue . . . the independence of the individual from all restraint and invasion by authority" (72). The crucial term here, I believe, is "invasion." Invasion suggests, not interference in public acts, but interference in private decisions. It suggests entry into the personal sphere of the individual. In this context, the "restraint" takes on personal resonance as well, and the entire statement appears to reflect an underlying model of happiness as personal—thus, prototypically, romantic—choice.

Goldman makes the point more explicitly in "Was My Life Worth Living?" There she answers the question of why she "maintained such a noncompromising antagonism to government." She briefly mentions economic issues, then goes on to a more heartfelt response. Government "comes into private lives and into most intimate personal relations, enabling the superstitious, puritanical, and distorted ones to impose their ignorant prejudice and moral servitudes upon the sensitive, the imaginative, and the free spirits" (434). She goes on to treat the literal relations between government and romantic union, discussing divorce laws and the enforcement of marriage. Here, Goldman is not only seeing government regulation as similar to interference in romantic love. She is pointing to a direct governmental role in preventing romantic union and substituting coerced marriage. In other words, a key point in her brief against government is its direct role as a blocking figure in real love stories.

In "Marriage and Love," she implicitly sees government as being still more actively destructive in this regard. Specifically, she suggests that government sets out even to uproot love. However, in keeping with the common idealization of love in romantic tragicomedy, she asserts that this is impossible: "All the laws on the statutes, all the courts in the universe, cannot tear it from the soil, once love has taken root" (212). It is interesting that Goldman uses a metaphor that is closely associated with nationalism. Again, having roots in the soil is one way in which a people's relation to a national place is commonly imagined. Goldman takes up this standard nationalist metaphor and makes it thoroughly personal and individual—

and thoroughly antinational. The soil is the lover's heart, not a physical place marked off by the boundaries of a state; the love is a feeling of one individual for another, not the loyalty of a person to an in-group and the "traditions" it imposes, which almost invariably include constraints on romantic union.

In "The Individual, Society and the State," Goldman characterizes "progress" in a way that is fully consistent with these points. She does not understand progress in terms of, say, dominating nature or satisfying physical needs. Rather, she explains progress as the "enlargement of the liberties of the individual with a corresponding decrease of the authority wielded over him by external forces" (110). What is striking about this statement is that Goldman clearly intends it to cover everything from government to such physical necessities as food. Thus, Goldman subsumes not only the social but the physical happiness prototype beneath the personal happiness prototype. In other words, in Goldman's scheme, increasing plenty is simply a way of increasing individual freedom—and that freedom has free choice in marriage as its prototype.

In the same essay, Goldman mentions those nonconformist thinkers who managed to express beauty and who "served as the beacon light" for others (115). These great rebels "dreamed of a world" different from our own. But it was not a world of greater bounty or (heroic) accomplishment. It was a world of the "heart's desire" (115). The phrase applies most readily to one's romantic beloved. Here too, then, Goldman tacitly models the ideal society on the prototype of personal (not social or even physical) happiness, romantic union.

Finally, it is worth noting that Goldman extends her implicit critique of the heroic emplotment by addressing the religious sanction given to social hierarchy. Thus, in "The Individual, Society and the State," she ridicules the claim that "power" is "divine" and arguments claiming "to prove the sanctity of the State" (114). She is unremitting in her condemnation of the ways in which supernatural ideas have been used to bolster social hierarchy. She even goes so far as to claim that "All progress has been essentially an unmasking of 'divinity,'" of what is "alleged" to be "sacred" (114).

Militarism

In the next section, Goldman turns from the internal aspect of the heroic plot (social hierarchy and government) to the external aspect—war. In the heroic narrative, this is invariably represented as a matter of threat and defense. However, in the real world, claims of danger, and assertions that one is engaging only in self-defense, are routinely used to justify aggression and conquest. Goldman's critique of militarism is straightforward. She demystifies the process of war as one of "cold-blooded, mechanical" killing (52) in which individuals are degraded to the condition of tools in the hands of commanders. Her first aim in saying this is to deheroicize war. She wishes to separate the real thing from the narratives that portray war as an occasion for glorious individual achievement, a time when brave individuals undertake the salvation of their society from a demonic enemy. She directly contrasts the main principle of military society, "unquestioning obedience," with a founding tenet of American society, "life, liberty, and the pursuit of happiness." She contends that the latter is not defended by the former, but disallowed by it. This is true most obviously within the armed forces, for the soldier is asked to surrender his or her individuality to the military authorities and the government. As a result, he or she cannot be said to have liberty, and cannot make the individual choices involved in the pursuit of happiness. But the conflict between militarism and the pursuit of happiness applies outside the armed forces as well. Under the guise of defending itself against an external threat, governments make even a "free country" into "an imperialistic and despotic power" (52).

It is also suggestive that Goldman refers to the buildup of a standing army as a loss, not only of money, but of the "hearts' blood" of the people. Had she merely said "blood," one might have inferred that her objection was to the loss of life. But by including the word "heart," she suggests again a romantic element. One's "heart's blood" is not simply the physical blood in one's veins, the blood that defines one's physical life. Rather, it is the feeling that makes that life worthwhile, the passion—especially, the passion of romantic love. Of course, Goldman is not claiming here that the military buildup has directly caused people to lose romantic love (though she does suggest that this may partially be the case). Rather, her claim is that militarism creates a society that is directly opposed to the ideal society, and that ideal society, again, is modeled on romantic union. Militarism, she contends, "is indicative of the decay of liberty and of the destruction of all that is best and finest in our nation" (54). She understands and evaluates that general decay of liberty against the prototype of liberty in romantic choice. Any decline from that prototype is aptly metaphorized as a loss of hearts' blood.

Goldman goes on to criticize the heroic emplotment of war by asserting "human brotherhood" (55) over the dehumanization of enemies. She exposes the unheroic perversity of those who wish "to hurl dynamite bombs upon defenseless enemies from flying machines" (54). She calls on ordinary people to reject both heroic and sacrificial emplotments, by saying to "their masters" that "We have sacrificed ourselves and our loved ones long enough" (54–55).

Here, too, other essays repeat and elaborate on the main ideas. In "The Individual, Society and the State," Goldman takes a stand on identity categories that anticipates recent research on the formation of in- and out-groups. The "State," she contends "is nothing but a name." To treat it as a reality is "to make a fetish of words" (113). In a remarkable response to the divinization of the nation, she goes on to say that "The State has no more existence than gods and devils have" (113). These claims run directly against the heroic emplotment of society. They reject the in-group identity such emplotment fosters and sanctifies. They repudiate the ways in-groups use that emplotment to mobilize aggression against putatively demonic enemies. In contrast with the heroic view, Goldman argues that "the only reality" is "the individual" (113). The nation exists "only" as "a collection of individuals" (111). Of course, Goldman is not unaware that many people believe an individual has certain definitive or essential properties that make him or her part of a group. These are, of course, precisely the properties that are used, not only to command patriotism and self-sacrifice for the nation, but also to block romantic union. The lovers cannot be joined because he is white and she is black, he is Muslim and she is Christian, he is a Montague and she is a Capulet. Unsurprisingly, Goldman rejects all such identity categories, thus all such limitations on love as well as all commands for patriotic devotion. "The living man," she tells us, "cannot be defined; he is the fountain-head of all life and all values; he is not a part of this or that; he is a whole" (111).

Goldman devotes an entire essay—"Preparedness: The Road to Universal Slaughter"—to what is, effectively, a critique of the threat/defense scenario and its hypocritical invocation in aggression and conquest. The central claim of the essay is that a stress on defense is not a way of preventing war, but a way of provoking it. In Goldman's words, "Supposedly, America is to prepare for peace; but in reality it will be the cause of war" (353). She goes on to treat, not only munitions, but identity categories as part of "defense." She explains that "the most dominant factor of military preparedness and the one which inevitably leads to war, is the creation of group interests" (354). Wars are allowed by the definition of in- and out-groups, and by claims about interests of the in-group—as well as the related dehumanization of "enemy" out-groups. In connection with this, during a period when European colonialism was spreading across the globe, she reversed the standard opposition between the civilized Europeans and the primitives they were taking in hand. She sought to undermine this particular in-group/out-group division and its dehumanization of the out-group. With obvious irony, she speaks of "savage tribes, who know nothing of Christian religion or of brotherly love" as being the only humans who are not in "the deathly grip of the war anesthesia." Using "race" to refer to humans, not to subgroups, she explains that "the rest of the race is under" a "terrible narcosis" (347).

Finally, Goldman suggests a more direct opposition between romantic love and war. In connection with this, she follows the general optimism of romantic emplotment and asserts the ultimate triumph of romantic love. For example, in "Marriage and Love," she writes that "Man has conquered whole nations, but all his armies could not conquer love" (211). The implication is that there is a literal contradiction between love and war. In other words, there is not only a conflict in social models between the heroic and the romantic; there is a more direct, practical conflict as well.

Free Speech and Religion

The next section of "What I Believe" treats freedom of expression and freedom of association. These have obvious relations to the romantic plot. The links are particularly clear in the case of association, for freedom of association is just what the blocking figures deny to lovers. Despite this, Goldman's discussion of these topics does not seem to draw very significantly on romantic models. The advocacy of free speech and association are certainly related to her tacit romantic emplotment, as is clear elsewhere in the essay (particularly in the concluding section). In this section, however, her treatment of these issues is more straightforwardly pragmatic.

The brief fifth section treats religion. Here, Goldman returns to her inversion of the civilized/primitive hierarchy. She first explains that "Religion is a superstition that originated in man's mental inability to solve natural phenomena" (56). Here, Goldman clearly suggests that science is superior to religion. But Goldman's concern is not purely epistemological. Science is progress because, in giving us genuine understanding of the natural world, it increases our freedom. Again, this view of progress is bound up with Goldman's tacit use of the romantic prototype. But does this construal mean that the "civilized" world of Europe is superior to the supposedly "primitive" world of, say, Africa. In other words, does this criticism of religion justify a colonialist division between an in-group and an out-group? Here, again, Goldman challenges a hierarchy that is central to colonialist heroic emplotment. She states that "Organized churchism has stripped religion of its naïveté and primitiveness" (56). In other words, modern religion has set aside the initial, prescientific functions of religion. However, this has not given rise to an increase in freedom, thus progress. Rather, modern "churchists" have "turned religion into a nightmare that oppresses the human soul and holds the mind in bondage" (56–57).

These passages suggest a connection between religion and the sorts of social constraint that are the primary obstacle to happiness in the romantic narrative. Elsewhere, Goldman opposes religion to romantic union more directly. Specifically, she discusses conventional morality, which is invariably underwritten by religion. In combination with economic coercion, conventional morality results in mental illness and the spread of venereal disease. Specifically, "Morality" allows a woman to experience "the raptures of love, the ecstasy of passion, which reaches its culminating expression in the sex embrace" only when married. But economic coercion prevents marriage except when the man has enough money "to establish a home and . . . to provide for a family" (171). The result is "hysteria" and a "joyless" existence for the woman, and venereal infection for the man. The man's infection comes from contact with a prostitute, who is herself "the victim of Morality, even as the withered old maid is its victim" (172). In short, religion (along with political economy) is the cause of great crimes. These crimes are, paradigmatically, crimes against romantic union. It is interesting to see how Hitler and Goldman take up some of the same social problems—prostitution and venereal infection—yet treat them so differently. Hitler, again, places venereal disease in the context of a sacrificial narrative that makes it part of social punishment for a sexual sin. For Hitler, this punishment can be ended only through sacrifice, particularly sacrifice of the putative sinners. Goldman, in contrast, places prostitution and infection in a romantic context, viewing them as the outcome of authoritarian inhibition on free love. Thus, Hitler responds with an assertion of authoritarianism while Goldman responds with an affirmation of freedom.

Marriage and Love

Goldman ends her overview of Anarchism with a discussion of marriage and love. This is not only the final component of her Anarchist program; it is also the culminating topic. She treats six areas in which Anarchism seeks to transform society. She saves romance for the concluding and most important position. She opens this section with a passage that retrospectively makes clear the importance of free speech to her romantic emplotment. Marriage and love, she writes, "are probably the most tabooed subjects in this country." One cannot discuss these topics without "scandalizing" people. But it is crucial to have "an open, frank, and intelligent discussion" of them (57).

She goes on to contrast marriage and love, maintaining that marriage "furnishes the State and Church with a tremendous revenue" and a "means of prying into" people's lives (57). Here, she indicates quite clearly why a romantic model of politics leads her to a rejection of both state and church. She also once again identifies interference in romantic union as the prototypical social evil. Similarly, in her essay on jealousy, Goldman maintains that "Every love relation should by its very nature remain an absolutely private affair. Neither the State, the Church, morality, or people should meddle with it" (215). Conversely, "legal, religious, and moral interference are the parents of our present unnatural love and sex life" (219; the metaphor of "parents" here is not unrelated to the romantic narrative prototype). Despite these dismal consequences of church and state repression, Goldman goes on to affirm the optimism of romantic tragicomedy. Specifically, she asserts that "from time immemorial," love "has defied all man-made laws," thus state-based legal systems, as well as "conventions in Church and morality" (57).

Thus far in this section, Goldman has indicated that her opposition to government and church, as well as her strong support for free speech—hence three of her five components of Anarchism—derive at least in part from a tacit establishment of romantic union as the prototype of happiness. She goes on to explain that marriage is opposed to love by making the woman "chattel" for her husband. Here, we glimpse the romantic model behind her criticism of property as well. In "Jealousy," she elaborates on the point, claiming that "monogamy . . . came into being as a result of the domestication and ownership of women" and that "the Church and the State" have "justified jealousy as the legitimate weapon of defense for the protection of the property right" (217). This leaves only the opposition to war. She has already discussed how war is a mechanization of murder. In this section, she discusses motherhood and love as forming the only possible source for the safe and secure production of new life. The contrast with war and its production of death is implicit but unmistakable. In short, this culminating section indicates clearly that Goldman's deepest concerns—about property, government, militarism, free speech, and religion—are inseparable from her modeling of happiness on romantic union and her emplotment of social oppression and liberation in terms of romantic tragicomedy.

Finally, Goldman extends her treatment of love beyond the topics treated so far by taking up feminism. She writes that the liberation of women will involve several things. First, it will entail "loving a man for the qualities of his heart and mind," not for his money. This may seem to make the woman dependent on the man. But it does not. This choice presumes economic autonomy on the part of the woman. However, Goldman does not bother to mention this because, for her, that economic independence is not an end in itself. Plenty and domination are not her goals. For her, again, the exemplary case of happiness is the union of lovers. Economic autonomy is simply a necessary condition for achieving that end. Second, emancipation means that women will "follow that love without let or hindrance from the outside world" (58). I should emphasize that she does not say, "follow that man," but "follow that love." This is not a matter of the woman subordinating herself to the man. That happens in cases of economic dependency. Following one's love, in contrast, is a matter of the woman—and the man—pursuing the one paradigmatic good. Here, the romantic narrative is unmistakable, for that narrative concerns, precisely, following one's love, and how that free action is blocked by hindrance from the outside world. Finally, the liberated woman will affirm "free motherhood" (58). This is Goldman's own development of the narrative structure. It is sometimes the case that romantic tragicomedy extends beyond the simple union of the lovers to the birth of a child. Goldman takes up, emphasizes, and elaborates on this part of the story. Here, too, her view contrasts with that of heroic and sacrificial nationalists, who stress the posterity of the nation, not that of lovers. Moreover, she again takes up the common nationalistic image of the citizen as a plant. But, in this case as well, she reverses its significance. Specifically, she maintains that a free, loving couple provides the only atmosphere in which "the human plant"—thus a plant that is not defined by any national or other in-group—"can grow into an exquisite flower" (58). Even the imagery here (the flower) draws on the standard, springtime imagery of romantic union (for a range of examples from different traditions, see my "Literary Universals and Their Cultural Traditions.")

Needless to say, the ideas in this section are developed in other writings as well, most obviously in the essay "Marriage and Love." There, too, the relation of her political views to the romantic prototype is unmistakable. For example, with respect to feminism, she takes up the paternalistic—and, roughly, heroic—idea that a woman needs the "protection" of a man. She responds that a woman does not need any "protection" beyond "love and freedom" (211). Indeed, in that same essay, Goldman celebrates love in terms that should eliminate any lingering doubts about her tacit prototype for happiness and her tacit emplotment of social action. "Love," she writes, is "the strongest and deepest element in all life, the harbinger of hope, of joy, of ecstasy"; it is "the defier of all laws, of all conventions"; it is "the freest, the most powerful moulder of human destiny" (211).[15]

In sum, Whitman provided us with a moving portrait of what America could be if all Americans accepted his gentle, embracing vision of nationalism. Repudiating heroic and sacrificial models, with their pain and death, he substituted an unabashedly sexual, romantic story for the nation. But, ultimately, this vision fails as nationalism. Whitman's tacit story pushes inexorably beyond nationalism or any in-group/out-group division to a sense of international unity across all people, perhaps even across all sentient beings. In my view, that failure is the greatest value of the poem, and of the ideas it expresses.

Similarly, Goldman provides us with a remarkable instance of romantic emplotment. But, in her case, it is never an emplotment of nationalism. From the outset, it is an emplotment of humanity undivided by national or other boundaries. Her activism and her more abstract reflection were oriented by a prototype of happiness as romantic love, and a correlated prototype of sorrow as romantic separation. Her thinking about social change was organized by a romantic emplotment that included standard dramatis personae (such as the interfering father) and even standard imagery. Her opposition to government, private property, religion, war, restrictions on speech and assembly was bound up with her imagination of an ideal world in terms of romantic comedy and her associated rejection of heroic and sacrificial emplotments. The result was, in my view, a deeply humane vision

---

15. After her discussion of substantive Anarchist goals, Goldman has a concluding section on the means of achieving those goals. This section is largely irrelevant to the concerns of this chapter. However, Goldman does in effect criticize the justification of violence through standard heroic emplotments. Thus, she argues against the usual heroic story in which revolutionaries are cast in the role of illegitimate usurpers. She explains that it is hypocritical to condemn revolutionaries, since "Every institution today rests on violence; our very atmosphere is saturated with it" (59). At the same time, she differentiates her position from the usual revolutionary narrative as well (see 60). That narrative is itself a heroic story in which the currently dominant group (e.g., the bourgeoisie) has usurped the place of the society's rightful leadership (e.g., the proletariat, itself guided by the vanguard party). In this way, the section continues her criticism of heroic emplotment.

of society. Goldman's work suggests the power—or perhaps I should say beauty—of a romantic, therefore antinationalistic imagination of human social life. But it also suggests why the romantic prototype has existed only at the margins of political discourse. That discourse has, it seems, invariably been dominated by the terror and counterterror of heroic and sacrificial nationalisms. Goldman's optimism is inspiring. Sadly, it does not seem warranted.

WORKS CITED

Abélès, Marc. "Die Inszenierung der republikanischen Nation durch François Mitterrand." In François, Siegrist, and Vogel, *Nation und Emotion,* 274–88.
Abrahams, Peter. *Mine Boy.* Portsmouth, NY: Heinemann, 1989.
Ackermann, Volker. "Staatsbegräbnisse in Deutschland von Wilhelm I. bis Willy Brandt." In François, Siegrist, and Vogel, *Nation und Emotion,* 252–73.
Adolphs, Ralph, and Antonio Damasio. "The Relationship between Affect and Cognition: Fundamental Issues." In *Handbook of Affect and Social Cognition.* Ed. Joseph Forgas, 27–49. Mahwah, NJ: Lawrence Erlbaum, 2001.
Allen, Brooke "Our Godless Constitution." *The Nation* (February 21, 2005). Available at http://www.thenation.com.
Ambady, Nalini, Joan Y. Chiao, Pearl Chiu, and Patricia Deldin. "Race and Emotion: Insights from a Social Neuroscience Perspective." In Cacioppo, Visser, and Pickett, *Social Neuroscience,* 209–27.
American Heritage Dictionary of the English Language. Boston: Houghton Mifflin, 1981.
Amin, Samir. *The Liberal Virus: Permanent War and the Americanization of the World.* Trans. James H. Membrez. New York: Monthly Review Press, 2004.
Anderson, Benedict. *Imagined Communities: Reflections on the Origin and Spread of Nationalism.* Rev. ed. New York: Verso, 1991.
Anderson, Sarah, Phyllis Bennis, and John Cavanagh. "Coalition of the Willing or Coalition of the Coerced? How the Bush Admin-

istration Influences Allies in Its War on Iraq." Institute for Policy Studies, February 26, 2003. Available at http://www.ips-dc.org/COERCED.pdf.

Angelova, Penka "Narrative Topoi nationaler Identität: Der Historismus als Erklärungsmuster." In Reichmann, *Narrative Konstruktion nationaler Identität*, 83–106.

Anscombe, G. E. M. *Intention.* 2nd ed. Ithaca, NY: Cornell University Press, 1963.

Appadurai, Arjun. "How to Make a National Cuisine: Cookbooks in Contemporary India." *Comparative Studies in Society and History* 30.1 (1988): 3–24.

Arendt, Hannah. *The Origins of Totalitarianism.* New ed. with added prefaces. San Diego, CA: Harcourt Brace and Company, 1979.

Aristotle. *Poetics. Aristotle's Theory of Poetry and Fine Art with a Critical Text and Translation of the Poetics.* Ed. and trans. S. H. Butcher. 4th ed. New York: Dover, 1951.

Atwood, Margaret. *Surfacing.* New York: Fawcett Crest, 1972.

Awolalu, J. Omosade. *Yoruba Beliefs and Sacrificial Rites.* Harlow, UK: Longman, 1979.

Baer, Michael, and Dean Jaros. "Participation as Instrument and Expression: Some Evidence from the States." *American Journal of Political Science* 18.2 (May 1974): 365–83.

Balakrishnan, Gopal, ed. *Mapping the Nation.* London: Verso, 1996.

Balakrishnan, Gopal. "The National Imagination." In Balakrishnan, *Mapping the Nation*, 198–213.

Balibar, Etienne. "Racism and Nationalism." Trans. Chris Turner. In Balibar and Wallerstein, *Race, Nation, Class*, 37–67.

Balibar, Etienne, and Immanuel Wallerstein. *Race, Nation, Class: Ambiguous Identities.* New York: Verso, 1991.

Bandura, A. *Aggression: A Social Learning Analysis.* Englewood Cliffs, NJ: Prentice-Hall, 1973.

Barker, Colin. "Fear, Laughter, and Collective Power: The Making of Solidarity at the Lenin Shipyard in Gdansk, Poland, August 1980." In Goodwin, Jasper, and Polletta, *Passionate Politics*, 175–94.

Barsalou, Lawrence W. "Ad Hoc Categories." *Memory and Cognition* 11.3 (1983): 211–27.

Baxmann, Inge. "Der Körper der Nation." In François, Siegrist, and Vogel, *Nation und Emotion*, 353–65.

Befu, Harumi. "Hegemony of Homogeneity in the Politics of Identity in Japan." In Dominguez and Wu, *From Beijing to Port Moresby*, 263–91.

Ben-Amos, Avner. "Der letzte Gang des großen Mannes. Die Staatsbegräbnisse in Frankreichs Dritter Republik." In François, Siegrist, and Vogel, *Nation und Emotion*, 232–51.

Benhabib, Selya. "Germany Opens Up." *The Nation* (June 21, 1999): 6–7.

Bennington, Geoffrey. "Postal Politics and the Institution of the Nation." In Bhabha, *Nation and Narration*, 121–37.

Berezin, Mabel. "Emotions and Political Identity: Mobilizing Affection for the Polity." In Goodwin, Jasper, and Polletta, *Passionate Politics*, 83–98.

Berkowitz, Leonard. "More Thoughts about the Social Cognitive and Neoassociationistic Approaches: Similarities and Differences." In Wyer and Srull, *Perspectives on Anger and Emotion*, 179–97.

Berkowitz, Leonard. "Towards a General Theory of Anger and Emotional Aggression: Implications of the Cognitive-Neoassociationistic Perspective for the Analysis of

Anger and Other Emotions." In Wyer and Srull, *Perspectives on Anger and Emotion*, 1–46.
Bhabha, Homi K., ed. *Nation and Narration*. New York: Routledge, 1990.
Biber, Douglas, Susan Conrad, and Randi Reppen. *Corpus Linguistics: Investigating Language Structure and Use*. Cambridge, UK: Cambridge University Press, 2006.
Black, Eric. "Resolution 242 and the Aftermath of 1967." *Frontline* (June 2002). Accessed November 11, 2007, at http://www.pbs.org/wgbh/pages/frontline/shows/oslo/parallel/8.html.
Blair, R. "A Cognitive Developmental Approach to Morality: Investigating the Psychopath." In *Cognition* 57 (1995): 1–29.
Blakey, Michael L. "Scientific Racism and the Biological Concept of Race." *Literature and Psychology* 45.1, 45.2 (1999): 29–43.
Bloom, William. *Personal Identity, National Identity, and International Relations*. Cambridge, UK: Cambridge University Press, 1990.
Book of Dede Korkut. Trans. Geoffrey Lewis. New York: Penguin, 1974.
Bosma, Harke A., and E. Saskia Kunnen. *Identity and Emotion: Development through Self-Organization*. Cambridge, UK: Cambridge University Press; Paris: Editions de la Maison des Sciences de l'Homme, 2001.
Bourdieu, Pierre. *Sociology in Question*. Trans. Richard Nice. London: Sage, 1993.
Bower, G. H. "Affect and Cognition." *Philosophical Transactions of the Royal Society of London, Series B* 302 (1983): 387–402.
Boyer, Pascal. *Religion Explained: The Evolutionary Origins of Religious Thought*. New York: Basic Books, 2001.
Bradley, Sculley, Richmond Croom Beatty, E. Hudson Long, and George Perkins, eds. *The American Tradition in Literature*. 4th ed. New York: Grosset & Dunlap, 1974.
Brennan, Timothy. "The National Longing for Form." In Bhabha, *Nation and Narrative*, 44–70.
Breuilly, John. "Approaches to Nationalism." In Balakrishnan, *Mapping the Nation*, 146–74.
Breuilly, John. *Nationalism and the State*. New York: St. Martin's Press, 1982.
Brothers, Leslie. *Friday's Footprint: How Society Shapes the Human Mind*. Oxford: Oxford University Press, 1997.
Brown, David. *Contemporary Nationalism: Civic, Ethnocultural and Multicultural Politics*. London: Routledge, 2000.
Brown, Judith M. *Gandhi: Prisoner of Hope*. New Haven, CT: Yale University Press, 1989.
Buchanan, Mark. *Nexus: Small Worlds and the Groundbreaking Theory of Networks*. New York: W. W. Norton, 2002.
Buckley, Anthony D., and Mary Catherine Kenney. *Negotiating Identity: Rhetoric, Metaphor, and Social Drama in Northern Ireland*. Washington, DC: Smithsonian Institution Press, 1995.
Burleigh, Michael. *Death and Deliverance: 'Euthanasia' in Germany c. 1900–1945*. Cambridge, UK: Cambridge University Press, 1994.
Bush, George W. "Address to a Joint Session of Congress and the American People." September 20, 2001. Available at http://www.whitehouse.gov/news/releases/2001/09.
Bush, George W. "President's Remarks at National Day of Prayer and Remembrance." September 14, 2001. Available at http://www.whitehouse.gov/news/releases/2001/09.
Butler, Judith. "Imitation and Gender Insubordination." In Fuss, *Inside/Out*, 13–31.

Butola, B. S. "The Paradoxes of National Integration." In Malla, *Nationalism, Regionalism and Philosophy of National Integration*, 138–53.

Cacioppo, John T., Penny S. Visser, and Cynthia L. Pickett, eds. *Social Neuroscience: People Thinking about Thinking People*. Cambridge, MA: MIT Press, 2006.

Campos, J. J., K. C. Barrett, M. E. Lamb, H. H. Goldsmith, and C. Stenberg. "Socioemotional Development." In *Handbook of Child Psychology: Vol. 2. Infancy and Developmental Psychobiology.* 4th ed. Ed. M. Haith and J. Campos. New York: Wiley, 1983.

Cannadine, David. "The Context, Performance and Meaning of Ritual: The British Monarchy and the 'Invention of Tradition,' c. 1820–1977." In Hobsbawm and Ranger, *The Invention of Tradition,* 101–64.

Carrasco, David. *Quetzalcoatl and the Irony of Empire: Myths and Prophecies in the Aztec Tradition.* Chicago: University of Chicago Press, 1982.

Carroll, James. "The Pope's True Revolution." *Time: Online Edition* (April 11, 2005). Available at http://www.time.com/time/.

Carter, Cameron S., Todd S. Braver, Deanna M. Barch, Matthew M. Botvinick, Douglas Noll, and Jonathan D. Cohen. "Anterior Cingulate Cortex, Error Detection, and the Online Monitoring of Performance." *Science* 280 (May 1, 1998): 747–49.

Caspi, Arie. "Running Out of Time." *Ha'aretz Magazine* (June 8, 2001): 4–5.

Chari, V. K. *Walt Whitman in the Light of Vedantic Mysticism.* Lincoln: University of Nebraska Press, 1964.

Chatterjee, Partha. *The Nation and Its Fragments: Colonial and Postcolonial Histories.* Princeton, NJ: Princeton University Press, 1993.

Chein, Jason M., and Julie A. Fiez. "Dissociation of Verbal Working Memory System Components Using a Delayed Serial Recall Task." *Cerebral Cortex* 11 (November 2001): 1003–14.

Chikamatsu, Monzaemon. *Major Plays of Chikamatsu.* Ed. and trans., Donald Keene. New York: Columbia University Press, 1990.

Chomsky, Noam. *9–11.* New York: Seven Stories Press, 2001.

Chomsky, Noam. *Failed States: The Abuse of Power and the Assault on Democracy.* New York: Metropolitan Books, 2006.

Chomsky, Noam. *Hegemony or Survival: America's Quest for Global Dominance.* New York: Henry Holt, 2004.

Chomsky, Noam. *Knowledge of Language: Its Nature, Origin, and Use.* New York: Praeger, 1986.

Chomsky, Noam. *The New Military Humanism: Lessons from Kosovo.* Monroe, ME: Common Courage Press, 1999.

Chomsky, Noam. *Rules and Representations.* New York: Columbia University Press, 1980.

Chomsky, Noam, and Gilbert Achcar. *Perilous Power: The Middle East and U. S. Foreign Policy, Dialogues on Terror, Democracy, War, and Justice.* Ed. Stephen R. Shalom. Boulder, CO: Paradigm, 2007.

Chowdhury, Abhijit. "Internalising the Concept of National Movement in India: Some Problems of Cognition (with a reference to Tagore-Gandhi Debate)." In Malla, *Nationalism, Regionalism and Philosophy of National Integration*, 86–137.

Chua, Beng-Huat, and Eddie Kuo. "The Making of a New Nation: Cultural Construction and National Identity in Singapore." In Dominguez and Wu, *From Beijing to Port Moresby,* 35–67.

Chun, Allen J. "The Culture Industry as National Enterprise: The Politics of Heritage in Contemporary Taiwan." In Dominguez and Wu, *From Beijing to Port Moresby,* 77–113.

Cialdini, Robert B., Richard J. Borden, Avril Thorne, Marcus Randall Walker, Stephen Freeman, and L. R. Sloan. "Basking in Reflected Glory: Three (Football) Field Studies." *Journal of Personality and Social Psychology* 34.3 (1976): 366–75.
Clore, Gerald L., and Andrew Ortony. "Cognition in Emotion: Always, Sometimes, or Never?" *Cognitive Neuroscience of Emotion*. Ed. Richard D. Land and Lynn Nadel with Geoffrey L. Ahern, John J. B. Allen, Alfred W. Kaszniak, Steven Z. Rapcsak, and Gary E. Schwartz. Oxford: Oxford University Press, 2000, 24–61.
Cockburn, Alexander. "Terrorism as Normalcy." *The Nation* (July 1, 2002): 9.
Cohen, Ed. "Who Are 'We'? Gay 'Identity' as Political (E)motion (A Theoretical Rumination)." In Fuss, *Inside/Out*, 71–92.
Cohn, Bernard S. "Representing Authority in Victorian India." In Hobsbawm and Ranger, *The Invention of Tradition*, 165–209.
Conway, M. A., and D. A. Bekerian. "Situational Knowledge and Emotions." *Cognition and Emotion* 1.2 (1987): 145-91.
Correll, J., B. Park, C. M. Judd, and B. Wittenbrink. "The Police Officer's Dilemma: Using Ethnicity to Disambiguate Potentially Threatening Individuals." *Journal of Personality and Social Psychology* 83 (2004): 1314–29.
Cullen, L. M. "The Cultural Basis of Modern Irish Nationalism." In Mitchison, *The Roots of Nationalism*, 91–106.
Damasio, Antonio R. *Descartes' Error: Emotion, Reason, and the Human Brain*. New York: Avon, 1994.
Damasio, Antonio R. *Looking for Spinoza: Joy, Sorrow, and the Feeling Brain*. Orlando, FL: Harcourt, 2003.
Daniel, S. C. "Philosophy of National Integration in Indian Context: A Holistic Approach." In Malla, *Nationalism, Regionalism and Philosophy of National Integration*, 51–65.
Das Gupta, Uma. *Rabindranath Tagore: A Biography*. New Delhi, India: Oxford University Press, 2004.
Davis, Dick. "Introduction to Reuben Levy's Translation of Ferdowsi's *Shāh-nāma*." In Ferdowsi, *The Epic of the Kings*, xxv–xxxvii.
Debbarma, K. "Insurgency and Counter Insurgency in Tripura." In Malla, *Nationalism, Regionalism and Philosophy of National Integration*, 176–95.
Decety, Jean, and Thierry Chaminade. "The Neurophysiology of Imitation and Intersubjectivity." In Hurley and Chater, *Perspectives on Imitation*, vol. 1, 119–40.
Deng, Francis Mading. *The Dinka and Their Songs*. Oxford: Clarendon Press, 1973.
de Sousa, Ronald. "The Rationality of Emotions." In *Explaining Emotions*. Ed. Amelie Oksenberg Rorty. Berkeley: University of California Press, 1980, 127–51.
Devine, P. G. "Stereotypes and prejudice: Their automatic and controlled components." *Journal of Personality and Social Psychology* 56 (1989): 5–18.
Dib, Mohammed. *La grande maison*. Paris: Editions du Seuil, 1952.
Dittmer, Lowell, and Samuel S. Kim, eds. *China's Quest for National Identity*. Ithaca, NY: Cornell University Press, 1993.
Dittmer, Lowell, and Samuel S. Kim. "In Search of a Theory of National Identity." In Dittmer and Kim, *China's Quest for National Identity*, 1–31.
Dittmer, Lowell, and Samuel S. Kim. "Whither China's Quest for National Identity?" In Dittmer and Kim, *China's Quest for National Identity*, 237–90.
Dohrn, Bernardine. "Homeland Imperialism: Fear and Resistance." *Monthly Review* 55.3 (July–August 2003): 130–34.
Domingez, Virginia R., and David Y. H. Wu, eds. *From Beijing to Port Moresby: The Politics of National Identity in Cultural Policies*. Amsterdam, Netherlands: Gordon and Breach, 1998.

Dreyfus, Robert. "Iraq: The Other Surge." *The Nation* (October 29, 2007): 6–8.
Duckitt, John H. *The Social Psychology of Prejudice.* New York: Praeger, 1992.
Dundas, Paul. *The Jains.* New York: Routledge, 1992.
Durán, Lucy. "Introduction." In Bamba Suso and Banna Kanute. *Sujata.* Trans. Gordon Innes, with the assistance of Bakari Sidibe. Ed. Lucy Durán and Graham Furniss. New York: Penguin, 1999.
During, Simon. "Literature—Nationalism's Other? The Case for Revision." In Bhabha, *Nation and Narration,* 138–53.
Dutt, Romesh Chunder. *The Economic History of India.* 2 vols. London: Routledge and Kegan Paul, 1950.
Dutta, Binayak. "Trends in Indian Nationalism: Regionalism an Obvious Derivative." In Malla, *Nationalism, Regionalism and Philosophy of National Integration,* 196–213.
Eich, Eric, and Dawn Macaulay. "Fundamental Factors in Mood-Dependent Memory." In Forgas, *Feeling and Thinking,* 109–30.
Eisenberg, Nancy. "Emotion, Regulation, and Moral Development." *Annual Review of Psychology* 51 (2000): 665–97.
Ellis, A. B. *The Yoruba-Speaking Peoples of the Slave Coast of West Africa.* Oosterhout, Netherlands: Anthropological Publications, 1970, 111–14.
Emmerich, Roland, dir. *Independence Day.* 20th Century Fox, 1996.
Engelhardt, Tom. "The Cartography of Death." *The Nation* (October 23, 2000): 25–34.
Erikson, Erik. *Gandhi's Truth: On the Origins of Militant Nonviolence.* New York: W. W. Norton, 1969.
Ess, Kristen. "The Stage Is Set for Ethnic Cleansing." *ZNet* (26 July 2003). Available at http://www.zmag.org/content/showarticle.cfm?SectionID=22&ItemID=3961.
Euripides. *The Trojan Women.* In *Euripides: Ten Plays.* Trans. and ed. Moses Hadas and John McLean. New York: Bantam Books, 1960, 173–204.
Evans, Richard J. "Parasites of Plunder?" (Review of Götz Aly, *Hitler's Beneficiaries: Plunder, Racial War, and the Nazi Welfare State.*) *The Nation* (January 8/15, 2007): 23–28.
Faiz, Faiz Ahmed. *The True Subject: Selected Poems of Faiz Ahmed Faiz.* Princeton, NJ: Princeton University Press, 1988.
Ferdowsi, Abolquasem. *The Epic of the Kings: Shāh-nāma.* Abridged trans., Reuben Levy. Costa Mesa, CA: Mazda Publishers; New York: Bibliotheca Persica, 1996.
Fiedler, Leslie. *Love and Death in the American Novel.* Rev. ed. New York: Doubleday, 1992.
Fischer, Louis, ed. *The Essential Gandhi.* New York: Vintage Books, 1962.
Fish, Stanley. "Critical Self-Consciousness, or Can We Know What We're Doing?" *Doing What Comes Naturally: Change, Rhetoric, and the Practice of Theory in Literary and Legal Studies.* Durham, NC: Duke University Press, 1989.
Fiske, Susan T., Lasana T. Harris, and Amy J. C. Cuddy. "Why Ordinary People Torture Enemy Prisoners." *Science* 306.5701 (November 26, 2004): 1482–83.
Flapan, Simha. *The Birth of Israel: Myths and Realities.* New York: Pantheon, 1987.
Fletcher, Bill. "Can U.S. Workers Embrace Anti-Imperialism?" *Monthly Review* 55.3 (July–August 2003): 93–108.
Forgas, Joseph P. "Affect and Information Processing Strategies: An Interactive Relationship." In Forgas, *Feeling and Thinking,* 253–80.
Forgas, Joseph P., ed. *Feeling and Thinking: The Role of Affect in Social Cognition.* Cambridge: Cambridge University Press; Paris: Editions de la Maison des Sciences de l'Homme, 2000.

Foster, Kevin. *Fighting Fictions: War, Narrative and National Identity.* London: Pluto Press, 1999.
François, Etienne, Hannes Siegrist, and Jakob Vogel. "Die Nation." In François, Siegrist, and Vogel, *Nation und Emotion,* 13–35.
François, Etienne, Hannes Siegrist, and Jakob Vogel, eds. *Nation und Emotion: Deutschland und Frankreich im Vergleich 19. und 20. Jahrhundert.* Göttingen, Germany: Vandenhoeck and Ruprecht, 1995.
French, Howard W. "Sympathy for Japan's Leader Ebbs in a String of Gaffes." *New York Times* (May 26, 2000): A3.
Frijda, Nico H. *The Emotions.* Cambridge: Cambridge University Press; Paris: Editions de la Maison des Sciences de l'Homme, 1986.
Fromm, Erich. *The Anatomy of Human Destructiveness.* Greenwich, CT: Fawcett Crest, 1973.
Fuss, Diana. *Inside/Out: Lesbian Theories, Gay Theories.* New York: Routledge, 1991.
Gallagher, Catherine, and Stephen Greenblatt. *Practicing New Historicism.* Chicago: University of Chicago Press, 2000.
Gallese, Vittorio. "'Being Like Me': Self-Other Identity, Mirror Neurons, and Empathy." In Hurley and Chater, *Perspectives on Imitation,* vol. 1, 101–18.
Gandhi, Mohandas K. *An Autobiography: The Story of My Experiments with Truth.* Trans. Mahadev Desai. Boston: Beacon Press, 1957.
Gandhi, Mohandas K. *Collected Works of Mahatma Gandhi.* 90 vols. New Delhi, India: Publications Division of the Government of India, 1958–1984.
Gans, Chaim. *The Limits of Nationalism.* Cambridge: Cambridge University Press, 2003.
Ghurye, G. S. *Indian Costume.* 2nd ed. Bombay: Popular Prakashan, 1966.
Gilbert, Daniel T., and Timothy D. Wilson. "Miswanting: Some Problems in the Forecasting of Future Affective States." In *Feeling and Thinking: The Role of Affect in Social Cognition.* Ed. Joseph P. Forgas, 178–97. Cambridge: Cambridge University Press, 2000.
Gilman, Sander. *The Jew's Body.* New York: Routledge, 1991.
Glasgow University Media Group. *War and Peace News.* Milton Keynes, UK: Open University Press, 1985.
Goldberg, Michelle. *Kingdom Coming: The Rise of Christian Nationalism.* New York: W. W. Norton, 2006.
Golden, Peter B. *An Introduction to the History of the Turkic Peoples.* Wiesbaden, Germany: Otto Harrassowitz, 1992.
Goldman, Emma. *Red Emma Speaks: An Emma Goldman Reader.* Ed. Alix Kates Shulman. New York: Schocken Books, 1982.
Gonglah, H. "Insurgency in Northeast India: Deeper than Politics." In Malla, *Nationalism, Regionalism and Philosophy of National Integration,* 154–64.
Goodwin, Jeff, and Steven Pfaff. "Emotion Work in High-Risk Social Movements: Managing Fear in the U.S. and East German Civil Rights Movements." In Goodwin, Jasper, and Polletta, *Passionate Politics,* 282–302.
Goodwin, Jeff, James M. Jasper, and Francesca Polletta, eds. *Passionate Politics: Emotions and Social Movements.* Chicago: University of Chicago Press, 2001.
Goodwin, Jeff, James M. Jasper, and Francesca Polletta. "Why Emotions Matter." In Goodwin, Jasper, and Polletta, *Passionate Politics,* 1–24.
Green, Mary Jean. *Women and Narrative Identity: Rewriting the Quebec National Text.* Montreal, Quebec, and Kingston, Ontario: McGill-Queen's University Press, 2001.

Greenfeld, Liah. *Nationalism: Five Roads to Modernity.* Cambridge, MA: Harvard University Press, 1992.

Greenspan, Ezra, ed. *Walt Whitman's "Song of Myself": A Sourcebook and Critical Edition.* New York: Routledge, 2005.

Greenwald, Anthony, Mahzarin Banaji, Laurie Rudman, Shelly Farnham, Brian Nosek, and Marshall Rosier. "Prologue to a Unified Theory of Attitudes, Stereotypes, and Self-Concept." In Forgas, *Feeling and Thinking,* 308–30.

Habermas, Jürgen. "The European Nation-State—Its Achievements and Its Limits: On the Past and Future of Sovereignty and Citizenship." In Balakrishnan, *Mapping the Nation,* 267–80.

Hajjar, Lisa. "Torture and the Politics of Denial." *In These Times* 28.15 (2004).

Hardt, Michael, and Antonio Negri. *Empire.* Cambridge, MA: Harvard University Press, 2000.

Hardt, Michael, and Antonio Negri. *Multitude: War and Democracy in the Age of Empire.* New York: Penguin Press, 2004.

Harris, Paul, Tjeert Olthof, Mark Terwogt, and Charlotte Hardman. "Children's Knowledge of the Situations that Provoke Emotion." *International Journal of Behavioral Development* 10 (1987): 319–43.

Harvey, Paul, ed. *The Oxford Companion to Classical Literature.* Oxford: Oxford University Press, 1984.

Hastings, Adrian. *The Construction of Nationhood: Ethnicity, Religion and Nationalism.* Cambridge: Cambridge University Press, 1997.

Hatfield, Elaine, John T. Cacioppo, and Richard L. Rapson. *Emotional Contagion.* Cambridge: Cambridge University Press, 1994.

Haugland, Kjell. "An Outline of Norwegian Cultural Nationalism in the Second Half of the Nineteenth Century." In Mitchison, *The Roots of Nationalism,* 21–29.

Hauser, Marc D. *Moral Minds: How Nature Designed Our Universal Sense of Right and Wrong.* New York: HarperCollins, 2006.

Head, Bessie. *A Question of Power.* Oxford: Heinemann, 1974.

Hébert, Anne. *Le Premier Jardin.* Paris: Éditions du Seuil, 1988.

Herb, Guntram H. "National Identity and Territory." In Herb and Kaplan, *Nested Identities,* 9–30.

Herb, Guntram H., and David H. Kaplan, eds. *Nested Identities: Nationalism, Territory, and Scale.* New York: Rowman and Littlefield, 1999.

Herman, Edward S. "Road Map to Sustainable Ethnic Cleansing." *ZNet* (July 5, 2003). Available at http://zmag.org/content/showarticle.cfm?SectionID=22ItemID=3860.

Herman, Edward S., and David Peterson. "The Dismantling of Yugoslavia: A Study in Inhumanitarian Intervention—and a Western Liberal-Left Intellectual and Moral Collapse." *Monthly Review* 59.5 (October 2007): 1–62.

Herzfeld, Michael. *Cultural Intimacy: Social Poetics in the Nation-State.* New York: Routledge, 1997.

Higgins, Lesley, and Marie-Christine Leps. "'Passport Please': Legal, Literary, and Critical Fictions of Identity." In *Un-Disciplining Literature: Literature, Law and Culture.* Ed. Kostas Myrsiades and Linda Myrsiades. New York: Peter Lang, 1999, 117–68.

Hirschfeld, Lawrence A. *Race in the Making: Cognition, Culture, and the Child's Construction of Human Kinds.* Cambridge, MA: MIT Press, 1996.

Hitchens, Christopher. "Fallen Idols." *The Nation* (April 2, 2001): 9.

Hitchens, Christopher. "Israel Shahak, 1933–2001." *The Nation* (July 23/30, 2001): 9.

Hitler, Adolf. *Mein Kampf.* Ed. and trans. John Chamberlain et al. New York: Reynal and Hitchcock, 1940.

Hitler, Adolf. *Mein Kampf.* München, Germany: Zentralverlag der NSDAP, 1943.
Hobsbawm, Eric. "Introduction: Inventing Traditions." In Hobsbawm and Ranger, *The Invention of Tradition*, 1–14.
Hobsbawm, Eric. "Mass-Producing Traditions: Europe, 1870–1914." In Hobsbawm and Ranger, *The Invention of Tradition*, 263–307.
Hobsbawm, Eric. *Nations and Nationalism Since 1780: Programme, Myth, Reality.* Cambridge: Cambridge University Press, 1990.
Hobsbawm, Eric, and Terence Ranger, eds. *The Invention of Tradition.* Cambridge: Cambridge University Press, 1983.
Hoffmann, Stefan-Ludwig. "Mythos und Geschichte: Leipziger Gedenkfeiern der Völkerschlacht im 19. und frühen 20. Jahrhundert." In François, Siegrist, and Vogel, *Nation und Emotion*, 111–32.
Hogan, Patrick. *Camps on the Hearthstone.* Dublin, Ireland: C. J. Fallon, 1956.
Hogan, Patrick Colm. "Allegories of Political Maturity: Labour, Marxism, and the ANC in Peter Abrahams' *Mine Boy*," *Journal of Commonwealth and Postcolonial Studies* 6.2 (1999): 37–56.
Hogan, Patrick Colm. "Bessie Head's *A Question of Power*: A Lacanian Psychosis." *Mosaic: A Journal for the Interdisciplinary Study of Literature*. 27.2 (June 1994): 95–112.
Hogan, Patrick Colm. *Cognitive Science, Literature, and the Arts: A Guide for Humanists.* New York: Routledge, 2003.
Hogan, Patrick Colm. *Colonialism and Cultural Identity: Crises of Tradition in the Anglophone Literatures of India, Africa, and the Caribbean.* Albany: State University of New York Press, 2000.
Hogan, Patrick Colm. *The Culture of Conformism.* Durham, NC: Duke University Press, 2001.
Hogan, Patrick Colm. *Empire and Poetic Voice: Cognitive and Cultural Studies of Literary Tradition and Colonialism.* Albany: State University of New York Press, 2004.
Hogan, Patrick Colm. "Identity and Imperialism in Margaret Atwood's *Surfacing*." In McLeod, *Commonwealth and American Women's Discourse*, 181–90.
Hogan, Patrick Colm. "Literary Universals and Their Cultural Traditions: The Case of Poetic Imagery." *Consciousness, Literature, and the Arts* 6.2 (August 2005). Available at http://www.aber.ac.uk/~drawww/journal.
Hogan, Patrick Colm. *The Mind and Its Stories: Narrative Universals and Human Emotion.* Cambridge: Cambridge University Press; Paris: Editions de la Maison des Sciences de L'Homme, 2003.
Hogan, Patrick Colm. "A Minimal, Lexicalist/Constituent Transfer Account of Metaphor." *Style* 36.3 (2002): 484–502.
Hogan, Patrick Colm. "Narrative Universals, Nationalism, and Sacrificial Terror: From *Nosferatu* to Nazism." *Film Studies: An International Review* 8 (Summer 2006): 93–105.
Hogan, Patrick Colm. "Narrative Universals, National Sacrifice, and *Dou E Yuan*." *Ex/Change* (Hong Kong) 12 (2005): 18–25.
Hogan, Patrick Colm. *On Interpretation: Meaning and Inference in Law, Psychoanalysis, and Literature.* Athens: University of Georgia Press, 1996.
Hogan, Patrick Colm. "On the Very Idea of Language Sciences." In *The Cambridge Encyclopedia of the Language Sciences.* Ed. Patrick Colm Hogan. Cambridge: Cambridge University Press, 2009.
Hogan, Patrick Colm. "Revolution and Despair: Allegories of Nation and Class in Patrick Hogan's *Camps on the Hearthstone*." *The Canadian Journal of Irish Studies* 25.1/25.2 (1999): 179–201.

Holland, John H., Keith J. Holyoak, Richard E. Nisbett, and Paul R. Thagard. *Induction: Processes of Inference, Learning, and Discovery:* Cambridge, MA: MIT Press, 1986.
Horowitz, Donald. *Ethnic Groups in Conflict.* Berkeley: University of California Press, 1985.
Hudson, R. A. *Sociolinguistics.* Cambridge: Cambridge University Press, 1980.
Hurley, Susan, and Nick Chater, eds. *Perspectives on Imitation: From Neuroscience to Social Science. Volume 1: Mechanisms of Imitation and Imitation in Animals; Volume 2: Imitation, Human Development, and Culture.* Cambridge, MA: MIT Press, 2005.
Ismail, Manal. "Inside the Cable Beast." *Extra!* 16.5 (October 2003): 24–25.
Ito, Tiffany, and John Cacioppo. "Affect and Attitudes: A Social Neuroscience Approach." In *Handbook of Affect and Social Cognition.* Ed. Joseph Faogas, 50–74. Mahwah, NJ: Erlbaum, 2001.
Ito, Tiffany A., Geoffrey R. Urland, Eve Willadsen-Jensen, and Joshua Correll. "The Social Neuroscience of Stereotyping and Prejudice: Using Event-Related Brain Potentials to Study Social Perception." In Cacioppo, Visser, and Pickett, *Social Neuroscience,* 189–208.
Jamail, Dahr. "Who Are the Insurgents?" *The Progressive* (January 2008): 37–38.
Jameson, Fredric. *The Political Unconscious: Narrative as a Socially Symbolic Act.* Ithaca, NY: Cornell University Press, 1981.
The Jerusalem Bible. Ed. Alexander Jones et al. Garden City, NY: Doubleday, 1966.
Johnson-Laird, Philip N. *The Computer and the Mind: An Introduction to Cognitive Science.* Cambridge, MA: Harvard University Press, 1988.
Jordens, J. T. F. "Gandhi and the *Bhagavadgita.*" In Minor, *Modern Indian Interpreters of the Bhagavadgita,* 88–109.
Kádár-Fülop, Judit. "Culture, Writing, and Curriculum." In *Writing Across Languages and Cultures: Issues in Contrastive Rhetoric.* Ed. Alan C. Purves. Newbury Park, CA: Sage, 1988, 25–50.
Kahneman, Daniel, and Dale T. Miller. "Norm Theory: Comparing Reality to Its Alternatives." *Psychological Review* 93.2 (1986): 136–53.
Kaplan, David H. "Territorial Identities and Geographic Scale." In Herb and Kaplan, *Nested Identities,* 31–49.
Kaplan, Justin. *Walt Whitman: A Life.* New York: HarperCollins, 1980.
Kaschuba, Wolfgang. "Die Nation als Körper: Zur symbolischen Konstruktion 'nationaler' Alltagswelt." In François, Siegrist, and Vogel, *Nation und Emotion,* 291–99.
Kasfir, Neslon. "Cultural Sub-Nationalism in Uganda." In Olorunsola, *The Politics of Cultural Sub-Nationalism in Africa,* 51–148.
Kateb, George. *Patriotism and Other Mistakes.* New Haven, CT: Yale University Press, 2006.
Kauṭilya. *Arthaśāstra, 6th ed.* Trans. R. Shamasastry. Mysore: Mysore Printing and Publishing, 1960.
Kennedy, Miranda, and Matthew Power. "The Buddha's Teardrop." *In These Times* 27.15 (June 23, 2003): 20–23.
Kerr, David, with Stephen Chifunyise. "Southern Africa." In *A History of Theatre in Africa.* Ed. Martin Banham. Cambridge: Cambridge University Press, 2004, 265–311.
Khalidi, Rashid I. "Contrasting Narratives of Palestinian Identity." In Yaeger, *The Geography of Identity,* 187–222.
Kiberd, Declan. *Inventing Ireland.* Cambridge, MA: Harvard University Press, 1995.

King-Casas, Brooks, Damon Tomlin, Cedric Anen, Colin F. Camerer, Steven R. Quartz, and P. Read Montague. "Getting to Know You: Reputation and Trust in a Two-Person Economic Exchange." *Science* 308.5718 (April 1, 2005): 78–83.
Klinge, Matti. "'Let Us Be Finns'—the Birth of Finland's National Culture." In Mitchison, *The Roots of Nationalism*, 67–75.
Kondo, Hirohito, Naoyuki Osaka, and Mariko Osaka. "Cooperation of the Anterior Cingulate Cortex and Dorsolateral Prefrontal Cortex for Attention Shifting." *NeuroImage* 23 (2004): 670–79.
The Koran. Trans. N. J. Dawood. 5th ed. New York: Penguin, 1993.
Kosslyn, Stephen. *Image and Brain: The Resolution of the Imagery Debate*. Cambridge, MA: MIT Press, 1994.
Kövecses, Zoltán. *Metaphor: A Practical Introduction*. Oxford: Oxford University Press, 2002.
Kövecses, Zoltán. "Metaphor, Universals of." In *The Cambridge Encyclopedia of the Language Sciences*. Ed. Patrick Colm Hogan. Cambridge: Cambridge University Press, 2009.
Krendl, Anne C., C. Neil Macrae, William M. Kelley, Jonathan A. Fugelsang, and Todd F. Heatherton. "The Good, the Bad, and the Ugly: An fMRI Investigation of the Functional Anatomic Correlates of Stigma." *Social Neuroscience* 1 (2006): 5–15.
Kuan Han-ch'ing. *Snow in Midsummer*. In *Selected Plays of Kuan Han-ch'ing*. Trans. Yang Hsien-yi and Gladys Yang. Beijing: Foreign Languages Press, 1958, 21–47.
Kunda, Ziva. *Social Cognition: Making Sense of People*. Cambridge, MA: MIT Press, 1999.
Lakoff, George. *Don't Think of an Elephant! Know Your Values and Frame the Debate: The Essential Guide for Progressives*. White River Junction, VT: Chelsea Green Publishing, 2004.
Lakoff, George. *Women, Fire, and Dangerous Things: What Categories Reveal About the Mind*. Chicago: University of Chicago Press, 1987.
Lakoff, George, and Mark Johnson. *Metaphors We Live By*. Chicago: University of Chicago Press, 1980.
Lakoff, George, and Mark Turner. *More than Cool Reason: A Field Guide to Poetic Metaphor*. Chicago: University of Chicago Press, 1989.
Lamprecht, Gerhard, dir. and writer. *Somewhere in Berlin*. Deutsche Film (DEFA), 1946.
Lang, Peter J. "The Network Model of Emotion: Motivational Connections." In Wyer and Srull, *Perspectives on Anger and Emotion*, 109–33.
Langer, Gary. "Advantage Bush: New Poll Shows Bush in Lead." *ABCNews.com* (September 9, 2004). Accessed November 9, 2007, at http://www.abcnews.go.com/sections/politics/Vote2004/bush_campaign_poll_040909.html.
Langlois, J. H., and I. A. Roggman. "Attractive Faces Are Only Average." *Psychological Science* 1 (1990): 115–21.
Laver, James. *English Costume of the Eighteenth Century*. Drawn by Irish Brooke. New York: Barnes and Noble, 1931.
Lawrence, D. H. *Studies in Classic American Literature*. New York: Penguin, 1961.
The Laws of Manu. Ed. and trans. Wendy Doniger, with Brian K. Smith. New York: Penguin, 1991.
LeDoux, Joseph. *The Emotional Brain: The Mysterious Underpinnings of Emotional Life*. New York: Touchstone, 1996.
LeDoux, Joseph. *Synaptic Self: How Our Brains Become Who We Are*. New York: Viking, 2002.

LeDoux, Joseph E., and Elizabeth A. Phelps. "Emotional Networks in the Brain." In Lewis and Haviland-Jones, *Handbook of Emotions,* 157–72.
Leventhal, Howard. "A Componential, Self-Regulative Systems View of Berkowitz's Cognitive-Neoassociationistic Model of Anger." In Wyer and Srull, *Perspectives on Anger and Emotion,* 135–46.
Levi, Werner. *Contemporary International Law: A Concise Introduction.* Boulder, CO: Westview Press, 1979.
Lewis, Michael, and Jeannette M. Haviland-Jones, eds. *Handbook of Emotions.* 2nd ed. New York: Guilford Press, 2000.
Li, Wai-yee. "Full-Length Vernacular Fiction." In *The Columbia History of Chinese Literature.* Ed. Victor H. Mair. New York: Columbia University Press, 2001, 620–58.
Lieberman, Matthew D., and Naomi I. Eisenberger. "A Pain by Any Other Name (Rejection, Exclusion, Ostracism) Still Hurts the Same: The Role of Dorsal Anterior Cingulate Cortex in Social and Physical Pain." In Cacioppo, Visser, and Pickett, *Social Neuroscience,* 167–87.
Lincoln, Abraham. "Address at Gettysburg, Pennsylvania: Address delivered at the dedication of the Cemetery at Gettysburg." In *Speeches and Writings 1859–1865.* Ed. Don E. Fehrenbacher. New York: Library of America, 1989, 536.
Luo Guanzhong. *Three Kingdoms: A Historical Novel, Abridged.* Ed. and trans. Moss Roberts. Berkeley: University of California Press, 1999.
Lyons, F. S. L. *Culture and Anarchy in Ireland 1890–1939.* New York: Oxford University Press, 1979.
Maas, Annette. "Der Kult der toten Krieger: Frankreich und Deutschland nach 1870/71." In François, Siegrist, and Vogel, *Nation und Emotion,* 215–31.
MacDonald, Angus W., Jonathan D. Cohen, V. Andrew Stenger, and Cameron S. Carter. "Dissociating the Role of the Dorsolateral Prefrontal and Anterior Cingulate Cortex in Cognitive Control." *Science* 288. 5472 (June 9, 2000): 1835–38.
Mack, Maynard, gen. ed. *The Norton Anthology of World Masterpieces.* Expanded Ed. Vol. I. New York: W. W. Norton, 1995.
MacPhee, Graham. "Recalling Empire: Anglo-American Conceptions of Imperialism and the Decline of the Nation-State." *College Literature* 35.1 (Winter 2008): 198–208.
Mahapatra, Sitakant, ed. and trans. *Staying Is Nowhere: An Anthology of Kondh and Paraja Poetry.* Calcutta, India: Writers Workshop, nd.
Maja-Pearce, Adewale, ed. *The Heinemann Book of African Poetry in English.* Oxford: Heinemann, 1990.
Malla, N., ed. *Nationalism, Regionalism and Philosophy of National Integration.* New Delhi, India: Regency Publications, 1998.
Mann, Michael. "Nation-States in Europe and Other Continents: Diversifying, Developing, Not Dying." In Balakrishnan, *Mapping the Nation,* 295–316.
Marcus, G. E. "Emotions in Politics." *Annual Review of Political Science* 3 (2000): 221–50.
Marx, Karl, and Frederick Engels. *Manifesto of the Communist Party.* Beijing: Foreign Languages Press, 1975.
McAdams, Richard H. "Conformity to Inegalitarian Conventions and Norms: The Contribution of Coordination and Esteem." *The Monist* 88.2 (April 2005): 238–59.
McHugh, Roger, ed. *Dublin 1916.* New York: Hawthorn Books, 1966.
McLeod, Alan L., ed. *Commonwealth and American Women's Discourse: Essays in Criticism.* New Delhi, India: Sterling Press, 1996.

Mészáros, István. "Militarism and the Coming Wars." *Monthly Review* 55.2 (June 2003): 17–24.
Miller, James E., Jr. *Leaves of Grass: America's Lyric-Epic of Self and Democracy.* New York: Twayne, 1992.
Milton, John. *The Works of John Milton.* Ed. Frank Patterson et al. 18 vols. New York: Columbia University Press, 1932.
Minor, Robert N., ed. *Modern Indian Interpreters of the Bhagavadgita.* Albany: State University of New York Press, 1986.
Mitchell, Jason P., Malia F. Mason, C. Neil Macraw, and Mahzarin R. Banaji. "Thinking about Others: The Neural Substrates of Social Cognition." In Cacioppo, Visser, and Pickett, *Social Neuroscience,* 63–82.
Mitchison, Rosalind, ed. *The Roots of Nationalism: Studies in Northern Europe.* Edinburgh: John Donald Publishers, 1980.
Mitchison, Rosalind. "Some Conclusions." In Mitchison, *The Roots of Nationalism,* 159–67.
Monroe, Kristen Renwick, James Hankin, and Renée Bukovchik van Vechten. "The Psychological Foundations of Identity Politics." *Annual Review of Political Science* 3 (2000): 419–47.
Morgan, Prys. "From a Death to a View: The Hunt for the Welsh Past in the Romantic Period." In Hobsbawm and Ranger, *The Invention of Tradition,* 43–100.
Mo Tzu. "Mo Tzu's Doctrines of Universal Love, Heaven, and Social Welfare." In *A Source Book in Chinese Philosophy.* Trans. and ed. Wing-Tsit Chan. Princeton, NJ: Princeton University Press, 1963, 211–31.
Moyers, Bill. "Blind Faith." *In These Times* (February 28, 2005): 22–23.
Mumby, Dennis K., ed. *Narrative and Social Control: Critical Perspectives.* Newbury Park, CA: Sage, 1993.
Naipaul, V. S. *The Mimic Men.* New York: Penguin Books, 1967.
Nairn, Tom. *Faces of Nationalism: Janus Revisited.* London: Verso, 1997.
Nandy, Ashis. *Exiled at Home.* Delhi, India: Oxford University Press, 1998.
Nandy, Ashis. *The Illegitimacy of Nationalism: Rabindranath Tagore and the Politics of Self.* Delhi, India: Oxford University Press, 1994.
Nandy, Ashis. *The Intimate Enemy: Loss and Recovery of Self Under Colonialism.* Delhi, India: Oxford University Press, 1983.
Nandy, Ashis. *Traditions, Tyranny, and Utopias: Essays in the Politics of Awareness.* Delhi, India: Oxford University Press, 1987.
Nandy, Ashis, Shikha Trivedy, Shail Mayaram, and Achyut Yagnik. *Creating a Nationality: The Ramjanmabhumi Movement and Fear of the Self.* In Nandy, *Exiled at Home.*
Narayan, R. K. *The Ramayana.* New York: Penguin, 1972.
Nārāyaṇa. *Hitopadeśa.* Trans. and ed. M. R. Kale. Delhi, India: Motilal Banarsidass, 1967.
Nesse, R. M. "An Evolutionary Perspective on Panic Disorder and Agoraphobia." *Ethology and Sociobiology* 8 (1987): 73S–83S.
Ng-Quinn, Michael. "National Identity in Premodern China: Formation and Role Enactment." In Dittmer and Kim, *China's Quest for National Identity,*, 32–61.
Ngũgĩ wa Thiong'o. *Petals of Blood.* New York: Penguin, 1977.
Nichols, John. "Winter Soldiers Return." *The Nation* (December 10, 2007): 5.
ní Fhlathúin, Máire. "The Anti-Colonial Modernism of Patrick Pearse." In *Modernism and Empire.* Ed. Howard J. Booth and Nigel Rigby. Manchester, UK: Manchester University Press, 2000, 156–74.

Niane, D. T. *Sundiata: An Epic of Old Mali.* Trans. G. D. Pickett. Harlow, UK: Longman, 1965.

Nicolson, Harold. *Monarchy.* London: Weidenfeld and Nicolson, 1962.

Nigosian, S. A. *The Zoroastrian Faith: Tradition and Modern Research.* Montreal: McGill-Queen's University Press, 1993.

Nisbett, Richard E., and Lee Ross. *Human Inference: Strategies and Shortcomings of Social Judgment.* Englewood Cliffs, NJ: Prentice-Hall, 1980.

Nusbaum, Howard C., and Steven L. Small. "Investigating Cortical Mechanisms of Language Processing in Social Context." In Cacioppo, Visser, and Pickett, *Social Neuroscience,* 131–52.

Nussbaum, Martha C. *The Fragility of Goodness: Luck and Ethics in Greek Tragedy and Philosophy.* Cambridge: Cambridge University Press, 1986.

Nussbaum, Martha C. "Patriotism and Cosmopolitanism." In *For Love of Country?* Ed. Joshua Cohen, 3–17. Boston: Beacon Press, 2002.

Nussbaum, Martha C. *Upheavals of Thought: The Intelligence of Emotions.* Cambridge: Cambridge University Press, 2001.

Oatley, Keith. *Best Laid Schemes: The Psychology of Emotions.* Cambridge: Cambridge University Press; Paris: Editions de la Maison des Sciences de l'Homme, 1992.

Oatley, Keith. *Emotions: A Brief History.* Malden, MA: Blackwell, 2004.

Oatley, Keith. "Why Fiction May Be Twice as True as Fact: Fiction as Cognitive and Emotional Simulation." *Review of General Psychology* 3.2 (1999): 101–17.

Oatley, Keith, and P. N. Johnson-Laird. "Toward a Cognitive Theory of Emotions." *Cognition and Emotion* 1.1 (1987): 29-50.

O'Brien, Edna. *Mother Ireland.* New York: Penguin, 1978.

O'Casey, Sean. *Three Plays.* London: Macmillan, 1978.

O'Connor, Ulick. *A Terrible Beauty is Born: The Irish Troubles 1912–1922.* London: Hamish Hamilton, 1975.

O'Flaherty, Wendy Doniger. "The Clash between Relative and Absolute Duty: The Dharma of Demons." In *The Concept of Duty in South Asia.* Ed. Wendy Doniger O'Flaherty and J. Duncan M. Derrett, 96–106. London: South Asia Books/School of Oriental and African Studies, 1978.

Olorunsola, Victor A., ed. *The Politics of Cultural Sub-Nationalism in Africa.* Garden City, NY: Anchor Books, 1972.

Ong, Walter J., S.J. "Nationalism and Darwin." *In the Human Grain: Further Explorations of Contemporary Culture.* New York: Macmillan, 1967, 83–98.

Ortony, Andrew. "Beyond Literal Similarity." *Psychological Review* 86 (1979): 161–80.

Ortony, Andrew, Gerald Clore, and Allan Collins. *The Cognitive Structure of Emotions.* New York: Cambridge University Press, 1988.

Ostriker, Alicia. "Loving Walt Whitman and the Problem of America." In Greenspan, *Walt Whitman's "Song of Myself,"* 98–106.

Pal, Amitabh. "Empire Unbound." *The Progressive* (February 2004): 40–44.

Panksepp, Jaak. *Affective Neuroscience: The Foundations of Human and Animal Emotions.* New York: Oxford University Press, 1998.

Panksepp, Jaak. "Emotions as Natural Kinds within the Mammalian Brain." In Lewis and Haviland-Jones, *Handbook of Emotions,* 137–56.

Parekh, Bhikhu. *Colonialism, Tradition, and Reform: An Analysis of Gandhi's Political Discourse.* New Delhi, India: Sage, 1989.

Parenti, Christian. "Postcard from Kabul" (October 9, 2004). Available at http://www.thenation.com.

Parenti, Christian. "Who Rules Afghanistan." *The Nation* (November 15, 2004). Available at http://www.thenation.com.
Peterson, Indira. "Cilappatikāram." In Mack, 1995, 1248–52.
Phelan, James. *Living to Tell About It: A Rhetoric and Ethics of Character Narration*. Ithaca, NY: Cornell University Press, 2005.
Philip, Alan Butt. "European Nationalism in the Nineteenth and Twentieth Centuries." In Mitchison, *The Roots of Nationalism*, 1–9.
Philippi, Donald L. *Songs of Gods, Songs of Humans: The Epic Tradition of the Ainu*. San Francisco: North Point Press, 1982.
Pilkington, C. M. *Judaism*. Lincolnwood, IL: NTC/Contemporary Publishing, 1995.
Pinker, Steven. *How the Mind Works*. New York: W. W. Norton, 1997.
Plantinga, Carl. "The Scene of Empathy and the Human Face on Film." In Plantinga and Smith, *Passionate Views*, 239–55.
Plantinga, Carl, and Greg M. Smith, eds. *Passionate Views: Film, Cognition, and Emotion*. Baltimore, MD: Johns Hopkins University Press, 1999.
Pollak, Vivian R. *The Erotic Whitman*. Berkeley: University of California Press, 2000.
Preston, Stephanie D., and Frans B. M. de Waal. "Empathy: Its Ultimate and Proximate Bases." *Behavioral and Brain Sciences* 25 (2002): 1–72.
Prinz, Jesse J. "Imitation and Moral Development." In Hurley and Chater, *Perspectives on Imitation*, vol. 2, 267–82.
Quint, David. *Epic and Empire: Politics and Generic Form from Virgil to Milton*. Princeton, NJ: Princeton University Press, 1993.
Railton, Stephen. "'As If I Were with You'—The Performance of Whitman's Poetry." In Greenspan, *Walt Whitman's "Song of Myself,"* 7–26.
Ranger, Terence. "The Invention of Tradition in Colonial Africa." In Hobsbawm and Ranger, *The Invention of Tradition*, 211–62.
Reich, Bernard, and David H. Goldberg. *Political Dictionary of Israel*. London: Scarecrow Press, 2000.
Reichmann, Eva, ed. *Narrative Konstruktion nationaler Identität*. St. Ingbert, Germany: Röhrig Universitätsverlag, 2000.
Renan, Ernst. "What Is a Nation?" Trans. Martin Thom. In Bhabha, *Nation and Narration*, 8–22.
Roberts, Lee, Riyadh Lafta, Richard Garfield, Jamal Khudhairi, and Gilbert Burnham. "Mortality before and after the 2003 Invasion of Iraq: Cluster Sample Survey." *The Lancet* 364.9448 (November 20, 2004). Available at http://www.thelancet.com.
Roberts, Moss. "Afterword to the Unabridged Edition: About *Three Kingdoms*." In *Three Kingdoms: A Historical Novel*. Attributed to Luo Guanzhong. Abridged Ed. Trans. Roberts. Beijing: Foreign Languages Press; Berkeley: University of California Press, 1999.
Robin, Corey. *Fear: The History of a Political Idea*. Oxford: Oxford University Press, 2004.
Rogers, Timothy T., and James L. McClelland. *Semantic Cognition: A Parallel Distributed Processing Approach*. Cambridge, MA: MIT Press, 2004.
Rosen, Steven, ed. *A Survey of World Conflicts*. Pittsburgh, PA: University of Pittsburgh Center for International Studies, 1969.
Roshwald, Aviel. *The Endurance of Nationalism: Ancient Roots and Modern Dilemmas*. Cambridge: Cambridge University Press, 2006.
Rothschild, Matthew. "Israel Isn't David . . . It's Goliath." (Interview with Irena Klepfisz.) *The Progressive* (July 2001): 27–29.

Rubin, D. L. "Nonlanguage Factors Affecting Undergraduates' Judgments of Nonnative English-Speaking Teaching Assistants." *Research in Higher Education* 33 (1992): 511–31.

Rubin, David. *Memory in Oral Traditions: The Cognitive Psychology of Epic, Ballads, and Counting-Out Rhymes.* New York: Oxford University Press, 1995.

Rushdie, Salman. *Midnight's Children.* New York: Penguin Books, 1980.

Said, Edward. *Orientalism.* New York: Pantheon, 1978.

Said, Edward. "The End of Oslo." *The Nation* (October 30, 2000): 4–5.

Santayana, George. *The Life of Reason, or, The Phases of Human Progress: Reason in Common Sense.* New York: Scribner's, 1905.

Santasombat, Yos. "Buddhist Cultural Tradition and the Politics of National Identity in Thailand." In Dominguez and Wu, *From Beijing to Port Moresby,* 305–51.

Sargeant, Winthrop, trans. *The Bhagavad Gītā.* Albany: SUNY Press, 1994.

Schacter, Daniel L. *Searching for Memory: The Brain, the Mind, and the Past.* New York: Basic Books, 1996.

Schank, Roger C. "Scripts." *The Cambridge Encyclopedia of the Language Sciences.* Cambridge: Cambridge University Press, 2009.

Schank, Roger C., and Robert P. Abelson. *Scripts, Plans, Goals, and Understanding: An Inquiry into Human Knowledge Structures.* Hillsdale, NJ: Lawrence Erlbaum, 1977.

Scheer, Robert. "Cultivating Opium, Not Democracy." *The Nation* (November 23, 2004). Available at http://www.thenation.com.

Scheer, Robert. "The Pope Pleaded. We Didn't Listen." *Los Angeles Times—latimes. com* (April 12, 2005). Available at http://www.latimes.com.

Schivelbusch, Wolfgang. *The Culture of Defeat: On National Trauma, Mourning, and Recovery.* Trans. Jefferson Chase. New York: Henry Holt, 2003.

Schmidgall, Gary. *Walt Whitman: A Gay Life.* New York: Dutton, 1997.

Sen, Amartya. *Identity and Violence: The Illusion of Destiny.* New York: W. W. Norton, 2006.

Service, John. "Foreword to the Unabridged Edition." In Luo, *Three Kingdoms,* xiii–xv.

Shakespeare, William. *The Life of Henry the Fifth.* In *The Norton Shakespeare.* Ed. Stephen Greenblatt, Walter Cohen, Jean E. Howard, and Katharine Eisaman Maus, 1454–1521. New York: W. W. Norton & Company, 1997.

Sharma, R. P. "Gandhian Nationalism and Its Variant Readings." In Malla, *Nationalism, Regionalism and Philosophy of National Integration,* 23–50.

Shaver, Phillip, Judith Schwartz, Donald Kirson, and Cary O'Connor. "Emotion Knowledge: Further Exploration of a Prototype Approach." *Journal of Personality and Social Psychology* 52.6 (1987): 1061–86.

Sicherman, Carol. *Ngũgĩ wa Thiong'o: The Making of a Rebel. A Sourcebook in Kenyan Literature and Resistance.* New York: H. Zell, 1990.

Sidhwa, Bapsi. *Cracking India.* Minneapolis, MN: Milkweed Editions, 1991.

Simpson, David. "Destiny Made Manifest: The Styles of Whitman's Poetry." In Bhabha, *Nation and Narration,* 177–96.

Simpson, Joseph R, Jr., Wayne C. Drevets, Abraham Z. Snyder, Debra A. Gusnard, and Marcus E. Raichle. "Emotion-Induced Changes in Human Medial Prefrontal Cortex: II. During Anticipatory Anxiety." *PNAS* 98.2 (January 16, 2001): 688–93.

Sinai, Ruth. "Government Report: 1.65 Million Israelis Living Below Poverty Line." *Haaretz.com* (September 5, 2007). Accessed on November 10, 2007, at http://www.haaretz.com/hasen/spages/900677.html.

Sirota, David. "The Upside of Nationalism: America-first fervor could be the driving force behind economic populism." *In These Times* (April 2008): 32–33, 47.
Sisòkò, Fa-Digi. *The Epic of Son-Jara: A West African Tradition.* Trans. and ed. John William Johnson. Bloomington: Indiana University Press, 1992.
Smith, Anthony D. *The Ethnic Origins of Nations.* Oxford: Blackwell, 1986.
Smith, Anthony D. "Nationalism and the Historians." In Balakrishnan, *Mapping the Nation,* 175–97.
Smith, Greg M. *Film Structure and the Emotion System.* Cambridge: Cambridge University Press, 2003.
Snyder, Timothy. *The Reconstruction of Nations: Poland, Ukraine, Lithuania, Belarus, 1569–1999.* New Haven, CT: Yale University Press, 2003.
Sommer, Doris. "Irresistible Romance: The Foundational Fictions of Latin America." In Bhabha, *Nation and Narration,* 71–98.
Soyinka, Wole. *The Strong Breed.* In *Collected Plays 1.* New York: Oxford University Press, 1973, 113–46.
Soyinka, Wole. *The Swamp Dwellers.* In *Collected Plays 1.* New York: Oxford University Press, 1973, 79–112.
Spolsky, Bernard. *Language Policy.* Cambridge: Cambridge University Press, 2004.
Stephens, James. *The Insurrection in Dublin.* New York: Macmillan, 1917.
Stern, Jessica. *Terror in the Name of God: Why Religious Militants Kill.* New York: HarperCollins, 2003.
Stevenson, Robert W. "Tilak and the *Bhagavadgita*'s Doctrine of Karmayoga." In Minor, *Modern Indian Interpreters of the Bhagavadgita,* 44–60.
Szabo, Eliza. "Civilian Casualties in Afghanistan: Fatal Neglect." *Counterpunch,* July 20, 2007. www.copunterpunch.org.
Tagore, Rabindranath. *The Home and the World.* Trans. Surendranath Tagore. New York: Penguin, 1985.
Tagore, Rabindranath. *Nationalism.* New York: Macmillan, 1917.
The Tale of the Heike. Trans. Helen Craig McCullough. Stanford, CA: Stanford University Press, 1988.
Tan, Ed S. H., and Nico H. Frijda. "Sentiment in Film Viewing." In Plantinga and Smith, *Passionate Views,* 48–64.
Tangney, June Price. "Moral Affect: The Good, the Bad, and the Ugly." *Journal of Personality and Social Psychology* 61.4 (1991): 598–607.
Tlatli, Moufida, dir. *The Silences of the Palace.* Cinétéléfilms and Mat Films, 1994.
Tolstoy, Leo. *Anna Karenina.* Trans. David Magarshack. New York: New American Library, 1961.
Treibel, Annette. "Transformationen des Wir-Gefühls: Nationale und Ethnische Zugehörigkeiten in Deutschland." In *Transformationen des Wir-Gefühls: Studien zum Nationalen Habitus.* Ed. Reinhard Blomert, Helmut Kuzmics, and Annette Treibel. Frankfurt, Germany: Suhrkamp, 1993.
Trevor-Roper, Hugh. "The Invention of Tradition: The Highland Tradition of Scotland." In Hobsbawm and Ranger, *The Invention of Tradition,* 15–41.
Trumpener, Katie. *Bardic Nationalism: The Romantic Novel and the British Empire.* Princeton, NJ: Princeton University Press, 1997.
Tversky, Amos. "Features of Similarity." *Psychological Review* 84 (1977): 327–52.
Vālmīki. *Srimad Vālmīki Ramayanam.* 3 vols. Trans. N. Raghunathan. Madras, India: Vighneswara Publishing, 1981/1982.
van Dijk, Teun. *Communicating Racism: Ethnic Prejudice in Thought and Talk.* Newbury Park, CA: Sage, 1987.

Vaziri, Mostafa. *Iran as Imagined Nation: The Construction of National Identity.* New York: Paragon, 1993.
Verdery, Katherine. "Whither 'Nation' and 'Nationalism'?" In Balakrishnan, *Mapping the Nation*, 226–34.
Vietnam Veterans Against the War. *The Winter Soldier Investigation: An Inquiry into American War Crimes.* Toronto: Beacon Press, 1972.
Vogel, Jakob. "Militärfeiern in Deutschland und Frankreich als Rituale der Nation (1871–1914)." In François, Siegrist, and Vogel, *Nation und Emotion*, 199–214.
von Trotta, Margarethe, dir. *The Promise.* Bioskop, 1995.
Wachtel, Andrew Baruch. *Making a Nation, Breaking a Nation: Literature and Cultural Politics in Yugoslavia.* Stanford, CA: Stanford University Press, 1998.
Walby, Sylvia. "Woman and Nation." In Balakrishnan, *Mapping the Nation*, 235–54.
Walcott, Derek. *Omeros.* New York: Farrar, Straus, and Giroux, 1990.
Wallerstein, Immanuel. "Neither Patriotism Nor Cosmopolitanism." In *For Love of Country?* Ed. Joshua Cohen. Boston: Beacon Press, 2002, 122–24.
Weeks, William. *John Quincy Adams and the American Global Empire.* Lexington: University Press of Kentucky, 1992.
Weinberger, Eliot. "What is Happening in America?" *Vorwarts* (June 8, 2003). Available at http://www.dvmx.com/weinberger.html.
Wexler, Bruce E. *Brain and Culture: Neurobiology, Ideology, and Social Change.* Cambridge, MA: MIT Press, 2006.
Wheeler, M. E., and S. T. Fiske. "Controlling Racial Prejudice: Social Cognitive Goals Affect Amygdala and Stereotype Activation." *Psychological Science* 16 (2005), 56–63.
White, Hayden. *Metahistory: The Historical Imagination in Nineteenth-Century Europe.* Baltimore: Johns Hopkins University Press, 1973.
Whitman, Walt. "Song of Myself." In *Leaves of Grass.* Ed. Sculley Bradley and Harold W. Blodgett. New York: W. W. Norton, 1973, 28–89.
Wierzbicka, Anna. "Emotions." In *Semantic Primitives.* Trans. Wierzbicka and John Besemeres, 57–70. Frankfurt am Main, Germany: Athenaum Verlag, 1972.
Wigoder, Geoffrey, ed. *The New Standard Jewish Encyclopedia,* 7th ed. New York: Facts On File, 1992.
Wilkinson, Richard G. *Mind the Gap: Hierarchies, Health and Human Evolution.* New Haven, CT: Yale University Press, 2000.
Williams, Glanmor. "Wales–the Cultural Bases of Nineteenth and Twentieth Century Nationalism." In Mitchison, *The Roots of Nationalism*, 119–29.
Williams, Mark. "Mansfield in Maoriland: Biculturalism, Agency and Misreading." In *Modernism and Empire.* Manchester, UK: Manchester University Press, 2000, 249–74.
Wimmer, Andreas. *Nationalist Exclusion and Ethnic Conflict: Shadows of Modernity.* Cambridge, UK: Cambridge University Press, 2002.
Wolpert, Stanley. *Gandhi's Passion: The Life and Legacy of Mahatma Gandhi.* Oxford: Oxford University Press, 2001.
Wolpert, Stanley. *A New History of India.* 4th ed. New York: Oxford University Press, 1993.
Wyer, Robert S., Jr., and Thomas K. Srull, eds. *Perspectives on Anger and Emotion.* Hillsdale, NJ: Lawrence Erlbaum, 1993.
Yaeger, Patricia. *The Geography of Identity.* Ann Arbor: University of Michigan Press, 1996.
Yeats, William Butler. *The Collected Plays of W. B. Yeats.* New York: Macmillan, 1953.

Zajonc, Robert B. "Feeling and Thinking: Closing the Debate over the Independence of Affect." In Forgas, *Feeling and Thinking,* 31–58.
Zeami Motokiyo. "Atsumori." Trans. Arthur Waley. In *Masterpieces of the Orient.* Expanded ed. Ed. G. L. Anderson. New York: W. W. Norton, 1977.
Zinn, Howard. *Terrorism and War.* Ed. Anthony Arnove. New York: Seven Stories Press, 2002.

INDEX

Abigail of Carmel, 225
abortion, 145–46
Abrahams, Peter, 136, 308n3
Absolom, 226
actions: and affectivity, 104, 109–11, 178, 179; in epilogue of suffering, 210, 257, 262; in heroic tragicomedy, 209; and metaphors, 166; in narratives, 11–12, 167–68, 171, 172, 182, 185, 192, 200; and national ideologies, 212, 212n24; in sacrificial tragicomedy, 20, 292; in techniques of nationalization, 66. *See also* motivations; thought and action
activists, 39–40, 39n12, 41n13, 42, 141, 235–36, 302
adharma, 290, 296
Aeneid, 191
Aeoina-kamui, 122, 122n28
aesthetic appreciation, 106, 240. *See also* awe; wonder

affective mimicry, 96–97
affectivity: fostering in narratives, 169; and identity categories, 93–118; in identity hierarchies, 9, 9n14, 63–65, 63n24, 92–123; and in-groups, 5, 63, 67, 93–102, 108, 114–19, 121, 122, 180, 181, 260; and land, 63, 67, 102–5, 118–19; and language, 83; in "My Country 'tis of Thee," 163; and out-groups, 5, 63, 67, 94, 97–99, 101, 104–16, 119, 122, 180, 181, 260; and religion, 118–23; in "Song of Myself," 310, 317, 320. *See also* emotion
Afghanistan: and American collective memory of war, 140; and American group ideals, 49; causes and consequences of conflict in, 12; emotions regarding war in, 99; identity conflicts over

war in, 57; narrative of war in, 169, 170, 173, 183–87, 184nn12–13, 187n15, 240, 243–44, 256
Africa: affectivity toward land in, 118; cultural practices in, 40, 43; divinization of authority in, 119; durability in, 92; in metaphors, 135–36, 143, 146–47, 153–54; portrayal in *Independence Day*, 239. *See also* specific countries
African Americans, 31–32, 45–46, 97, 234, 236, 239, 317, 318, 321
Africans, 137–38, 150, 152–53, 153n17, 282
aggression, 172n5, 178, 179, 183, 200. *See also* violence
ahiṃsā, 288–90, 302. *See also* violence, Gandhi on
Ahinoam of Jezreel, 225
Ahriman, 122
Ainu, 122–23, 122n28
al-Aqsa Intifada, 218–19, 219n7
Algeria, 160
alignment nationalism: and affectivity, 114, 115, 119; and identity conflicts, 55–57; in *Mein Kampf*, 268; and metaphors, 142–43; and opposability, 86, 87, 87n12; and "Song of Myself," 319. *See also* nonelective alignment nationalism
allegories, 11n15, 135–37, 144, 146–47, 161, 225, 290, 307n3. *See also* narratives
al Qaeda, 107, 169, 170, 173, 183, 186, 187, 187n15, 243, 245
Alsace-Lorraine, 144
Amalekites, 223–26, 229
Ambady, Nalini, 47, 97
Ambedkar, B. R., 32
American character, 135–36, 138–39
American nationalism: and Brown's account of nationalism, 64n25; and global economic policies, 3n1; Goldman on, 330; in heroic tragicomedy, 17–18, 231, 237, 238, 238n18, 240, 246–47, 252, 254, 255, 260; identity conflicts in, 57; in "Song of Myself," 318, 322; study of, 7. *See also* United States
Amnesty International, 220, 220n7

amygdala, 31, 32, 47, 63, 97. *See also* neurological structures
anarchism: Goldman's goals regarding, 336, 336n15; and government, 328; and marriage and love, 333; and property, 325, 326; in romantic tragicomedy, 21, 308. *See also* Goldman, Emma
"Anarchism: What It Really Stands For" (Goldman), 328
"Anasaktiyoga" (Gandhi), 292
ancestry, 132n3, 149, 156–59, 164, 164n22, 165, 191, 192. *See also* family
Anderson, Benedict: on affectivity, 95; on durability, 91; on flag displays, 69; on imagination, 124; on metaphors, 142, 143, 156, 161; on prevalence of nationalist conflict, 2; on salient events, 74; on understanding of national community, 10
anger: in causal sequences, 176–79, 183, 187; emotions relating to, 200; in heroic tragicomedy, 240, 241, 247, 248, 253; and in-group/out-group division, 31, 106, 109–14, 109n19; metaphors for, 126–29; types of, 111–13
ANGER IS HEAT metaphor, 126–27
animal sacrifices, 294, 294n12
anniversaries, 92. *See also* holidays
Anscombe, Elizabeth, 177
anticolonialism, 4, 39–40, 42, 43, 285, 286, 290, 294, 301. *See also* colonialism
Antiochus, 227
anti-Semitism, 207, 271. *See also* Jews; *Mein Kampf* (Hitler)
Apartheid South Africa, 86
Appadurai, Arjun, 85
Area 51, 237, 238
Arendt, Hannah, 3n1, 56, 120, 122
Argentina, 120
Aristotle, 173, 249
Ark of the Covenant, 226, 227
Arndt, Ernst Moritz, 76
art, 40, 76, 103, 104
artha. *See* authority
articulatory metaphors, 129–30
artifacts. *See* public objects

Asian Americans, 97
Asians, 107, 150
Assamese, 160
assimilation, 40, 279
Ataturk, Kemal, 215
ātman, 297–98, 311, 314
Atsumori, 259
attachment, 103–5, 110, 117, 200, 291–93, 299, 300, 302
attentional focus, 6–7, 174, 175n7, 178n9, 184, 186
Atwood, Margaret, 141, 145–46
Australia, 40, 239
Austria, 92, 120, 269, 273, 276, 277
authority: divinization of, 119; as happiness goal, 196, 197; in heroic tragicomedy, 12, 195, 199, 216, 232, 240, 249, 253; in homogenization, 88; in in-group hierarchies, 115; in metaphors, 142, 157, 159, 166; rejection of, 53–54; in romantic tragicomedy, 195, 307, 315, 320, 324, 326–29, 333; and ruminative anger, 112; in sacrificial tragicomedy, 19; usurpation of in narrative, 12, 188, 194. *See also* dominance; hierarchies; national leaders
awakening, 141–42
awe, 117–18, 120, 240, 249. *See also* aesthetic appreciation; wonder
Aylmer, John, 120, 122

Baamba, 35
Babylonia, 119
"bad boss/bureaucracy" scenario, 53–54
Balakrishnan, Gopal, 216n4
Balibar, Etienne, 155n19
Bandura, A., 111
Banyoro, 35
Barbie dolls, 14–15
Barrès, Maurice, 144
basal ganglia, 63
Batoro, 35
Baxmann, Inge, 144, 148
BBC's *Nine O'Clock News,* 155
Befu, Harumi, 56
Bekerian, D. A., 196
Belgians, 36

benevolent/malevolent categorization: and divinization of national authority, 120; in emotional causality, 179–81, 179n11; in epilogue of suffering, 257, 259; in *Independence Day,* 235–37; and in-group/out-group division, 97–100; in King David story, 228; and land, 102–3; in national narratives, 171, 182, 183; in September 11 attacks emplotment, 243, 247, 250, 252, 254. *See also* heroes; villains
Bengal, 33, 135, 288
Bengalis, 56
Ben-Gurion, David, 225
Benhabib, Selya, 78
Bennington, Geoffrey, 173n6
Berkowitz, Leonard, 108, 178, 179
Berlin, 278
Bhabha, Homi, 151, 167
Bhagavad Gītā, 19, 42, 286–89, 303. *See also Mahābhārata*
Bharati, Uma, 159
Bharatiya Janata Party, 215
bias, 46–47, 152, 152n16, 173, 210
Biber, Douglas, 41
biblical stories, 17, 121, 229, 235n17. *See also* Christian fall and redemption story; King David story
Big Demon (Ainu), 122
Bihar earthquake, 285, 303
bin Laden, Osama, 107, 115, 170
birth, 144–47, 158, 161. *See also* pregnancy
The Birth of a Nation, 144
Black Demon, 122
blame, 178, 179
blood, 250, 250n23, 330
Bloom, Leopold, 190
Bloom, William, 5n8
body, 133, 142–48, 165, 166, 271, 272, 275, 278–80, 283
Bogle Corbet (Galt), 141
Bolívar, Simón, 159
Bombay, 307
The Book of Dede Korkut, 119, 122, 123, 215, 224
Book of Martyrs (Foxe), 121
border control, 162
Bose, Subhash, 118

Bosma, Harke A., 9n14
Botswana, 150–51
Bourdieu, Pierre, 25n2, 35, 142
Bower, G. H., 175–76
Boyer, Pascal, 33, 59, 127, 179, 181, 261
brahmacharya, 284, 296
brahman, 297–98, 311, 314. *See also* spirituality
bravery, 231, 245–46, 248, 250, 251, 276, 281
Breuilly, John, 7n9, 40, 168, 173n6
Brown, David, 6n8, 20, 39n12, 64n25
Brown, Judith, 286, 286n10, 302–3
Buckley, Anthony D., 161
Buddhism, 40
buildings. *See* public objects
Burma, 56
Bush, George W., 18, 49, 120, 162, 209–10, 218, 237, 240–56
Butola, B. S., 150

Cacioppo, John T., 176
Caesar, Julius, 158n20
calendar organization, 74–75
California, 233
Caliphate, 119
Calley, Lieutenant, 262
Cambodia, 140
Camden, William, 90
Canada, 141, 145–46, 146n14, 158
Canadians, 39
cancer, 143
Cannadine, David, 70, 72, 92, 119
Cape Gooseberry, 150–51
capitalism, 326
capitals, 70
Caribbean, 80, 150
Caspi, Arie, 218–20, 230
caste system, 88n12, 287–89, 306, 319. *See also* dharma
categorial identities: and affectivity, 98; cultural practices of, 38–41, 41n13, 43; definition and description of, 8, 8nn12–13, 9, 29; and emotion, 9, 9n14; interaction with practical identities, 24–37; in *Mein Kampf,* 277; in narratives, 16, 191, 194; and opposability, 81, 88; prototypes of, 16, 44–50; in September 11 attacks emplotment, 246; in social world, 34–35; in "Song of Myself," 309, 309n4, 312, 319, 320. *See also* identity categories; labeling
categorial unification, 80–82
Cathleen ni Houlihan (Yeats), 158, 161
Catholics, 24, 33, 52, 57, 62, 69–70, 120, 140, 276, 302
Caucasians, 97. *See also* European-Americans
causal attribution: and emotion, 174–81, 176n8; in national narratives, 12, 169–71, 173, 181–86; in September 11 attacks emplotment, 241. *See also* causal sequences
causal sequences: components of, 173; and emotion, 173–88; endings of, 12, 183–88, 241, 242; in epilogue of suffering, 257; Gandhi on, 208, 295–301; in heroic tragicomedy, 217; in identity forms, 33; inference of, 11n16, 201; in *Mein Kampf,* 269, 271–72, 279, 281, 282; and metaphors and narratives, 11n15; in national narratives, 167–68; of pride, 100–101; role of interest in, 174; in sacrificial tragicomedy, 265; and September 11 attacks, 12, 242, 243, 245, 254. *See also* causal attribution; resolution
CBS News polls, 24n1
La Chanson de Roland, 215
chastity, 284, 284n9. *See also* sex; sexual union
Chatterjee, Partha, 32
Chattopadhyay, Bankimchandra, 157, 159
Chein, Jason M., 178n9
Chiao, Joan, 97
Chifunyise, Stephen, 92
Chikamatsu Monzeamon, 197
children: identity hierarchies in rearing, 51; in *Independence Day,* 239, 239n19; in *Mein Kampf,* 280, 282; in metaphors, 137–38, 157–62, 164; in romantic tragicomedy, 305–7; in *Winter Soldier Investigation,* 261, 262
China, 2, 80, 85, 119, 157
Chinese, 56, 82

Chipasula, Frank, 160, 161
Chomsky, Noam, 28, 68, 143, 220n7, 258
Christian fall and redemption story: Gandhi's allusion to, 292; in *Mein Kampf,* 269, 278, 280–83; as sacrificial prototype, 14, 265; and shame, 113; theory of, 205
Christianity: as American group ideal, 49; clothing of, 87n12; and divinization of nation, 120, 123; and King David story, 217–18, 229; in *Mein Kampf,* 274; in metaphors, 137; and opposability, 62; in September 11 attacks emplotment, 255
Christian nationalism, 17, 267n1
Chronicles, 222, 222n13, 223, 226–29
Chua, Beng-Huat, 84, 86
Cialdini, Robert B., 37
Cilappatikāram, 190
citizenship, 77–79, 103, 104, 132–33, 149, 162
civilian casualties, 244, 244n22
Civil War, 144
class: of activists, 39n12; and cultural practices, 42; durability of, 60; and family metaphor, 10; in heroic tragicomedy, 251; in metaphors, 136; in narratives, 189; opposability of, 62; in romantic tragicomedy, 194, 195, 306, 318, 319; in sacrificial tragicomedy, 272, 275, 281; and social closure, 38n10
cleansing metaphor, 114, 143, 155, 155n19
Clore, Gerald L., 37, 47, 111, 175
clothing, 40, 86–88, 87n12, 105
coalition-building, 22n21, 100, 125n1, 206, 237–38, 254
Cockburn, Alexander, 226
cognitive contents, 59
cognitive neuroscience, 5–6. *See also* neurological structures
cognitive principles: of affectivity, 96, 97, 100, 109–11, 176, 179, 181; and emotion and categorial identity, 9n14; of heroic tragicomedy, 217; of human compassion, 250; of imagination, 124; in *Independence Day,* 231n15; of in-group/out-group division, 5, 31; of inhibition, 177, 177n9; of King David story, 222n13; of metaphors, 125n1, 126–28; in narratives, 172, 172n5, 173, 182, 183, 192, 207; in national identification, 64n25; of nationalist feelings, 3n3, 4n4, 5n7; of sacrificial tragicomedy, 266, 269–70; of salience, 58n18; in September 11 attacks emplotment, 250–51, 250nn23–24, 251n25
Cohn, Bernard S., 119
Cold War, 63
collective behaviors, 64n25, 73–76, 181, 286. *See also* group formation; group ideals; GROUPS ARE INDIVIDUALS metaphor
collective memory, 139
collective self-punishment, 284–304. *See also* divine punishment; self-sacrifice
Collins, Allan, 37
colonialism: and affectivity, 119; and categorial and practical identities, 35–36; and durability, 91; and governmental autonomy, 21n21; in metaphors, 137–38, 141, 143, 146, 151–54, 160; and nationalist feelings, 3n1; and opposability, 80; in romantic tragicomedy, 306, 331–33; in sacrificial tragicomedy, 266, 267, 281. *See also* anticolonialism; postcolonial literature
Columbus Day, 91–92
Commemoration of the Leipzig People's Battle of 1813, 76
communication, 129–30, 168. *See also* language
communists, 207, 270
compassion, 250–51. *See also* empathy
conceptual metaphors, 10–11, 124–25
conflicts: among identity categories, 54–58, 63, 268; identities in subnational, 36; and ideology, 230; metaphors for, 130, 131; monitoring of, 177, 177n9; opposability in, 88–89; patriotism in international, 23; prevalence of nationalist, 1–2. *See also* ethnic conflict; war
conformity, 50, 50nn15–16, 168. *See also* nonconformity

Congo, 36
Conrad, Susan, 41
consequences: of differences in identity categories, 54–55; in Goldman's political views, 209; of in-group/out-group division, 31, 33–34, 36, 37; of King David story, 17, 220, 221; of *Mein Kampf*, 267, 268; of metaphors, 125n1, 166; nationalism as force with, 5; in national narratives, 167–69, 172, 173, 178–79, 181, 182, 186, 188, 194; in romantic tragicomedy, 308n3; in sacrificial tragicomedy, 14, 284, 301; of social activists, 40
constructivism, 64n25
contents, 6, 8
Conway, M. A., 196
cooperative renewal, 267n2. *See also* resolution
coronations, 92
corpus striatum, 103
cortical processes, 177, 177n9, 183. *See also* neurological structures
countervailing emotions. *See* inhibition
Cracking India (Sidhwa), 143, 144
Crandell, William, 260
creation. *See* procreation
Cromwell, Oliver, 122
Cuddy, Amy, 32
cuisine. *See* food
Cullen, L. M., 84
cultural difference, 8
cultural narratives, 14
"cultural nationalism," 40n13
cultural patterns, 35
cultural practices, 37–44, 56, 76
The Culture of Conformism (Hogan), 279

Dahomeyans, 56
Damasio, Antonio R., 175
Daniel, S. C., 159
Davis, Dick, 215–16
death, 144–45, 149, 153, 293
Dedalus, Stephen, 190
defiance, 253–54, 258
dehumanization, 99, 229, 230, 254, 259, 261, 261n28, 330–32

democracy, 145, 148, 238, 238n18, 253. *See also* elections
Democracy in America (Tocqueville), 37
Deng, Francis, 121
deportation, 55
de Waal, Frans, 98
Dharasana, 303
dharma, 196, 287–90, 299, 302. *See also* caste system; *specific dharmas*
Dib, Mohammed, 160
dictatorships, 143, 164, 170
difference: focus of attention on, 6–7; in identity categories, 54–55; and identity hierarchies, 51; in in-group/out-group division, 43; in literary interpretation, 204–5; in metaphors, 131; in narratives, 15, 190, 192, 202; role in causal sequences, 174, 181, 187. *See also* opposability
Dinka poems, 121
disease: and affectivity, 114; in epilogue of suffering, 258; Gandhi on, 297; Goldman on, 333; as metaphor, 142–43, 271–72, 275, 278–83; pacifism as, 258, 278; in sacrificial tragicomedies, 264. *See also* disgust
disgust, 32, 32n8, 106, 114–15, 142–43
distrust, 106–7, 117, 181, 235n17. *See also* trust
Dittmer, Lowell, 1
diversity, 29, 56–57, 229, 314, 318–19
divine election: and affectivity, 119, 120; Goldman on, 331; in heroic tragicomedy, 214; in *Independence Day*, 231, 233–36, 238, 240; and in-group/out-group division, 48, 121, 121n27; in sacrificial tragicomedy, 270, 276, 304; in September 11 attacks emplotment, 242, 246–49, 252, 253, 255. *See also* religion
divine punishment, 264, 265, 279, 283, 285. *See also* collective self-punishment; religion
Dohrn, Bernardine, 107n18

dominance, 48–49, 101, 242. *See also* authority; hierarchies; superiority
Don't Think of an Elephant (Lakoff), 125n1
dorsolateral prefrontal cortex, 178n9
dress. *See* clothing
Dreyfus, Robert, 3n1
Dublin, 190
Duckitt, John H., 36, 45–46, 81n8
Duncan, Don, 263
durability: of clothing, 86–87; enhancing in narratives, 169; of happiness prototypes, 200, 200n19; in heroic tragicomedy, 213, 214, 233, 240; of holidays, 75; in identity hierarchies, 9, 60–63, 60n19, 89–92; of land in narrative, 192; of language, 83; of metaphors, 149, 155, 164, 165; of public objects, 69, 70, 72; of race in "Song of Myself," 310. *See also* history; memory systems
Dura, Mohammed, 219
During, Simon, 168
Dutt, Romesh Chunder, 294
Dutta, Binayak, 160
duty. *See* dharma

earthquakes, 285, 295, 303
economic conscription, 109
economy: in ethnic conflict, 61n22; globalization of, 85; Goldman on, 325, 327, 328, 333, 335; and nationalist feelings, 3n1; nation as unit of, 2; in "Song of Myself," 318; of U.S. and Iraq, 3. *See also* money
education, 83–84, 91, 96, 103, 139–40. *See also* schools
Egypt, 119, 239
Eisenberg, Nancy, 178
eisteddfod, 76
elections, 76, 101–2, 139, 148. *See also* democracy
elective alignment strategy, 55–56
elective identity categories, 60
Elizabethans, 90
Emmerich, Roland, 218
emotion: competition of, 177–78, 177n9; dissipation of, 110, 185; effect on categorial identification, 64n25; and environment, 176, 177, 179; and governmental autonomy, 21n21; in GROUPS ARE INDIVIDUALS metaphors, 135, 142–43; and happiness prototypes, 196, 197, 200; in heroic tragicomedy, 213, 214, 217, 240; and in-group/out-group division, 31, 36; and metaphors, 126–30, 132, 146n14, 165, 166; in narratives, 11, 13, 15, 168–69, 172–88, 174n7, 190, 192–94, 200–202, 210; in NATION IS A FAMILY metaphor, 154, 156, 157, 159; and prevalence of nationalism, 2; in prototype formation, 46–47; role in nationalist feelings, 5, 5n7, 6; in techniques of nationalization, 67; triggers of, 98, 99, 174–83; and understanding national community, 10. *See also* affectivity; protoemotion systems
emotional contagion, 96–97
empathy: decrease in, 172; in epilogue of suffering, 259, 261; and exempla, 96–97; in King David story, 228; in narratives, 172, 194, 195; in September 11 attacks emplotment, 244, 246, 247, 251; triggers of, 98, 99; in *Winter Soldier Investigation*, 257. *See also* compassion
emplotment: of epilogue of suffering, 210–11, 211n23, 218, 228, 256–63; explicit and implicit, 201–12, 266; of heroic tragicomedy, 201, 206, 208, 211–18, 260; of *Independence Day*, 201, 218, 230–40; of King David story, 201, 218–30; of *Mein Kampf*, 202, 207–8, 267, 268–84; of national narratives, 168, 169, 192, 197, 201–12; of real events, 189; of romantic tragicomedy, 208, 209, 211–12, 305–9; of sacrificial tragicomedy, 207, 208, 211–12, 264–68, 267n1, 273n8, 293–94, 298, 304; of September 11 attacks, 241–56; of "Song of Myself," 202, 208–9, 309–23; of war narratives, 182, 184, 188
England. *See* Great Britain

The Epic of Son-Jara, 189–91, 197, 215
epics, 189, 189n16, 215, 217, 236, 257. *See also specific titles*
epilogue of suffering: ambivalence in, 257, 257n27; description of, 18–19; emotional responses to, 194; emplotment of, 210–11, 211n23, 218, 228, 256–63; ethical values in, 195; and *Independence Day,* 239; as narrative, 203n20; in "Song of Myself," 321. *See also* heroic tragicomedy; suffering
episodic memory, 6, 26, 67, 175–76
Erikson, Erik, 286n10
Èṣù, 265
ethics: as goal of life, 196; in heroic tragicomedy, 208; in in-group/out-group division, 48; in metaphors, 137; in narratives, 195, 200; in sacrificial tragicomedy, 14, 208, 279, 281, 282, 288, 293
"ethnic cleansing," 114. *See also* genocide
ethnic conflict, 1, 2, 30n7, 61n22, 63n24
ethnic groups, 38n10, 72, 86, 95
ethnicity: affectivity of, 114, 180–81; distinction from nationalism, 3; and family metaphor, 10; functionality of, 61, 77; in heroic tragicomedy, 206, 251; as identity, 3n3, 4n4, 24, 29, 31, 32, 36, 40, 54, 55, 57; in *Mein Kampf,* 269, 276; in metaphors, 131, 155, 155n19, 156, 159; in narratives, 189; opposability of, 81, 85; in romantic tragicomedy, 306; in "Song of Myself," 310, 318, 319; Wimmer's models on, 64n25
Euripides, 197
Europe: colonialism of, 137–38; cultural practices in, 43; happiness-eliciting conditions for children in, 200; nationalism in, 2, 17; nonelective alignment nationalism in, 56; opposability in, 62, 106, 106n17; sleeping/waking metaphor in, 142
European-Americans, 45–46, 105, 107, 317, 322. *See also* Caucasians
Evans, Richard J., 268n4

exempla, 26–27, 95–97, 115–17, 214–15, 251
exile, 194, 224, 224n14, 228, 260, 263, 274, 305
explanations, plausible, 203–8, 211
expulsion, 114
extermination, 114, 279, 283

facial feedback, 96–97
Faiz, Faiz Ahmed, 160
familiarity, 95, 103, 104, 179, 179n11, 181, 190
family: in epilogue of suffering, 257–59, 262; in *Mein Kampf,* 273; in metaphors, 10, 11n15, 132–34, 132n3, 163, 166; in romantic tragicomedy, 305, 327. *See also* ancestry; children; NATION IS A FAMILY metaphor; parents
fascism, 142–43, 155, 266, 268. *See also* Nazism
Fauconnier, Gilles, 153
fear: in American schools, 107n18; in causal sequences, 176, 179, 185, 187; and divinization of national authority, 120; Gandhi on, 292, 295, 297, 300, 303; in in-group hierarchies, 115–17, 115n21, 116n22; and in-group/out-group division, 31, 32, 98, 101, 106–8, 110, 112; in narratives, 195, 241, 249
Federal Republic of Germany, 26n2
feminism, 34, 335–36
Ferdowsi, Abolquasem, 215–16
Fernando and Isabella, 56
festivals, 74–75. *See also* holidays
feudal nations, 119
fictional narrative, 217, 236, 304, 307, 307n2, 308n3
Fiedler, Leslie, 322n13
Fierstein, Harvey, 233
Fiez, Julie, 178n9
film, 189, 190, 217. *See also specific titles*
Finland, 91
Finnegans Wake (Joyce), 105
Fish, Stanley, 229
Fiske, Susan, 32
flag displays: after September 11 attacks, 68, 252, 253; in epilogue of

suffering, 260; in *Independence Day*, 232, 237; Israeli, 222; and pride, 102; salience of, 69n2; as technique of nationalization, 9
Flapan, Simha, 221
Fletcher, Bill, 107
Folk High Schools (Norway), 83
food: Gandhi on, 284–85, 292–95, 299, 302–3; as happiness goal, 199–200; in heroic tragicomedy, 213; identity through, 40; and in-group/out-group division, 106; in *Mein Kampf,* 273–74, 277, 280, 282; in moral prototypes, 172n4; and opposability, 84–85; in sacrificial tragicomedy, 14, 195, 264. *See also* hunger
Foster, Kevin, 12n16, 99, 120, 155–56, 214
founding fathers, 10, 155–58, 310. *See also* NATION IS A FAMILY metaphor; parents
Foxe, John, 121
FOX News/Opinion Dynamics Poll, 24n1
France: and divinization of nation, 119, 121, 122; durability of celebrations in, 92; in metaphors, 144, 153, 159, 160; opposability in, 84; as out-group in *Mein Kampf,* 277; public objects in, 70; salience of military in, 75; on U.S. invasion of Iraq, 23–24, 24n1, 53, 89, 186. *See also* French
François, Etienne, 2, 9n14, 71, 76
François, Gérard, 159
Franco-Prussian war, 148
Freedman, J. L., 196
freedom: Goldman on, 327, 329, 330, 332–36; as happiness goal, 196; in *Independence Day,* 231–33, 235, 236, 238, 239; in Iraq war narrative, 214; in "My Country 'tis of Thee," 164, 165; in narratives, 195; in romantic tragicomedy, 307; in September 11 attacks emplotment, 246, 253, 255; through death in sacrificial tragicomedy, 293
French, 106, 138. *See also* France
Frijda, Nico, 7, 108, 113, 174, 177
frustration, 110–11, 113, 177, 178

functionality: and affectivity, 95; of clothing, 87; of fear, 108–9; of heroic tragicomedy, 214, 240; in identity hierarchies, 9, 60–63, 60n21, 61n22, 64n25, 77–79, 78n7; of metaphors, 132, 165; of race in "Song of Myself," 310, 317; in war narratives, 185, 187, 187n15

Gallagher, Catherine, 106
Galloway, Joseph, 147
Galt, John, 141
Gandhi, Indira, 157, 158
Gandhi, Mohandas ("Mahatma"): on clothing, 87; comparison to Hitler, 286n10; on dharmas and violence, 287–89; explanations and interpretations of views, 208; on faith, 292; on flood, 298–99; on individual, 297–98, 311; on obedience to God, 297; on penance, 295–96; sacrificial tragicomedy of, 19–20, 267–68, 284–304; on salt regulations, 302–3; on self-defense, 301–2; on self-denial, 296–97, 301, 303; on service, 294–95; on social order, 284, 285, 295; on submission, 292; on three "virtues," 300; on unity of good and evil, 297–98; on war, 289–304
Gans, Chaim, 2, 40, 40n13
Gaza, 219n7
Gellner, Ernest, 1, 2
gender cues, 31–32
genocide: and Columbus Day celebrations, 92; cultural homogenization of survivors of, 40; disgust as motivation for, 114; and identity conflicts, 55, 58; and in-group/out-group division, 37; in Israel, 170n2; and *Mein Kampf,* 268, 268n5; and nonelective alignment nationalism in Germany, 56; in sacrificial tragicomedies, 19, 265
George V, king of Great Britain, 92
George VI, king of Great Britain, 92
German Democratic Republic, 26n2
Germania, 72, 147
Germans: and metaphors, 137, 138,

142, 144, 148, 155; nationalism during World War II, 268, 268n4; stereotypes of, 106; unity of, 306n1

Germany: categorial identity in, 38; and divinization of nation, 120, 122; durability in, 90; emplotment of nationalism, 267; functionality of citizenship in, 78; heroic tragicomedy in, 214; in-group hierarchy in, 117; in metaphors, 161; nonelective alignment nationalism in, 56; opposability in, 86; sacrificial tragicomedy in, 19, 207, 268–84; salience of military in, 75–76; on U.S. invasion of Iraq, 24n1; version of nationalism in, 8; in war narratives, 170

Gettysburg Address, 10, 90, 144, 158, 238n18

Ghana, 153–54

Ghurye, G. S., 87

Gikuyu, 118

Gilbert, Daniel T., 176

Gilgamesh, 218, 257

Gilman, Sander, 114

globalization, 1–2, 21n21, 85, 260, 308, 309, 323, 336. *See also* internationalism

goals, 11–12, 185–88, 192–93, 244, 292, 336, 336n15. *See also* happiness goals; resolution

"God Save the King," 163

Godwin, William, 141

Goldberg, Michelle, 17, 267n1

Goldman, Emma: on consumption, 326; on equality, 326; on freedom of speech and religion, 329, 332–34, 336; on government, 327–29, 330, 334, 336; on jealousy, 334; on marriage and love, 325–29, 333–37; on militarism, 329–32, 334; and patriarchal repression, 316n11; on philosophical principles, 209; on physical and mental appreciations, 326, 329; on property, 325–27, 334, 336; romantic tragicomedy of, 21, 209, 308, 324–37; on self-defense, 330, 331; on social action, 336–37; on social oppression, 335; on social relations, 325, 327; on transformation of society, 333–34

Goliad, 321

Goliath, 221, 221n10, 224, 236, 237, 244

Gonglah, H., 159–60

Goodwin, Jeff, 75–76

government, 4, 327–30, 334, 336

governmental autonomy, 21n21, 154. *See also* independence; national autonomy; self-determination

La Grande Maison (Dib), 160

Great Britain: divinization in, 119, 121–22; durability in, 90–92; in *Independence Day*, 237–38; in-group/out-group division in, 106; in *Mein Kampf*, 277; in metaphors, 141, 143, 144, 148, 155–56, 160–65; outlawing of Scottish dress, 87; in romantic tragicomedy, 306; in sacrificial tragicomedy, 266, 284, 286, 289–91, 294, 298, 302, 303; in "Song of Myself," 310

Greece, 56, 90, 91, 277

Greek epics, 189, 189n16

Greenblatt, Stephen, 106

Greenfeld, Liah: on affectivity, 119, 120, 122; on durability, 90; on heroic tragicomedy, 214; and in-group/out-group division, 36, 37; on metaphors, 134, 137, 147, 153, 159

Greenspan, Ezra, 20

Greenwald, Anthony, 49

grief: and benevolent/malevolent categorization, 98, 99; and happiness prototypes, 196; in heroic tragicomedy, 248; metaphor for sharing, 133; persistence of, 110; in September 11 attacks emplotment, 241, 241n20, 242, 246. *See also* sorrow

Griffiths, D. W., 144

group formation, 24–25, 29, 38–40, 38n10, 132. *See also* collective behaviors

group ideals, 44–50, 50n16, 53. *See also* collective behaviors; ideals

GROUPS ARE INDIVIDUALS metaphor, 134–36, 134n6, 141, 147–48, 159–60

guilt, 141, 265, 291
Gujarat, 32–33
Gujarati speakers, 39
Gulf War, 234, 235, 236
Guy Mannering (Scott), 162
Gypsies, 56

Ha'aretz Magazine, 218, 220
Habermas, Jürgen, 2
habituation, 172
habitus, 25n2
Hankin, James, 36, 37, 58, 168
Hanukah, 227
happiness goals: cross-cultural studies of, 196–201; in heroic tragicomedy, 216; in narrative prototypes, 13, 15–16, 192, 193, 193n17, 194–201; in sacrificial tragicomedy, 273–74. *See also* goals
happiness prototypes, 196–201, 324, 325, 327–30, 333–36
Hapsburg monarchy, 92
Haram al-Sharif, 191, 228
Hardman, Charlotte, 200
Hardt, Michael, 21n21
Harris, Paul, 32, 200
Haugland, Kjell, 83
Head, Bessie, 141, 150–51
health, 199–200, 213
Hébert, Anne, 158
Hegel, G. W. F., 138
Henri IV (of France), 159
Henry V, king of England, 121–22
Henry VIII, king of England, 56
Herb, Guntram H., 102, 103
Herman, Edward S., 58, 170n2
heroes, 117, 122, 123, 186–88, 190, 210, 234. *See also* benevolent/malevolent categorization; heroic tragicomedy
heroic nationalism, 64n25
heroic tragicomedy: benevolent/malevolent categorization in, 182; Bush's speech as, 240–56; characters in, 232–34, 235n17, 239n19; as cross-cultural narrative prototype, 198–200, 217; as default for nationalism, 16, 20; descriptions of, 12, 17–18; development principles of, 188–89; divinization of in-groups in, 121; emplotment of, 201, 206, 208, 211–18, 260; happiness goals in, 13, 15–16, 193–201; and "My Country 'tis of Thee," 163, 165; organization of, 222–23, 222n13; popular, 217, 231; pride in, 100; rewards and punishments in, 199; and romantic tragicomedy, 21, 306, 320, 321, 324, 327–31, 333, 335–37, 336n15; and sacrificial tragicomedy, 266, 269, 270, 273, 273n8, 276–78, 280, 281, 283, 288, 290–92, 295, 297, 298, 300–304; significance of place in, 191; social conditions for, 209, 216; social impact of, 17; structures of, 14, 188; and Winter Soldier Investigation, 19. *See also* epilogue of suffering; heroes; *Independence Day;* King David story; war
Herzfeld, Michael, 133, 180
hierarchies: affectivity in in-group, 115–18, 115n21, 116n22; and anger, 112, 114; of categorial and practical identities, 9; coercion in identity, 52; divinization of authority in political, 120; downward comparisons in, 36; effect of fear on, 108–9; in ethnic conflict, 61n22; in group ideals, 48–49; in heroic tragicomedy, 213, 240, 248, 249, 253–55, 276; identities in social, 50–54; and identity conflicts, 57–58; and metaphors, 132, 137, 142, 143, 154, 157, 159, 166; and narrative prototypes, 16, 216; parameters of identity category, 58–67; preferences for, 64n25; religion in, 119; role of social in narrative, 188, 194–95; in romantic tragicomedy, 21, 306–8, 320, 321, 323, 324, 327, 329, 331–33; in sacrificial tragicomedy, 276, 288, 301–2; Swazi political, 92. *See also* authority; dominance
Hind Swaraj (Gandhi), 290
Hindus: categorial and practical identities of, 32–34; collective memory of, 140; divinization of nation, 122; ethical theory, 286–89;

Gandhi on conflict with Muslims, 295–96; in heroic tragicomedy, 14, 215, 217; in metaphors, 135, 144, 159; opposability of, 62, 84, 86; in romantic tragicomedy, 14, 307; and sacrificial tragicomedy, 19, 267; significance of place to, 191–92; situational identification of, 43. See also *Bhagavad Gītā*
historical events, 60n19, 89–92
historical particularity, 8
history: and affectivity, 93, 96, 101, 103, 176; in allegory, 136; and differences in categorial identities, 64n25; and elective alignment strategy, 56; emplotment of, 189; in epilogue of suffering, 18–19; and heroic tragicomedy, 217, 217n5, 240; of hunger in India, 294; in King David story, 221; in *Mein Kampf*, 270, 271, 278, 283–84; in metaphors, 11n15, 138–41, 152–53, 158, 159, 164; in narratives, 12–14, 16, 16n19, 191; nationalism in, 3, 3n3, 40; nationality of, 73n3; role in nationalist feelings, 5–7, 7n9; in romantic tragicomedy, 307; in sacrificial tragicomedy, 19, 207, 304; in September 11 attacks emplotment, 245, 246, 255; as university discipline, 91; in war narratives, 170. See also durability; memory systems
Hitchens, Christopher, 225
Hitler, Adolf: comparison to Gandhi, 286n10; comparison to Goldman, 333; on divinization of national authority, 120; and emplotment of *Mein Kampf*, 202, 267; metaphor for, 143; nonelective alignment nationalism of, 56; on unification of Germans outside Germany, 306n1; use of prototypes in *Mein Kampf*, 273, 273n8. See also *Mein Kampf* (Hitler)
Hobbes, Thomas, 147
Hobsbawm, Eric, 69, 72, 83, 89, 92, 118, 148, 155–57
Hoffmann, Stefan-Ludwig, 76, 142, 155

holidays, 74–75, 88, 91–92, 227. See also specific holidays
Holinshed, Raphael, 90
Holocaust, 170, 218, 221n10, 267, 268
Holy Roman Empire, 119
home: and affectivity, 103–5; Gandhi on, 301; in King David story, 221, 227; in *Mein Kampf*, 268, 269, 271, 273, 274; in metaphors, 161–62, 227; in narratives, 191, 194, 199; in sacrificial tragicomedy, 265, 266, 291; in September 11 attacks emplotment, 245, 254. See also housing; land
The Home and the World (Tagore), 135, 160
Homeland Security, Department of, 162, 245
Homer, 90
homogenization: and affectivity, 63, 95; and identity conflicts, 54–56; and identity hierarchies, 50–51; and metaphors, 138, 152; of outgroups, 81, 81n8; through collective activities, 76; through cultural practices, 40–43, 40n13, 81–85, 81n9, 87, 87n12, 88; through self-concepts and group ideals, 44
homophobia, 114
homosexuality, 29, 233, 312–14, 313n10, 316, 322, 322n13. See also pansexuality; sex
Horowitz, Donald, 30, 30n7, 56, 60n20, 61n22, 62, 63n24, 97
housing, 85–86. See also home
Hubbard, Al, 259, 260
Hudson, R. A., 28
human life cycle: in metaphors, 147. See also birth; death
human sacrifice, 299, 299n13
humiliation, 113, 325
humility, 300
Hungary, 92, 143
hunger: binding effect of, 105; emotions relating to, 200; in heroic tragicomedy, 216; and in-group/out-group division, 106; in sacrificial tragicomedy, 264, 266, 267, 267n2, 269, 274, 277, 278, 294, 295, 303, 304. See also food

Hussein, Saddam, 3, 115, 164, 169, 178–79, 183, 214, 245
hybridization, 151

Iblis (Satan), 122
Iceland, 215
ideals, 14, 15, 105–6, 120, 326, 330. *See also* group ideals
Identity and Emotion (Bosma and Kunnen), 9n14
identity categories: conflicts among, 54–58, 63, 268; elective vs. nonelective, 55; in emotional causality, 180–81; functionality in times of conflict, 61n22; and ideology, 230; metaphors for, 132, 133, 142–43; parameters of hierarchization of, 58–67; in romantic tragicomedy, 306, 307, 323, 331; social function of, 61; in war narratives, 186, 194, 232, 241. *See also* categorial identities
identity divisions, 16
identity formation, 8, 10, 29. *See also* categorial identities; practical identities
identity groups, 37–44, 61, 166, 232, 254
ideology: of American nationalism, 231, 237, 238, 238n18, 252, 254, 255; Brown's view of nationalism as, 64n25; of Israeli nationalism, 229, 230; in narrative emplotment, 212, 212n24; in prototype formation, 47
idiosyncratic narratives, 198, 202, 210
Illiad, 189, 211n23, 218, 235
imagination: and affectivity, 106–11, 113, 120; in heroic tragicomedy, 214, 219, 221; and metaphors, 129, 135, 137; of nation, 124; and national emplotment, 200; of unity in "Song of Myself," 312–13
imitations, 96
immaterial labor, 22n21
immigration, 55, 150–51, 151n15, 162, 164, 164n22
immortality, 145
inaugurations, 92

Inca empire, 119
independence, 195, 266, 286, 294, 295, 297, 303. *See also* governmental autonomy; national autonomy; self-determination
Independence Day, 18, 201, 205, 211, 218, 230–40, 254
Independence Day of United States (July 4), 75, 92
India: affectivity toward land in, 118; categorial and practical identities in, 32–34; cultural practices in, 42; divinization of authority in, 119, 122; durability in, 89–91; functionality in, 61; heroic tragicomedy in, 14, 215, 217, 224n14; human sacrifice in, 299n13; idea of individual in, 297–98, 311; in metaphors, 135, 137, 138, 143, 144, 148, 157, 159, 160, 162; narratives set in, 189–92; opposability in, 62, 84, 85, 86, 87; reception of Gandhi's views in, 208, 286; romantic tragicomedy in, 14, 307; sacrificial tragicomedy in, 19, 266, 267, 284–304; version of nationalism in, 8
"Indian Tamils," 56
individuals: and affectivity, 95–96, 117, 181; Gandhi on, 292, 297–98; happiness goals of, 13; in heroic tragicomedy, 216, 253, 281; identity of, 8n13; in *Mein Kampf*, 281, 282; in metaphors, 10, 133–48, 134n6, 166; in narrative prototypes, 16, 199; and rational self-interest, 64n25; in romantic tragicomedy, 307, 329–31; in "Song of Myself," 311, 315–16. *See also* swadharma
"The Individual, Society and the State" (Goldman), 329, 331
Indonesia, 161
inegalitarian social equilibrium, 51n17
inferential metaphors, 129–31, 135
ingenuity, 231, 233, 238, 239, 250
in-groups: and affectivity, 5, 63, 67, 93–102, 108, 114–19, 121, 122, 180, 181, 260; boundary with out-group, 38n10; categorial and practical identities of, 29–34,

30n6, 36–37; cognitive principles of, 5; cultural practices of, 37–38, 40, 43, 44; durability of, 60n19, 91; in epilogue of suffering, 259; happiness goals in narrative, 193, 194; in heroic tragicomedy, 12, 13, 213, 216, 226, 228, 232, 235–36, 243, 244, 247, 250, 252–54; and identity formation, 8–9; and identity hierarchies, 53, 64n25; in metaphors, 132, 137, 138, 141, 142–43; in narratives, 186, 191, 199; opposability of, 80, 81, 85–87, 87n12; prototypes of, 45–50, 50n15; in romantic tragicomedy, 306–8, 331–33, 336; in sacrificial tragicomedy, 19, 264, 265, 266, 269, 276, 277, 279, 281, 283, 291, 296

inhibition: as anger trigger, 109–10; in emotional causality, 177–80, 177n9, 183; emotions relating to, 200; and in-group/out-group division, 32, 194; of joy and sorrow, 105; in narratives, 201; in romantic tragicomedy, 305, 333

"initiating events," 182–83

The Injustice Done to Tou Ngo, 116n24

insanity, 141

insula, 32, 63

internal enemies, 19, 113–15

internationalism, 270–72, 275, 281, 283, 307, 308. *See also* globalization; transnational affiliations; universalism

international solidarity, 8, 21

interpretations, reportable, 203–8, 211

Iran, 3, 119, 122, 215–16

Iraq: allusion to in *Independence Day,* 233, 234, 237–38, 240; and American collective memory of war, 140; functionality of identities in, 61n22; identity conflicts over war in, 57; narrative of war in, 169, 170, 187, 214, 256; nationalism in, 3n1; opposability of U.S. decision to invade, 23–24, 89, 186; and September 11 attacks, 68, 243–45; U.S. demoralization of, 118; U.S. ideals in invasion of, 44, 49; U.S.

identity hierarchy in invasion of, 53; U.S. invasion of, 2–3

Iraq Veterans Against the War (IVAW), 256

Ireland: affectivity toward land in, 118; civil war in, 156; collective memory in, 140; and divinization of nation, 122; durability in, 91; in metaphors, 153n18, 158–61; in narratives, 190; sacrificial tragicomedy in, 267. *See also* Northern Ireland

Irish character, 138

Irish diet, 106

Irish nationalists, 84, 155, 158–59, 190

Ishbaal (son of Saul), 226

Islam, 63. *See also* Muslims

isolation. *See* exile

Israel, 191, 219, 219n7, 221, 238, 243. *See also* King David story

Israeli Defense Forces, 219n7

Israeli nationalism, 17, 18, 170, 170n2, 217–20, 220n9, 229–30

Italy, 85

Ito, Tiffany, 31, 32, 176

Ivory Coast riots, 56

Jain self-starvation, 293

Jaipur, 86

Japan, 56, 119, 121, 197, 238

Java, 33

Jela, Ban, 119–20

Jerusalem, 191, 222, 226, 227

Jerusalem Bible, 229

Jesus, 265, 280

Jews: clothing of, 87n12; and disgusting associations, 114–15; and divinization of nation, 121; festivals of, 227; functionality of citizenship in Eastern Europe, 78; and heroic tragicomedy of Muhammad, 230; images of, 218, 220; in *Independence Day,* 23, 233, 239; in *Mein Kampf,* 207, 268, 269, 271, 275–76, 279, 280, 282–83; metaphors for, 143; and nonelective alignment nationalism in Germany, 56; and opposability, 62, 84, 86; significance of place to,

191; stereotypes of, 106. *See also* King David story
Jezreel, 224, 225
John Paul II, Pope, 57
Johnson, Mark, 126
Jones, John Paul, 321
Jordens, J. T. F., 286
journeys. *See* tourism
joy, 99–101, 105, 110. *See also* pride
Joyce, James, 105, 190
Judah, 191, 221, 225–27, 229
Juergensmeyer, Mark, 113
July 4th. *See* Independence Day
jus sanguinis, 78, 79
jus soli, 78, 79
justice. *See* law

Kádár-Fülop, Judit, 83
Kahneman, Daniel, 7, 174
kāma. *See* pleasure
Kaplan, David, 3n3
Kaplan, Justin, 313
Kasfir, Nelson, 35–36
Kennedy, Miranda, 161
Kenney, Catherine, 161
Kenya, 118, 143, 146–47
Kerr, David, 92
Kerry, John, 117, 117n25, 218, 256, 258
khadi, 87
Khan, Mehboob, 158
kilts, 86–87
Kim, Samuel, 1
King David story: allusion to in *Independence Day*, 233; in Arab world, 221, 229–30; division of story, 222, 222n13; emplotment of, 201, 218–30; as heroic tragicomedy, 17, 18; interpretations of, 205; journey in, 191; as paradigmatic narrative, 217–18. *See also* Goliath
King Lear (Shakespeare), 141
King, Martin Luther, 19
1 Kings, 222, 222n13, 226, 228, 229
Kirson, Donald, 196–97
Klepfisz, Irena, 221n10
Klinge, Matti, 91
Kohn, Hans, 121
Kondh people, 299n13

Kondo, Hirohito, 178n9
Kosovo Temple of Ivan Meštrović, 69–70
Krendl, Anne C., 32, 47
kṣatriyadharma, 287, 288, 289, 291, 299
Kunda, Ziva, 31, 46, 47
Kunnen, Saskia, 9n14
Kuo, Eddie, 84, 86
Kurds, 40, 82–83, 143

labeling, 36–38, 36n9, 63. *See also* categorial identities
Labor Day, 75
Lakoff, George, 124–27, 125n1
Lamprecht, Gerhard, 267n2
land: and affectivity, 63, 67, 102–5, 118–19; durability of, 90; functionality of, 78; in heroic tragicomedy, 206, 232; in metaphors, 10, 132–34, 144, 148–54, 163–66; in narratives, 188–92; in sacrificial tragicomedy, 283; salience of, 70–72. *See also* home; territory; tourism
Landsmal, 83
Langer, Gary, 117n25
language: affectivity of, 114; affirmation of American in "Song of Myself," 310; Brown's three conceptual, 64n25; functionality of, 77, 78, 82–83; and identity conflicts, 55, 56; identity through, 28, 35, 38–42, 38n11, 41n13. *See also* communication; speech
Latimer, Hugh, 120
Latin America, 156–57, 159, 306–7
Latin American literature, 16n18
law: and affectivity, 116, 116n24; collective memory of, 140; functionality of, 77–79; homogenization through, 83; as inclusion criterion, 132; in metaphors, 148; as requirement for statehood, 4; in sacrificial tragicomedies, 265; as technique of nationalization, 9
Lawrence, D. H., 314
Leaves of Grass (Whitman), 20, 308. *See also* "Song of Myself" (Whitman)

Leviathan, 147
Levi, Werner, 4, 132, 144, 148
Lewin, Nathan, 226
lexical connections, 127–28, 130
liberalism, 306, 306n1
Liberation Tigers of Tamil Elam (LTTE), 284n9
Lincoln, Abraham, 10, 144, 158
Lincoln memorial, 234
literary theories, 204–7, 205n21
literature: and affectivity, 103, 115; divinization of nation in, 121–22; durability of, 90–91; epilogue of suffering in, 218; happiness prototypes in, 197–200; identity through, 40; land in, 190; and narrative prototypes, 192, 193. *See also* narratives; poetry
Li, Wai-yee, 214n1
London, 70
Los Angeles, 235–36, 238
love: emplotment in poetry, 202; forbidden in "Song of Myself," 316–23; Goldman on, 324, 325, 327, 333–37; as happiness goal, 196, 197; in narratives, 188. *See also* romantic relations; romantic tragicomedy
"A Love Poem for My Country" (Chipasula), 160
loyalty, 48, 53, 152
Lunda empire, 92
Luo, Guanzhong, 157
lust, 105, 128
Lyons, F. S. L., 153n18

Maas, Annette, 90, 189, 214
MacPhee, Graham, 3n1
Mahābhārata, 218, 257, 288–304. See also *Bhagavad Gītā*
Maharashtra, 288
Malaysian citizenship, 56
malevolence. *See* benevolent/malevolent categorization
Mali, 157, 191, 197, 215
Malinowski, S. Bronislow, 92
Malvinas/Falkland Islands War, 12n16, 99, 120, 155–56, 214
Mandeville (Godwin), 141

"Manifesto on *Ars Poetica*" (Chipasula), 161
Mann, Michael, 2
Manu (Gandhi's assistant), 284
Marathi speakers, 39
marriage: Goldman on, 325–29, 333–37; in "Song of Myself," 317, 320–22, 322n13
"Marriage and Love" (Goldman), 325–28, 332, 335
Martin Luther King Day, 74–75
martyrdom. *See* self-sacrifice
Marxists, 34, 109, 125n1, 136, 270, 279
mascots, 147
Mau Mau revolutionaries, 143, 147
McDonald's, 84, 84n10, 85
McHugh, Roger, 153n18
Mecca, 191
media: and affectivity, 99–101, 107, 115, 116, 116n24, 179; durability of, 90; and metaphors, 139; and popular heroic tragicomedy, 231; role in war narrative, 184, 184n13, 187, 214; and salience, 72–73, 73n4
medial prefrontal cortex, 30. *See also* neurological structures
Mein Kampf (Hitler), 19, 202, 207–8, 267–84
"melting pot," 42. *See also* homogenization
Memorial Day, 75
memorials, 91–92. *See also* holidays
memory systems: and affectivity, 93, 98, 99, 108–11, 113; description of, 6; and durability, 60n19; in emotional causality, 177, 178, 178n9, 183; in heroic tragicomedy, 231n15; and identity formation, 26; and metaphors, 129, 138–41, 139n10; role in causal sequences, 174, 175–76; salience for, 175, 177, 181. *See also* durability; history; *specific types of memory*
Meštrović, Ivan, 69–70
Mészáros, István, 2
Metahistory (White), 16n19
metaphors: "blends" of, 153, 153n18; and concrete images, 129; description of, 124–25, 125n1; for disgust,

114; in epilogue of suffering, 258; framing through, 125n1; homological forms of, 133–34; in *Mein Kampf,* 268, 271; in "My Country 'tis of Thee," 163–66; national character in, 135–36, 138–39; nation as family, 154–62; nation as individual, 134–48; nation as land, 148–54; patterns of, 126–34; public objects as, 69; religious, 119; social generalization of, 127; in "Song of Myself," 310–11; spatial and temporal mappings on body, 144–45; as technique of nationalization, 67; types of, 129–30; for understanding national community, 10–12, 11n15. *See also* schemas; *specific metaphors*
Midnight's Children (Rushdie), 89, 144, 162, 308n3
military: and affectivity, 109, 112, 117–18; cognitive tendencies toward aggression of, 172n5; functionality of, 79; Goldman on, 329–32, 334; in heroic tragicomedy, 216, 228, 230, 234–36, 241–42, 244–46, 248, 250–52, 254–56; in metaphors, 142, 156; in narratives, 195; opposability of, 88; in romantic tragicomedy, 306; in sacrificial tragicomedy, 276, 278, 280–81, 288, 294, 298, 300–304; salience of, 75–76. *See also* war; *Winter Soldier Investigation* (Vietnam Veterans Against the War)
Miller, James, 7, 174, 312
Milton, John, 122
mimeticist, nation as, 136–37
The Mimic Men (Naipaul), 150
mind, 137, 141–42
The Mind and Its Stories (Hogan), 94, 193, 193n17, 202
Mine Boy (Abrahams), 136
minorities, 56
mirrors, 96, 172, 315
miscegenation, 281–83, 313
Mitchell, Jason P., 30
Mitchison, Rosalind, 3
modern states, 3–5, 4nn4–5, 7, 18, 64n25

money, 72, 280, 282, 296. *See also* economy
Monroe, Kristen Renwick, 36, 37, 58, 168
monuments. *See* public objects
mood congruent processing, 175–76, 175n8
Moodie, Susanna, 140
mood repair, 175, 175n8
moral evaluations: prototypes of, 171–72, 172n4, 172n5; in romantic tragicomedy, 333, 334; in sacrificial tragicomedy, 264–65, 279, 280, 290, 291, 295–301; in war narratives, 170–73, 182, 244, 244n22, 249, 256, 257, 260
moral principles, 188, 194, 195
Morgan, Prys, 71
mothers, 11n15, 157, 163, 334, 335. *See also* parents; women
motivations: and affectivity, 93, 109, 178, 179; in epilogue of suffering, 218; and governmental autonomy, 21n21; and identity conflicts, 57; for individual and collective behaviors, 64n25; and in-group/out-group division, 36, 109; and metaphors, 166; in narratives, 13, 172; for nationalist feelings, 5; and prevalence of nationalism, 2; salience of, 68; in September 11 attacks emplotment, 243. *See also* actions; goals
Moyers, Bill, 17
Mueller, Adam, 147, 148
Muhammad, 119, 191, 229–30
Mumbai, 39
Mumbi, 118
Mumby, Dennis, 12n16, 168
Murnau, F. W., 267n2
museums, 90. *See also* public objects
music, 40, 103, 104. *See also* "My Country 'tis of Thee"; national anthems
Muslims: categorial and practical identities of, 32–34; collective memory of, 140; cultural practices of, 43, 44; and divinization of nation, 123; Gandhi on conflict with Hindus, 295–96; on heroic tragi-

comedy of Muhammad, 229–30; in *Independence Day*, 239; in metaphors, 135, 137, 144, 159; and nonelective alignment nationalism, 56; opposability of, 62, 63, 84, 86; in romantic tragicomedy, 307; and September 11 attacks, 68; significance of place to, 191; and Temple Mount conflict, 228; in war narrative, 170
Mussolini, Benito, 143
Mwindo Epic, 218, 224, 257
"My Country 'tis of Thee," 10, 163–66
My Lai massacre, 262
mysticism, 42
mythology, 91, 215, 230

Nagaland, 160
Naipaul, V. S., 150
Nairn, Tom, 7n9
Nandy, Ashis, 32, 42, 43, 86, 91, 138, 285, 288
Narrative and Social Control (Mumby), 12n16, 168
narrative middle, 193, 193n17, 197, 241, 241n20, 242, 254, 281
narratives: affectivity in, 93, 117; characters in, 186, 188–92; development principles of, 169, 188–92; disgust in, 114; family metaphors in, 154, 157; goals and actions in, 11–13, 11nn15–16; hierarchies in American national, 53; mental structures of, 201–12; organization of, 203, 207–8, 244, 249; patriotic metaphors in, 163; public objects in, 69–70; structures of patriotic, 167–69; as technique of nationalization, 67, 166; on war, 12, 169–73, 181–88, 194. *See also* allegories; heroic tragicomedy; literature; romantic tragicomedy; sacrificial tragicomedy
national anthems, 73–76, 102, 102n14, 157, 163, 215
national autonomy, 3, 3n1, 21n21, 54. *See also* governmental autonomy; independence; self-determination
National Cathedral (Washington, D.C.), 218, 242

national center, 191–92, 227
national consciousness, 142
nationalism: criticism of, 166; definition of, 4; prevalence of, 1–5; role of social trends in, 5–6; study of histories of, 7–8
nationalization, techniques of, 9, 66
national leaders, 157–58. *See also* authority; presidents
nation-building, 56, 154
NATION IS A FAMILY metaphor: description of, 144–45, 154–62; Lakoff on, 125n1; in September 11 attacks emplotment, 253–55; in "Song of Myself," 310, 314, 318, 322. *See also* family; founding fathers
NATION IS A GARDEN metaphor, 153
NATION IS A HOME metaphor, 161–62, 227. *See also* home
NATION IS AN INDIVIDUAL metaphor, 145, 146, 148. *See also* individuals
NATION IS THE LAND metaphor, 149–54, 163–66. *See also* land
NATION IS A MOTHER metaphor, 11n15. *See also* mothers
NATION IS A PERSON metaphor, 72, 136, 221n10, 247, 248, 250, 309, 311
nation-state, 2, 3n1, 21n21, 79, 168
Nation und Emotion (François, Siegrist, and Vogel), 9n14
Native Americans, 42, 141, 268n5, 317, 322
naturalization, 78–79
Nazism: affectivity of, 114–15, 118; and Christian nationalism, 267n1; development of party, 283; on disabled, 280; and elective alignment strategy, 56; on food and hunger, 277; metaphors in, 143; and opposability, 86; in sacrificial tragicomedy, 207, 265, 267. *See also* fascism; *Mein Kampf* (Hitler)
Negri, Antonio, 21n21
Nehru, Jawaharlal, 302
neighborhood metaphor, 162
Nepal, 200
Nesse, R. M., 103
network theory, 21n21

neurological structures: and affectivity, 63, 103, 180–81; as basis for modern nationalism, 64n25; in categorial and practical identities, 30–31, 33, 36, 37; and inhibition, 177, 177n9; in prototype formation, 27n4, 47. *See also* amygdala; cortical processes
Nevada, 237
New Mexico, 232
news, 24n1, 73, 73n4; emplotment of, 189. *See also* media
New York, 233, 235, 236, 243
New York Times, 99
New Zealand, 118
Ngũgĩ wa Thiong'o, 146–47, 308n3
Nicolson, Harold, 92, 119
Nigeria, 160
Nihonjinron, 56
Nisbett, Richard E., 46
Njalssaga, 215
Njegoš, Petar, 119–20
nonconformity, 53. *See also* conformity
nonelective alignment nationalism, 56, 279. *See also* alignment nationalism
nonelective identity categories, 60
nonordinary. *See* difference
nonstories, 207–10, 217
nonviolence. *See* ahimsā; violence
normalcy: in epilogue of suffering, 203n20; in moral prototypes, 172n5; role in narrative structure, 11n15, 174, 184, 187, 188, 192; in sacrificial tragicomedies, 265, 270; in September 11 attacks emplotment, 241, 241n20, 242, 245
Northern Ireland, 33, 61, 62, 161. *See also* Ireland
Norwegian nationalism, 83
Nosferatu, 114, 267n2
novels, 202
novelty. *See* difference
Nusbaum, Howard C., 31
Nussbaum, Martha, 93, 114–15, 314, 316, 316n11, 317

Oatley, Keith, 93, 100, 103, 175, 180–81
object categorization, 58–59

O'Brien, Edna, 158–59
O'Casey, Sean, 153n18
O'Connor, Eugene, 158n20
O'Connor, Ulick, 196–97
Ofeimun, Odia, 160
O'Flaherty, Liam, 156
Olorunsola, 36
Olthof, Tjeert, 200
Olympics, 101
Omeros (Walcott), 135–36, 152–53, 153n17
Ong, Walter, 147
opposability: in heroic tragicomedy, 213, 214, 240; in identity hierarchies, 9, 62, 63, 80–89; of metaphors, 132, 138, 146, 149, 163, 165; in sacrificial tragicomedy, 277; in "Song of Myself," 310, 317, 319. *See also* difference
oral tradition, 91
Ortony, Andrew, 37, 111, 175
out-groups: and affectivity, 5, 63, 67, 94, 97–99, 101, 104–16, 115n21, 119, 122, 180, 181, 260; boundary with in-group, 38n10; categorial and practical identities of, 29–34, 30n6, 36–37; cognitive principles of, 5; cultural practices of, 38, 43, 44; and disgust, 32, 32n8; and durability, 60n19; in epilogue of suffering, 259; in heroic tragicomedy, 12, 13, 182, 213, 216, 223, 228, 235–37, 235n17, 242–44, 246, 247, 252–54; and identity formation, 8–9; and identity hierarchies, 53, 64n25; in metaphors, 137, 138, 142–43, 166; in narratives, 16, 186, 199; opposability of, 80–82, 81n8, 85, 87, 87n12, 88; prototypes of, 45–50; in romantic tragicomedy, 306, 307, 308, 314, 331–33, 336; in sacrificial tragicomedy, 19, 264, 265, 266, 277, 279, 289, 291, 296; threat and domination in narrative, 193, 194; transition from in-groups to, 186n14

pain, 98, 172n5, 178, 219, 219n7, 301. *See also* suffering
Paine, Tom, 259

Pakistan, 33, 144
Palestine: and King David story, 17, 191, 218–20, 221n10, 225–26, 229, 230; pain in conflict with Israel, 219, 219n7; and September 11 attacks, 68, 173, 243
Palestinian Authority, 220
Panjab, 288
Panksepp, Jaak, 103, 109, 109n19, 176
pansexuality, 208–9, 312–16, 312n8, 321–22. *See also* homosexuality; sex
pan-Slavic activists, 120, 122
paradigmatic narrative, 217, 236, 257–59, 261, 267, 321. *See also* King David story
Parekh, Bhikhu, 42
Parenti, Christian, 183, 184n12
parents: in *Mein Kampf*, 273, 275, 282; in metaphors, 157–62, 162n21; in romantic tragicomedy, 195, 305, 306, 325, 326, 327, 334. *See also* founding fathers; mothers
passports, 78
Patañjali, 42
Pater Patriae, 158n20
patriotism: in epilogue of suffering, 259; in heroic tragicomedy, 215, 251; and ideas and practices, 23; as identity, 23–24, 53; in metaphors, 153, 153n18, 159–61, 163–66; narrative structures of, 167–69; and prevalence of nationalism, 2; and techniques of nationalization, 66
Pearl Harbor, 236, 251
Pearse, Padraic, 155
penance, 265–66, 269, 289, 295–96, 304
PEOPLE ARE PLANTS metaphor: description and uses of, 129–31, 133, 149–53, 166; and family metaphor, 158; Goldman's use of, 335; and immigration, 151, 151n15; in *Mein Kampf*, 271, 275. *See also* roots
people's exchange (between Turkey and Greece), 56
perceptual experiences, 129, 175
personification, 135, 148, 158, 163, 165

Petals of Blood (Ngũgĩ wa Thiong'o), 146–47, 308n3
Peter I, tsar of Russia, 119, 158
Peterson, Indira, 58, 190
Petöfi, Sándor, 143
Pfaff, Steven, 76
Phelan, James, 14
Philip, Alan Butt, 55–56
Philistines, 223–25, 229
physical injury, 109–10
pilgrimages, 90. *See also* tourism
Pindar, 105
place attachment, 103–5. *See also* land; territory
Plantinga, Carl, 96
plants. *See* PEOPLE ARE PLANTS metaphor
plays, 202
pleasure, 196, 200, 295
plot junctures, 202
The Plough and the Stars (O'Casey), 153n18
Poema de Mio Cid, 215
poetry, 103, 121, 160–61, 202, 215, 240. *See also* literature; *specific titles*
polarization. *See* opposability
Poles, 73, 78
policies and practices, 16–17, 19–20
political movements, 40, 270, 275, 281, 283
political treatises, 202
politicians, 139
politics: emotions in, 9n14; of Gandhi, 208, 284–86, 290, 292, 295, 296; of Goldman, 209, 324–37; identity through, 34, 35; and in-group/out-group division, 30n7, 31, 32; and metaphors, 125n1, 144, 150, 155–56, 159; and nationalist feelings, 3, 3n1, 3n3; in national narratives, 168, 229, 230; in romantic tragicomedy, 21, 21n21, 307; in sacrificial tragicomedy, 304; Wimmer's models on, 64n25
Pope, 57, 235, 302
population, 4
postage stamps, 72
postcolonial literature, 144. *See also* colonialism

potatoes, 106
poverty, 171–72, 172n4, 219n7, 274–75
power: as happiness goal, 13, 196, 197, 199; in Israel/Palestine conflict, 219–20; in King David story, 221, 228; lack of as violence trigger, 113; and pride, 101; in September 11 attacks emplotment, 244
Power, Matthew, 161
practical alienation, 38–40, 42, 57
practical identities: in collective behaviors, 76; coordination of, 81–85, 87, 87n12, 88; definition and description of, 8, 8nn12–13, 25–26, 25n2; and emotion, 9n14; hierarchies in, 50–51; and identity conflicts, 55–57, 81, 81n9; interaction with categorial identities, 24–37; in metaphors, 138; shared and different, 28; through cultural practices, 38–39, 41–44, 41n13; through language, 28, 35
Pranami Hindus, 32–33, 43. *See also* Hindus
pregnancy, 135–36, 146. *See also* birth
Le Premier Jardin (Hébert), 158
"Preparedness: The Road to Universal Slaughter" (Goldman), 331
presidents, 90, 157, 232–38. *See also* national leaders
Presidents' Day, 74, 92
prestige, 13, 101
Preston, Stephanie D., 98
pride, 100–102, 104, 109, 240, 252–53, 260, 298, 300. *See also* joy; superiority
priming affects, 111, 127–32, 244, 250, 250n23, 269, 271
primordialism, 64n25
privacy limits, 162
problem-solving, 126, 128–29
procedural memories, 6, 26
procedures, 27
processes, 6, 8
procreation, 313–14
The Promise (von Trotta), 307n2
propaganda function, 62–63
prosperity, 196, 199
prostitution, 275–76, 280–82, 325, 333
protection seeking, 108, 116–17, 120, 213
Protestants, 24, 33, 62, 140, 302
protoemotion systems, 94, 105. *See also* affectivity; emotion
protoidentification, 39
prototypes: and affectivity, 63, 95–96; averaging in formation, 45–46; of categorial identities, 44–50, 50nn15–16; cognitive construction in *Independence Day*, 231n15; "corrective processes" in formation, 47; in emotional causality, 174, 176, 177, 181, 187; happiness goals in, 15–16; and identity formation, 9; and identity hierarchies, 52; and in-group/out-group division, 105–7, 115; and memory systems, 6; of morality, 171–72, 172n4; of national narratives, 168, 169, 171, 172, 192–201; nature of, 26–27, 27n4; social impact of narrative, 13–14, 17; of suicide bombers, 239; types of, 12. *See also* heroic tragicomedy; romantic tragicomedy; sacrificial tragicomedy; stereotypes
provocation. *See* causal attribution
psychological dimension, 5n8, 30–31, 30n7, 36, 60n21, 286n10
public objects, 69, 70–72, 89–91, 103–4
purgative sacrificial nationalism: description of, 19, 266, 304; examples of, 267n2; in *Mein Kampf*, 267–84; and romantic tragicomedy, 306, 306n1

Québec, 158
queer theory, 29. *See also* homosexuality
A Question of Power (Head), 141, 151
Quint, David, 215
Qur'ān, 230

Rabinowitz, Peter, 102n14, 186n14, 235n17, 239n19, 251n25, 309n4
race: and affectivity, 97, 114, 180–81; functionality of, 61, 77; Goldman

on, 332; in heroic tragicomedy, 251; and identity, 31–32; and identity conflicts, 54, 55; in *Mein Kampf,* 269, 270–71, 273, 275–77, 279, 280–83; in metaphors, 141–43, 155, 156; opposability of, 62, 80–81, 81n9, 86; in prototype formation, 45–46; in romantic tragicomedy, 20, 21, 194, 195, 208; salience of, 59, 75; in "Song of Myself," 310–23, 322n13. *See also specific races*
racism, 12n16, 37, 114, 168
Railton, Stephen, 313n10
Rajasthan, 33
Rāma, 295
Ramah, 224
Rāmāyaṇa, 14, 122, 189–92, 215, 217, 224n14
Ranger, Terence, 89, 119
rape, 161
rational choice, 64n25
Ratnam, Mani, 307
reactionary traditionalism, 42–45
rebellion, 213
regionalism: and cultural practices, 41n13; functionality of, 77; and identity conflicts, 57; in King David story, 225, 226; in narratives, 189, 190–92; and opposability, 82, 85; in romantic tragicomedy, 20; and salience of national holidays, 75; in "Song of Myself," 311–12, 318–19, 322, 323
relational salience, 59, 59n18
religion: affectivity of, 94, 114, 118–23; authoritarianism of, 164; durability of, 60; in epilogue of suffering, 261n28; and family metaphor, 10; functionality of, 61, 77; Goldman on, 329, 332–34, 336; in heroic tragicomedy, 213, 251, 255–56; and identity conflicts, 54–57; identity hierarchies in, 51, 52; identity through, 24, 29, 33–34, 36, 40, 41; and metaphors, 142–43, 153n18, 159, 165; and nationalist feelings, 3n3, 191; and opposability, 62, 81, 86, 87n12; in romantic tragicomedy, 20, 306; in sacrificial tragicomedy, 284, 285, 297, 298; salience of, 69–70, 74, 75; in "Song of Myself," 310, 313–14, 319, 320, 323. *See also* divine election; divine punishment; King David story; *specific denominations;* spirituality
Renan, Ernst, 140
Reppen, Randi, 41
representational memories, 6, 26
resolution: in causal sequences, 12, 183–88; in epilogue of suffering, 211, 262; in romantic tragicomedy, 305, 307, 317; in September 11 attacks emplotment, 241, 241n20, 242, 247–49, 254; through regeneration of land, 149, 152, 153; through resurrection, 145, 272, 283. *See also* cooperative renewal; goals
revenge, 111, 112
revolutionaries, 336n15
revolutions, 117, 143, 147, 153
Rhys, Jean, 141
Robin, Corey, 116n22
Roman Empire, 3n3
Romanov dynasty, 92
romantic relations, 106, 160–61, 165, 176, 200. *See also* love; sex
romantic tragicomedy: antinationalist, 307–8, 307n3, 336; benevolent/malevolent categorization in, 182; characters in, 195, 305, 328, 332; as cross-cultural narrative prototype, 198–200; descriptions of, 12–13, 20–21; development principles of, 188–89; emplotment of, 208, 209, 211–12, 305–9; happiness goals in, 15–16, 193–201; and heroic tragicomedy, 216; in *Independence Day,* 237; and Malvinas/Falkland Islands War, 12n16; in *Mein Kampf,* 273, 274, 277; nationality in, 306; patriarchal repression in, 316n11; and sacrificial tragicomedy, 273n8; social ideas and practices in, 17, 21; structures of, 14, 188, 307–8, 307n3. *See also* love
Rome, 119
Romeo and Juliet, 326, 327
Roosevelt, Franklin, 251

roots, 149–51, 328–29. *See also* PEOPLE ARE PLANTS metaphor
Rosen, Steven, 1
Roshwald, Aviel, 2
Ross, Lee, 46
Rubin, D. L., 31
"Running out of time" (Caspi), 218
Rushdie, Salman, 144, 162, 308n3
Russia, 24n1, 92, 117–19, 134, 238, 277

sacrificial nationalism, 8, 64n25
sacrificial tragicomedy: benevolent/malevolent categorization in, 182; descriptions of, 12, 19–20; emplotment of, 207, 208, 211–12, 264–68, 267n1, 273n8, 293–94, 298, 304; happiness goals in, 15–16, 193–201; and heroic tragicomedy, 216; influence of prototype, 14; and romantic tragicomedy, 21, 306, 331, 333, 335–37; shame in, 100; social impact of, 17; structures of, 188; and suicide bombing, 113; theory of, 204–5
sacrificial victims, 265, 266, 292, 299, 299n13
sādhāraṇadharma, 287–89. *See also* universalism
Said, Edward, 103
salience: and affectivity, 95, 101, 121, 175, 177, 181; of clothing, 87; in epilogue of suffering, 210; of flags, 69n2; of food, 84, 85, 304; of Gandhi's views, 208; of happiness-eliciting conditions, 200; in heroic tragicomedy, 206, 213, 231n15, 239n19, 240, 251, 252; of housing in Singapore, 86; in identity forms, 30–31; in identity hierarchies, 9, 54, 58–63, 58n18, 67–76; of language, 83; of metaphors, 127, 132, 165; of narrative prototypes, 211; in "Song of Myself," 310, 313, 317; through education, 91; of travel in narratives, 191
sallekhana, 293
salvation, 145
1 Samuel, 222, 222n13, 225
2 Samuel, 222, 222n13, 225, 226, 228

Sanskrit epics, 189, 189n16
Santasombat, Yos, 40
Santayana, George, 139–41, 139n10
Satyagraha Ashram, 285, 286, 293, 302–3
Saul, 221, 223–26
scapegoats, 299, 300
Scarry, Elaine, 284
Scheer, Robert, 184
schemas: definition of, 26, 26n3; in heroic tragicomedy, 215; and identity formation, 26–27; in narratives, 168, 188, 192; in September 11 attacks emplotment, 248, 250; in "Song of Myself," 310–11. *See also* metaphors
Schivelbusch, Wolfgang, 269
Schlegel, Friedrich, 147–48
schools, 107n18. *See also* education
Schwartz, Judith, 196–97
science, 271–72, 277, 279, 281, 332
Scots, 86–87, 190
Scott, Walter, 141, 162
scripts, 26n3
security. *See* protection seeking
segmentation, 173, 181–82, 185, 187
segregation, 55, 86
selection, 173, 176, 181–82, 185, 187, 210, 244
self-concepts, 29, 44–50, 60, 64, 81, 100–101, 163–64, 246–47
self-consciousness, 121, 177, 201
self-criticism, 252
self-definition, 308, 309, 309n4, 311, 312, 314, 319
self-determination, 3, 3n1, 4, 36–37. *See also* governmental autonomy; independence; national autonomy
self-dharma. *See* swadharma
self-discipline, 195, 296. *See also* self-sacrifice
self-esteem, 36–37
self-interest, 36, 64n25
self-sacrifice: of Gandhi, 19, 267, 284–304; of heroes, 214, 239; in *Mein Kampf*, 268, 268n4, 272; in metaphors, 153, 153n18; in narratives, 14; in sacrificial tragicomedies, 264, 283; in September 11 attacks emplotment, 250–51, 255. *See also* collective self-punishment

semantic memories, 26, 48, 67, 175–76, 192
Sen, Amartya, 33–35, 55
senility, 137–38
September 11 attacks: and affectivity, 99, 104, 107, 108, 245; and Brown's account of nationalism, 64n25; in causal sequence, 12, 178–79, 186; as crime, 209, 236, 242, 244, 255; in heroic tragicomedy, 18, 209–10, 218, 236, 240–56; narrative of, 169–70, 173, 214; and pacifism as disease, 258; salience of, 68–69, 74; and surge of U.S. nationalism, 2
Serbia, 143
Serbian nationalists, 120
Serb identity, 58, 168
Serbo-Croatian nationalists, 82
sex: and categorial identity, 29–30; functionality of, 61; Gandhi on, 284–85, 293, 295, 296, 300–301; Goldman on, 325, 333; in *Mein Kampf*, 271, 280; opposability of, 62; role in romantic feelings, 176; in sacrificial tragicomedies, 195, 264, 267n1. *See also* homosexuality; pansexuality
sexism, 114
sexual desire, 200
sexual orientation, 29–30, 32. *See also* homosexuality; pansexuality
sexual union: as happiness goal, 196; and out-group stereotypes, 106; in "Song of Myself," 312–14, 312n6, 317–23, 336
Shāh-nāma, 122
Shâhnâme, 3, 215, 235
Shah of Iran, 119, 122
Shakespeare, William, 90, 121–22, 141, 189
shame, 100, 102, 112–13
Shaver, Phillip, 196–97
Shaw, George Bernard, 153n18
Sheehan, Canon, 153n18
"Shock and Awe" campaign, 118
Shui-hu hou chuan, 214n1
Sicherman, Carol, 143
sidekicks, 186, 187
Sidhwa, Bapsi, 143, 144
Siegrist, Hannes, 2, 9n14, 71, 76
Sikhs, 34

The Silences of the Palace, 146
Simpson, Joseph, 175n7, 318
sincerity, 300
Singapore, 84, 86
sins: Gandhi on, 285, 289, 291, 293, 295–301, 303; in *Mein Kampf*, 269–72, 279–83, 333; in sacrificial tragicomedies, 194, 264–66, 267n1; and self-concept and group ideals, 49
Sirota, David, 3n1
Sisòkò, Fa-Digi, 215
situational identification, 42–43
situationalism, 64n25
slavery, 138, 152–53, 310, 317–19
sleeping/waking metaphor, 141–42
Small, Steven, 31
Smith, Greg, 93
Smithsonian Museums, 90
"The Sniper" (O'Flaherty), 156
Snyder, Timothy, 5n7, 7n9
social authority, 4, 324, 326, 327, 329. *See also* government
social category cues, 32, 52
social closure, 38n10
Social Democratic Party (German), 275
social devastation, 188, 194, 264–65, 267n2, 269–70, 272, 276, 278, 279, 281–83, 304
social groups, 60, 60nn19–20, 108, 132–33
social happiness, 193, 196, 216, 242
social identity, 36, 37, 101–2, 113
socialists, 275, 325
social tragicomedy, 325
The Society of Antiquaries, 90
Solomon, 221, 223, 225–29
Somewhere in Berlin, 267n2
Sommer, Doris, 16n18, 20, 306–7
"Song of Myself" (Whitman): contradictions in, 311; emplotment of, 202, 208–9, 309–23; equality in, 315; national Absolute in, 311, 314; patriarchal repression in, 316, 316n11; as romantic tragicomedy, 20, 21, 308, 336
sorrow: in Goldman, 336; and happiness prototypes, 196, 197; in heroic tragicomedy, 237, 241–42, 247; inhibition of, 105; in narra-

tives, 193, 193n17; persistence of, 110. *See also* grief
soul cravings, 326, 326n14
South Africa, 80, 86, 136, 141, 160
South Asia, 88n12, 196
sovereignty. *See* self-determination
Soviet Union, 2, 63, 80, 164
Soyinka, Wole, 153
Spanish character, 138
speech, 31. *See also* language
spinning-wheel movement, 292, 294–96
spirituality: in epilogue of suffering, 262; as happiness goal, 196; in metaphors, 133, 134, 136–38, 145, 147, 165, 166; in sacrificial tragicomedies, 265, 290, 293, 297–98. *See also Bhagavad Gītā;* brahman; religion
Spolsky, Bernard, 38n11
sports, 73–74, 88–89, 101
Sri Lanka, 56
state, 115, 117, 118
state formation, 56
statehood requirements, 4
"statist nationalism," 40n13
St. David's Day (1 March), 76
Stephens, James, 160–61
stereotypes: and cultural practices, 42, 43; in emotional causality, 181; in heroic tragicomedy, 233, 234; in identity forms, 36; in metaphors, 138; and neurological structures, 47; opposability of intra-European, 106, 106n17. *See also* prototypes
Stern, Jessica, 113, 265
Stevenson, Robert W., 137
stories, 15, 201–12, 202n20, 217
structuration, 173, 181–82, 185, 187, 210
structures, cognitive, 6, 8
St. Vitus Day Temple, 69–70
subgroups, 94–95
subnationalisms: and affectivity, 118; in categorial and practical identities, 35, 36; and Columbus Day celebrations, 91–92; and cultural practices, 38–39; in *Independence Day,* 232–34, 239, 240; inhibition in narratives, 169; in King David story, 225, 226; in *Mein Kampf,* 272, 281; and memory, 139–40; in metaphors, 141, 143, 156, 159, 160; in narrative prototypes, 16, 188–92; and opposability, 81, 82, 85, 86, 88; in romantic tragicomedy, 20–21, 195, 208, 211, 306, 306n1, 307; and September 11 attacks emplotment, 241–42, 251–52; in "Song of Myself," 310, 311, 315, 317, 319, 320; study of, 8
śūdradharma, 287, 294
suffering, 172, 173, 194, 213, 248, 255, 297. *See also* epilogue of suffering; pain
suicide, 293, 294, 297, 303
suicide bombing, 113, 239, 284n9
summer soldiers, 259
superiority, 100, 104, 121, 121n27, 137. *See also* dominance; pride
Surfacing (Atwood), 141, 145–46, 146n14
Survey of World Conflicts (Rosen), 1
swadeshi movement, 135
swadharma, 287, 302. *See also* individuals
The Swamp Dwellers (Soyinka), 153
Swazi *Incwala* ceremony, 92
symbolic integration, 71–72. *See also* public objects
syncretism, 42
syphilis, 143, 271, 275, 280. *See also* disease

Tagore, Rabindranath, 135, 143, 160, 216, 216n2, 285, 308n3
Taiwan, 2, 82
Taj Mahal, 90
The Tale of the Heike, 218, 257, 259, 262–63
Taliban, 164, 169, 183, 186, 186n14, 187
Tamil epic, 190
Tamil rebels, 161
Tan, Ed, 174
Tangney, June Price, 113
temperature metaphors, 126–29
Temple Mount, 191, 228
tempter figures, 269, 271, 275, 276, 278, 279, 281–83, 291. *See also* villains

territory: and elective alignment strategy, 56; Goldman on, 328–29; identity through, 35–36; as requirement for statehood, 4, 4n5; in "Song of Myself," 313, 315, 320, 323. *See also* land
terrorism, 63, 254, 265, 288. *See also* war on terror
Terwogt, Mark, 200
testimonies, 202–3. *See also Winter Soldier Investigation* (Vietnam Veterans Against the War)
Thailand, 40
Thanksgiving, 92
theft, 171, 172, 285
thought and action: emplotment of, 201; in epilogue of suffering, 211n23; in heroic tragicomedy, 17, 217, 218, 222–23, 222n13, 254; in practical identity, 26; role in nationalist feelings, 6; in romantic tragicomedy, 21; in sacrificial tragicomedy, 285, 303, 304; salience of, 67. *See also* actions
threat/defense sequence: description of, 199, 213; in heroic tragicomedy, 12, 215n1, 216, 240, 254–55; in *Independence Day*, 231; in King David story, 221, 222n13; in *Mein Kampf*, 270, 276; in narratives, 188, 194; and romantic tragicomedy, 321, 324, 328–31; in September 11 attacks emplotment, 243, 244, 253, 258
Three Kingdoms (Luo), 157
Tilak, Bal Gangadhar, 137, 286
Tishah B'Av, 227
Tlatli, Moufida, 146
Tocqueville, Alexis de, 37
Togolese, 56
tolerance, 42, 195
Tolstoy, Leo, 177
tombs of Unknown Soldiers, 69
torture, 172n5
tourism, 70–71, 103, 119, 190–92, 224–25, 232–34, 240. *See also* land; pilgrimages; public objects
tradition invention, 89, 92
tragicomedies, 193, 193n17, 249. *See also* heroic tragicomedy; romantic tragicomedy; sacrificial tragicomedy
trained reason, 285
transnational affiliations, 88, 143, 241–42, 310. *See also* internationalism
trauma, 141, 152–53
Treaty of Lausanne, 56
Treaty of Versailles, 268
Treibel, Annette, 25n2, 38
Trevor-Roper, Hugh, 86
Tripura, 118
Trumpener, Katie, 121, 141, 161, 162, 190, 306
trust: and affectivity, 95–97, 103, 108–9, 116–17, 117n25, 120; in heroic tragicomedy, 235, 235n17, 249; in narratives, 195; neurological structures for, 63. *See also* distrust
truth, 285, 288
Tunisia, 146
Turkey, 40, 56, 119, 143, 215
Turkish nationalists, 82, 83
Turner, Mark, 126, 153
Tyrol, 118

Uganda, 56
Ukraine, 277
Ulster Plantation Uprising, 141
Ulysses (Joyce), 190
Umutomboko ceremony, 92
United Nations, 220n7
United States: affectivity in, 115, 118, 179; biblical stories in, 17, 229; coalition-building by, 22n21; collective memory of, 140; desire for peace, 247, 249, 252, 331; durability in, 91–92; in epilogue of suffering, 258; fear of outgroups in, 107; functionality in, 61, 78–79; group ideals of, 49–50; in heroic tragicomedy, 18–19, 209, 217, 240–56; homogenization in, 40, 42, 82; identity hierarchies in, 52–53; in *Independence Day*, 206, 231–40; in-group/out-group division in, 37, 43–44; invasion of Iraq, 2–3, 23–24, 24n1, 89; and King David story, 217–18,

221n10; in *Mein Kampf,* 277; and metaphors, 145–47, 156, 163–66; opposability in, 62, 80, 85, 86; policies leading to Afghanistan and Iraq invasions, 240, 243, 245, 254, 256; romantic tragicomedy in, 20–21, 308–9, 336; and sacrificial tragicomedy, 19; salience in, 68, 70, 74–75; shared pride in, 101–2; in "Song of Myself," 208, 319; surge of nationalism in, 2; techniques of nationalization in, 9; Vietnam veterans' identity with, 211; in war narratives, 170, 173, 186, 187. *See also* American nationalism

unity: in Goldman's ideal society, 326–27; in heroic tragicomedy, 214, 215, 233, 238, 251–52, 254; in *Mein Kampf,* 268, 269, 271–75, 277, 283, 306n1; and metaphors, 10, 143, 144, 147, 148, 154, 164–66; in romantic tragicomedy, 306, 307; in "Song of Myself," 310–21, 323

universalism. *See* internationalism; *sādhāraṇadharma*

universals: of metaphor, 138; of narrative, 204

unmotivated metaphors, 130

untouchables, 88n12

USA PATRIOT Act, 44, 249

usurpation/restoration sequence: description of, 199, 213; in heroic tragicomedy, 306; in *Independence Day,* 231, 236, 237; in King David story, 222n13, 224–26; in *Mein Kampf,* 270, 278, 281; in *Rāmāyaṇa,* 224n14; and romantic tragicomedy, 320, 321, 324, 328, 336n15; in September 11 attacks emplotment, 253

utopia, 213, 226–29, 327

valencing, 176, 177

Vālmīki, 90

value. *See* functionality

van Vechten, Renée, 36, 37, 58, 168

varṇadharma, 287, 288, 302

Vaziri, Mostafa, 215

Vedāntic metaphysics, 137

Verdery, Katherine, 41, 136

Vietnam, 56

Vietnam Syndrome, 118, 258

Vietnam Veterans Against the War (VVAW). *See Winter Soldier Investigation* (Vietnam Veterans Against the War)

Vietnam War, 140, 234. See also *Winter Soldier Investigation* (Vietnam Veterans Against the War)

villains, 186–88, 214, 219–20, 277. *See also* benevolent/malevolent categorization; internal enemies; tempter figures

violence: anger as motivation for, 112, 113; collective memory of, 140; dharma of, 288; fear as motivation for, 108–9; Gandhi on, 208, 284, 285, 288, 290, 291, 295, 298, 299, 301, 302; Goldman on, 336n15; and in-group hierarchies, 115, 116, 116n23; and King David story, 228, 230; in metaphors, 141, 160; and national narratives, 168, 170. *See also* aggression; war

Virgil, 191

Vogel, Jakob, 2, 9n14, 71, 75, 76

von Clausewitz, Carl, 302

von Trotta, Margarethe, 307n2

Wachtel, Andrew Baruch, 35, 69–70, 119–20, 139–40, 159, 216

Waddington, Augusta, 87

Walcott, Derek, 135–36, 152–53, 153n17, 308n3

Wales, 71, 76, 87, 120, 121, 157

war: and affectivity, 99–101, 108, 109, 112, 117, 118, 121; American nationalism during, 7, 234; connection to nationalism, 216n4; emplotment of, 202, 209–10, 213, 214, 220, 224, 241–56; functionality of, 79; Gandhi on, 289–304; identity hierarchies in, 61n22; in metaphors, 130, 153, 156; narratives on, 12, 169–73, 181–88, 194; and national holidays, 75–76; opposability in, 82, 88; prevalence of ethno-nationalist, 1–2; and romantic tragicomedy, 315, 321, 324, 329–32, 334, 336; in sacrificial tragicomedies, 273–74, 289–304. *See also* conflicts; heroic tragicomedy; kṣatriyadharma; military; violence; *Winter Soldier Investigation* (Vietnam Veterans Against the War)

war crimes, 256. *See also Winter Soldier Investigation* (Vietnam Veterans Against the War)

Warner, William, 90

war on terror, 63, 120, 169, 256. *See also* terrorism

Warsaw Uprising, 221n10

Washington, D.C., 232, 234–35

Washington Post, 143

"Was My Life Worth Living" (Goldman), 324, 328

water, 313, 315, 316, 320–22

weapons, 284

weapons of mass destruction, 169, 214, 244

Weber, Max, 38n10

Weeks, William, 231

Weinberger, Eliot, 107, 214

West Bank, 224, 225

Wexler, Bruce, 33

"What I Believe" (Goldman), 324–37

White, Hayden, 16n19, 202

Whitman, Walt, 232. *See also* "Song of Myself" (Whitman)

Wide Sargasso Sea (Rhys), 141

Wilkinson, Richard G., 113

Williams, Glanmor, 73, 76

Williams, Mark, 118

Wills, T. A., 36

Wilson, Timothy, 176

Wimmer, Andreas, 1, 2, 38n10, 39n12, 56, 61n22, 64n25

Winter Soldier Investigation (Vietnam Veterans Against the War): description of, 18–19; emplotment of, 210–11, 211n23, 218, 256–63; narrative organization of, 203, 210, 257; ruminative anger in, 112

"Winter Soldier: Iraq and Afghanistan" hearings, 256

winter soldiers, 259–60

Wolpert, Stanley, 284, 286n10, 302

women, 163, 239n19, 316, 316n11, 334. *See also* mothers

wonder, 104–5, 104nn15–16. *See also* awe

work, 168, 325

working memory, 6

World Trade Center, 104

World War I, 170, 207, 267, 269–71, 276, 278

World War II, 232–33, 236, 251, 268, 268n4

yajña (sacrifice), 294, 294n12, 295, 296, 301

Yeats, W. B., 158, 161

Yoga-Sūtra (Patañjali), 42

Yom Kippur, 227

Yoruba beliefs, 265, 299

Yüan dynasty, 7, 7n10, 116n24

Yugoslavia, 35, 58, 69–70, 82, 139–40, 159, 168, 216

Yugoslav wars, 2

Zajonc, Robert B., 95, 172, 175

Zeami, Motokiyo. *See The Tale of the Heike*

Zinn, Howard, 99

Zoroastrianism, 122

www.ingramcontent.com/pod-product-compliance
Lightning Source LLC
Chambersburg PA
CBHW031959220426
43664CB00005B/75